THE
ELVIS
READER

THE ELVIS READER

TEXTS AND SOURCES

ON THE KING OF

ROCK 'N' ROLL

EDITED BY

KEVIN QUAIN

ST. MARTIN'S PRESS   NEW YORK

Design by Judith A. Stagnitto

Library of Congress Cataloging-in-Publication Data

The Elvis Reader: texts and sources on the king of rocks 'n' roll / [selected by] Kevin Quain.

p.   cm.

ISBN 0-312-06966-9

1. Presley, Elvis, 1935-1977. I.Quain, Kevin.

ML420.P96E44 1992

782.42166'092—dc20   91-33832

                                                 CIP

                                                 MN

First Edition

10 9 8 7 6 5 4 3 2 1

TABLE OF CONTENTS

▬

REFERENCE SECTION

ACKNOWLEDGMENTS

Grateful acknowledgment is hereby made to the following for permission to reprint previously published material.

ALL SHOOK UP? by Richard Middleton from *Elvis: Images and Fancies,* Edited by Jac Tharpe, University Press of Mississippi, 1977. Reprinted by permission of University Press of Mississippi.

PRESLEY AND THE GOSPEL TRADITION by Charles Wolfe from *Elvis: Images and Fancies,* Edited by Jac Tharpe, University Press of Mississippi, 1977. Reprinted by permission of University Press of Mississippi.

THE MAN IN THE BLUE SUEDE SHOES by James and Annette Baxter from *Harper's Magazine,* April 1957. © by *Harper's Magazine.* All rights reserved. Reprinted from the April 1957 issue by special permission.

ELVIS, THE INDIGENOUS by Mr. Harper from *Harper's Magazine,* January 1958. Copyright © by *Harper's Magazine.* All rights reserved. Reprinted from the January 1958 issue by special permission.

THE ROCK IS SOLID from *Time* magazine, November 4, 1957. © 1957 Time Warner Inc. Reprinted by permission.

LONELY & SHOOK UP from *Time* magazine, May 27, 1957. © 1957 Time Warner Inc. Reprinted by permission.

Thanks to Jim Fitzgerald, Alex Kuczynski, Mojo Nixon, Peter Guralnick, Albert Goldman.
Special thanks to David Johnston.

With love to my favorite girls:
Antje MacEachern
Paola Marcon

PREFACE

RRRRRIIIINNNNGGGG!!!! RRRRRIIIIINNNNNGGGGG!!!

I'm not answering the phone. This crazed Canadian is pestering me to write an intro for his book. Some nutjob named Kevin Quain, who for all I know could be a Serbo-Croatian one-eyed albino midget with firearms and a weird Elvis fixation.

RRRRRIIIIINNNNNGGGG!!!!!

OK, OK, I'll write the damn thing. Hell, I even like this boy's twisted tirade. With enuff eyeballin' of this tome, you can begin to glimpse the Great American Dream in all its rabid glory. Now, some of you nonmusic types may be wondering why ole kooky Kev is picking on me. Well, a few years back I pontificated this semihit song "Elvis Is Everywhere," which explains the King's influence on the Pyramids and the Bermuda Triangle, the ANTI-ELVIS (Michael J. Fox), and the undeniable fact that ELVIS IS EVERYWHERE, ELVIS IS EVERYTHING, ELVIS IS EVERYBODY, AND ELVIS IS STILL THE KING!

Now, I didn't sit down with greed in my heart and conjure up some exploitation of the American Messiah; hell, two-thirds of the song literally poured outta me onstage one night when I was ranting and raving about something else. On a good day, I like to think of myself as a lightning rod hit by the collective Elvis energy and psychosis of the universe. Once the song and the video were released, people began giving me all kinds of relics from the uncrowned King's empire. Being a nutcase magnet for all kinds of Elvis-information overload, I've got a few recurring themes I wanna let loose on ya:

1. **It's OK to make fun of Elvis.** My song is a celebration of Elvis, Elvis-mania, and his fans. That doesn't mean that Elvis didn't do some pretty stupid things or that some of his fans aren't completely whacked. Elvis seemed to be able to do the coolest thing & the shlockiest thing in the same five minutes and not know the difference. That's what makes him great; that's what makes him the Great American Zen Riddle.

2. **The passing of Elvis from the mortal plane has started the foundations of a new religion.** Now, I don't wanna offend any o' y'all, but look at all this stuff: we've got shrines (Graceland, Sun Studio), we've got holy relics (hunks of clothing and the King's bottled sweat), and the spontaneous orgy of mourning that erupted after the Big E's last exit has mutated into an annual festival in Memphis, sorta like Christmas, Easter, and Hallowe'en rolled into one. Anyway, seems like everybody's written their own gospel about the King of rock 'n' roll, followed their own disciples, come up with their own life-after-death theories, and damned any false prophets who don't agree with 'em. Now, maybe that ain't religion, but it sure looks an awful lot like it sometimes.

   I think people wanna believe Elvis is alive because if Elvis, the American Messiah, the New World Royalty, can die, then *so can they*. Our culture loves to pretend that death doesn't happen, and when the point man for postwar liberation goes down the tubes, the collective anguish and denial is amazing.

3. **Never underestimate the effect Elvis had in his first ten years.** Forget about the fat Vegas Elvis at the end and remember that ONE OUT OF THREE AMERICANS SAW ELVIS ON "ED SULLIVAN" IN 1956! And to paraphrase Texas songwriter Butch Hancock, Elvis wiped out four thousand years of Judeo-Christian uptightness about sex in fifteen minutes of TV. The King shook

the fig leaf away and the kids on "The Donna Reed Show" would soon find themselves high as a kite and fornicating in the mud at Woodstock . . .

So get up and feel the Elvis vibration! Move your lip, move your hip! Blast through the rancid puke of the Nelson twins and let **everybody,** let **each** and **every** voice rise up and make a **joyful** noise! Let us all SING LIKE THE KING!!

Elvisly yours,

Mojo Nixon
June 1991

INTRODUCTION

Elvis is the definitive pop culture hero; infinitely flexible, he encompasses everything American from the sublime to the grotesque. He is as much a tribute to the essential optimism of the American Dream as he is an indictment of its falseness and its pitfalls. The Elvis Myth has a completeness and beauty that rivals that of the best of American fiction: He represents a unique meeting of folk hero and media event. Few figures in American history have evoked the extreme responses Elvis Presley has, and fewer still have endured after death as a myth, an industry, and a cult figure to the degree Elvis Presley has. Whether Elvis's achievements as an artist or a human being warrant this type of treatment is debatable, but his status as a unique cultural phenomenon is undeniable. The real question now is: *Why?*

The most popular American artists have always been larger than life. We like them big, we like them loud, and we like them consistent. It has always seemed important to American audiences and critics alike that artists retain the role they assumed when they first came to our attention. Good girls have to stay good, bad boys have to stay bad, drunks have to keep drinking . . . but on the other hand, we have pretty short attention spans, even shorter memories, and we bore easily. And a good Decline and Fall has always been a big attention getter. We always want the Next Big Thing and the Same Old Thing at the same time, even though we often can't tell the difference anyway. We're rough and demanding with our artists. If they play by our rules and we don't get bored of them, we just might let them live. Like kings. And every once in a while we turn them into gods.

Since his death in 1977, Elvis has gradually wormed his way into our everyday consciousness, becoming a potent figure in pop iconography. His first name alone has worldwide currency and almost unlimited evocative power. He may not have been all things to all people, but he was many things to many people. To the hip cynical school of Letterman and "Doonesbury," Elvis is little more than a sick joke; but he is a joke we all recognize and understand. And the huge masses of the faithful, those aging teenagers of the fifties who first embraced Elvis and refused to let go are as familiar, in all their lunatic glory, as the man they worship. To his following Elvis was not merely a singer, he was a heroic ideal, the embodiment of a success story complete with a Decline and Fall that rivals anything ever concocted in Hollywood. Clearly, something about Elvis attracts us and repulses us at the same time, and we need to figure out why. For one reason or another, Elvis continues to loiter on the fringes of our collective consciousness with a maddening persistence.

We have a way of feeding on celebrities with such voraciousness that we often have little appetite or interest in their work itself. It's always been much easier to pay attention to someone's nasty habits than it is to concentrate on his or her artistic accomplishments. Bad Behavior competing with Good Art. Thus we get Jackson Pollock, the Drunken Cowboy Painter; and Hemingway, the Tough Writer; and Elvis, the Hillbilly Singer. These artists came with nifty new packaging we'd never seen before, and some of us became so entranced with the cardboard and cellophane we forgot to look inside. Our loss. Fair enough, everybody lives and dies by those rules, whether they like it or not. Elvis stuck around long enough to shed some labels and acquire others. And if at times it seemed like he was ignoring the script, maybe it was only because the script he had was different but no less familiar to us. It seems like a lot of people missed the point of Elvis—the point being that there is no point; he provided something for everyone to grab on to. If Elvis was inconsistent in his packaging, he was at least consistent in the fact that he always had an easily recognized package. He left us with a variety of images of himself to mix and match. Pick your favorite. The images sometimes clash; but again, that's the whole idea, only it puts you in the position of having to defend one Elvis against another, the raw, bluesy Elvis hailed as a genius by contemporary rock journalists versus the vulgar and sentimental Vegas Elvis. Cat clothes v. jumpsuits. We're uneasy in our assessment of Elvis because even if he was the hippest, he was also the cheesiest, the tackiest. He was an effortless genius and a jaded hack. He was fat, he was thin, he was beautiful, he was ugly, he was straight, he was stoned. He was everybody. He was Elvis. Who are you?

Some people believe Elvis is alive. Others claim to have had supernatural experiences involving Elvis. These beliefs have been absorbed by the myth: Elvis Is Alive and Elvis Beyond the Grave stories have been a staple of the tabloid press since 1977, and jokes about those same stories are commonplace. The two conflicting types of story coexist and flourish easily: The Elvis myth is rich in irony, paradox, and sheer surrealism. Of course, the question we need to ask at this point is not "Is Elvis Alive?" but rather: "Why are we still talking about him?" The demands of myth are such that truth need not be factual and facts need not be truthful. And Elvis's story is essentially true in that it can serve to reaffirm our values, our beliefs, and our sense of how the world operates, regardless of our point of view. From one angle it is a cautionary tale, a graphic lesson in the dangers of success and excess. From another angle his story pays tribute to a political and cultural climate in which an individual can rise from poverty and obscurity to wealth and fame. Conversely, his story can be interpreted as proof of the hollowness of such a transformation. Any good myth will always accommodate many different readings and interpretations; flexibility is a prerequisite for longevity. Fifteen years after his death, Elvis is as flexible and accommodating as ever. An examination of this myth-making process offers us a glimpse of ourselves engaged both in creation and consumption and ultimately can reveal as much of ourselves as it does of Elvis.

In many ways Elvis is still here. His music has never really gone away; almost every RCA LP ever released is still in print, and dozens more appear each year, earning sales that any living singer would envy. His thirty-one movies, those bland and colorful travelogues, have become a familiar part of late-night television programming and are heavily rotated during the two holy weeks on the Elvis calendar: the week of his birth, January 7, and the week of his death, August 16. Yet his artistic output itself represents only part of the phenomenon; the concept of Elvis as the subject of a religious cult is implicit in the Beyond the Grave genre of stories and is even more evident in the "secondary" industries that sprang up in the wake of his death. The awe and reverence with which Elvis's home, his personal possessions, and even his imitators are treated is far beyond that accorded to any other American historical figure. The persistence of Elvis as a myth, an industry, and a religion is a truly remarkable phenomenon, one that reflects, for better or for worse, the values of our time.

Either way, in *real* life Elvis is dead, dead, dead. Or rather the poor southern kid who gave flesh and blood to myths and American Dreams is dead. Maybe the real reason Elvis died was that he was just an ordinary human being who cracked under the weight of all that Elvisness. Maybe being Elvis was just too big a job for any one human being to handle, which would explain why so many Elvis imitators just do it part-time. I think Elvis was an inevitable part of American history, and if he had not existed, it would most certainly have been necessary to invent him, if only as a way of getting from the fifties to the sixties with our sanity intact. Perhaps creating (and disposing of) Elvis was America's greatest achievement, a collective work of art both of ourselves and outside of ourselves, infinitely beautiful and mysterious.

So what have we got here? A popular singer who was just different enough to be hailed as a revolutionary cultural figure. Elvis sure didn't invent rock 'n' roll, but he gave it a face and a name. All the evidence indicates that popular music had made moves in that direction many times; from the jump music of Louis Jordan to the sophisticated pop of Cab Calloway and Billy Eckstine to Glen Miller's "In the Mood," to the urban blues of Muddy Waters and Howlin' Wolf. So let's say that Elvis was in the right place at the right time. Last but not least, Elvis put a white face on what was largely a black musical tradition, a fact that makes him an ambivalent figure among some of today's popular black musicians. If Elvis can be credited with helping break down racial and cultural barriers through popular music, he also serves to remind us of those barriers. To some, Elvis may evoke a nostalgic yearning for simpler times, but to others the fifties were years of racism and oppression, not "Happy Days" at all. And no one should kid themselves into thinking that the motives of Elvis and his management had anything to do with breaking down racial and cultural barriers. But while we ponder the racial implications of the Elvis phenomenon, it might help to remind ourselves that American musical traditions have always been based on fusions of existing styles, fusions that often mix colors and cultures.

Of course, there is something slightly unsettling about the tenacity of our hold on the Elvis image. There must be something about that image that seems necessary to hold on to, even if only to disparage it. Throughout his lifetime, Elvis made an easy target for cynics, and in death it's so easy to knock him you have to wonder why anybody would bother. But Elvis is accommodating in that respect, too; somebody was always using him as a whipping boy for some reason or another, and now that he's dead he cares even less. None of that "You won't have old Elvis Aron Presley to kick around" stuff from Elvis. No way. You're talking about someone who made a living out of squeezing his bloated body into shiny jumpsuits and singing songs such as "Big Hunk o' Love" without a trace of irony. Elvis can absorb our contempt with the same magnanimity with which he took the love and adoration.

It seems foolish for anyone to say that Elvis *let us down* by getting fat, old, and tacky, but they say it all the time. They say a lot of things. Maybe Elvis was a hypocrite for harboring a deep dislike for the sixties counterculture he helped create. Maybe he was hypocritical for condemning drug addicts even as he gleefully toyed with vast and varied combinations of pharmaceuticals. But that judgment might be hasty. We do, after all, judge these people by a different yardstick, and didn't our initial attraction hinge on his ability to embrace contradictions? Maybe what we sometimes think of as hypocrisy is merely the difference between what we see and what is really there. The difference between what we want and what we get. Or maybe the explanation is darker than that. When we start to hate the things we once loved, the things we created in the first place, it throws a shadow on our already blurry sense of identity. Besides, if we worship something as effortless as youth and despise something as blameless as age, we're willing participants in our own disappointment and disillusionment. Only those who die young can fail to disappoint us.

Of course, even the dead aren't really safe. Lately we seem to take a lot of pleasure in kicking around people we used to drool over. We get a morbid thrill out of displaying the old dirty laundry of people we used to think didn't have laundry. That's all right, I guess. We build 'em up. We tear 'em down. But maybe the picture of your favorite celebrity as Dirty Sinner is just as flat and one-dimensional as the haloed portrait it replaces. My question is this: Are we prepared to accept a legend that is as complex and as contradictory and as individual as we are?

Elvis didn't fade away. He disintegrated right in front of us. He got fat, he got old. Every performance became an act of faith in which he put his dignity on the line, along with his gut, out in front of those lights. He held a mirror up to his audience, and you can never predict how people are going to react to their own reflection, or even if they'll recognize it. If he showed us a dazzling vision of youth and beauty, of impossible hipness and dangerous sexuality, he also showed us the downside: the loneliness, the ridicule, the physical price of age and excess. He stopped being hip, as did his audience—most of whom didn't love him any less in his decaying state.

To many, Elvis was—and is—a personification of all our ills, corruption, drug abuse, obesity, racism, lust, greed, and selfishness. Some writers have suggested that Americans reveal their own corruption and foolishness by persisting in their deification of someone so weak. If only a fraction of the allegations are true, clearly Elvis had some problems. He had a weakness for food and drugs, a violent streak. He was perhaps selfish, self-centered, and self-destructive. He often betrayed his gift and his audiences with bad performances and bad music. Above all, his greatest sin was mortality; he died young enough for us to remember his youth and old enough for us to witness his pathetic decline. But perhaps his weaknesses only serve to bring him closer to us by giving flesh, blood, and all the complexities of humanity to a gilded image that was obviously false and incomplete. The vices that Elvis is condemned for are no different than those of his own generation, which was just as reluctant to display its weakness to the rest of the world. If we initially cheered Elvis as a mythic symbol of our youth, beauty, and promise, we must accept the logical completion of that myth, even if it makes us feel guilty to do so. The crux of the problem lies in the fact that while Elvis is thoroughly dead (rumors to the contrary are greatly exaggerated), we're still alive, making it a relationship fraught with practical and spiritual dilemmas.

I'm hesitant to draw any real conclusions about Elvis; it's difficult to come up with any final word on him. Maybe the time for projecting all our fantasies onto him is over, and now it's time to project our theories and dogmas about American Culture onto him. I'm reluctant to participate; for me Elvis has always been a marvelously ambiguous figure, and I'm content to accept him as such, a kinetic sculpture, a hall of mirrors, a force of nature. Dead well over a decade and we keep seeing new things in him; he continues to reveal new aspects of himself to us. Ultimately, Elvis is a riddle that cannot be solved, but he gives us a great deal to think about and a lot of great music to listen to while we're thinking.

The book you now hold in your hands is an attempt to delve into some of the Elvis images that still linger on the fringes of our imaginations. There's a lot of different viewpoints between these covers, and lots of them conflict. That's as it should be. Draw your own conclusions. This book isn't just about Elvis, it's about a time and a place and people called Americans who worship strange new gods and do terrible things and wonderful things and do them with a strange blend of pomposity and casual indifference that still astonishes the rest of the world. Elvis, for better or for worse, is part of American history and culture, a uniquely American Myth. If you want to understand America, sooner or later you're going to have to deal with Elvis. His music has been on the radio, his name on our lips, and his images splattered all over our popular media much too long for us to write him off as a temporary aberration, a brief twitch of madness, or a fad.

Maybe all the strangeness will fade and Elvis will acquire a warm sepia-tone immortality, a patina of respectability, and we'll treat him with the deference we reserve for the dull, the harmless, and the safely dead. It won't be the tearful, solemn Elvis Was a Saint reverence, it'll be the cold and indifferent respect we pay to those Great Americans whom history has embalmed. That's all right, as long as there's a few young people with ears who can still hear music underneath the layers of nostalgia and sentiment. After all, that's what started this whole mess: music. Rhythms that made you shake and twitch, a voice that gave you chills, and a greasy-haired southern kid who had the world by the tail and couldn't care less.

That music broke its promises of freedom and eternal youth long ago but still weaves a powerful spell. At its best, it achieved the absolute purity of Great Art without even trying. And if you can do that in America, maybe you *can* stay young forever, a king in life and a god in death.

THE
MUSICAL
ELVIS

Whatever social and cultural implications the arrival of Elvis heralded, it was his musical impact that produced the most palpable changes. These pieces delve into the origins of his style and examine the complexities of the cross-cultural musical environment of the urban South in the early fifties.

ALL SHOOK UP?

■

Innovation and Continuity
in Elvis Presley's Vocal Style

by Richard Middleton

This piece, by author and music lecturer Richard Middleton, first appeared in Southern Quarterly *(Fall 1979). It is one of the few pieces of serious writing that deals with Elvis's stylistic innovations in a practical and technical manner.*

One way of looking at Elvis Presley is as a great American success story. From a life of anonymity and poor-white Southern poverty to enormous wealth and the kind of fame so pervasive that "all one has to do is appear";[1] undisputed king of popular music from 1956 to the advent of the Beatles, with world record sales estimated in 1971 as about 155 million singles and 25 million albums; top of the American popular record charts for 55 out of 104 weeks in the period from 1956 to 1958; and so on, and so on. Yet paradoxically this triumphant progress can also be read as a kind of failure. Certainly most rock critics take this line, seeing Elvis's career as a progressive sell-out to the music industry, a transition from "folk" authenticity (the Sun singles of 1954–55) to a sophisticated professionalism (epitomized by the ballads and movies of the 1960s) in which the dollars multiplied but musical values went by the board. Greil Marcus is the

[1]Greil Marcus, *Mystery Train* (Dutton, 1976), p. 139.

only writer on Elvis I have come across who tries to resist this Faustian scenario—which in essence is just as romantic as the great American success legend, its apparent obverse—but even he, when he comes to make his crucial distinction, places it between the Sun Golden Age, "a space of freedom," and a subsequent decline into a "riskless aesthetic of smooth-it-away" which "gives an all-encompassing Yes to his audience."[2]

There are big theoretical difficulties with such an analysis. Cultural fields, particularly in modern mass societies, do not work in this simple way. Of course there *are* different markets and different kinds of music but the processes of creation, production and consumption are too dynamic and interactive to permit rigid historical, typological or evaluative dividing lines. It is probably safe to say that in postwar America a pure "folk" role, untouched by commercial influences, had become impossible. The dissemination of music by radio and gramophone record permeated the whole country and every social stratum. The performers whom the young Elvis heard, and presumably learned from—gospel music singers, bluesmen like Arthur Crudup, Bill Broonzy, Junior Parker and Howlin' Wolf, country-and-western stars such as Bob Wills, Hank Williams and Roy Acuff—were *commercial* artists; they, like Elvis himself, did not separate themselves off from the whole wash of music that was available. When Sam Phillips, founder of Sun Records and "creator" of Elvis Presley, said "If I could find a white man who had the Negro sound and the Negro feel, I could make a billion dollars,"[3] the twin motivations, artistic and commercial, were not separated or separable.

If we look at the music Elvis produced through his career, we find equally strong *empirical* objections to the "decline-and-fall" view. All too often commentators stress a change in "sound" (for example, the "primitive"—hence "authentic"—acoustic of the Sun records giving way to the "sophisticated"—hence "manipulative"—methods of RCA, with their more elaborate use of amplification, vocal backing groups, strings) at the expense of other characteristics of the musical style, which may show continuity. I want to argue for the existence of important continuities.

Compared to his two great rock and roll contemporaries, Chuck Berry and Little Richard, the *scope* of Elvis's significance is limited. Unlike them, he was not a songwriter; unlike Chuck Berry, he was

[2]Ibid., pp. 141, 166, 199.
[3]Quoted in Jerry Hopkins, *Elvis: A Biography* (New York: Simon & Schuster, 1972), p. 66.

4

not an important instrumental stylist. Musically his contribution lies almost wholly in his singing, and it is this I want to discuss. His productivity was enormous, covering singles, albums and movies, but the center of his work was the single, and because of this, and to limit the boundaries of the discussion, I shall confine my examples to his most successful singles, as compiled on RCA's "Golden Records" series, together with the earlier singles made at Sun.[4]

Elvis's two most notable contributions to the language of rock and roll singing are firstly, the assimilation of "romantic lyricism" and secondly, what I shall call boogification. Both techniques can be found in classic form in his first national hit, "Heartbreak Hotel" (1956). This was by origin a country song but its vocal has the shape of a typical blues shout. Nevertheless the rough tone, spontaneous, irregular rhythms, and "dirty" intonation that most blues singers would have used are for the most part conspicuously absent from Elvis's performance; his tone is full, rich and well produced, his intonation is precise, stable and "correct," the notes are sustained and held right through, and the phrasing is legato. All this is particularly clear on the words "broken hearted lovers," "been so long on lonely street" and "take a walk down lonely street," but the lyrical spirit is important throughout. At the same time this lyrical continuity is subverted by boogification. As in boogie-woogie, the basic vocal rhythms are triplets (♪♪♪ , ♪♪) and, again as in boogie-woogie, the *off*-beat quaver is often given an unexpected accent (e.g. ♪♪), producing syncopation and cross-rhythm. The effect is physical, demanding movement, jerking the body into activity. Elvis, however, extends the technique. He adds extra off-beat notes not demanded by words or vocal line, often splitting up syllables or even consonants, slurring words together, disguising the verbal sense. So we have

lo - one - ly stree - ee - eet , be - o so lo - one - ly he - a - by

heart - break ho - tel - I - I I'll - ll be , they'll ne'er ley 'o 'er look be - ack'll make you so

Occasionally, when it would not really be possible actually to notate subdivisions of the beat, there is on a "sustained" note something like a rhythm vibrato (in triplet rhythm): listen for instance to "Although" at the start of the second and last choruses, "Now" at the start of the third, and "Well" at the start of the fourth. Boogification

[4] *The Elvis Presley Sun Collection* (RCA HY1001, English), *Elvis's Gold Records,* vols. 1, 2, 3 and 4 (RCA 1707, 2075, 2765, 3921).

is often accompanied by characteristic "vocal orchestration": usually this involves deep, resonant chest-tone, designed to sound erotic, but Elvis also uses simulation of physical effort and distress, by means of spitting out words and gasping for breath. The overall effect of the boogification technique is of course sexy but it is also a bit jittery and absurd. The sensuality seems almost out of control, perhaps one of the earliest examples in rock of irrational "living for kicks," and indeed it may be that Elvis's development of the technique stems from his own erotic movements as a performer, which it is clear were, originally at least, spontaneous and involuntary.[5] The combination of boogification with romantic lyricism in "Heartbreak Hotel"—the two elements are perfectly integrated, or rather held in tension—produces a style already, at this early stage in Elvis's career, teetering on the edge of that melodrama into which he was so often to fall.

In fact, the same fusion of techniques can be found even earlier, while Elvis was still recording for Sun. "Milkcow Blues Boogie" (1955) is perhaps the best example since, again, the techniques are so well integrated, though Elvis's treatment of the song is at such a quick tempo that the operation of the techniques themselves is less clear than in "Heartbreak Hotel." The lyrical approach—the rich tone, the singing *through* the note, the sustained legato, the controlled phrase-ending—is most apparent for the last line of each chorus. Boogification pervades the entire vocal, though the quick tempo means there is less scope for *accenting* off-beat notes, and often the effect is so fast as to be a rhythm vibrato. The tempo also makes accurate notation harder. However, at the beginning we hear something like this:

Well— ah woke- up— this-a-morning a-and sh-ah loo-ooked ou-ou-out the door—

Later:

You're gon-na nee-eed your a-lo-o-vin'-a-da-a-ddy here some day

(here the quavers are very short: almost an aspect of the articulation—slurring the words together—rather than of the rhythm). And again: And again:

Well-ll a tried ev'ry thi-ing to git a-long with-a-you-ou—

[5]See Henry Pleasants, *The Great American Popular Singers* (London: Gollanez, 1974), pp. 271–2.

Again boogification is accompanied by vocal orchestration, this time including sudden falsettos.

A third important vocal technique appears in "Milkcow Blues Boogie"—though in terms of Elvis's overall development it is less important than the two already mentioned: this is the influence of gospel music. Obviously this derives from his upbringing (attending services and revival meetings at the Pentecostal church his parents belonged to in Tupelo—though in any case the music, white and black, was all around in the culture in which Elvis grew up), and it shows up in vocal tone (ecstatic—listen especially to the introductory "Well" at the start of the first chorus and again at Elvis's re-entry after the guitar solo) and in the use of elaborate melismata, a typical gospel technique. In "Milkcow" these occur most prominently in the last line of each chorus, on one particular word (italicized here): ". . . since that *cow* been gone," ". . . treating *me* this way," ". . . when your *baby's* not around." In a way "gospelization" is an equivalent in the area of pitch to what boogification does in the area of rhythm. In both cases the squareness and regularity of the lyrical traditions of white popular song are broken up, on the one hand through off-beat accents and rhythmic complexity, on the other, through "off-*tune*" melodic patterns. In both cases rational control is heard as being threatened by hints of ecstasy, physical or spiritual, and therefore by a touch of the irrational. The relationship is particularly clear when, as is often the case, the two techniques are combined in the same song. "Trying to Get to You" (1956, though recorded in 1955) is a good example, its rocking medium-tempo boogie rhythm perfectly matching the gospel-ish phrasing and tone of the vocal.

Gospelization was not just a "folk" technique which Elvis subsequently forgot. As with boogification and romantic lyricism, he continued to use it in his early Victor recordings—and indeed throughout his career. "Anyway You Want Me" (1956) is in a direct line from "Trying to Get to You" (the only important change being the addition of a backing vocal group), and later songs like "One Night" (1958) and "Fame and Fortune" (1960) carry on the tradition.

What we do see in that tradition, however, is an example of a kind of stylistic specialization. This is also true of the other vocal techniques I have mentioned. While all of them continue to appear throughout Elvis's career, songs which *integrate* them, like "Milkcow Blues Boogie" (or "Mystery Train") in the Sun period or "Heartbreak Hotel" in the early Victor period, become less common. In particular the two main techniques, lyricism and boogification, tend to diverge, the former channelled into ballads, the latter into a particular kind of rock and roll song which I shall call mannerist. Elvis's huge ballad repertoire needs little commentary here, save to point out that it derived from both country and Tin Pan Alley sources— "I'll Never Let You Go" *and* "Blue Moon" (both 1956, though recorded in 1955 and 1954 respectively)—and that it began not with the move to RCA but at Sun, "Love Me Tender" (1956) and "That's When Your Heartaches Begin" (1957) being preceded by equally sentimental ballads cut for Sam Phillips; indeed, it began earlier: when as a boy Elvis was entered for a talent contest at the Mississippi-Alabama Fair, it was "Old Shep" that he sang. Mannerist rock is more interesting. It is associated most clearly with a series of songs, many written for Elvis by Otis Blackwell, starting with "Don't Be Cruel" (1956) and "All Shook Up" (1957) and stretching down to "Please Don't Drag that String Around" (1963). The techniques of boogification are exaggerated, over-played, even parodied. Placed in a context where they are not tempered by rock and roll shout, gospel ecstasy or lyrical passion—in short, by anything *serious*—and where instead they are associated with (deliberately introduced, tongue-in-cheek?) musical clichés, they move from the area of sexual excitement towards that of laughter. By pushing the techniques of "living for kicks" into mannerism, Elvis distances himself from their demands, physical and psychological. In "All Shook Up," for example, the old techniques are there:

♪ ♩ ♪ | ♩ ♪ ♪ ♪ ♪ ♩ ♪ ♪ | ♪ ♪ ♪ ♩ ♪ ♩
a-well-a-bless-a-my soul-a-what's-a-wrong with me

but the triviality of the lyrics (from the powerful blues sex-imagery of "Milkcow" to a portrayal of love as no more than "itching like a man in a fuzzy tree" is the size of the transformation) and Elvis's light, amused vocal tone (no "vocal orchestration" here) tell us that this is not serious, it is a performance.

Mannerism is usually seen as an RCA development; Charlie Gillett, for instance, describes it in terms of the decline-and-fall myth.[6] But once again we find that it was already developing during the Sun period, notably in "Baby Lets Play House" (1955). The boogification here is very fast and complex, and, coupled with sudden falsettos, it produces a hiccoughing effect which is almost absurd. Certainly it is deliberately exaggerated so that it now expresses not instinctive enjoyment but self-aware technique: Elvis's confidence in

[6]Charlie Gillett, *The Sound of the City* (Souvenir Press, 1971), pp. 66–7.

his own powers is so unquestioned as to reach the level of ironic self-presentation. Stylistically each chorus divides into two. The first half is rock and roll shout, and contains threats to his girl ("You may go to college . . . but . . .," "I'd rather see you dead little girl Than to be with another man," etc.); the second half is mannerist and expresses Elvis's refusal to take himself seriously, the easy self-confidence of parody. To use a vogue concept, the myth to which the song speaks is "deconstructed" and the deconstruction takes place *in the song itself.*

Just as there are no easy distinctions to be made between Sun and Victor recordings, so commonly made categorizations based on "black" and "white" material are hard to maintain too. Both at Sun and at RCA the two principal techniques, romantic lyricism and boogification, were used indiscriminately in songs derived from or in either the rhythm and blues tradition or the country and western tradition. Elvis's first commercial release (1954) couples a rhythm and blues number, Arthur Crudup's "That's All Right," and Bill Monroe's country song, "Blue Moon of Kentucky." He sings the blues with all the lyrical control at his command, his tone rich and sustained, his phrasing rather square and precise, his intonation for the most part legitimate, the phrase-endings beautifully finished off. Blues lament is turned into confident self-presentation. Conversely "Blue Moon of Kentucky" is speeded up and the vocal boogified (though the lyrical style is retained for the "bridge)". Again the final effect of Elvis's version is of a celebration of his own charisma and power. Much the same still happens in some RCA recordings. Elvis's version of Chuck Willis's "I Feel So Bad" (1961) is a lyricized blues to compare with "That's All Right," while even a ballad as sentimental as "Good Luck Charm" (1962) has a vocal carrying traces of boogification. The usual interpretation of such songs—Elvis was crossing cultures and singing the blues on a country song, creating "hillbilly blues" or rocking up ballads—is far too simple, as Marcus has pointed out.[7] Elvis was transforming all of these into something new, something unique, something of himself—or as Sam Phillips put it in the recording studio while Elvis was working out his "Blue Moon of Kentucky," "Fine, *fine,* man, hell, that's different! That's a *pop song* now, little guy! That's good!"[8]

Elvis's originality, then, lay not so much in the cultural mix which he helped to bring into being—that was in the air and would have

[7]See Marcus, pp. 191–3.
[8]Quoted Ibid., p. 192.

9

happened anyway—as in what he did with it. He himself, when asked by Sam Phillips's assistant who he sang like, quite justifiably replied, "I don't sound like nobody."[9] And this was not the result of an unselfconscious "folk" process (which subsequently gave way to a more "professional" production-line approach at RCA): even at Sun the evidence is that he was a self-aware artist who worked hard at building up a style, rehearsing a recording and creating a performance technique.[10] From the start his music had an "authentic multiplicity"[11] of styles. When he first turned up at the Sun studio and was asked what kind of song he did, his answer was "I sing all kinds."[12] He was always a performer. As Marcus says, "It may be that he never took *any* of it seriously, just did his job and did it well, trying to enjoy himself and stay sane—save," he adds, "for those first Tennessee records"[13]—though I would argue that the seeds of "performance" are already present in those Sun days, in "Baby Lets Play House" for example. The ballad style for which he has been so criticized by rock writers was not a fall from grace; it was always inherent in his singing, as "That's All Right" shows. Even at that early stage, "Elvis was . . . hellbent on the mainstream. . . . With Southern power in his music, Elvis had mainstream savvy in his soul."[14]

The only workable categorization of Elvis's output is not historical but by song-types. These run continuously throughout his career. Admittedly different types do correspond to some extent to different vocal techniques—though, as we have seen, this is not the whole story since any one technique can be used in several song-types; moreover, the best songs are beyond category, integrating the different techniques. What *does* happen historically is that integrated songs become gradually less common through the course of Elvis's career. The song-types tend to diverge, as the relatively small, well defined audience of the Sun days gives way to a large, heterogeneous market demanding different types for different sub-sections. Elvis is all things to all men *throughout* his career, but the nature of the audience changes. At least the following song-types can be identified:

[9]Quoted in Hopkins, p. 64.
[10]See Marcus, pp. 172–3; Hopkins, pp. 70–1, 85–6, 149–52.
[11]Marcus, p. 185.
[12]Quoted in Hopkins, p. 64.
[13]Marcus, p. 143.
[14]Ibid., pp. 182, 198.

1. Blues (from "That's All Right" [1954] to "I Feel So Bad" [1961])

2. Fast rock and roll (from "Good Rocking Tonight" [1954] through "Hound Dog" [1956] to "A Big Hunk o' Love" [1959])

3. Mannerist rock and roll (from "Baby Lets Play House" [1955] through "All Shook Up" [1957] to "Please Don't Drag that String Around" [1963])

4. Slow ballad, out of country music or Tin Pan Alley (from "I Love You Because" or "Blue Moon" [1956] to "Are You Lonesome Tonight" [1960], "It's Now or Never" [1960] and a multitude of other examples)

5. Up-tempo ballad (from "Blue Moon of Kentucky" [1954] through "A Fool Such as I" [1959] to "His Latest Flame" [1961])

6. Gospelized ballad (from "Trying to Get to You" [1956] through "Anyway You Want Me" [1956] to "It Hurts Me" [1963])

The unifying factor is Elvis himself—or more precisely, Elvis constructed as a particular category: "Elvis as romantic hero." He turns all his songs into celebrations of his own power, exercises in self-presentation. Even the blues are transformed from a lament in the face of evil reality into a charismatic transcending of reality: "Elvis's blues were a set of musical adventures, and as a blues-singing swashbuckler, his style owed as much to Errol Flynn as it did to Arthur Crudup. It made sense to make movies out of it."[15] He always knew he would be somebody (his mother told him). The hints of narcissism about his character and his music gain currency from the evidence of his parents' attitude to him (he was heavily spoiled as a child), from the outrageously flashy clothes he wore even as an unknown adolescent, and from the fondness he showed for his long, continually groomed hair (he went to a beautician, not a barber).[16] Indeed, if one is looking for psychoanalytic evidence within childhood, the combination of apparent ordinariness (Elvis seems to have been shy, unnoticed, *average*) and parental pampering might go far to explain the intensity of his search for self-fulfillment.

Elvis managed to combine in his singing and his image both the principal strands in what can perhaps be called "commercial romanti-

---

[15]Ibid., p. 182.
[16]See Hopkins, pp. 22–24, 37–40, 61–62, 273–74.

11

cism": first, the desire for peace, escape, a dream-world where everything is safe and lovely, and secondly, the fascination, half obsessive, half afraid, with "the dark side," the irrational world of wild revolt and self-gratification. Needless to say, these are associated in the music with the techniques of romantic lyricism and boogification respectively, and the fact that they are not opposed but complementary—both can be seen as "escapes" from mundane everyday existence, the one into fantasy and self-transcending tears, the other into the self-abnegating madness of "Saturday night rebellion"—explains the fact that both musical techniques can be used, often together, in *different* song-types, and also the seemingly strange mixture in Elvis's character and "image" of rebelliousness and conservatism. To locate these elements a little more precisely, one can find them in that familiar fusion of "good old Southern conservatism" on the one hand and "good old Southern (especially poor-white) stubborn, sometimes sullen revolt" on the other. Like any other Southern poor-white boy, he had to kick over the traces, and his culture made him enough of an outsider vis-à-vis the American mainstream to enable him to do it; at the same time, he felt himself intensely as part of a community, with its own myths and values, its own ways of dealing with and escaping the hardship of everyday reality. In a South which since pre-bellum days had represented "a cosmic conspiracy against reality in favour of romance" (W. J. Cash), a conspiracy intensified by defeat, isolation and neglect, Elvis's singing can be seen as the re-articulation of an old cultural dynamic, worked out, however, in a form that, because of changing social circumstances and economic structures within America and indeed the Western world as a whole, could appeal to a national and international audience equally hungry for rebellion and a fantasy of freedom.

PRESLEY AND THE GOSPEL TRADITION

by Charles Wolfe

Any discussion of Elvis's musical origins inevitably revolves around blues and country music. In this essay, Charles Wolfe, author and English professor at Middle Tennessee State University, explores the often-ignored influence of gospel music on Elvis as well as the influence of Elvis on gospel music.

The few serious attempts to trace the origins of Elvis Presley's music have traditionally focussed on two sources: country music, as exemplified by the honky-tonk and bluegrass styles as they came out of the 1940s, and blues, as represented by the early urban styles of Big Boy Crudup, Howlin' Wolf, and B. B. King. Doubtless these two musical sources can account for much of the very early Presley music, through the Sun years and into the mid-1950s. But for the bulk of Presley's career—through the 1960s and 1970s—these sources can account for only a part of his music. These are the years when Presley outgrew his classification as a rock singer and stepped into the center of mainstream American popular music. His sound and style throughout most of this period is a dense, eclectic complex of a number of influences, and one of the influences I want to explore in this essay is one which has been vaguely acknowledged and talked around for years, but which no one has confronted directly: the influence of white gospel music.

13

One of the reasons most people have shied away from talking about this third major influence on Presley is that very little has been written about the history of white gospel music. No one has yet written a serious history of the genre, and most of the information currently available has to be drawn from original research or from various self-serving press releases and fan newspapers. Numerous gospel performers, such as the Blackwood Brothers, the Speer Family, and Jimmy Swaggert, have written "biographies," and while these are useful to an extent, they are more often than not designed as "inspirational" reading rather than factual accounts. The very term gospel music has become confusing to the average reader; in recent years the term (which originated in white "revivalist" hymns of the 1890s) has been appropriated by scholars to describe black religious singing, though it is still generally used by the public (and the musicians) to refer to white singing. While there has been some overlap between the two singing traditions, the black and white gospel traditions remain quite distinct and have in common primarily only the fact that both musics focus on religion. During the late 1940s, when Elvis Presley was growing up in Mississippi, the term *spiritual* was usually applied to black groups and *gospel* reserved pretty much for white groups. The National Academy of Recording Arts and Sciences preserves this distinction in its awarding of the Grammy honors; separate categories exist for Soul Gospel and Traditional Gospel. While it is virtually certain that Presley was exposed to both types of these gospel traditions while growing up, and while it is quite likely that, directly or indirectly, he was influenced by the black tradition, this particular study will deal primarily with the white tradition, an influence Presley often acknowledged.

I

No one familiar with the history of music in the Memphis area can deny the role of gospel music. The Deep South states of Alabama and Mississippi have always been hotbeds of gospel music activity, ranging all the way from Sacred Harp meetings to the more sedate singing schools of James D. Vaughn and Stamps-Baxter. More than any other Southern city, Memphis became a center and a melting pot for the various gospel styles. This development had little to do with Memphis's alleged reputation as a home of the blues, but was more a reflection of the city's emergence as a media center in the 1920s. By 1923 the city had a powerful radio station, WMC, and by 1927 it was a center for Southern recording activities of major phonograph companies. Many of these records contained important early examples of Southern gospel music, both white and black; in fact, the first white performers to record in Memphis were a group of gospel singers headed by a man named George Long, from Presley's home town of Tupelo, Mississippi. (Their recording was "I'm Going Home to Die No More.") Memphis radio continued to attract gospel music to the area; by the late 1940s the Delmore Brothers and Wayne Rainey were mixing country, gospel, and a blues-cum-boogie sound that captivated the whole Arkansas-Tennessee-Mississippi area. By the time Presley had his first hit record, Memphis had become the site for the annual national gospel quartet convention.

Not only was Presley aware of this tradition, but as a young man he intensely wanted to be a part of it. His attention was especially attracted to the group which became the most popular quartet in the Memphis area—indeed, in the nation—in the early 1950s, the Blackwood Brothers. Since they were to form such an important part of Presley's early musical ambitions, it is useful to look at them in more detail.

The early career of the Blackwood Brothers is in many ways typical of the process through which many amateur gospel quartets throughout the South became "professionalized" in the 1930s and 1940s. The group was originally a family affair, made up of the sons of sharecroppers from Choctaw County in North Central Mississippi; three young brothers, Roy, James, and Doyle Blackwood, along with Roy's son R. W., began performing in the mid-1930s over station WJDX in Jackson, Mississippi, and over KWKH in Shreveport, Louisiana. They performed in the gospel quartet style that originated with music book publisher James D. Vaughn about 1910; Vaughn found that he could popularize and advertise his songbooks by sending quartets around the country to sing at church gatherings and all-day singings. The original sound of these quartets was not unlike that of some popular barbershop quartets of the day; songs were performed unaccompanied (in most cases), with each singer taking a different harmonic line. In the 1930s Vaughn's major rival in the songbook business was the Texas firm of Stamps-Baxter, and it was V. O. Stamps who heard the Blackwood Brothers and signed them up to be "representatives" of the powerful Stamps-Baxter company.

For a time the group played over KMA in Shenandoah, Iowa, and, after the interruption of World War II and several personnel changes, moved to Memphis in 1950. By this time the group was well established with gospel music fans. While in Shenandoah, they had started their own record company; and in Memphis they expanded this and added a publishing company. Yet their real fame was just beginning. In 1951 they signed a contract with a major label, RCA Victor, and soon had a nationwide hit on their hands, a song called "The Man Upstairs." They also achieved more nationwide fame in 1954 when they won first prize at the Arthur Godfrey Talent Scout Show on CBS. Shortly after the Godfrey show, however, in late June 1954, two members of the quartet were killed in a tragic plane crash in Gulfport, Mississippi. After some soul-searching, the group decided to continue in music, and found replacements for the two members they had lost. One of the new members was a powerful bass singer named J. D. Sumner, who was later to play a major role in Presley's music.

Throughout 1954 and 1955, the years when Presley was beginning his own musical career for Sam Phillips's Memphis-based Sun Record Company, the Blackwoods continued to be the most highly visible and exciting musical group in the Memphis area. By 1954 they were honorary Tennessee Colonels (under Gov. Frank Clement) and the entire quartet was on the staff of Mississippi Governor Coleman, who claimed the Blackwoods as cousins. Compared to the pablum being dished out in the popular music of the day—crooning by Perry Como and innocuous ditties by Patti Page—the Blackwoods' music was lively, fresh, and exciting; and furthermore, young aspiring singers of the time could easily look upon it as the epitome of commercial success and respectability.

There is certainly evidence that Presley did. As a young man in Memphis in 1953 he constantly hung around programs that featured the Blackwoods; on his lunch breaks, Presley would routinely watch the noon radio show over WMPS which featured country artists during the first half, and gospel groups—including the Blackwoods—during the second half. (The show's emcee, Bob Neal, was later to become one of Presley's first managers.) He would also attend concerts by the Blackwood Brothers. Bass singer J. D. Sumner recalls: "I first met him when he was a kid in Memphis living in the projects. In fact, I used to sneak him in the back of Ellis Auditorium so he could see our show." James Blackwood, the leader of the Blackwood Brothers, tells an even more revealing story: "When Elvis was eighteen, when he was driving the truck, my nephew Cecil and three other boys had a gospel quartet they called the Songfellows. They thought one of the boys was gonna leave, and so Elvis auditioned and he would-a joined them in singing around the Memphis area, except the other boy changed his mind. That finished it, and I think Elvis was disappointed, but he still sang with the boys from time to time, during rehearsals. And he often came to our all-night gospel sings at the auditorium."

Cecil later joined the regular Blackwood Brothers quartet, and J. D. Sumner reports that in later years Presley was in fact offered a job with "a major quartet," though he does not specify it as the Blackwood Brothers. "After Elvis started hitting it big in rock 'n' roll, one of the quartets called him back and offered him a job. Elvis went to his father and said, 'Daddy, what am I going to do?' His father said, 'Well, son, you're doing all right the way you're going now, so I would just keep it up.'" The fact that Presley, while starting to change the face of American music with his new rock music, would even seriously consider an invitation to join a major gospel group suggests how much gospel music counted in his musical values at the time.

Nor was the musical climate at Sun Records devoid of gospel music influences. While it is true that Sam Phillips recorded a surprisingly small percentage of gospel music, his major artists were very much a part of this tradition, and Phillips knew this. Of the four major figures who started on Sun—Elvis, Jerry Lee Lewis, Carl Perkins, and Johnny Cash—two have since authored "inspirational" books about their lives and gospel music (Perkins, Cash). Jerry Lee Lewis engaged in long theological debates with Phillips, one of which, fortuitously captured on tape at the beginning of a session that produced "Great Balls of Fire," is reprinted in Greil Marcus's book *Mystery Train*. (Lewis's cousin, Jimmy Swaggert, has emerged to become one of the major evangelists and gospel music performers of the 1970s.) But the most famous symbol of the gospel aspect of the Sun years is the so-called Million Dollar Quartet session. For years rumors had persisted that Phillips had taped an impromptu jam session featuring Elvis, Jerry Lee Lewis, Johnny Cash, and Carl Perkins gathered around the piano singing old gospel standards. Friends of Elvis have often reported that he liked to play piano and gather friends around to sing old gospel songs, so the story gained some credence. Finally, in 1978 producer Shelby Singleton, who had purchased all the old non-Elvis tapes from Sun, located a 35-minute tape that dated from 1957 and did, in fact, include the four giants of country music singing numbers like "Just a Little Talk with Jesus" and "I'm Gonna Walk that Lonesome Valley." Lawsuits stopped Singleton from releasing the tape as an LP, but the incident dramatized the role gospel music played in the careers of each of these different artists. Sam Phillips himself summed up the religious feeling at Sun records back in the mid-1950s, when he was producing the music that many traditional Southern Protestants saw as the devil's own. Phillips said: "I dare say that there were never any 'infidels'—or agnostics, even—that came in my studio. There was a deep-seated feeling for God, very much so, in probably every artist I ever worked with. Whether they knew how to express it in any way, they showed it to me in the way they did what they did." Thus, while preachers across the land thundered against the rock and roll revolution, the instigators of the new sound debated original sin with Phillips or gathered around the piano to do another chorus of "Jesus, Jesus, Jesus."

II

During Elvis Presley's twenty-three year career on stage, in films, and on records, he continually used established gospel groups among his back-up musicians. Three major groups dominated his back-up music: the Jordanaires (1956–67), the Imperials (1969–71), and J. D. Sumner and the Stamps Quartet (1972–77). In each case, the group came to Presley after establishing a secure name in the gospel field. In each case, the group worked very closely with Presley in developing the texture of the sound that he presented to the public. And in each case, the group found itself to some extent trading off the integrity of its gospel repertoire for increasing popularity in pop music as opposed to country or gospel. The effect that the constant exposure to such groups, and singing styles, had on Presley is not as easy to determine.

The Jordanaires appeared as part of the studio musicians on Presley's first post-Sun session for RCA Victor in January 1956; their first record with him was "I Was the One," which became the "B" side of Presley's first giant hit, "Heartbreak Hotel." The group was well-known at the time: they had made records of their own, done other back-up work, and were regular members of the WSM Grand Ole Opry. Yet their background was in many ways strikingly different from that of Presley's earlier mentors, the Blackwood Brothers. The original Jordanaires came out of Missouri in the mid-1940s, a group of young Midwesterners who specialized in singing barbershop quartet songs and what were then called spirituals. The group had success in Nashville over WSM, not as a country group but as a pop group, but finally decided to return to Missouri. The name Jordanaires was purchased by some local singers who thought such

18

a group could still work; one of them was Gordon Stoker, a tenor who had worked as a piano accompanist on the staff of WSM. He was soon joined by Neal Matthews and Hoyt Hawkins, and the key members of the group were in place. Matthews and Stoker were from Tennessee, and Hawkins was from Kentucky; but unlike the Blackwoods, all three had had college training, and all had had experience in nongospel types of music. Like the Blackwoods, they had attracted a national audience by winning on the Arthur Godfrey Talent Scouts, and by 1956 they had made a conscious decision to "add country, pop, and rock & roll music to their repertoire" (to quote from one of their own press releases).

It's unclear who had the idea of backing Elvis with the Jordanaires, though Chet Atkins had responsibility for drafting the sidemen for the session. Other sources claim that Elvis asked for the Jordanaires, though it seems unlikely that even Elvis, at his first major label session, would have felt secure enough to demand particular sidemen. Atkins, who had been putting together sessions for Victor for several years, knew that the Jordanaires had the ability to work out "head" arrangements: on the spot, improvised back-up arrangements featuring different vocal parts. Whatever the actual reason, the Jordanaires were relegated to strictly a back-up position; none of the publicity of the time, nor any of the resulting records, in any way indicated that this was an active collaboration between Elvis and a famous gospel group.

This situation was to change in 1957. As Presley's career skyrocketed throughout 1956, he developed what would today be called an image problem: across the country, parents' groups and church leaders protested his "spastic gyrations" and "primitive jungle-beat rhythm." Partly to counteract this image, Presley, in his second Sullivan appearance in 1957, sang a slow, almost sedate (even by gospel standards) version of an old country and western standard, "Peace in the Valley," which had been popularized by Red Foley some years before. (Ironically, it is not generally known that the song was in fact composed by black gospel composer Thomas A. Dorsey.) Audience reaction was favorable, and within weeks RCA had rushed out a 45 rpm extended play album containing "Peace in the Valley" and three other gospel standards. The liner notes to the set reflected the attempt to "right" Presley's image by stressing his love for gospel music, but also represented a sincere attempt to reflect Presley's genuine love for the music. Since this was Presley's first attempt to present such music before a wider audience, Calvin Helm's notes are worth quoting:

To a great many people Elvis Presley has been a surprise. They have been surprised at his style of singing, at his disarming frankness and most of all at his rapid success. To them this album will also be a surprise. But to any of the fortunate folks who have known Elvis, whether as a schoolboy, movie usher, delivery man or performer, PEACE IN THE VALLEY will be no surprise.

Little older than five was Elvis when he started singing in church in his native deep Southland. Its music was his earliest and he is quick to credit this early and sustained background for its contribution towards his style. In fact, prominent in his personal record collection are most of the records available by the Statesmen Quartet, the Blackwood Brothers Quartet, the Jordanaires and other sacred groups of the South.

It was, then, no real surprise when on a recent Ed Sullivan TV show Elvis decided to do the title song of this set. Nor were the folks at RCA Victor surprised the very next day when the deluge of wires and letters descended suggesting, requesting and demanding that the selection be recorded by Elvis. This album is the result and it is interesting to note that on these four great sacred numbers Elvis chose to use only the men he normally employs on his popular recording; Scotty Moore on guitar, Bill Black on bass, D. J. Fontana on drums and The Jordanaires. If you are not impressed by the results, I will be surprised.

This was the first real public acknowledgment of Presley's long-time interest in gospel music, but it is significant that the tunes of the EP album were not closely identified with the gospel quartet tradition *per se*. Two were by Thomas Dorsey (the other besides "Peace in the Valley" was "Take My Hand, Precious Lord," a standard in both black gospel and white country music), one was a pop gospel song associated with Billy Graham, "It Is No Secret What God Can Do," by Stuart Hamblen, and the last was "I Believe," then popular as a "church special" among tenor soloists. Though the Jordanaires backed Presley on all four songs, they functioned strictly as a back-up unit to Elvis's lead. This use of "popular" gospel songs as opposed to those associated with the quartet tradition was to continue throughout Presley's career.

During the next ten years the Jordanaires continued to back Presley on recordings and, starting with *Loving You* in 1957, in films.

The group grew increasingly close to Presley during his Hollywood years, and they seemed to have a psychological function as well as a practical function. Gordon Stoker recalls one episode during the filming of *Jailhouse Rock* that illustrates this point: "It was morning and Elvis went to the piano and began to play spirituals, his first love. We all fell in with him, all the Jordanaires and Bill and Scotty and D. J. We sang all morning with Elvis, probably not even thinking about the songs for the film, certainly not rehearsing or recording them. And then we broke for lunch." When the group returned, Elvis went right back to the piano and began singing gospel. Studio officials asked them to stop, to get busy on the songs for the film. Furious, Elvis walked out and the day was cancelled. "What the studio didn't realize," recalls Stoker, "was that Elvis hadn't sung in a studio in some while and this was his way of warming up, getting in the mood. . . ."

In spite of this close psychological and personal affinity for the Jordanaires, Presley did not record many gospel numbers with them during these years. In 1960 he did produce *His Hand In Mine,* the LP follow-up to the *Peace in the Valley* EP. The cover photo showed a sedate looking Elvis seated at a piano; the songs included a curious mixture of genuine spirituals, such as "Joshua Fit the Battle of Jericho," "I'm Gonna Walk Dem Golden Stairs" and "Working on a Building," and more traditional gospel material, such as Albert Brumley's "If We Ever Meet Again." The album did well enough to receive a gold record award, but it never rose very high in the national charts. The only other relevant piece recorded during this period was "Crying in the Chapel" in 1965; though not strictly gospel, it was a million-seller and rose to #3 in the national charts. The song was included in the 1967 album *How Great Thou Art,* and, along with the title song, helped the album garner over one million dollars in sales. Other titles in this album, his second full gospel LP, were rather formal church songs, such as "In the Garden," "Where No One Stands Alone," and "Further Along," songs that attained their greatest popularity not as gospel quartet performances, but as church "specials" or revival specials as sung by George Beverley Shea, lead singer with evangelist Billy Graham. These two albums, though, were only two of twenty-four released during this time by Elvis; they represent a rather small percentage of the total output. But if Presley didn't record many actual gospel songs with the Jordanaires, he continued to use the group constantly on his other recordings, and once complained bitterly to RCA when he felt the producers were mixing an album so as to emphasize the sound of his own voice too much over that of the group.

The Jordanaires, meanwhile, were expanding their own activities. With Presley not touring and confining his activities to films and studio albums, the group was free to develop work for other artists. They began to split their work between Nashville, New York, and Hollywood and found themselves doing back-up work for country singers like Marty Robbins, David Houston, and Loretta Lynn, as well as pop singers like Patti Page, Ernie Ford, Connie Francis, and Rick Nelson. By 1965 they were voted the fifth most popular singing group in the world by *Record Mirror,* a British trade publication. Their press office was claiming that the group had "initiated a new type of vocalizing by providing a background of vocal harmonizing for a lead singer," a curious claim that has more truth in it than might at first appear.

By 1969, when Presley was ready to make his "comeback" and resume touring, the Jordanaires had pretty much completed the transition to pop music and had all the studio and recording work they could handle. Though they continued to record with Presley on occasion, they began to cut down on the tours; Gordon Stoker reported that the group was simply tired of touring and didn't feel up to signing on with Elvis. In their place, Elvis got the Imperials, another group which had been known only in gospel circles; in fact, in 1969 the first year of the Gospel Music Association's prestigious Dove awards, the Imperials won the honors for the Best Gospel Group. Though they had been organized in the mid-1960s, the group was just peaking in popularity (at least among gospel circles) in 1969, the year Presley asked them to join him as a back-up group.

Even to gospel fans the Imperials were known as a slick, modern, upbeat group and were in many ways untypical of the classic quartet style represented by the Blackwood Brothers, the Statesmen, or the other groups of Presley's formative years. The group's leader was Tony Moscheo, a full-blooded Italian and former Catholic who had a degree in music from Florida State; he dressed sharply, had a New York accent, and was outspoken about the changes the Imperials made in gospel music. He argued that the Imperials, in fact, was the first gospel group to shed the quartet identity along with the "slicked-down hair and patent-leather shoes." "I don't like the identity associated with gospel groups. When a guy introduces us as the Imperials Quartet, it offends me." Another step was taken in shedding this image in 1971 when the Imperials became the first white gospel group to add a black member, Sherman Andruss.

The Imperials worked with Elvis for only three years, but they managed to appear in the film *That's the Way It Is* and to back him on some important records, including *He Touched Me,* the album that won Presley a Grammy for the best gospel album of the year in 1972. Presley's taste in gospel music—in both style and content—by now seemed closely aligned with that of the gospel music industry in Nashville. *He Touched Me* contained a copy of older gospel standards, such as "Amazing Grace," but generally was weighted toward modern songs by contemporary gospel figures, ranging from the pseudo folk stylings of Ralph Carmichael to the songs of Andrae Crouch, a contemporary black group attracting a wide crossover audience. He often performed, with the Imperials, "Why Me, Lord," a Kris Kristofferson song that was enjoying widespread popularity and which modern gospel groups were eager to perform. Unlike the Jordanaires, though, the Imperials never really broke out of gospel into mainstream pop music; at the same time that they backed Presley on RCA Victor, they continued to record on their own for exclusively gospel labels like Heart Warming and Impact.

Soon the Imperials tired of the touring circuit, and Presley turned to the man who was to become his closest liaison to the world of gospel music, John Daniel Sumner. Next to the legendary "Big Chief," Wetherington of the Statesmen, J. D. Sumner had the most famous bass voice in gospel music. He had joined the Blackwood Brothers in 1954, after the plane crash had killed the group's original bass singer, and had known Elvis since the earliest Memphis days. It was Sumner who had founded the National Quartet Convention and brought it to Memphis in 1955, and this had made him into one of the leading figures in the commercialization of the gospel music industry. In 1963 he and James Blackwood had purchased the Stamps Quartet Music Company in Dallas, one of the oldest and most prestigious gospel publishing houses, and in 1965 Sumner left the Blackwoods to become manager and singer for the Stamps Quartet. Following the modernizing trend in the industry, the group soon shortened its name to "J. D. Sumner and the Stamps." Shortly thereafter, they joined Presley and remained with him for the last whirlwind years of his career.

In an interview given shortly after Presley's death, Sumner reflected on the long-time attraction gospel music had held for Presley. "No one has ever loved bass singing like Elvis did. He told me one time if he could have his choice he would have been a bass singer. He used to have the Stamps come up to his room and sing gospel music for him and he always joined in singing bass. Elvis did more to change music than anyone. He was raised listening to gospel music and was raised in the Pentecostal church where they have always

23

had great feeling in their music. He got his beat in his music from the Pentecostal church. He took white gospel, black gospel, and country and that was where his music came from." Sumner also felt that Elvis's interest in the Stamps was part of his larger return to his roots manifested in the last five years of his career. "At first (when Presley first asked the group to back him) I was just going to take my boys up to sing while I took a little vacation. But then Elvis said he wanted me to sing and he would get me a microphone by myself. You see, he used to listen to me back in his younger days when I was a gospel star and he was just a country boy." Sumner's voice comes through on many of Presley's later records, and the Stamps were prominently featured in a segment of one of Presley's last television specials. In 1974 Presley's recording of "How Great Thou Art" won another Grammy, and by this time many of his fans—including some original fans from 1956 who were entering middle age—were responding more favorably to his gospel music than to other aspects of his music. Though the Stamps and Sumner appeared on an increasing number of concert recordings—they did about 100 concerts annually with Presley in the mid-1970s—the percentage of gospel in Presley's repertoire remained relatively low.

Gospel music played a larger role in the typical Presley concert of the 1970s. Sumner felt that "during the last six years he didn't sing much rock and roll. . . . He had one song, 'Burning Love,' that he wouldn't sing on stage. Even though the people liked it, he didn't. He preferred to sing songs like 'My Way' or 'Lord You Gave Me A Mountain.' I never heard a man sing 'How Great Thou Art' with such humbleness and dignity as Elvis did." Sumner often helped Elvis sing songs like "Why Me Lord" (Kristofferson) and "Help Me" (by country singer Larry Gatlin) on concerts and was fond of claiming that the gospel segment of the concerts was becoming the highlight of the shows.

Sumner also gives Presley credit for giving gospel music wider exposure in his 1970s concerts and often putting the Stamps on stage "to sing gospel music to people who have never before heard it." Elvis was, in other words, using his pop credentials to sell a music that his audience would not normally respond to. "If Elvis had been a gospel singer," says Sumner, "he wouldn't have reached the masses of people like he did." The Stamps would often, in their personal appearances without Presley, sing songs they did with him, but with only a fraction of the impact on their audience. "A lot of times we'll do a show and the biggest song on it is a gospel song. I would say to Elvis, 'that's a gospel song, but if we sang it it just wouldn't go over the same.' Elvis answered, 'That bugs me too.'"

J. D. Sumner also became a close personal friend of Presley's, and since Sumner was a major figure in the Gospel Music Association, Presley gained some entree into the highest echelons of the world of professional gospel music and its promotion. During the last year of his life he became involved in the attempt to build a Gospel Music Hall of Fame to parallel the Country Music Hall of Fame in Nashville. At one point Presley had agreed to give a benefit concert to get funds for the building started, but became angry when he found out that J. D. himself had not yet been elected to the Hall of Fame. Negotiations proceeded, however, and plans for such a benefit were actually being made when the officers of the GMA received word of Presley's death in August 1977. (Speaking from the stage of the 1978 National Gospel Quartet Convention, Sumner went into more detail about Presley's interest in gospel music and stated he felt that had Presley lived another six months, he would have converted his career into that of a full-time gospel singer.)

III

The influence of country music and blues on Presley's music can be readily seen by anyone who looks closely at his repertoire. This is not the case with the third influence, white gospel music. The Presley discography contains relatively few examples of gospel music, and none of them was among his biggest sellers. Nor were they all self-contained examples of classic Southern gospel quartet music; they were a mixture of traditional spirituals, black gospel, popular pseudo gospel pieces, quartet songs, and what the Gospel Music Association likes to call inspirational pieces. Whatever influence the classic Southern gospel music had on Presley, it was not in the content of his songs. There is a good deal of evidence to suggest, though, that this influence was felt in Presley's singing style and performing style.

Any discussion of the Presley singing style has to be prefaced by a caution. In the first place, singing style (as opposed to songs or content) is perhaps the most understudied aspect of folk or country music. No accepted vocabulary exists to describe popular singing techniques in an analytical way. Furthermore, as we have noted, no one has seriously examined the origin and nature of the gospel quartet style as it emerged in the early 1950s to captivate young Elvis

Presley. What did the Blackwood Brothers or the Statesmen really sound like in 1954, and what made their sound different or appealing? We don't really know, and until we do we can't be sure about any gospel influence on the Presley style. We can, though, venture a few tentative theories.

Among all the reports about how much Elvis loved gospel music, few give us any indication about why he liked it, or what elements of it appealed to him. An exception is a revealing account given by singer Johnny Rivers and quoted by Jerry Hopkins in *Elvis: A Biography:* "One of his idols when he was young was a man named Jake Hess, who was the lead singer for the Statesmen Quartet. If you'll listen to some of their recordings, you'll hear some of that style that is now Elvis Presley's style, especially in his ballad singing style. He was playing some of their records one day and he said, 'Now you know where I got my style from. Caught—a hundred million records too late.' It was really funny. I think he idolized Jake. Jake and the Statesmen and the Blackwoods." Listening to early records of the Statesmen that feature Jake Hess, and listening from the broader perspective of pop music rather than gospel, one is struck by the similarities of Hess's dramatic, forceful lead style and Presley's ballad style. But one is equally impressed with the way in which Hess uses the background quartet to highlight and even propel his singing; were it not for the content of the songs, in fact, one could almost mistake Hess and the early Statesmen for one of the doo-wop groups of the early years of rock and roll. The ultimate origins of this style may well lie in classic black gospel music, where singing with the emphasis on interplay between a lead voice that does the main lyric in front of responding voices is referred to as "Dr. Watts style." J. D. Sumner has hinted that Elvis was fascinated with this sort of group-lead interplay as well; speaking of Elvis, he recalls: "He remembered how I used to sing and he said he wanted some of those old endings I used to do—some of those '56 endings is what he called them. I used to go DOOOOOooooo and slur down to a low note. So he made me sing." Elvis's constant concern with using gospel groups as his back-up singers, and insisting that these groups maintain an integrity and identity (as opposed to relegating them to an anonymous studio sound), suggests that he was conscious of their role in the Presley sound.

To be sure, Presley did have a genuine interest in the content of gospel song as well, and he tried repeatedly in his career to use his own popularity to promote gospel music. These attempts met with limited success; he never really succeeded in elevating any of the gospel quartets he worked with to anything approaching his own level of popularity. The only group that came close was the Jordanaires, and their relative popularity can probably be ascribed to the fact that they themselves moved out of the specific gospel tradition into a broader based music. The element of gospel music that Presley was able to successfully get across to his vast audience was the integrated solo-group singing style. Gospel music became part of his aesthetic, if not part of his values, and some day, when the full story of modern Southern gospel music has been told and placed in perspective, we can make some serious judgments about the origins of a singing style that changed the face of American popular music.

A Note on Sources

This essay has been written using a wide variety of traditional printed sources, newspaper clippings, record company data, and interviews. The only two serious attempts to write about white gospel music in book form are Jesse Burt and Duane Allen *The History of Gospel Music* (Nashville: K & S Press, Inc., 1971) and Lois S. Blackwell, *The Wings of the Dove: The Story of Gospel Music in America* (Norfolk, Virginia: The Donning Company, 1978). A prime collection of material on individual gospel groups and singers can be found in Linnell Gentry *History and Encyclopedia of Country Western and Gospel Music,* 2nd ed. (Nashville: Clairmont, 1971). Some of the quotes about Elvis and gospel (especially in the early years) come from Jerry Hopkins, *Elvis: A Biography* (New York: Simon and Schuster, 1972); others come from the extensive clipping files on J. D. Sumner, the Imperials, and others maintained by Linnell Gentry, and I am deeply indebted to his willingness to make these available to me. Also special thanks to the Country Music Foundation Archives and Media Center, Nashville, and to members of the Gospel Music Association, and especially to Don Cusie.

THE
MYTHICAL
ELVIS

*Examinations of Elvis in the popular press, re-
flections of our shifting attitudes toward him, and
attempts to come to terms with a legend in our
own time: These are glimpses of ourselves in
poses of shock, disdain, bemusement, and wonder
as we struggle with (and against) a pure and endless fascination with Elvis.*

THE MAN IN THE BLUE SUEDE SHOES

■

by James and Annette Baxter

Originally published in Harper's Magazine *in 1958, this article is one of the first serious assessments of the Elvis phenomenon ever attempted. The authors' observations about Elvis and the generation that he so strongly affected are as valid today as they ever were, and their appraisal of Elvis's vocal capabilities is truly ahead of its time.*

Ol' Elvis Presley may be a better musician than most people dare to admit—and he might be offering the kids a commodity their parents can't recognize.

As a subject for polemic Elvis Presley has few peers, and too many people have experienced sudden shifts in blood pressure—either up or down—for him to be regarded as anything but an authentic barometer of the times. But, even now that he has been on the national scene for more than two years, he may be telling us more about ourselves than we would care to admit.

Presley's climb to fame, in the winter of 1955–56, followed upon the appearance of that raucous brand of popular music, primitive and heavy-footed, known as rock-and-roll. Untouched by subtlety, rock-and-roll seemed to signal a total collapse in popular taste, the final schism between a diminishing group sensitive to tradition and the great bulk of those who make entertainment to sell. Suddenly there was Elvis, not merely a manifestation of rock-and-roll, but of lascivious gyrations of the torso that older generations quickly recognized—the classic bump and grind of the strip-teaser.

Television compounded the jeopardy: Elvis could come lurching into any living-room, and he did, and the chorus of adolescent shrieks was swelled by shrieks from the parents. The stomping blatancy of "Blue Suede Shoes" and the insinuations of "I Want You, I Need You, I Love You" were sufficiently distressing, but the foot-spread stance and the unmistakable thrust—well, "The Pelvis" was going too far.

He went too far in every direction. Elvis was making millions of dollars, owning white Continental Mark IIs, getting into fights and reviving sideburns and being prayed over and building a house for his parents. The legend should have swallowed him out of sight, but it was all true—all, furthermore, palpably American. He may not actually have arrived for his Army physical in a Cadillac with a Las Vegas show girl and announced that he wanted to be treated just like everyone else—but the story was pure Elvis. Anyway, the gawky, loose-limbed, simple boy from Tupelo, Mississippi, was a genuine *tabula rasa,* on which the American populace could keep drawing its portrait, real and imaginary, and keep rubbing it out.

Admonished that there were those who found his hip-swiveling offensive, Elvis is said to have replied, "I never made no dirty body movements." And this is believable; Elvis moves as the spirit moves him; it all comes naturally. Hormones flow in him as serenely as the Mississippi past Memphis, and the offense lies in the eye of the beholder, not in Elvis's intentions.

By constantly reminding his teen-age listeners of what he so obviously was—a simple boy from Tupelo who had suddenly become famous—Elvis somehow removed the sting from the sexuality that could easily have terrified them. Valentino had to become an exotic in order to keep from frightening the ladies of an earlier era with his own heavy-lidded gaze; Elvis could remain the boy next door. He was even able to capitalize on his innocence: in his television appearances he could find himself flinging a Svengali-like finger out toward his audience and, when they squealed, he couldn't keep from giggling. He was as amused as they were by his idiotic power to hypnotize and, although the spell was on, the curse was off.

But Presley's stunning rapport with his own generation must

hinge on something more than the ageless call of the wild. Appealing to the youthful imagination in some way inscrutable to the parents of the teen-agers who worship him, Elvis fills some kind of need that the older generation can't fathom, and more significantly, doesn't feel. Why? Perhaps because they have run out of dreams.

Parents for whom the introduction of television in the late 'forties begat the era of the great giveaway need no dreams—they are already living one. Ranch-style homes, organization-man jobs, and exalted community status have outrun whatever hopes they brought from a meager past, and adults are too delightedly clutching these tangible evidences of a dream-come-true to bother projecting a more fanciful one. Their smartly-executed station-wagon psyches, jauntily upholstered and gleamingly trimmed, leave no room for excrescences and irrelevancies. But their offspring, a generation of poor little rich children, whom no part of the postwar bonanza has the power to enthrall, remain desperately in need of an enchanter.

THE MYSTERIOUS SOUTH

To meet this historic contingency Elvis is blessed not only with sex but with authentic Southernness. His primitivism carries conviction; when he intones the monotonous phrases of "I Got a Woman," Southern medium espouses Southern temperament. The range of verbal expression is precisely as limited and as colorful as we feel Elvis's own vocabulary must be. The voice, on the other hand, insisting on the subtlest of shifts in mood and timing, suggests that the man from whom it issues is, like his music, elusive.

The sum of Presley's qualities matches the national image of the Southland. For the South today popularly represents what the West once did: the self-sufficient, the inaccessible, the fiercely independent soul of the nation. With the taming of the West completed, only the deep South retains a comparable aura of mystery, of romantic removal from the concerns of a steadily urbanized and cosmopolized America.

The removal is two-fold: it combines an indifference to grammatical niceties, which the rest of the country benightedly associates with "civilization," with an old confidence in the private, intuitive vision. The rationalism of the "progressive" sections of the nation has always seemed to the Southerner inadequate to penetrate the darker corners of his experience, and these components of the Southern mind are central to a Presley performance.

The adolescent is far more responsive to them than his parents

33

could be. In the backwoods heterodoxies of Elvis he recognizes a counterpart to his own instinctive rebellion. And when Elvis confesses that he's "Gonna Sit Right Down and Cry," the accents of lament are felt as genuine; there's none of the artifice of the torch-singer in his wail. Elvis is for real, and in his voice the teen-ager hears intimations of a world heavily weighted with real emotion.

Most real emotions, the teen-ager knows without coaching, are daily discredited by his parents and teachers. Their own equably democratic temperaments and cheerfully enlightened code of behavior seem to deny the world that Elvis affirms. And the teen-ager, when he pounds convulsively at the sight and sound of Elvis, is pounding for entrance into that more enticing realm.

He is pounding his feet, however; ultimately the music Elvis makes must be given some credit for his popularity. And there is probably an ugly, awesome little truth in the deduction that he is prodigiously gifted. To those attentive to the music itself the most conspicuous feature of Elvis's singing is the versatility with which he exploits the tradition of the Negro "blues-shouter." He can shift without apparent strain from the blasting stridency of "Hound Dog" to the saccharine ooze of "I'll Never Let You Go," covering, when called upon, every transitional pose between: the choke-and-groan of "Love Me," the plaintive nasal whine of "How's the World Treating You," the gravel-throated bellow of "Long Tall Sally," or the throb-and-tremolo of "I Got a Woman."

Vocal pyrotechnics he has indeed (to what must be the everlasting despair of his imitators), but they would remain merely curiosities were he not able to manipulate them into an organic whole. His twisting of a tonal quality possesses a diabolical inevitability, and his phrasing is as flawless as it is intricate. Marianne Moore's comment about e. e. cummings—"He does not make aesthetic mistakes"—might with only brief hesitation be applied to Elvis Presley. Elvis has got the beat, and "Don't Be Cruel" will bear scrutiny by any but the most outraged of his captious audience.

LAUGHING AT US

But there is in Presley's delivery something much more subtle and hard to get at. From some fathomless and unstudied depth he has managed, in a whole series of songs, to call forth irony. Elvis is laughing at us, and at himself, without knowing it, and while remaining altogether serious. The throbbing sentimentality is at once wholly fake and sterling pure; listen for it in "I'm Counting on

You," or "Tryin' to Get to You." And so is the pompousness of "One-Sided Love Affair" and the mawkishness of "Old Shep." In his interpretation of these songs there are ambiguities that are surely unsuspected even by such an uninhibited and highly sophisticated primitive as Elvis himself.

This neither-fish-nor-fowl quality can be a frightening thing to adults, who suppose that they have fully identified themselves in an identifiable environment. But to adolescents, who detest above all the status quo—who want the world to be so limitless in its potentials that they cannot fail to find their changeling selves somehow secure within it—to them it is the throbbing substance of life itself. And when combined with the frenetic pulsations, the hectic, nervous quiverings of rock-and-roll, the rhythms of their own vacillations, it is enough to make Elvis a millionaire.

Whither Presley? When his present public finds itself, as it someday must, demesmerized by time, and when the mage-like fascination of Elvis gives way to some new and less inspired teen-age melodrama, what's to become of this young man whose life and legend are by now indistinguishable?

Will Elvis himself be able to salvage a personality from among the accumulated debris of prolonged public exposure? Will he choose one of several paths systematically trodden by the once great: lucratively "advising" the producers of "The Elvis Presley Story," lecturing across the country on the prevention of juvenile delinquency, opening with moderate hoopla a restaurant in Atlantic City, appointing a respectable hack to ghost his memoirs, or posing rakishly for a Chesterfield ad?

Some indication that Elvis has a notion of the responsibility of his mission is his plan for a fifteen-acre Elvis Presley Youth Foundation in Tupelo, reported in *Time*. How far this project may go is uncertain, but if it takes him back to Mississippi for spiritual recuperation from time to time, it will be both good for him and for the youth who want him, need him, and love him.

ELVIS, THE INDIGENOUS

███

by Mr. Harper

This brief item appeared in Harper's *in April 1957 and hints at the kinds of debates that Elvis sparked among observers of American society, as well as his popularity abroad. The quip about Elvis being "drafted" and "deprived of his sideburns" is particularly prophetic.*

ELVIS, THE INDIGENOUS

A correspondent from Communist Czechoslovakia writes me as follows:

> I heard about rock 'n' roll. Is it a new style of jazz, or does it belong to popular music? I would be glad to hear it. How does Elvis Presley sing? I had lent a Canadian journal *Liberty*, issue from August 1956, and in this is a picture from Elvis Presley while singing and playing on guitar. He looks as in ecstasy. Please, be so kind as to write me something about it.

This came at about the same time as a clipping from the *New York Times* ("Presley Records a Craze in Soviet") which stated that Elvis discs, cut on discarded hospital X-ray plates, are selling in Leningrad for $12.50 apiece. "Returning travelers report," wrote Harrison Salisbury, "that the singer is the latest craze of the Soviet zoot-suiters, or *stilyagi,* as they are called."

Yes, Virginia, there is an Elvis Presley.

Actually, from a strictly Marxist-Leninist viewpoint, you probably realize that he is a typical example of capitalist exploitation. Presley is an authentic folk-artist, in the tradition of the Negro blues-shouters, who has cleverly masqueraded as a *stilyagi* in order to capture the attention of the proletariat. Dismayed by his success, the American warmongers have urged their lackey intellectuals (like the formalist hyena Burke, of *High Fidelity*) to discredit Presley. Only the jazz scholar John A. Wilson has had the courage to point out that Presley is merely "mixing a genuine musical heritage with a musical fad that was well under way long before he gained any prominence. . . ."

That's about the story to date, though it is rumored that the State Department—ever the servant of imperialism—is facilitating the anti-Presley campaign by importing large numbers of calypso singers, by banana boat, from the American satellites in the Caribbean. If the situation becomes desperate, we are reliably informed that Presley will be drafted into the mercenary armies of Wall Street and deprived of his sideburns.

—Mr. Harper

THE ROCK IS SOLID

from *Time* magazine, November 1957

This item featured in the music column was typical of music critics' handling of rock 'n' roll in its early years. This particular critic notes wistfully that Elvis and rock 'n' roll seem to be enduring despite a trend toward ballads.

Is the golden glottis gurgling to a stop? Is there a quiver to those rosebud lips, a beginning of wilt to those poodle-wool sideburns? For two years, lovers of peace, quiet and a less epileptic kind of minstrelsy have waited for Elvis Presley and the adenoidal art form, rock 'n' roll, to fade. But knowledgeable disk jockeys and trade bulletins offer such purists little hope. In spite of previously noted tremors, last week rock 'n' roll looked solid as Gibraltar, and Elvis—with a new stomp-and-holler hit, *Jailhouse Rock* (RCA Victor)—was perched right on top.

The new Presley disk hit second place on *Billboard*'s authoritative top-tunes listing in its second week on the chart, and by last week Victor claimed to have shipped 2,000,000 copies (total Presley sales of single disks so far: a staggering 28 million). The movie-bred lyrics of *Jailhouse Rock* (*see* CINEMA) suggests a powerful argument for penal reform, but no clues to the record's whopping success.

Everybody in a whole cell block
Was dancing to the jailhouse rock . . .
[Mumble, mumble] crash, boom, bang
The whole rhythm section was a purple gang.

No New Sound. Philosophizes Chicago Deejay Marty Faye on rock 'n' roll: "The kids have accepted this twanging guitar, this nasal unintelligible sound, this irritating sameness of lyrics, this lamentable croak. They've picked a sound all their own, apart from anything the adults like. Rock 'n' roll is still as strong as ever, and we'll have to live with it until the kids find a new sound."

For a while last summer, it looked as if the kids might have found one. Calypso jounced and jingled into earshot, but in the end turned out to be loss *lieder*. Industry plotters pegged Hawaiian music for the next turntable fad, found the kids not in a hula mood. Rock 'n' roll faltered slightly when ballads (*Love Letters in the Sand, Tammy*) began catching on again, and a few of the U.S.'s disk jockeys report that ballads are continuing to cut into rock 'n' roll popularity. From staid Boston, WBZ's Bill Marlowe states flatly that "Rock 'n' roll has had it. The teenagers are beginning to look to better music." But in Los Angeles the craze is just as strong as ever, and in Atlanta, jukebox operators and record shop proprietors say that rock 'n' roll is still by far the most popular music.

No Steady Starlets. Elvis, unworried, continues to live off what most parents would agree is the fat of teenagers' heads. As befits a solid citizen (possible 1957 gross, $1 million), he has lately eschewed fist-fights and steady starlets, projected a 15-acre Elvis Presley Youth Foundation in Tupelo, Mississippi, his birthplace.

GOLDEN GLOTTIS PRESLEY

Living off the fat of the heads.

As Elvis gets older (22), he grows more conservative: his favorite vehicle, his handlers report, is not his black Harley-Davidson motor-cycle, his royal purple Lincoln Continental, his red Messerschmidt, his yellow Isetta, his pink or his yellow Cadillac, but a sumptuous, black, bankerish Cadillac limousine. If austerity and decorum shroud Presley's personal life, his fans need not worry that the old megalo-mania is disappearing. His tour manager explains that the reason Elvis has not graced TV this season is that no network has met his

$100,000-an-hour fee allowed that "if there were a program of half-hour duration, Elvis might make a concession and take $75,000."

Meanwhile, Elvis has prepared a surprise package for the nation that is likely to be the most serious menace to Christmas since *I Saw Mommy Kissing Santa Claus*. Victor is planning to release an album of Yule songs by Presley, accompanied by guitar and organ, the selections including *Silent Night* and *Santa, Bring My Baby Back to Me*.

LONELY & SHOOK UP

---

from *Time* magazine, May 1957

*This piece reflects the problem of journalists who neither liked nor under-
stood Elvis and his music but were obliged to write about him if only because
of his massive popularity and unprecedented earnings. This item, like most,
is not overtly mean spirited, but its teasing tone is indicative of how a great
many adults felt about rock 'n' roll in general and Elvis in particular.*

Cavorting sullenly before Hollywood cameras last week, Sexhibi-
tionist Elvis Presley got all shook up by his pelvic pulsations, dis-
lodged a cap prettifying one of his teeth, inhaled the bit of porcelain
into his lung. While thousands of bobby-soxers fretted next day over
the voice that was stilled, surgeons removed the object with forceps
and bronchoscope.

It was just one of those minor disasters that pave the way to greatness, and Elvis had plenty of material consolations for his pain. For
his antics in his third film *Jailhouse Rock,* Metro-Goldwyn Mayer
will pay him an unheard-of $250,000 plus 50% of the net profits.
This gives him a clear shot at coining the most money ever earned
by a star on a single film. Moreover, just to keep Elvis rocking con-
tentedly, M-G-M also tossed to Elvis Presley Music, Inc. the handling of the sheet music and disks, provided an executive suite in its
studios for Elvis and his menage of mentors, flacks and professional
pals.

But was Elvis really happy? Sensing the sadness that lurked behind Millionaire Presley's pout, the New York *Herald Tribune*'s keen-nosed Joe Hyams asked for an interview, was invited by to watch Elvis eat a modest lunch (a bowl of gravy, a bowl of mashed potatoes, nine slices of crisp bacon, a quart of milk, a big glass of tomato juice, lettuce salad, six slices of bread, four pats of butter).

Excerpts:

Q. *Do you plan to be a power for good, and direct some of your fans' energy into useful channels, such as combatting juvenile delinquency?*
A. Juvenile delinquency isn't long hair or a leather jacket. . . . I never thought of using my power in a good way. . . . I've just been taking it as it comes.

Q. *Do you feel secure yet as an entertainer?*
A. Man, I'll tell you I don't know. I'm not sure whether I've got it made.

Q. *Have you everything you want now?*
A. No, I'll tell you one thing, sometimes I get lonely as hell!

Q. *According to reports, you've chosen some remarkable parts of the human anatomy to sign autographs.*
A. That's not true. I've written on arms, legs and ankles—any place decent where someone can take soap and wash it off. . . . I don't want no daddy with a shotgun after me.

Q. *What part does Colonel Tom Parker [Presley's managerial mastermind] play in your career?*
A. I've got an idea of how to handle me better than anyone else has as far as keeping me in line. Colonel Parker is more or less like a daddy when I'm away from my own folks.

DEVITALIZING ELVIS

by John Lardner

This item appeared July 1956 in "Lardner's Week," a regular Newsweek *column, and deals with Elvis' controversial appearance on "The Steve Allen Show" in which Elvis, dressed in a tuxedo and later in a cowboy outfit, was a willing participant in what many saw as an attempt on Allen's part to mock and embarrass him.*

Along with the lively baseball, or rabbit pill, modern civilization has produced the lively vocalist, or rabbit singer. Outstanding among the twitching Carusos of the present day is a chap named Elvis Presley. There is nothing to be said against Elvis—and many people have said it—except that when placed in front of a microphone, he behaves like an outboard motor.

Pardon me. I stand corrected. Professor Klein, the Yale sociologist, who is peering over my shoulder as I write this, asks me to note that what Elvis acts like is a lovesick outboard motor.

Well and good. There has been no movement to stabilize or deaden the rabbit ball, and offhand there would seem to be no clear need to stabilize or deaden the rabbit vocalist. Live and let live—that is how most of us boys in the upper crust of sociology look at it. Nonetheless, we all watched with interest last week when one of our number, Steve Allen (who has his own show, as we say in the scientific game), made a public attempt to neutralize, calm, or detwitch Elvis Presley, the lively singer.

THE RIVAL CULTURES

Allen did this, one assumes, in what he personally considers the best interests of civilization. For him, it was logical. Civilization today is sharply divided into two schools which cannot stand the sight of each other. One school, Allen's, is torpid and dormant in style; it believes in underplaying, or underbidding, or waiting 'em out. The other, Presley's, is committed to the strategy of open defiance, of confusing 'em, of yelling 'em down. The hips and the Adam's apple, this school believes, must be quicker than the eye.

Each school has its own habits and markings, off stage and on. Members of the lively, or rabbit school tend to wear their sideburns long, if they do not actively bust out in goatees. In private life, they ride motorcycles—or, on especially gay week ends, the motorcycles ride them, the effect being much the same. During public performances, they seldom focus their eyes. The eye, in fact, is a vestigial organ among them, like the necktie and the vermiform appendix. When singing, this species is addicted to splitting or bisecting the notes. As in:

> Lo-uving yo-ou e-uternally
> Wi-yith a-ull my-igh har-ut!

The Allen or play-it-down school wears its hair much shorter. Like Primo Carnera, the time his *vastus lateralis* was paralyzed, members do not react when stuck with pins. They play pianos, as being less jumpy than guitars, and sing:

> Love *yaternally* (Sister),
> *Withal mott.* (Now and then adding a casual "Vo-de-o-do" to show they are still there.)

When Allen made his move last week to mute and frustrate Presley, for the good of mankind, the proceedings were instructive, but somewhat saddening. Allen was nervous, like a man trying to embalm a firecracker. Presley was distraught, like Huckleberry Finn, when the widow put him in a store suit and told him not to gap or scratch.

Allen's ethics were questionable from the start. He fouled Presley, a fair-minded judge would say, by dressing him like a corpse, in white tie and tails. This is a costume often seen on star performers at funerals, but only when the deceased has specifically requested it in his will. Elvis made no such request—or for that matter, no will. He was framed.

A DOSE OF JOE MILLER

Later in the experiment, Allen fighting with no holds barred for the survival of the take-it-easy school, made a comic out of Presley, and fed him a couple of torpid punch lines.

"Who was that lady I seen you with last night, Elvis?" said Allen, sticking his thumb in the victim's eye and turning it slowly around.

"That was no lady, that was my git-tar," said Elvis morosely.

Now, I do not claim that that was exactly the gag that was used; but at any rate, it was a gag from which no ordinary twitching vocalist, or rabbit singer, could be expected to recover. Elvis recovered. As he left the hall, more dead than alive, he found the street hip-deep in bobby-soxers. And he bloomed like a rose, they tell me, and writhed again as of old.

A STAR IS BORNE

by Janet Winn

This facetious review of Love Me Tender *appeared in the* New Republic *in December 1956 and is typical of the ridicule directed at Elvis and his audiences by many writers and critics. The implicit assessment of Elvis's lackluster film debut, however, is a reasonable one and one shared by most viewers and critics who were not under the spell of teenage hysteria at the time.*

I went to see *Love Me Tender* last night, and I liked it enormous. Elvis Presley isn't a bit obscene or lewd; he's just *different*. He certainly stood out from everybody else in the picture—it takes place back in Civil War times when they didn't hardly have no rock 'n' roll yet—and not only because of his singing and virileness; but also because of his acting.

Elvis didn't just *memorize* his lines. He seemed to sense, deep down inside somewhere, what almost every word meant. That's why his portrayal of Clint, a nice Southern boy who helps his mother around the house, and does bumps and grinds to raise money for the new school, and then all of a sudden goes insane with jealousy, was so moving.

But that Debra Paget! She's so *vapid*. Elvis and her are married and everything, but she likes the brother. That's why Elvis goes

46

insane of jealousy in the end. I don't mean that Debra and Richard Egan (he's the brother) *do* anything, but *still*. She and Vance (he's Richard Egan) had gone around with each other before the war. The minute, however, she hears he was killed, she marries Elvis who was too young to fight. But the brother wasn't really killed, and when he comes back she still has a thing about him. For a long time Elvis doesn't suspect nothing, but finally it dawns on him.

He's real hurt. "Ya never loved me tender. Ya always loved *him* tender," he says. She don't say nothing. He shakes her. "When *yer* lyin' beside a me, ya wish it was Vay-ance, don't ya? DON'T YA? DON'T YA? *DON'T YA?*" She still don't say nothing, so he starts to kill her, only somebody stops him. But the best scene was the one where Elvis dies this tragic death. It was so poignant. A lot of movies they don't make you feel crumby when the hero dies; but this one you really do, like when Laurence Olivier dies in *Hamlet,* the famous play by William Shakespeare. Elvis doesn't die slowly, but he doesn't die quickly either. He dies just right, whimpering and gasping and drooling. He dies in Debra's arms. The next scene shows his gravestone. Mom and the boys are there, and so is a minister. They all look pretty broken up. But then a wonderful occurrence happens. Elvis (not all of him, just his face) appears, and he's singing the haunting ballad they took the title of the movie off of. "Love Me Tender." I didn't feel so bad anymore, because I knew he was still with them in spirit.

I might as well mention something about the plot. It's about some money Richard Egan and his buddies stole during the war from the Yankees. It wasn't really *during* the war, but Richard Egan and his buddies thought it was, because no one had told them the war was over. When they found out the war *was,* they didn't know what to do with the money, on account of they couldn't find Lee. So they kept the money.

The really thought-provoking thing about this movie isn't the plot though, but Elvis. I think in this movie, Elvis demonstrates once and for all how downright unfair it is to call him a teenage menace. Nobody in the audience yowled or shrieked or moaned or went out of their mind or anything. Everybody just *sat* there. That's because they realized Elvis is a real actor, and I think that when Marilyn Monroe does *The Brothers Karamazov,* like she said she would, Elvis ought to be in it too. He'd be just *great* as the other brother.

47

A LONELY LIFE ENDS ON ELVIS PRESLEY BOULEVARD

by Clark Porteous

This was the headline and front-page story of the Memphis Press-Scimitar *the day after Elvis died, and it reflects the confusion and disbelief of a legion of fans who could not conceive of a world without Elvis.*

The King is dead.

Elvis Presley—the jiggling, jiving, rock 'n' roll king—lived just 42 years, seven months and eight days.

It was an exciting but frustrating life which ended in Baptist Hospital, where Elvis was pronounced dead at 3:30 p.m. yesterday of a heart attack.

Elvis made millions of dollars and literally was worshiped by millions of fans. But he was lonesome much of the time, paid a high price for privacy and could not do many things he would have liked to do because he always drew a crowd of admirers.

Elvis, with a pleasant singing voice and a new style, strumming a guitar and gyrating his pelvis—which brought him the name in early days of "Elvis the Pelvis"—made millions, was able to buy anything he wanted, yet happiness seemed to elude him.

Elvis gave away countless thousands, giving funds to numerous Memphis institutions just before Christmas every year. He would give his friends—and occasionally even strangers—expensive automobiles.

Yet as the years passed, many of his friends seemed to have faded away, not generally because they wanted to, but some said Elvis had changed.

Elvis Aron Presley was written about on his 40th birthday, and friends were quoted as saying he was "fat and forty" and refused to see anybody until his weight got down to his regular trim 180 pounds. He was staying in his mansion, Graceland, on Elvis Presley Boulevard, a part of Bellevue renamed by city fathers to honor Elvis.

He became more and more of a recluse in his last few years. Red West and other close friends, who used to be called the "Memphis Mafia," were no longer with him.

Elvis, already a living legend and somewhat of a folk hero to many, was found unconscious at Graceland at 2:30 p.m. yesterday.

Maurice Elliott, Baptist Hospital vice president, said Joe Esposito, Presley's road manager and long-time friend, called an ambulance and tried to revive Elvis with mouth-to-mouth resuscitation and heart massage until the ambulance arrived. Efforts to revive Presley continued in the ambulance and in the emergency room at Baptist Hospital.

Finally, according to Elliott, Dr. George C. Nichopoulos, Elvis's personal physician, discontinued efforts and pronounced the singer dead at 3:30. Nichopoulos indicated a heart attack and this was shown to be correct by an autopsy.

Elvis's friends, who followed the ambulance to the hospital, were overcome with grief and kept expressing hope that the king was not dead. Many nurses and others in the hospital had tears in their eyes when word spread that Elvis was really dead.

And at Graceland, fans gathered—many weeping—at a requiem in front of the gate which is decorated with musical notes.

The Presley epic started in a small frame house where he was born in Tupelo, Miss. Now an Elvis shrine, the house was built by his father and grandfather. He was the surviving member of twin boys whom his mother, Gladys Presley, named Elvis Aron and Jessie Garon. His twin died in infancy.

Elvis was grief-stricken when his mother died Aug. 14, 1958, while Elvis was serving in the Army in Texas. Mrs. Presley, who also died of a heart attack, was the same age as Elvis when he died—42. The 19th anniversary of her death was two days before Elvis died.

Elvis bade his mother farewell on a little wooded knoll in Forest Hill Cemetery, where he later placed an impressive white marble and rose-red granite memorial.

"Goodby, darling, goodby—I loved you so much," a sobbing Elvis said before leaving the burial site. "I lived my whole life just for you."

Elvis once recalled that in his boyhood his mother was very possessive of him, probably due to the loss of the twin. The Presleys had no other children.

"My mama never let me out of her sight," Elvis said. "I couldn't go down to the creek with the other kids. Sometimes, when I was little, I used to run off. Mama would whip me and I thought she didn't love me."

Elvis knew extreme poverty as well as extreme wealth.

His father, Vernon, who has shared in his son's success, did odd jobs and farmed in Tupelo, but the family was poor. When Elvis was 14, the family moved to Memphis. They lived in a one-room apartment on Alabama in North Memphis at first, later moved into Lauderdale Courts, one of the two first public housing projects built in Memphis in the mid-'30s.

Elvis went to Humes High, where he made such friends as Red West and George Klein. Elvis failed to make the Humes football team, but long after he became a big success, he liked to play touch football with his friends.

He remained partial to Humes and bought concert tickets for Humes alumni. On one occasion, *The Press-Scimitar* ran a story about a senior student at Humes who was living with her grandmother because her father, an Army career man, was stationed elsewhere.

The girl was told she had to pay tuition and she didn't have the money and was afraid she would not be able to graduate. That night a big black car drove up to the little North Memphis house and Elvis personally delivered far more than enough money for the girl to continue at Humes and also buy some nice clothes. Yes, Elvis remembered the tough times he had.

As a boy, Elvis never studied music, but he had an inexpensive radio which he would listen to for hours at a time. He remembered liking the Grand Ole Opry and records by cowboy singers such as Roy Acuff and Hank Snow. But a special favorite was sweet-singing Gene Austin.

"I sang some with my folks in the Assembly of God Church choir," Elvis said. "It was a small church so you couldn't sing too loud.

"Getting a guitar was Mama's idea. I beat on it a year or two and never did learn much about it. I still know only a few major chords. I don't read music, but I know what I like."

Elvis was graduated from Humes in 1953. He had been too small to make the football team, but he was interested in sports and learned to be an expert at karate.

After graduation from Humes, Elvis worked on the assembly line of a precision tool company, then at a furniture factory making plastic tables and then as a truck driver for Crown Electric Co. He also ushered at Loew's State, a theater which was later to show many of his movies.

In the summer of 1953, Elvis took the step which led to fame and fortune. He had "just an urgin" and went to Sam Phillips's Sun Record Co. He paid to have a recording made for his mother. Elvis said "it sounded like somebody beating on a bucket lid." But Elvis was told he had an unusual voice and someone might call him.

Months passed and Elvis kept driving a truck for $35 a week. At night he attended a trade school, studying to be an electrician.

Then in the spring of 1955, lightning struck and Phillips called Elvis and asked him if he could come to the studio and record a ballad called "Without You." But Elvis just couldn't sing it the way Phillips wanted him to. After a coffee break, Elvis started singing a song with a rock 'n' roll beat. Phillips and the others liked it. The king was on his way to fame and fortune. He recorded "That's All Right, Mama" and "I Don't Care if the Sun Don't Shine," backed up by "Blue Moon of Kentucky."

Elvis's recordings first were played on radio station WHBQ. Elvis hid in a theater because he was afraid people would laugh at him. "Some did and some are still laughing, I guess," Elvis said later. But the record sold 7,000 copies in Memphis that first week.

A few months later, Col. Thomas A. Parker, a country slicker from Madison, Tenn., who likes to talk like a rube, agreed to manage Presley and Parker has had much to do with the phenomenal financial success of Presley. Parker craftily handled Presley appearances, kept him out of the limelight at times, helped build the Elvis mystique.

Parker, whose motto has been "Don't try to explain it, just sell it," did quite a job of selling Elvis. Col. Parker booked Elvis on tours with such established stars as Hank Snow and Andy Griffith. By the fall of 1955, Manhattan was beginning to hear about the swivel-hipped rock-and-roll singer. Col. Parker induced RCA to buy Elvis's contract from Phillips for $35,000, a price which turned out to be a great deal for RCA. Elvis got a $5,000 bonus for signing, more money than he had ever seen, but just a taste of what was coming.

In cities such as Jacksonville and Norfolk, Elvis swiveled out onto the stage wearing pink silk shirts, tight black pegged pants and cat boots over pink and black socks. He would stand for a moment like a figure in a wax museum. Then he would spraddle his long legs into a pivoting stance, take a few swipes at his guitar which rested against his then-flat belly and he would start swinging his hips in a sexual swirl. In fact, he was so sexy that when he appeared on TV on the Ed Sullivan show, the camera focused above his hips. The TV people believed it was too hot for the audience.

Parker began to sell Elvis with pink bunnies, Teddy bears, pennants, posters, cutouts and stacks of records. Parker often wore gaudy hats and sports shirts with "Elvis" embroidered on all sides.

Parker got 20th Century–Fox to put Elvis in films and the story is that when Parker talked to Buddy Adler, the production boss, about Elvis, Adler said, "Would $25,000 be all right?" Parker said that would be "just fine for me. Now how about the boy." He got the ante upped for Elvis, got $50,000 for a single TV appearance, which was a lot at that time. Parker said he considered it "his patriotic duty to keep Elvis in the 90 per cent tax bracket," and he did. Parker got Elvis booked into Las Vegas and refused to accept a check, demanding cash in advance. And he got it.

He got Elvis signed for the Seattle World's Fair for $250,000. There were a series of inexpensive movies, with Elvis pleasing his growing horde of fans and finally learning to act just a bit. There were regular appearances at Las Vegas, concerts now and then, and the money rolled in.

Elvis lived in a nice house on Audubon, near the park, off Park Avenue. Then he bought the 18-room Graceland mansion on South Bellevue in Whitehaven. Graceland has been his home since. Elvis had other homes, but he said he would always live in Memphis, and he seemed to enjoy the privacy of Graceland with its music-note gate, stone fence and security guards to keep the public out. His uncle, Travis Smith, used to take cameras up to the mansion to take pictures for Elvis fans, when he felt like it.

There were almost always Elvis fans at the gate, fans from all over, fans who wanted blades of grass, leaves from Graceland as a souvenir.

The fans would wait for hours, hoping to get a glimpse of the king. Sometimes they would be rewarded. Sometimes Elvis would ride one of his many motorcycles, a tractor or other smaller vehicles around on his estate. Sometimes he would even go out the gate. On rare occasions—much less in recent years—he would stop and chat with his fans or sign autographs.

But when Elvis really wanted to go out, he would charter a skating rink, bowling alley, theater or other entertainment place and take his friends. He just couldn't make a public appearance alone fearful of being mobbed.

In later years, at concerts, Elvis would throw scarves out to the crowd, and these became prized souvenirs of those lucky enough to catch one.

Elvis's song hits rolled out regularly, with RCA Victor bringing out the first big one, "Heartbreak Hotel." It was followed by many more such as "Love Me Tender," "Blue Suede Shoes," "I Got a Woman," I Want You, I Need You," "Jailhouse Rock," "Hardheaded Woman" and many others. And the one his fans never let him forget, "Hound Dog."

Elvis had a handsome face, which prompted Danny Thomas at a Memphis show for St. Jude Children's Hospital to call him "Doll Face." The show was at old Russwood Park, before it burned, and Elvis appeared and gyrated, but he could not sing because of a Parker contract clause. But as usual, Elvis brought down the house and was a hit in competition with such movie stars as Jane Russell and Susan Hayward.

At the peak of his career, in 1958, Elvis was called into the Army. The draft was still in effect and it became Elvis's turn. Despite all the money he was making and the enormous taxes he was paying Uncle Sam, he made no effort to avoid going into service at a buck private's meager pay.

At the old Kennedy Hospital on Getwell, now part of Memphis State University, Elvis took and easily passed his physical. He was a fine specimen of a young man at the time. He was extremely courteous and he remained polite to his elders and to women the rest of his life. He "sirred" reporters and others. Hedda Hopper, the Hollywood gossip columnist, said she once told Elvis, "Call me Hedda, Elvis. Everybody else does." She said he replied "Yes, ma'am, Mrs. Hopper."

Once on a movie set, Jackie Gleason visited Elvis on the set and scolded him for calling him "sir" and "mister." Elvis told Gleason that his mama had told him that anybody a year older than him was "mister" and "Mr. Gleason, you're one year older than I am, I think, sir."

Elvis asked no special favors in the Army and apparently got few. He was a good soldier. He got his eight weeks of basic training at Fort Hood, Tex. He was sent to Germany and came home only for his mother's funeral. He served in a tank outfit in Germany and was promoted to sergeant.

While in Germany, Elvis met a girl, Priscilla Beaulieu, daughter of an Air Force officer. Apparently there was a spark for Elvis from the very first for the teen-ager. Elvis, who had dated Anita Wood, Ann-Margaret and many others, brought Priscilla home to Graceland.

She finished growing up at Graceland and attended Immaculate Conception High School, being taken to and from school in one of the Presley fleet of cars. Elvis had been car crazy since he began to earn big money and always had a number of fine cars, including a $34,000 Rolls Royce, which in 1968 he gave to SHARE, Inc., a Hollywood women's charity group to sell to the highest bidder.

Graceland, like other Elvis homes, had pinball machines, pool tables, jukeboxes and other gadgets to keep the king from being bored. Elvis always was a night owl, liking to stay up most of the night and sleep away daylight hours.

There were often rumors that Elvis was married to Priscilla, but they were wrong. In early 1967, when found at a 160-acre ranch he was interested in buying, near Days, Miss., Elvis made a slip. A reporter asked Elvis if she could go inside the house at the ranch and Elvis smiled and said, "No, people are asleep in there. My father and mother-in-law." The reporter jumped on that at once and asked Elvis if he were married, and Elvis finally said he meant to say his stepmother. His father Vernon had remarried.

Priscilla was only 14 and Elvis 25 when he met her in Germany. They were married in 1967, in Las Vegas, and a year later had a daughter, Lisa, now 9 years old. Lisa is the presumptive heir to most of Elvis's millions. Though he and Priscilla were divorced in 1973, blaming his career for their long separations, there were some who believed the couple might get back together, had Elvis lived. Friends say they talked on the telephone almost every night and that Elvis missed both Lisa and Priscilla. They live in California.

Elvis had made such movies as *Love Me Tender, Loving You, Jailhouse Rock* and *King Creole* before going in the Army. After he got out, he made more movies. He showed talent as a half Navajo Indian rodeo cowboy in *Stay Away, Joe,* and other movies. But then Col. Parker, apparently fearing overexposure, took him out of movies. The Presley movies were big money makers and at one time it was reported Elvis would star in the movie version of Rudolf Valentino.

After taking Elvis out of movies, Col. Parker began to let him star in high-price TV appearances. Elvis became even richer, and in addition to Rolls Royces had at one time five Cadillacs—white, pink, blue, canary yellow and gold.

In the late 1960s, Elvis went into semiretirement after selling 400 million records and making 31 movies. Then he came back in 1972 and found his fans still faithful—though many of the fans who had swooned at his appearances had children of their own. Even younger fans still got goose bumps over the king of rock 'n' roll, though he was approaching 40.

Presley the car fan would buy as many as a half-dozen cars at a time and would give friends fine ones for Christmas presents. In September 1973, he went into Schilling Lincoln Mercury, 987 Union, and bought five Continental Mark IV's from Raymond Surber, a car salesman. It was a $60,000 sale.

But with all his cars and other gadgets with which to have fun, all his girl friends, his fame and fortune, some who knew Elvis best did not believe he ever really found happiness.

Recently, Presley bought a 707 jet and named it Lisa Marie for his daughter.

Elvis always appeared before sell-out houses at his infrequent Memphis concerts, just as in other cities. He had a concert scheduled at the Mid-South Coliseum Aug. 27 and it sold out so quickly that a second was added for Aug. 28, and it also sold out. So Elvis fans who had planned to see and hear him at the Coliseum will have to settle for the final appearance of the King, in a silent trip to Forest Hill Cemetery, where lies his beloved mother, who—like her famous son—died at age 42 on a hot August day.

LAST STOP ON THE MYSTERY TRAIN

![black bar]

by Jay Cocks

This article from August 1977, shortly after Elvis's death, shows the extent to which he had been absorbed into a popular culture he helped define and the distance both he and his audience had covered since the days when his music was described as an "adenoidal art form."

> *Train I ride.*
> *Sixteen*
> *Coaches long*
> *Train I ride.*
> *Sixteen*
> *Coaches long*
> *Well, that long black train*
> *Carry my baby and gone.*
> *—Mystery Train*

As the legend goes, Elvis Presley had only a year's passing familiarity with a recording studio when he cut that record in the winter of 1955. He had wandered into Sun Records with his guitar, two summers before, plunked down $4 to sing a couple of tunes to his mother, Gladys, and left carrying a 10-in. acetate for her birthday

57

present. Sun Secretary Marion Keisker heard a mean, lowdown sweetness in the baritone voice, made a tape of the session and played it back later for her boss, Sam Phillips. He had been looking for a "black sound inside a white boy" to make Sun Records a national mark way beyond Memphis. Phillips listened, thought about Presley, took his time making a decision. There was no rush. Presley, then 18, was pulling down $35 a week as a truck driver for the Crown Electric Co. About the only audience who knew him were his high school classmates who had watched, stunned, as their shy schoolmate hot-wired a class amateur show. Finally, Phillips called Presley back into the studio, a year after he had left with his gift for Gladys. That marked the last time in his life things would go slowly for Elvis Presley.

A song that came out of those first sessions, *That's All Right, Mama,* became a substantial local hit. So did the next four singles. By the time the last, *Mystery Train,* was released, Presley had connected with a deadeye promoter named Colonel Tom Parker, who landed him a national contract with RCA Records for the outlandish sum of $35,000. In the winter of 1956, not six months after *Mystery Train* came out, Elvis Presley released *Heartbreak Hotel* and sent American popular culture into a collective delirium that came, after a while, to be called "the Rock Era."

Time passed to a heavy back beat. In a giddy blur, Presley went on the *Ed Sullivan Show,* intimidated the adults of America and drove their kids into a frenzy. Parents said Elvis was suggestive, lewd, a greaser. To kids that was just the point. Elvis reveled in his performances. He used his music as an open invitation to release, and kids took him up on it.

He inspired scores of imitators, sold millions of records. He got drafted into the Army, got his infamous D.A. and 'burns clipped, served a tour of duty in Germany, sold millions of records. He went to Hollywood, appeared in 33 movies, sold millions of records. He played Vegas, got married, filled amphitheaters, got divorced, lived a gaudy life so high and wide that it seemed like a parody of an American success story. And he kept selling records, well over 500 million in all. The music got slicker and often sillier, turned from rock toward rhinestone country and spangled gospel. Only the pace remained the same. Elvis Aron Presley always lived fast, and last week, at the age of 42, that was the way he died.

He was found lying on the bathroom floor in the afternoon. All attempts to revive him failed. Presley had died of "cardiac arrythmia"—a severely irregular heartbeat—brought about by "undetermined causes." Doctors said there was no evidence of any illegal drug use, although a new book co-authored by three former Presley bodyguards maintains that "E" consumed uppers, downers and a variety of narcotic cough medicines, all obtained by prescription. He also was wrestling halfheartedly with a fearful weight problem and was suffering from a variety of other ailments like hypertension, eye trouble and a twisted colon.

So the legend goes: nothing kills America's culture heroes as quickly and surely as success. Presley burnt himself out, as if on schedule. He had been thirsty for glory. Born in Tupelo, Miss., he was an only child whose parents scraped along on odd jobs until the family moved to Memphis when Elvis was 13. He was fanatically and unabashedly devoted to his mother. He was buried near her after the kind of awful, agonized public wake that attended the passing of Rudolph Valentino and Judy Garland. Eighty thousand fans jammed the street outside his Memphis mansion, Graceland, hoping for a view of the body; 30,000 were admitted to the house. Dozens swooned, cried, keened and passed out from the heat outside the mansion gates. Two people were killed when a drunken driver plowed into the crowd. After the funeral at Graceland, a cortege of 16 white Cadillacs led a slow procession down Elvis Presley Boulevard to the cemetery. There the lawn was banked with some 2,200 floral tributes—an imperial crown of golden mums, hortisculptured hound-dogs and guitars, sunflowers in wine bottles. Memphis ran out of flowers; reinforcements were sent in from California and Colorado.

Rock stars—all Presley stepkids in one way or another—paid him tribute. "I am very sad," said Rod Stewart. "His death is a great loss to rock 'n' roll." Said Brian Wilson of the Beach Boys: "His music was a great inspiration to us. His personality was a great inspiration to us. He was a fine gentleman." Meanwhile, radio stations canceled regular programming and even commercials to play lengthy homage to the fallen king. In Boston a fan lent his own Presley collection to fill the gaps in one station's library. Outside the Las Vegas Hilton, the flag was lowered to half-mast. Instant cottage industries in Elvis T-shirts blossomed. Stores everywhere sold out of Presley records, as if one spin on the turntable would keep him alive forever.

In a sense, of course, it will. Presley was not, as he has so often been called, "the father of rock 'n' roll," but he was the first to consolidate all its divergent roots into a single, surly, hard-driving style. Rock had its origins deep in rhythm and blues, which, in a time of strict musical segregation, was black music all the way. Presley gave rock and blues a gloss of country-and-western and a rock-a-billy beat, but he preserved the undertones of insinuating sexuality, accentuated rock's and blues' rough edges of danger from the sharp beat to the streetwise lyrics. "It was like a giant wedding ceremony," Marion Keisker said later, "like two feuding clans who had been brought together by marriage."

Those early Sun sides, typified by the wonderfully spooky, smoky *Mystery Train,* were arguably the best music Elvis ever made. The more familiar songs, like *Heartbreak Hotel, Hound Dog* and *Don't Be Cruel* are great tunes, joyful and sassy. They have become cultural artifacts, but no amount of historical respectability can fully dim their raucous vitality. They also represent a high point. Only four or five years after they came out, Presley's music had virtually become a patented mixture of heavy breathing and hokum.

After his Army hitch, and under the guidance of Colonel Parker, Elvis's new music was confined largely to sanctimonious spirituals and sound-track ditties off the string of brain-rotting movies he turned out, sometimes at the rate of three a year. At first, the movies—like *Jailhouse Rock*—tried for a little of the defiance and vitality Elvis got in his music, but such ambitions were quickly forsaken for formula. Elvis beefed about the scripts, which he once contemptuously dismissed as "travelogues," but Parker could point to the fact that each of the movies turned a profit—often a handsome one—and that the sound track from one of these travelogues, *Blue Hawaii,* was Presley's bestselling album ever. The Colonel was constantly nudging Presley away from rock, stuffing him into an entertainment package that offered a little something for everyone. Audiences stayed loyal, and Presley earned millions each year. No matter that with the coming of the Beatles a lot of rockers deserted him. Elvis had already set their style.

It was style as much as the songs he sang that made Elvis Presley such an immediate, and ultimately irreplaceable, phenomenon. Initially, it was all a matter of attitude, the low lids, the lip that curled up like a whitecap before breaking on the beach, the musky voice that seemed to take its honey coating from a lot of scruffy worldliness and its distinct throb from straight below the waist. His first appearances were small Pop cataclysms. The sensuous movements that headline writers called "gyrations" and that earned Presley nicknames he did not like—Swivel Hips, the Pelvis—had their roots in roistering responses of some fundamentalist congregations.

Offstage his deferential manner toward adults, his shy country-boy come-on to women, made him seem, whatever heights of fame he achieved, strictly and forever down home. He defined himself, as Critic Greil Marcus points out in an excellent Presley essay, "by presenting his authentic multiplicity. I am, he announced, a house rocker, a boy steeped in mother-love, a true son of the church, a matinee idol who's only kidding, a man with too many rough edges for anyone ever to smooth away. Something in me yearns for a settling of affairs, he said with his pale music and his tired movies; on the other hand, he answered with his rock 'n' roll and occasional blues, I may break away at any time."

He never did. Not really. His later stage shows were full of intentional self-parody; he took to telling audiences "this lip used to curl easier." Of late he made his entrance at concerts to the thundering strains of *Thus Spake Zarathustra*. He could still rock out when he wanted to cut loose with a fine, jagged version of *Hound Dog,* but he seemed increasingly bored with his music and more absorbed in the lavish trappings of his own celebrity.

In the first flush of his success, Elvis lived with the crazy vigor of a good ole boy who just had the whole world tucked snugly into the back pocket of his overalls. He surrounded himself with hometown cronies, kept them fed and cared for, dispensed lavish gifts. He gave away luxury cars—particularly the Cadillacs he doted on—like gumdrops. After a while, though, the cronies became heavies—bodyguards, procurers—and the gifts bribes to buy loyalty, or silence. He courted a girl, Priscilla Beaulieu, he had met during his Army hitch. He persuaded her father to let her come over from Germany to live and, when he got out of the Army, to go to school in Memphis. She was not yet 15 when they met. They got married when she was 21, and a year later, in 1968, they had a daughter. After that, Elvis spent a lot of time away from her until they divorced in 1973. Presley became reclusive, paranoid. He immured himself among roomfuls of flamboyant furniture in Graceland. He took up karate, amassed a vast collection of guns and police badges and, according to the trio of tattletale bodyguards, would travel not only with a brace of handguns but such heavy armaments as a Thompson submachine gun and an M-16 rifle.

Earlier, he had rented a Memphis movie theater and a roller rink for afterhours amusement. In recent years, his only forays out into the real world were concert tours that were carefully insulated. The routine was usually the same: private plane to private limo to back entrance of hotel to specially cleared elevator to penthouse suite; then, after a while, off to the concert, onto the stage, back to the hotel, then to the airport. Reality never intruded, except when the schedule faltered. In a 1972 documentary, *Elvis on Tour,* there is a quick scene of Elvis, stranded on an airport runway, waiting for the gangway of his private plane to roll out. He is caught in the glare of sunlight, and he looks up in the sky with startled curiosity, as if surveying an alien planet.

The world he left behind so quickly had still not quite recovered from the changes he brought down on it. In England, the punk rockers who are raising such a ruckus, spooking the music business and intimidating their elders, turn themselves out just like the Elvis of the '50s, in tight pants and defensive snarls. Their unadorned, assaultive music tries for the same fierce simplicity Elvis seemed to achieve so effortlessly. Back in Memphis, hysteria prevailed. Guards were posted outside the mausoleum to keep fans and fanatics from laying waste to the burial grounds. There were to be fresh shipments of Elvis records, re-releases of the old movies, TV retrospectives. Presley mourners talked about trying to reach his spirit through seances.

So the legend goes. And grows. From out of the barrage of funeral images, from the fragmented memory of dozens of Presley lyrics, one reaches for a single last memory, searches for an epitaph. Go way back, to another of those early Sun records and there is one that seems particularly appropriate. "Well," Elvis starts off, in a wild, raw drawl, then rushes into the verse:

> *I heard the news*
> *There's good rockin' tonight*

Now there is, for everyone. Elvis saw to that.

ALL SHOOK UP

■

by Maureen Orth

This article by Newsweek *reporter Maureen Orth gives an overview of Elvis's career and provides a front-line report of the unprecedented mass mourning that immediately followed reports of his death, as thousands of fans from all over the world converged on Memphis.*

Inside his Memphis mansion, Graceland, the king of rock 'n' roll lay silent in a copper coffin. Women hid tiny cameras in their bras to take one last picture as they filed past. Outside, hundreds of floral arrangements, some shaped like guitars and one like a hound dog, lined the long driveway and thousands of fans kept vigil on the tacky boulevard below in the sweltering heat. They had abandoned jobs, driven all night and flown in from abroad for one last glimpse of their idol. "Don't faint now," a mother warned her faltering daughter, "or I'll just have to leave you." A billboard down the way read: "In Memoriam" and the Beef and Liberty Restaurant sign directly across the street carried the message "Rest in Peace." But hardly anyone in Memphis could really believe that Elvis Presley was dead of a heart attack, at the age of 42.

Elvis—"Elvis-the-Pelvis"—was more than a pop superstar. With his sleepy, sensual looks, his sexy bumps and grinds and his black-sounding voice, he not only changed the course of pop music forever, he may have created the generation gap. Rarely does an entertainer so galvanize the unstated yearnings of an age and serve as a harbinger of the decade to come as Elvis did in the mid-1950s with the first of his long parade of hits, which included "Heartbreak Hotel," "Hound Dog" and "All Shook Up." After his famous first appearance on "The Ed Sullivan Show" in 1956, my aunt told me how foolish I was to sit screaming with joy at the spectacle of that vulgar singer on TV. It was then I knew that she and I lived in different worlds, and it was then that kids' bedroom doors slammed all over America. Boys wore greasy ducktail haircuts and tried to imitate Elvis's moves in front of the mirror. Girls gave up collecting charms for their bracelets for the forbidden charms of his 45-rpm records. Our parents hated Elvis and that was all right with us. From Elvis on, rock was rebellious.

His death aroused the same old frenzy—and pared away the sad spectacle of recent years when Elvis had become fat, reclusive and increasingly paranoid. Memphis florists had to fly in 5 extra tons of flowers to fill the orders going to him. Stores all over the country were sold out of Elvis's records, and the RCA plant in Indianapolis, which can press 250,000 albums a day, was working a 24-hour shift to catch up. Ballantine Books received what might be the largest single order in the history of publishing—for 2 million copies of "Elvis: What Happened?" an exposé by three disgruntled former bodyguards. Radio stations all over the world were playing hours of Elvis music. In Japan, music critics reportedly sobbed on television as they discussed him.

In London, hundreds of Teddy boys and their tattooed girlfriends prayed alongside housewives and their babies in a special church service. In Paris, L'Humanité, the Communist Party newspaper, headlined THE 'KING' IS DEAD. And back in Memphis, the reckless frenzy reached tragic proportions when hours before Elvis's private funeral, a drunk teen-age driver ran into three people keeping vigil outside Graceland, killing two young women and critically injuring another.

When he died, Elvis had sold over 500 million records—more than any other pop star. He was born dirt poor in the small rural town of Tupelo, Miss. His father worked at odd jobs and his mother spoiled her only child as much as their meager earnings allowed. When she died, Elvis was so distraught that local lawmen would try to cheer him up by taking him on daily helicopter rides. From his mother, Elvis, who was always shy and uncomfortable around strangers, learned his lifelong habit of "Sirring" and "Ma'aming" everybody.

In 1953, after the family had moved to Memphis, Elvis, who was 18 and working as a truck driver for $41 a week, had "just an urgin'" that prompted him to pull into Sam Phillips's Sun Records to make a record for his mamma's birthday. Phillips was looking for a certain kind of singer. "If I could find a white man who had the Negro sound and the Negro feel," said Phillips, "I could make a billion dollars." That's what he found, but Phillips eventually settled for $35,000—which RCA paid him for his contract a year after Elvis's first Sun single, a black rhythm-and-blues song called "That's All Right," became a regional hit.

The sale was engineered by Elvis's new manager, "Colonel" Tom Parker, a former carnival pitchman. Parker's credo was "Don't try to explain it, just sell it"—a motto his well-trained concessionaires followed last week when they hawked Elvis T-shirts for $5 in front of Graceland. The Colonel, as he was called, took absolute charge of Elvis's career and got top dollar for every job. He knew he had something special.

But Elvis didn't. "I don't think of it as an act," he told an early interviewer. "I just sing. It comes out this way and that's what I do. I never really think about it." But he did like to be different. His tight pants and pink silk shirts were extreme at the time. He experimented for hours with his black ducktail. He wore eye shadow for his first appearance on the Grand Ole Opry and heard an official there tell him, "We don't use nigger music at the Grand Ole Opry." Within a few years Elvis's style had nearly destroyed country music because every country boy wanted to sing just like Elvis—not like Webb Pierce. "He was white but he sang black," says the noted guitarist Chet Atkins, who was assistant producer on the early records at RCA. "It wasn't socially acceptable for white kids to buy black records at the time. Elvis filled a void."

In 1956, the Colonel parlayed Elvis's hits into a movie career that was enhanced sentimentally when Elvis got drafted and served two years in the Army. Long before Robert Redford, Elvis was earning a million dollars per picture for the corny B movies he later scorned as "Presley travelogues." The Colonel maintained it was his "patriotic duty to keep Elvis in the 90 per cent tax bracket"; he was loath to tamper with a successful formula, and along the way, Elvis never really grew up. "I never understood why he didn't try to make better records or movies," says an RCA executive. "He was like the Colonel, who felt that you don't really need quality because you'll always be popular."

In the '60s, Elvis the rock 'n' roll star was eclipsed by the very groups his music had spawned—the Beatles, the Rolling Stones, the Doors—and to most rock fans, he was nothing more than a golden oldie. For almost nine years, the Colonel kept him away from personal appearances. But in the late '60s, he reemerged with a glittering Las Vegas engagement. In recent years, he toured sporadically, overweight and musically lethargic. But he invariably sold out sports arenas to audiences of all ages.

Offstage, Elvis increasingly isolated himself from the public. He granted no interviews. He surrounded himself with an entourage of good-buddy yes-men, the "Memphis Mafia." He spent hours in his bedroom watching TV. For fun, he'd rent an amusement park or movie theater for himself and his friends. His generosity not just to friends but to strangers—upon whom he would sometimes lavish new Cadillacs—was legendary. But in 1972 his wife, Priscilla, whom he had married in 1967—their daughter, Lisa Marie, is now 9—finally grew tired of being a bird in a gilded cage and left him for her karate instructor. It was a blow he never recovered from.

Recently Elvis took to wearing a bulletproof vest during public appeareances. He also collected guns. One day a few years ago in Las Vegas, when he couldn't stand to watch Robert Goulet on television, he shot the screen out of the TV set. "He showed us the set," said Mickey, a blond secretary who knew Elvis in Las Vegas, as she stood at the gate outside Graceland the night before his funeral last week. "He told me it was OK because the hotel always put it on his bill. Toward the end, though, he was paranoid. He kept in his Bible the police report of two guys who tried to rush him on the stage in 1973. My purse was always searched for weapons before I could go into his suite, and once when the cork of a champagne bottle was popped he ducked for cover and his bodyguards completely surrounded me."

Were the rumors true that Elvis was hooked on pills—speed and downers? "He was so out of it sometimes he couldn't talk," Mickey said. "I was there one morning when he was ready to go to bed and his doctor passed out pills to everybody." Last week former bodyguard Sonny West said another guard tried to stop Elvis from taking drugs by roughing up the boys who delivered them. "He looked Red in the eye," West recalled, "and said, 'I need them, I need it.'"

But it was the legend of Elvis that mattered to the fans who came to Memphis to say goodbye. "I read the bodyguards' book and I don't believe it," said Margaret Carver, a 37-year-old housewife from Waldorf, Md. "Whatever's written about him, true or false, makes no difference to me, I have no other idols." The next day, 150 family members and friends sang "How Great Thou Art" at the private funeral service in Graceland, before the king of rock 'n' roll was laid to rest in the mausoleum at Forest Hill Cemetery. They heard TV evangelist Rex Humbard tell of how Elvis had invited him to Las Vegas last December. "He talked about religion," said Humbard. "He wanted to know if Jesus would be coming back soon."

THE HEARTBREAK KID

by Jack Kroll

This short meditation on the cultural impact of Elvis and his music appeared alongside Maureen Orth's "All Shook Up" in the August 29, 1977, issue of Newsweek.

The whole amazing story of Elvis is about heartbreak. His first giant hit just had to be "Heartbreak Hotel," in which Elvis mournfully rocked and rolled: "Now since my baby left me/I've found a new place to dwell,/Down at the end of Lonely Street/At Heartbreak Hotel/I'm so lonely,/I'm so lonely,/I'm so lonely,/That I could die."* That was in 1956, when Elvis was on fire with talent and success, but his "baby," all his babies did eventually leave him—his adored mother, his wife, his child, the urgent energy that sparked his talent. At the end, his Memphis Xanadu, the Graceland mansion, had long since become a luxurious Heartbreak Hotel, and poor Elvis bloated by the American ambrosias—peanut butter, Pepsi, pills and success—died in the midst of his own private lonely crowd.

It's no use sentimentalizing this story, but it's important to feel something for the man whose great contribution was feeling. An

---

*Words and music by Mae B. Aron, Tommy Durden and Elvis Presley. Copyright 1956 by Tree Publishing Co., Inc. Used by permission.

immortal moment in our cultural history materialized on TV screens before 54 million people when Ed Sullivan, puckered with befuddlement, introduced 21-year-old Elvis. "I don't know what he does," confessed Sullivan, "but it drives people crazy." And then Elvis was there, a baby slyness on his face, feinting once, twice, with his hips and guitar as the offscreen audience screeched each time, thinking he was going to start singing. And then he swiveled again, a Promethean twitch that brought a raunchy fire into the global village as he started to sing, "You ain't nothin' but a hound dog . . ." Legend has it that Sullivan stood in the wings, watching the unseemly saturnalia in his studio, muttering over and over, "Sonovabitch, sonovabitch . . ."

White Heat: Which was of course the only appropriate comment. Plato, almost two and a half millennia before, had predicted Elvis when he pointed out that "forms and rhythms in music are never changed without producing changes in the most important political forms and ways" and spoke of a new musical style that "goes on to attack laws and constitutions, displaying the utmost impudence." Elvis had the impudence and rock 'n' roll had the form and rhythm. America's postwar swarm of young people was a huge field of force—including economic—waiting to be mobilized. When Elvis exploded, kids were no longer just individual appendages on millions of American families. Rock 'n' roll fused their sensibilities—and their pocketbooks—together with the white heat of the music. A tribe was born.

This process of parturition really did scare Elvis's non-peers—the adults—and a kind of civil war was triggered that in different ways is still going on. But it began as the silliest of civil wars, epitomized by the minister who called Elvis "morally insane" and by Ed Sullivan's camera that chastely took Elvis in only from the waist up, like a host who stares fixedly at a dinner guest's face after noticing that his fly is open. The hue and cry was hardly logical. Elvis had incited a mass reaction, and that's what you get in a mass society. The grownups had been doing it for a long time—remember the Rudolph Valentino hysteria, and the middle-aged frenzy at political conventions, which have hardly been more edifying spectacles than the Dionysiac euphoria at Elvis's concerts.

Jackhammer Assault: Elvis really did start a revolution, but it was a revolution that should have had a broken heart as its shoulder patch, because it was both real and not real. The real part was the nearly total culture created for kids. At last they had their own music, their own whacked out rituals involving cars, girls, everything that went with Good Old Rock 'n' Roll. The unreal part was that all of this would soon be absorbed into the system, including Elvis. At first all you saw was Elvis's aggression, his jackhammer assault on the dead-centrism of the Eisenhower years. But if you looked closely at Elvis—as pop-artist Andy Warhol did—you saw the opposite of all this: you saw an almost androgynous softness and passivity in his punk-hood persona. Elvis and his revolution were vulnerability disguised as bravado.

Elvis was a rebel with two causes. The instigator of raunch-revolt was a good boy who loved his mother. The jailbird of "Jailhouse Rock" enjoyed ROTC training in high school and was a model draftee. Elvis played a Confederate in his first movie, "Love Me Tender." In one scene Mildred Dunnock tells him to drop his gun and he refuses. This simple scene required several retakes because Elvis instinctively kept dropping his gun as ordered. "You could see he was used to obeying older people, especially his mother," recalled the distinguished actress. "It was a touching thing." But rock writer Peter Guralnick has written that he and other Elvis fans couldn't reconcile the good-boy Elvis with the rebel: "We thought it was a joke. We thought that Elvis was putting us on; it seemed so clearly at odds with Elvis's rebel image and the mythology which . . . we had erected around a pop idol."

Innocence: When you lead a kids' revolution, the ironic part is that your subjects may grow up and get nostalgic about the good old rock 'n' roll days, but you still have to be King Kid. There have been many tragic figures in jazz, their lives cut short—Charlie Parker, Billie Holiday—but still they changed and developed as artists. As a force, as an artist—and he was one, a very special and powerful kind of contemporary folk-artist—Elvis really had just one moment, when he was a teenage truck driver recording for Sam Phillips's Sun Records in Memphis. You can experience that moment on Elvis's most wonderful record, "Elvis: The Sun Sessions" (RCA). An instinctive genius at synthesis, Elvis absorbed all the styles—black rhythm and blues, white country and Western, gospel, even the last, self-parodying groans of the crooners. What you hear is the energy of innocence, pure, pure rock 'n' roll.

There's still plenty of racial resentment at Elvis's unchallenged role as king of rock 'n' roll. Perhaps the greatest black rockers are Chuck Berry, still performing, and Little Richard, who's now a Seventh-day Adventist minister. They were measured, gallant and accurate last week in their appraisal of Elvis. "Blacks didn't have the airwaves Elvis had," said Berry, and then added, "He delivered what he obtained beautifully." "He was an integrator," said Little Richard. "Elvis was a blessing. They wouldn't let black music through. He opened the door for black music." Maybe Berry and Little Richard are lucky. The drug that killed Elvis was his own supersuccess. His very generosity was an attempt to shrink away the obesity of his affluence. "He was a rocker," said Little Richard. "I was a rocker. I'm not rockin' anymore and he's not rockin' anymore."

ELVIS!

███

by Roy Blount, Jr.

In this brief meditation on Elvis as prototypical rock star and teen hero, Blount ponders the mysteries of Elvis's endurance as a cultural icon.

When I was in the eighth grade, 1954, I got wind of "Annie Had a Baby" ("cain' wuck no mo'") and heard reports of black music shows in Atlanta from fellow adolescents more advanced than I who would wink at each other and repeat the catch phrase "hunchin' and a-jackin'." I don't know what song that was from, but it made more of an impression on me than Elvis Presley did. Of course, when Elvis came, he was on *The Ed Sullivan Show.* You didn't have to be cool to know about Elvis. "We've lost the most popular man that ever walked on this planet since Christ was here himself," said Carl Perkins when Elvis died.

The summer after eighth grade, I went to a party at the house of my Babe Ruth League coach, a wizened and taciturn mill worker whom you would not expect to figure in a pelvic revolution. But the coach's boys had organized the party, and one of Elvis's first singles was playing. My coach's equally wizened but more voluble elder son came up and asked me earnestly, "Do you think Elvis has got it?"

"Yes," I said. Though I was no authority. This was my first rock-criticism conversation—one of the few, in fact, that I have had over the years—and my soundest one. Elvis had managed to make music that hunched and jacked and yet could be heard in one's baseball coach's home. It didn't grab and unsettle me like "Annie Had a Baby," or like Ray Charles or Chuck Berry or Jerry Lee Lewis, and it still doesn't. But it had it. And it made it mellifluous.

There is a wonderful Alice Walker short story, "Nineteen Fifty-Five," about a black blues singer like Big Mama Thornton, who did the first version of "Hound Dog," and a white muddled megarocker like the late Elvis. The Elvis character is guiltily beholden to her, and she says things like, "It don't matter, Son." At the end of the story it comes over the TV that the Elvis character is dead. The Big Mama character doesn't want to watch his fans grieve. "They was crying and crying and didn't know what they was crying for. One day this is going to be a pitiful country, I thought."

And here's what Chuck Berry said when asked after Elvis's death what Elvis would be remembered for: "Oh boop, boop, boop; shake your leg; fabulous teen music; the Fifties; his movies."

But Elvis didn't just siphon off some negritude and slick it up. ("Hound Dog" was written by Leiber and Stoller, who added to the black culture they appropriated and didn't try to appropriate any more than they could carry.) His h-and-j was fired by poor-white disrepressed defiance, and to it he added mooniness, juvenility, niceness, hope, fuzz, hype, and androgyny. Rock 'n' roll.

Whereas Janis Joplin began by trying to sing the blues as unseasoned homely white-girl hysteria, Elvis's sudden rockabilly was fresh and centripetal. He took the guilt out of the blues, says Greil Marcus. That is like taking the grit out of the beach or the smell out of the collards, but Elvis did it. It got people—white people I guess I mostly mean, but aren't white people Americans too?—wiggling. The next thing you knew, there was a Youth Culture, which I think we may assume Elvis did not dream of in 1954. I know I didn't.

The Youth Culture took wiggling for granted, and Mick Jagger's pelvis was to Elvis's as a Cuisinart is to a mortar and pestle. But Elvis was an old redneck boy who loved gospel and drove a truck. He might just about as well have grown up to be Jerry Falwell. For a boy with Elvis's background to move the way he did suddenly proved something, as in 1929 when the *rich* started bailing out. The jump from not shaking that thing at all to shaking it was bigger than the segue from shaking it to undulation. It was Elvis, you could say with some justice, who goosed mainstream America into that jump.

Elvis didn't fit into the Youth Culture. He ballooned—began to wear a girdle, as decent girls did before he came along. He became a martyr: to the new level of profligate absurd glamour-power he established, and to his own abiding adolescence. After his death, when Big Mama Thornton was asked how she felt about having made a hundred dollars or so from "Hound Dog" compared with Elvis's millions, she said, "I'm still here to *spend* my hundred dollars."

Though ever a (naughty) mama's boy, Elvis sprang beyond Big Mama; special effects outjump flesh and blood every time. Even before the Pill, Elvis seemed to obviate the primacy of Jack-hunch-Annie-and-knock-her-up. Boy fans tended to approach him more reservedly than did the girls, to whom he seemed to be saying—*trustworthily*—that he could do you without getting you in trouble, and vice versa.

"Hound Dog" made grim traditional sense as a woman's song about a trifling man. Elvis's version was vaguely raunchy, mostly adorable. How could there be any downside to a man who looked both wholesome and sultry, a man whose sensual lips sang, "Don't be cruel, to a heart that's true"? "Sex is dynamite," generations of American mothers had been telling their daughters, and by *dynamite* they didn't mean fabulous. They meant ruination. Elvis probably would have said, "Yes'm, I know," to every one of those mothers, and yet he lit that dynamite and went pop. And grinned. Elvis's grin, like FDR's, was historic. It got young people on the road to concluding that they had nothing to feel guilty about but guilt itself, that parents were wrong about sex and probably everything else, that the system (parents), not the heart, was where all the shadows lay.

Over the long haul Elvis was more of a crooner than a rocker. But he was a frontiersman. Ray and Chuck and Jerry Lee remained cut-the-cards, you-*know*-what-I'm-carrying guys, who are never likely to be accused, as Elvis was in a cankered biography by Albert Goldman, of preferring that girls leave their panties on. The other night I watched a tape of Elvis's 1968 comeback concert. He looked like Martin Sheen, Jack Palance, Katy Jurado, Sal Mineo, Ann-Margaret (the mouth), and a touch of Grady Sutton. He was pretty, tough, vaunting, shy, dumb, wily, saturnine, and mercurial. Elvis wasn't just heteroerotic: he was close to Norman O. Brown's polymorphous perverse.

Rock 'n' roll evolved in that direction. (I wonder what Elvis made of David Bowie.) And so did American culture until about the time Elvis died. Now there's a different trend. Ronald Reagan, George

Shultz, Jesse Helms, George Will, and Frank Sinatra show few traces of the rock revolution. The culture seems to be doubling back, looking for something it dropped. Do you know what my adolescent kids are listening to? Besides Dire Straits' "Industrial Disease"? They are listening to a group called Stray Cats, who play rockabilly.

I HAVE ELVIS'S last afternoon paper. Or what would have been, if he had lived into the evening of August 16, 1977. I was in Nashville that day. When somebody brought the news into the greasy spoon where I was sitting, the jukebox—I swear—had just finished playing Elvis's latest hit, "Way Down."

ELVIS THE PELVIS, ELVIS LIVES, ELVIS'S EVILS, ELVIS IS VILE, ELVIS'S VEILS (oddly, Elvis disliked Levi's—too close to poverty britches I guess) all seemed to be in the nature of things, but ELVIS DEAD was a jolt. I flew to Memphis. "What's that?" I asked Fred Stoll, Elvis's gatekeeper, at Graceland late that night. "That's Elvis's last *Press-Scimitar*," said Stoll. So I stole it. It still had the rubber band on, until I opened it while writing this piece and the dried-out rubber snapped.

Elvis in his coffin was fat, glowering, and surrounded by similar-looking but vertical heavies who pushed us viewers along. Reportedly Elvis had died "straining at the stool" while reading a book about the discovery of Christ's remains. ELVIS DEAD, all right. But not at peace. He looked like he wanted to make another big leap, but couldn't. He didn't look cool.

Neither did the thousands of people who gathered at the gates of Graceland. People fainted left and right, from the heat, the crowding, and the historical moment. And because if you fainted, you got carried onto the grounds.

"He was really a good man," said a stringy woman wearing off-brand jeans and a halter top revealing a midriff with two moles and a fresh abrasion. "To achieve superstardom at that age and keep his basic Christian qualities. I don't see how he did it. I don't really know."

"He coulda lived another no telling how long," said a fat woman in lemon-lime shorts. "But he just kinda gave himself to the people."

A mother in her late thirties kept edging herself and her little girl, about four, toward the Graceland gate. The girl was crying. An altercation developed in front of them. I don't think anyone could tell what the roots of the disturbance were, but the police moved in and collared a black man. He yelled. He'd been waiting so long. One cop cuffed the man's hands behind his back and thrust a nightstick between the man's legs. Another cop grabbed the other end of the stick and they carried the man away like that, riding him out of Elvis Nation on a rail. The man made a strangled noise. The mother took the occasion to push her daughter, who was screaming now, beyond the barricades and through the gate and into the line, past banks of floral displays (and Styrofoam crosses and artificial roses and gilded plastic cardinals or blue jays), to see the dead man.

You might like Ray and Chuck and Jerry Lee better, and also Little Richard, but I doubt you would fly to see them, God forbid, in their coffins. Whatever else you think about Elvis, he was epochal.

Elvis Aron Presley had a twin brother, Jesse Garon, who was stillborn on January 8, 1935, in East Tupelo, Mississippi. When Elvis was three, his father, Vernon, served nine months in Parchman Penitentiary for forgery. In 1948 the town authorities alleged that Vernon had been selling moonshine; they gave him two weeks to leave town. The family moved to Memphis.

On his eleventh birthday Elvis got his first guitar—a $12.75 model his mother bought at the Tupelo Hardware Store. He caused a scene because he had wanted his mother to buy him a shotgun instead.

In the summer of 1953 Elvis, who was driving a truck for an electrical firm, stopped at the Memphis Recording Service, hoping that Sun Records owner Sam Phillips would discover him. Although Phillips was not in, his secretary recorded Elvis; the tapes did not impress him.

By 1954 Elvis had cut his first record for Sun; still, the next year he failed in his audition for the Arthur Godfrey show.

Phillips sold Elvis to RCA for forty thousand dollars; at his first recording session for his new company, he recorded "Heartbreak Hotel," which became number one on *Billboard* magazine's charts.

Ed Sullivan once said, "I wouldn't have Presley on my show at any time." Eventually Elvis did appear on the show—filmed from the waist up.

Elvis's gyrations upset many people. A clergyman once called him "the twirling dervish of sex." Hedda Hopper condemned Presley as a menace to society and a threat to innocent children. (She later recanted and did the Twist with him at a Hollywood party.)

Senator Estes Kefauver placed a tribute to Presley in the *Congressional Record*.

In 1956 Elvis dated Natalie Wood, who spent a week with the Presleys in Memphis.

While serving in the Army in Germany, Elvis met his future wife, Priscilla Beaulieu, at a party. She was fourteen. He brought her to

Memphis and enrolled her in a Catholic school. He showed his step-mother her picture, saying, "I've been to bed with no less than one thousand women in my life. This is the one, right here." After five years of marriage, Priscilla left Elvis for her karate instructor, Mike Stone.

A Christian churchgoer most of his life, Elvis, for a time, was a follower of Yogi Paramahansa Yogananda.

In 1971 the U.S. Jaycees gave Elvis an award for being one of the "Ten Oustanding Young Men in America." Ron Ziegler was another recipient that year.

He made thirty-one movies and two documentaries. He refused to see his movie *Jailhouse Rock* after its female lead, Judy Tyler (once Princess Summerfall Winterspring on TV's *Howdy Doody Time*) was killed in a car accident.

His favorite movie was *Lawrence of Arabia*. Two of his favorite actors were Tony Curtis and Marlon Brando; he once called James Dean a "genius." He developed a strong aversion to Robert Goulet and once fired a gun at a television screen during a Goulet performance.

He collected badges. Once, carrying a white walking stick and wearing a purple velvet suit and a cape, he came to Washington bent on obtaining a Federal Narcotics Bureau badge. A deputy bureau chief was cordial to Elvis—hoping that he would endorse the agency's campaign against drug abuse—but he firmly refused to give Elvis a badge. A short while afterward the chief received a call instructing him to bring a badge to the Oval Office. Elvis was there waiting for it.

He once flew his entourage a thousand miles for peanut-butter-and-jelly sandwiches.

Toward the end of his life he weighed as much as 230 pounds. At a 1976 New Year's Eve show in Pontiac, Michigan, his trousers split up the middle. Another night, in Memphis, Elvis lost the seat of his pants bending over to kiss one of the girls in front of the stage.

In his last year he dated nineteen-year-old Ginger Alden, Miss Memphis Traffic Safety of 1976. He gave her a Cadillac and an eighty-five-thousand-dollar ring.

He died on August 16, 1977, while sitting on the toilet reading *The Scientific Search for the Face of Jesus.* A tissue analysis of his body revealed the presence of depressant drugs Butabarbitol, codeine, morphine, Nembutal, pentobarbital, phenobarbital, Placidyl, Quäälude, Valium, and Valmid. He was buried wearing a diamond ring bearing the inscription *TCB*—short for his motto, Taking care of business. In his lifetime he had grossed more than a billion dollars.

After his death women claimed to have made love to his ghost. In 1978 impersonator Dennis Wise underwent facial surgery to improve his resemblance to Elvis.

THE KING IS DEAD—OR IS HE?

by Richard Corliss

This piece appeared in Time *on October 10, 1988, and is a brief update on the state of affairs in the Elvis world that year, a year that found him back from the dead and communicating from the grave at the same time.*

The night Elvis died, one of his fans came home to find that her Presley records had mysteriously melted. That same evening, a couple discovered that the Elvis statue in their den had inexplicably broken apart. Years later, a police officer tracked his missing son to Los Angeles through information supplied in a dream by Elvis. The singer's face suddenly materialized in the wood paneling of a woman's pantry door. His voice counseled an overweight woman to lay off junk food. The late star, a frequent hospital visitor, has offered words of comfort to a woman giving birth, to another in a near death experience, and to a young girl dying of complications from Down's syndrome, whose last words were "Here comes Elvis!"

At least, so reports Dr. Raymond A. Moody Jr. in *Elvis After Life* (Peachtree; 1987), a collection of interviews with people claiming psychic experiences involving the dead singer. Moody even cites a woman who believes her young son is the King reincarnated. Her son believes it too. "Yeah, I'm Elvis Presley," he affirms in a familiar drawl. "I died, and I came back."

On Aug. 16, 1977, when Presley's death was announced, a Hollywood mourner observed, "Good career move." Never was cynicism more prophetic. The singer's estate is valued today at $50 million, ten times what it was when he was alive. A new movie, *Heartbreak Hotel,* imagines a '70s teenager kidnapping Elvis to impress his mom, and *Elvis: An American Musical* is touring the country this fall. An Elvis postage stamp is probably next, once proponents agree on which image—that of the young or the middle-aged star—should appear on it. And one can call an 800 number and get details about a Memphis bank's brand-new Elvis MasterCard.

Elvismania transcends the usual devotion to a white-hot celebrity, even one who has died before his time. Rudolph Valentino, Will Rogers, James Dean and Marilyn Monroe may have left indelible niches in the hearts of their fans, but few built shrines to them. Rumors of their survival rarely blossomed into testimony of posthumous visitations. Nor did their homes become cathedral theme parks. Yet each year Graceland, Presley's residence in Memphis, welcomes more than half a million Elvisitors, and many are true believers. To commemorate the high holy day, Aug. 16, 10,000 acolytes hold a candlelight vigil.

For some the light holds hope for the King's return. Once the province of supermarket tabloids, reports of Elvis's resurrection now nestle in bookstores. Following on the heels of Moody's book, Gail Brewer-Giorgio's best-selling *Is Elvis Alive?* (Tudor; 1988) offers evidence to stoke the stories. Fact: on the singer's grave his middle name, Aron, is misspelled as Aaron. Possible conclusion: Elvis *Aron* Presley is not buried there. The book comes with a tape of a man who sounds like Elvis and offers Delphic hints of his postmortem life and times. If Brewer-Giorgio fails to convince skeptics, she has profitably tapped a rich vein of quasireligious longing. Millions may sneer along with *Doonesbury* and David Letterman at news of Presley's sanctified status, but many believe it. A star may have died, but something is being born. Maybe the Church of Elvis.

The Rev. Robert D. Martin thinks so. "This has the makings of the rise of a new religion," says the retired Episcopal minister from Hernando, Miss. "Elvis is the god, and Graceland the shrine. There are no writings, but that could be his music. And some even say he is rising again. The August week is more like people going to Lourdes than to an entertainment event. People genuflect before his grave. Women have come to Memphis to deliver babies, claiming Elvis is the father and that he will come down from heaven when the boy is 16 to anoint him—sort of like Jesus in the Jordan River."

Fine, but why Elvis? Not just because he was rock's first superstar, but also because as the pawn of his manager, Colonel Tom Parker, he was the last pop idol who did not control his own career. In 1956 he released his first million-seller, *Heartbreak Hotel,* and raised screams and hackles on TV variety shows. Then, too soon, he was devoured by Hollywood's makeover machinery, steered into a rut that would lead to 33 low-mediocre films. Parker's determination to slip Elvis into the old show-biz mainstream effectively neutered the emperor of sexual and musical threat. By 1964, when the Beatles conquered America, Presley was still in his 20s but already an anachronism. And in his later, Vegas years, he often looked the pathetic, self-parodying porker. He was the first Elvis impersonator and a prisoner of his own eminence—the King in exile.

All this was essential to the creation of a cult religion. Presley had to suffer in the only way a celebrity can, through self-humiliation. This soldered the bond between a onetime poor boy from Tupelo, Miss., and his blue-collar, blue-haired or red-white-and-blue fans. He was both above them and one of them.

And now, some of them believe, he is with them again. On the stone wall that surrounds the entrance to Graceland they scrawl messages to their elusive idol: OUR LOSS IS HEAVEN'S GAIN . . . ELVIS, WAS THAT YOU AT BURGER KING? . . . ARE YOU DEAD—OR JUST LONESOME TONIGHT? Infidels can look at the balance sheet and say that wherever the star may be, he is certainly taking care of business. Presleyterians know better: ELVIS is an anagram for LIVES.

I'VE SEEN ELVIS AND HE'S ALIVE AND WELL!

███

by Pete Cooke

This item is typical of the kind of article that has become a regular feature of many tabloid magazines. This article was one of the first of its kind (the Elvis Is Alive genre) and the story achieved a kind of legendary status, prompting a wave of Elvis sightings all over the country.

The stunning revelation that Elvis Presley faked his death and is still alive came as no surprise to Louise Welling, a Kalamazoo housewife who has seen The King twice!

But at the time of her first chance encounter with Elvis at a Michigan grocery store the mother of five was "speechless."

"I remember it very vividly," Mrs. Welling told *The NEWS*. "It was last September on a Sunday after church. I went to Felpausch's grocery store in Vicksburg with my grandson.

"I was at the checkout, picking up my groceries," Mrs. Welling said. "I looked up and there he was, Elvis. I couldn't believe it. I was speechless, I mean you're not expecting to run into Elvis Presley in the grocery store. I was shocked."

Mrs. Welling, 50, said Elvis was at the checkout buying a fuse.

"He was holding a motorcycle helmet and dressed in an all-white jumpsuit," she said. "It wasn't fancy or anything, just a white jumpsuit. He'd lost weight and he didn't have sideburns.

"I didn't speak to him," Mrs. Welling said. "I'm a shy person anyway and I wouldn't speak to him unless he spoke to me first."

Mrs. Welling said few people believed she'd really seen Elvis until a recent *NEWS* article detailed startling evidence that the superstar faked his death in August 1977 in order to escape from the spotlight and live a normal life.

The mind-boggling story of Elvis's secret life is documented in the new book by Gail Giorgio, *The Most Incredible Elvis Presley Story Ever Told.*

According to the author's account, Elvis was flown to Hawaii while a wax figure was placed on public display in a coffin at Graceland, his Memphis estate.

The blockbuster book reveals that Elvis grew a beard, changed his name to John Burrows and began traveling the world.

The author's sources said Elvis was last known to be living in Kalamazoo, Mich.

But that wasn't news to Mrs. Welling, who saw Elvis twice in the Kalamazoo area last fall.

The second encounter with The King came a couple of weeks after Mrs. Welling bumped into Elvis in the grocery store.

"He was in the Burger King on this particular Friday," Mrs. Welling said. "My 26-year-old daughter Linda and my grandson and I pulled into the parking lot. I was getting my grandson out of the car while Linda went ahead to the door.

"That's when Elvis came out of the Burger King," she said. "He walked right past Linda. He put on a pair of dark glasses, got into a small, light blue car and took off real fast."

Mrs. Welling, whose husband Edward is a General Motors millwright, said she knows that others have seen Elvis in and around Kalamazoo.

"Other people have seen him, but they are afraid to say anything publicly," Mrs. Welling said.

"I'm not an Elvis fan. I don't have any Elvis records or Elvis books. I'm not into Elvis. I'm just saying what I saw. I don't have any reason to lie and I'm certainly not making a cent out of this."

WHERE WERE YOU WHEN ELVIS DIED?

■■■■■

by Lester Bangs

This article was originally published in the Village Voice *a few weeks after Elvis's death and later appeared in* Psychotic Reactions and Carburetor Dung, *a collection of the late great Lester Bangs's effusive writing. As always, his ranting and raving is eloquent, funny, and right on target.*

Where were *you* when Elvis died? What were you doing, and what did it give you an excuse to do with the rest of your day? That's what we'll be talking about in the future when we remember this grand occasion. Like Pearl Harbor or JFK's assassination, it boiled down to individual reminiscences, which is perhaps as it should be, because in spite of his greatness, etc., etc., Elvis had left us each as alone as he was; I mean, he wasn't exactly a Man of the People anymore, if you get my drift. If you don't I will drift even further, away from Elvis into the contemplation of why all our public heroes seem to reinforce our own solitude.

The ultimate sin of any performer is contempt for the audience. Those who indulge in it will ultimately reap the scorn of those they've dumped on, whether they live forever like Andy Paleface Warhol or die fashionably early like Lenny Bruce, Jimi Hendrix, Janis Joplin, Jim Morrison, Charlie Parker, Billie Holiday. The two things that distinguish those deaths from Elvis's (he and they having

84

drug habits vaguely in common) were that all of them died on the outside looking in and none of them took their audience for granted. Which is why it's just a little bit harder for me to see Elvis as a tragic figure; I see him as being more like the Pentagon, a giant armored institution nobody knows anything about except that its power is legendary.

Obviously we all liked Elvis better than the Pentagon, but look at what a paltry statement that is. In the end, Elvis's scorn for his fans as manifested in "new" albums full of previously released material and one new song to make sure all us suckers would buy it was mirrored in the scorn we all secretly or not so secretly felt for a man who came closer to godhood than Carlos Castaneda until military conscription tamed and revealed him for the dumb lackey he always was in the first place. And ever since, for almost two decades now, we've been waiting for him to get wild again, fools that we are, and he probably knew better than any of us in his heart of hearts that it was never gonna happen, his heart of hearts so obviously not being our collective heart of hearts, he being so obviously just some poor dumb Southern boy with a Big Daddy manager to screen the world for him and filter out anything which might erode his status as big strapping baby bringing home the bucks, and finally being sort of perversely celebrated at least by rock critics for his utter contempt for whoever cared about him.

And Elvis was perverse; only a true pervert could put out something like *Having Fun with Elvis On Stage,* that album released three or so years back which consisted *entirely* of between-song onstage patter so redundant it would make both Willy Burroughs and Gert Stein blush. Elvis was into marketing boredom when Andy Warhol was still doing shoe ads, but Elvis's sin was his failure to realize that his fans were not perverse—they loved him without qualification, no matter what he dumped on them they loyally lapped it up, and that's why I feel a hell of a lot sorrier for all those poor jerks than for Elvis himself. I mean, who's left they can stand all night in the rain for? Nobody, and the true tragedy is the tragedy of an entire generation which refuses to give up its adolescence even as it feels its menopausal paunch begin to blossom and its hair recede over the horizon—along with Elvis and everything else they once thought they believed in. Will they care in five years what he's been doing for the last twenty?

Sure Elvis's death is a relatively minor ironic variant on the future-shock mazurka, and perhaps the most significant thing about Elvis's exit is that the entire history of the seventies has been retreads and brutal demystification; three of Elvis's ex-bodyguards recently got together with this hacker from the New York *Post* and whipped up a book which dosed us with all the dirt we'd yearned for for so long. Elvis was the last of our sacred cows to be publicly mutilated; everybody knows Keith Richard likes his junk, but when Elvis went onstage in a stupor nobody breathed a hint of "Quaalude. . . ." In a way, this was both good and bad, good because Elvis wasn't encouraging other people to think it was cool to be a walking *Physicians' Desk Reference,* bad because Elvis stood for that Nixonian Secrecy-as-Virtue which was passed off as the essence of Americanism for a few years there. In a sense he could be seen not only as a phenomenon that exploded in the fifties to help shape the psychic jailbreak of the sixties but ultimately as a perfect cultural expression of what the Nixon years were all about. Not that he prospered more then, but that his passion for the privacy of potentates allowed him to get away with almost literal murder, certainly with the symbolic rape of his fans, meaning that we might all do better to think about waving good-bye with one upraised finger.

I got the news of Elvis's death while drinking beer with a friend and fellow music journalist on his fire escape on 21st Street in Chelsea. Chelsea is a good neighborhood; in spite of the fact that the insane woman who lives upstairs keeps him awake all night every night with her rants at no one, my friend stays there because he likes the sense of community within diversity in that neighborhood: old-time card-carrying Communists live in his building alongside people of every persuasion popularly lumped as "ethnic." When we heard about Elvis we knew a wake was in order, so I went out to the deli for a case of beer. As I left the building I passed some Latin guys hanging out by the front door. "Heard the news? Elvis is dead!" I told them. They looked at me with contemptuous indifference. So *what.* Maybe if I had told them Donna Summer was dead I might have gotten a reaction; I do recall walking in this neighborhood wearing a T-shirt that said "Disco Sucks" with a vast unamused muttering in my wake, which only goes to show that not for everyone was Elvis the still-reigning King of Rock 'n' Roll, in fact not for everyone is rock 'n' roll the still-reigning music. By now, each citizen has found his own little obsessive corner to blast his brains in: as the sixties were supremely narcissistic, solipsism's what the seventies have been about, and nowhere is this better demonstrated than in the world of "pop" music. And Elvis may have been the greatest solipsist of all.

I asked for two six-packs at the deli and told the guy behind the counter the news. He looked fifty years old, greying, big belly, life still in his eyes, and he said: "Shit, that's too bad. I guess our only hope now is if the Beatles get back together."

Fifty years old.

I told him I thought that would be the biggest anticlimax in history and that the best thing the Stones could do now would be to break up and spare us all further embarrassments.

He laughed, and gave me directions to a meat market down the street. There I asked the counterman the same question I had been asking everyone. He was in his fifties too, and he said, "You know what? I don't *care* that bastard's dead. I took my wife to see him in Vegas in '73, we paid fourteen dollars a ticket, and he came out and sang for twenty minutes. Then he fell down. Then he stood up and sang a couple more songs, then he fell down again. Finally he said, 'Well, shit, I might as well sing sitting as standing.' So he squatted on the stage and asked the band what song they wanted to do next, but before they could answer he was complaining about the lights. 'They're too bright,' he says. 'They hurt my eyes. Put 'em out or I don't sing a note.' So they do. So me and my wife are sitting in total blackness listening to this guy sing songs we knew and loved, and I ain't just talking about his old goddam songs, but he totally *butchered* all of 'em. Fuck him. I'm not saying I'm glad he's dead, but I know one thing: I got taken when I went to see Elvis Presley."

I got taken too the one time I saw Elvis, but in a totally different way. It was the autumn of 1971, and two tickets to an Elvis show turned up at the offices of *Creem* magazine, where I was then employed. It was decided that those staff members who had never had the privilege of witnessing Elvis should get the tickets, which was how me and art director Charlie Auringer ended up in nearly the front row of the biggest arena in Detroit. Earlier Charlie had said, "Do you realize how much we could get if we sold these fucking things?" I didn't, but how precious they were became totally clear the instant Elvis sauntered onto the stage. He was the only male performer I have ever seen to whom I responded sexually; it wasn't real arousal, rather an erection of the heart, when I looked at him I went mad with desire and envy and worship and self-projection. I mean, Mick Jagger, whom I saw as far back as 1964 and twice in '65, never even came close.

There was Elvis, dressed up in this ridiculous white suit which looked like some studded Arthurian castle, and he was too fat, and the buckle on his belt was as big as your head except that your head is not made of solid gold, and any lesser man would have been the spittin' image of a Neil Diamond damfool in such a getup, but on Elvis it fit. What didn't? No matter how lousy his records ever got, no matter how intently he pursued mediocrity, there was still some hint, some flash left over from the days when . . . well, I wasn't there, so I won't presume to comment. But I will say this: Elvis Presley was the man who brought overt blatant vulgar sexual frenzy to the popular arts in America (and thereby to the nation itself, since putting "popular arts" and "America" in the same sentence seems almost redundant). It has been said that he was the first white to sing like a black person, which is untrue in terms of hard facts but totally true in terms of cultural impact. But what's more crucial is that when Elvis started wiggling his hips and Ed Sullivan refused to show it, the entire country went into a paroxysm of sexual frustration leading to abiding discontent which culminated in the explosion of psychedelic-militant folklore which was the sixties.

I mean, don't tell me about Lenny Bruce, man—Lenny Bruce said dirty words in public and obtained a kind of consensual martydom. Plus which Lenny Bruce was hip, too goddam hip if you ask me, which was his undoing, whereas Elvis was not hip at all, Elvis was a goddam truck driver who worshiped his mother and would never say shit or fuck around her, and Elvis alerted America to the fact that it had a groin with imperatives that had been stifled. Lenny Bruce demonstrated how far you could push a society as repressed as ours and how much you could get away with, but Elvis kicked "How Much Is That Doggie in the Window" *out* the window and replaced it with "Let's fuck." The rest of us are still reeling from the impact. Sexual chaos reigns currently, but out of chaos may flow true understanding and harmony, and either way Elvis almost singlehandedly opened the floodgates. That night in Detroit, a night I will never forget, he had but to ever so slightly move one shoulder muscle, not even a shrug, and the girls in the gallery hit by its ray screamed, fainted, howled in heat. Literally, every time this man moved any part of his body the slightest centimeter, tens or tens of thousands of people went berserk. Not Sinatra, not Jagger, not the Beatles, nobody you can come up with ever elicited such hysteria among so many. And this after a decade and a half of crappy records, of making a point of not trying.

If love truly is going out of fashion forever, which I do not believe, then along with our nurtured indifference to each other will be an even more contemptuous indifference to each others' objects of reverence. I thought it was Iggy Stooge, you thought it was Joni Mitchell or whoever else seemed to speak for your own private, entirely circumscribed situation's many pains and few ecstasies. We will continue to fragment in this manner, because solipsism holds all the cards at present; it is a king whose domain engulfs even Elvis's. But I can guarantee you one thing: we will never again agree on anything as we agreed on Elvis. So I won't bother saying good-bye to his corpse. I will say good-bye to you.

THE SOUTHERN ELVIS

Elvis in context of the South. The emphasis here is on the concept of the southern experience being distinct and separate from the rest of America and the ways in which the southern heritage of guilt, violence, and poverty shaped not only Elvis but our own perceptions of him.

ELVIS, OR THE IRONIES OF A SOUTHERN IDENTITY

---

by Linda Ray Pratt

In this essay, English professor Pratt provides a southern perspective of El-
vis's public persona, with all its inherent contradictions. She examines Elvis
in context of a mythology that is uniquely southern, full of paradox and
sentiment.

Elvis was the most popular entertainer in the world, but nowhere
as popular as in his native South. In the last years of his career, his
audience in other parts of the country was generally centered in the
original "fifties" fans whose youth and music were defined by Elvis,
and in the lower or working class people who saw in Elvis some
glamorized image of their own values. In the South, however, the
pattern of Elvis's popularity tended to cut across age barriers and
class lines which were themselves a less recognizable thing in a region in which almost no one is more than a generation or two away
from poverty, and where "class" in small communities might have
more to do with family and past status than with money. Among
Southern youth, Elvis was not a relic from a musical past; he was
still one of the vital forces behind a Southern rock, which though
different now from his, still echoes the rhythms which his music had
fused out of the region. His numerous concerts in the South could
not exhaust the potential audience. At his death, leading politicians

and ministers from the South joined the people on the street in eulogizing him. Local radio and television stations ran their own specials in addition to the syndicated or national programs. Halftime ceremonies at the Liberty Bowl were in tribute to him. When someone commented on national TV that the Presleys were "white trash," it was a regional slur, not just a personal one. The white South expressed love, grief, and praise for Elvis from all age groups at virtually every level of the social, intellectual, and economic structures.

The phenomenon of such widespread sectional regard and emotional intensity went beyond the South's usual pride in the success of "one of our own." The emotion became more puzzling if one listened to some of the reasons offered to explain it: Elvis loved his mother; Elvis's heart was broken; Elvis loved Jesus; Elvis was the American Dream. Such reasons for loving and mourning Elvis seemed strange because, on the surface at least, they were so tangential to Elvis himself or to the musical or cultural impact he unquestionably did have. How, in the face of his vitality and defiance of convention, could one love Elvis because he loved Jesus? And how, in a man expressing nothing if not undisguised sexuality, could one love Elvis because he was so good to his mother? But people, especially those beyond the age group of his original teen fans, often did say such things. Merle Haggard's "From Graceland to the Promised Land," with its emphasis on Elvis's mother's death and his faith in Jesus, is, after all, the perfect Southern folk song about Elvis. The South's involvement with Elvis is sincere, but most of the expressed reasons for it do not reach very far, and some of them seem patently false. They are the myths sent up to justify the emotion and to obscure its source. The emotions spring from associations with a reality the South collectively prefers to conceal and yet constantly experiences. The paradox of Elvis was that he was able simultaneously to reveal the reality of the modern South while concealing it in a myth of the American Dream. He was at once both "King" and outsider.

The myth of Elvis which the South voices is in part very familiar. He is the sharecropper's son who made millions, the Horatio Alger story in drawl. Almost everyone who knew him assured us that, despite the money and fame, "he never changed" (no one remarks how tragic such a static condition would be, were it possible). He never got over his mother's death (in 1958); he was humble and polite; he doted on his little girl; he loved his home town; he never forgot where he came from. He had wealth, yes; but in the tradition of those who love Jesus, he was uncomfortable with riches when others were poor and so gave millions of dollars away to the less fortunate. The American success story turned to altruism. Even his money was not tainted, just dollars freely given in exchange for entertainment so good it always seemed a bargain. Unlike some others whose success was a ticket out of the South and into the broader, happier American identity, Elvis remained in Memphis. His regional loyalty when he could have lived anywhere deeply complimented the South. Graceland was a new image of the Southern plantation, this time free from associations with slavery and a guilt-ridden past. The very gates had musical notes on them. He was a good boy and a good ole boy. Elvis himself seemed to believe this vision; certainly he played to it in his "family" movies, his sacred music, and in his "American Trilogy" dominated by "Dixie." It was a sentimental myth, but, then, W. J. Cash has called Southerners "the most sentimental people in history" (*The Mind of the South,* p. 130).

Elvis's fame initially grew out of an image in opposition to the one the myth attempts to disguise. He was scandalous, sexual, defiant of all authority. He was preached against from the pulpit as an immoral force. In a blackboard jungle, he was the juvenile delinquent. On the streets, he was a hood. Socially, he was a "greaser." Economically, he was "poor white," a gentler rendition of "white trash." Maybe he loved Jesus, but even his Christmas songs could be dirty. In songs like "Santa Claus Is Back In Town" he played with the conventions of Christmas music in order to startle and subvert.

This image of Elvis, the rocker with "a dirty, dirty feeling," "born standing up and talking back," never fully disappeared. His last few movies, like a lot of the lyrics he improvised in concert, were sprinkled with off-color jokes and plays on words. His 1976 image was as excessive and extravagant as his 1956 image, though not in the same ways. The violence still flowed out of the karate movements, the sexuality in such songs as "Burning Love." In concert, his emotional passion sometimes transfigured such schmaltzy songs of lost love and broken hearts as "Hurt" or "You Gave Me a Mountain" into rich autobiographical moments. Even the obscene subversion of Christmas showed up again in "Merry Christmas, Baby."

The Elvis of the sentimental myth would never have changed musical or cultural history, but the authentic Elvis who did so was transformed into a legend obscuring what the man, the music, or the image really meant. Although some elements of the myth were commonly associated with Elvis throughout the country, in the South—particularly the white South—the myth was insisted upon and pushed to its extremes. The question is why. Jimmy Carter loves his mother and Jesus, too, but the South has not rewarded him with uncritical devotion. The real Elvis, both early and late, might have been severely criticized, but even his drug-involved death is called a "heart attack," the ten drugs the autopsy found in his body merely the "prescription medicines" of a sick and heartbroken man who kept pushing himself because he did not want to disappoint the fans. Those who have argued that people projected onto Elvis anything they liked because his image was essentially vacuous are mistaken; if anything, the image is too rich in suggestion to be acknowledged fully or directly.

Some critics attribute the sentimental myth of Elvis to the cleverness of Colonel Parker and the cooperation of Elvis himself. To do so is to oversimplify a complex phenomenon and to misread a generation's genuine mythmaking as merely another shrewd "sell" campaign. For anyone less significant than Elvis, the path that Colonel Parker apparently advised by way of numbingly stupid movies and empty music would have been the path to sure oblivion. The 1968 Black Leather television special saved Elvis from that, but allegedly against the advice of Parker who wanted the show to be all Christmas music. Elvis, pursued by the myth and under pressure to confirm it, kept to himself and never told the public anything. The Colonel was smart enough to promote the myth, but it was the authentic handiwork of a society that needed a legend to justify the identification it felt with such a figure. After Elvis died, the Brentwood, Tennessee, Historical Society even supplied the Presley genealogy. The family was, of course, completely respectable, producing "renowned professors, doctors, judges, ministers" in every generation until poverty overcame them during Reconstruction.

C. Vann Woodward has said that the South's experience is atypical of the American experience, that where the rest of America has known innocence, success, affluence, and an abstract and disconnected sense of place, the South has known guilt, poverty, failure, and a concrete sense of roots and place ("The Search for Southern Identity" in *The Burden of Southern History*). These myths collide in Elvis. His American success story was always acted out within its Southern limitations. No matter how successful Elvis became in terms of fame and money, he remained fundamentally disreputable in the minds of many Americans. Elvis had rooms full of gold records earned by million-copy sales, but his best rock and roll records were not formally honored by the people who control, if not the public taste, the rewarding of the public taste. Perhaps this is always the fate of innovators; awards are created long after the form is created. His movies made millions but could not be defended on artistic grounds. *The New York Times* view of his fans was "the men favoring leisure suits and sideburns, the women beehive hairdos, purple eyelids and tight stretch pants" (*New York Times* story by Wayne King, 8 Jan. 1978). Molly Ivins, trying to explain in *The New York Times* the crush of people and "genuine emotion" in Memphis when Elvis died would conclude, "It is not required that love be in impeccable taste." Later, in the year after his death, Mike Royko would sarcastically suggest that Elvis's body and effects be sent to Egypt in exchange for the King Tut exhibit. ("So in terms of sheer popularity, no other American dead body can stand up to Presley's.") The "Doonesbury" cartoon strip would see fit to run a two-weeks sequence in which "Boopsie" would go visit Elvis's grave. Her boyfriend puts her down with, "2,000,000 necrophiliacs can't be wrong." Elvis's sheer commercial value commanded respect, but no amount of success could dispel the aura of strangeness about him. He remained an outsider in the American culture that adopted his music, his long hair, his unconventional clothes, and his freedom of sexual movement.

Although he was the world's most popular entertainer, to like Elvis a lot was suspect, a lapse of taste. It put one in beehives and leisure suits, in company with "necrophiliacs" and other weird sorts. The inability of Elvis to transcend his lack of reputability despite a history-making success story confirms the Southern sense that the world outside thinks Southerners are freaks, illiterates, Snopeses, sexual perverts, lynchers. I cannot call this sense a Southern "paranoia" because ten years outside the South has all too often confirmed the frequency with which non-Southerners express such views. Not even the presidency would free LBJ and Jimmy Carter from such ridicule. At the very moment in which Southerners proclaim most vehemently the specialness of Elvis, the greatness of his success, they understand it to mean that no Southern success story can ever be sufficient to satisfy a suspicious America.

And Elvis was truly different, in all those tacky Southern ways one is supposed to rise above with money and sophistication. He was a pork chops and brown gravy man. He liked peanut butter and banana sandwiches. He had too many cars, and they were too pink. He liked guns, and capes, and a Venus de Milo water fountain in the entry at Graceland. I once heard about 1958 that he had painted the ceiling at Graceland dark blue with little silver stars that twinkled in the dark. His taste never improved, and he never recanted anything. He was the sharecropper's son in the big house, and it always showed.

Compounding his case was the fact that Elvis didn't always appear fully white. Not sounding white was his first problem, and white radio stations were initially reluctant to play his records. Not to be clearly white was dangerous because it undermined the black-white rigidities of a segregated society, and to blur those definitions was to reveal the falseness at the core of segregation. Racial ambiguity is both the internal moral condemnation and the social destruction of a racist society which can only pretend to justify itself by abiding by its own taboos. Yet all Southerners know, despite the sternest Jim Crow laws, that more than two hundred years of racial mixing has left many a Southerner racially ambiguous. White Southerners admit only the reality of blacks who have some white blood, but, of course, the knife cuts both ways. Joe Christmas and Charles Bon. Désirée's Baby. In most pictures, Elvis might resemble a blue-eyed Adonis, but in some of those early black and white photographs, his eyes sultry, nostrils flared, lips sullen, he looked just that—black and white. And he dressed like blacks. His early wardrobe came from Lansky Brothers in Memphis. Maybe truck drivers wore greasy hair and long sideburns, but only the blacks were wearing zoot suits and pegged pants with pink darts in them. Country singers might sequin cactus and saddles on satin shirts, Marty Robbins would put a pink carnation on a white sport coat, and Johnny Cash would be the man in black. Only Elvis would wear a pink sport coat with a black velvet collar. "The Memphis Flash," he was sometimes called.

The music was the obvious racial ambiguity. Elvis's use of black styles and black music angered many Southern blacks who resented the success he won with music that black artists had originated but could not sell beyond the "race record" market of a segregated commercial world. In interviews today, these black blues musicians usually say that Elvis stole everything from them, an understandable complaint but one that nevertheless ignores his fusion of black music with white country to create a genuinely new sound. He was the Hillbilly Cat singing "Blue Moon of Kentucky" and "That's All Right (Mama)." Elvis's role in fusing the native music of poor Southern whites and poor Southern blacks into rock and roll is the best known aspect of his career and his greatest accomplishment.

Students of rock always stress this early music, but the sentimental myth gives it less attention, though the records always sold better in the South than in any other region. The music in the myth is more often the love ballads and the Protestant hymns. Yet the music that was in reality most important to Southerners was the music most closely tied to Southern origins. Elvis himself seemed to understand this; compare, for example, his 1974 concert album from Memphis's Mid-South Coliseum (the "Graceland" album) with any other concert album. The music I remember hearing most was music like "Mystery Train," "One Night," "Lawdy Miss Clawdy," "Heartbreak Hotel," "Peace in the Valley," "Blue Christmas," and "American Trilogy." For Southerners, this fusion of "Dixie," "All My Trials," and "The Battle Hymn of the Republic" has nothing to do with the rest of America, although its popularity around the country suggests that other Americans do relate it to their own history. The trilogy seems to capture Southern history through the changes of the civil rights movement and the awareness of black suffering which had hitherto largely been excluded from popular white images of Southern history. The piece could not have emerged before the seventies because only then had the "marching" brought a glimmer of hope. Even Elvis could not have sung this trilogy in New York's Madison Square Garden before there was some reason for pride and hope in the South. Elvis was right to make the song his; it is an appropriate musical history from one whose music moved always in the fused racial experiences of the region's oppressed. Rock and roll, taking inside it rhythm and blues and country, was the rhythm of Southern life, Southern problems, and Southern hopes. It is not coincidence that rock and roll emerged almost simultaneously with the civil rights movement, that both challenged the existing authority, and that both were forces for "integration."

The most stunning quality about Elvis and the music was the sexuality, yet the sentimental myth veers away from this disturbing complexity into the harmlessly romantic. Elvis might be "nice looking" or "cute" or perhaps "sexy," but not sexual. The sexuality he projected was complicated because it combined characteristics and appeals traditionally associated with both males and females. On one hand, he projected masculine aggression and an image of abandoned pleasure, illicit thrills, back alley liaisons and, on the other hand, a quality of tenderness, vulnerability, and romantic emotion. Andy Warhol captured something of this diversified sexuality in his portrait of Elvis, caught in a threatening stance with a gun in his hand but with the face softened in tone and line. The image made Elvis the perfect lover by combining the most appealing of male and female characteristics and satisfying both the physical desire for sensual excitement and the emotional need for loving tenderness. The music echoed the physical pleasure in rhythm and the emotional need in lyrics that said "Love Me," "Love Me Tender," "Don't," "I Want You I Need You I Love You," and "Don't Be Cruel." Unlike many later rock stars whose music would voice an assault on women, Elvis's music usually portrayed an emotional vulnerability to what women could do *to* him, as well as what he could do *for* them. When the public's notion of his heartbroken private life confirmed this sense of vulnerability, the image took on renewed power. Despite the evidence in the music or the long hair and lashes and full, rounded features, most Elvis fans would deny that his appeal is vaguely androgynous. Many male and female fans talk about Elvis as an ideal male image but would probably find it threatening to traditions of sexual identity to admit that the ideal male figure might indeed combine traditional male characteristics with some which are freely admitted only in women. In the South where sex roles are bound up with the remnants of a chivalric "way of life," open sexuality was allowable only in the "mysterious" lives of blacks, and permissible sexual traits in whites were rigidly categorized by sex. But the image of Elvis goes behind these stereotypes to some ideal of sexuality that combines the most attractive elements in each of them.

Women's sexual imaginations of Elvis have rarely been openly expressed, in part because women weren't supposed to have any explicit sexual fantasies and in part because those who did were perhaps least likely, because of the cultural and regional prohibitions, to admit them. Despite the mass of published material about Elvis, almost nothing of a serious nature by women has been printed. One remarkable exception is a short story by Julie Hecht, "I Want You I Need You I Love You" in *Harper's* (May 1978). Hecht's story makes the only serious effort I have seen to reveal those characteristics which gave Elvis's sexual appeal such complexity and power. The woman in the story remembers first imagining his kiss when she was twelve and didn't know what came after the kiss. Twenty years later in her fantasy of August 1977, she is able to "save" Elvis's life by getting him on a good health food diet. They become "best of friends," and she has her moment of tenderness: "I did get to touch him. I touched his hands, I touched his face, we hugged, we kissed, I kissed his hands, I kissed his face, I touched his face, I touched his arms, I touched his eyes, I touched his hair, I saw his smile, I heard his voice, I saw him move, I heard him laugh, I heard him sing" (*Harper's,* p. 67). This passage illustrates the obsessive physical attraction that combined with the illusion that Elvis was really sweet, tender, and in need of loving care. Seeing or hearing Elvis was never enough; one had to try to touch him. In life, such fans tore at his clothes and his person; in death, they visit his grave. Does any woman really care whether or not Elvis loved his mother or Jesus? But I never met a female fan who did not detest Priscilla. "Somebody ought to put a bullet through her," a pleasant faced middle-aged saleswoman in a bookstore once told me.

Elvis said he grew sideburns because he wanted to look like truck drivers, and many such men would later want to look like him. One important element in Elvis's sexual appeal for men seemed to be the acting out of the role of the "hood" who got the girl, won the fight, and rose above all the economic powerlessness of real hoods. Men who because of class and economic binds knew their own limitations seemed especially attracted to this aspect of the image. They wore their hair like his, affected his mannerisms, sang with his records. Men too sophisticated to betray themselves in such overt ways betrayed themselves in other ways. I remember a highly educated man rhapsodizing about how phallic the black leather suit was that Elvis wore in his 1968 television appearance. When Elvis aged and put on weight, men were his cruelest detractors. They seemed to take his appearance as a personal offense.

Beyond the money, the power, the fame, there was always at some level this aspect of Elvis, the American Dream in its Southern variation. Like other great Southern artists, Elvis revealed those characteristics of our culture which we know better than outsiders to be part of the truth. In Elvis was also the South that is bizarre, or violent, or darkly mysterious, the South called the grotesque in Faulkner or O'Connor. Perhaps this is why a book like *Elvis: What Happened?* could not damage the appeal. The hidden terrors, pain, and excesses of the private life which the book reveals, despite its mean-spirited distortions, only make the image more compelling in its familiarity. Even his drug problem had a familiar Southern accent—prescription medicines, cough syrups, diet pills.

Elvis's South is not the old cotton South of poor but genteel aristocrats. His Mississippi is not that of Natchez. Elvis is the Mississippi of pulpwood, sharecroppers, small merchants. His Memphis had nothing to do with riverboats or the fabled Beale Street. Elvis's Memphis was the post-World War II city of urban sprawl, racial antagonism, industrial blight, slums, Humes High. He walked the real Beale Street. Despite Graceland, and "Dixie" in Madison Square Garden, Elvis was the antithesis of the Rhett and Scarlett South. But no one living in the South today ever knew the Rhett and Scarlett South. Southerners themselves go to Natchez as to a tourist attraction. Elvis's South was the one that most Southerners really experience, the South where not even the interstate can conceal the poverty, where industrial affluence threatens the land and air which have been so much a part of our lives, where racial violence touches deep inside the home, where even our successes cannot overcome the long reputation of our failures. Even Graceland is not really beautiful. Squeezed in on all sides by the sprawl of gas stations, banks, shopping plazas, and funeral homes, Elvis's beloved home is an image of the South that has been "new" now for over fifty years.

Elvis evoked the South of modern reality with a fidelity he could not himself escape. The South rewarded him with its most cherished myths, but Elvis's tragedy was that he got caught in the contradictions. We only wanted to be able to claim that he was a good boy who loved Jesus. He apparently needed to become that, to live out the mythic expectations. He hungered for approval. The problem was that most of what Elvis really was could never be so transmogrified. He *was* the king of rock and roll, but he was uncomfortable with what the title implied. Linda Thompson has said that in his later years he hated hard rock. The further he moved from the conventions of the romantic myth, the more he proclaimed them. The more drugs he used, the more he supported law and order. When the counter culture he helped to usher in became widespread, he thought of helping the FBI as an undercover agent. How could he not be schizophrenic at the end, balancing the rock myth he created, the sentimental myth he adopted, and the emotional needs that made him like anyone else? He was destroyed by having to be what he was and wanting to be what he thought he ought to be. The Jesus-loving boy singing dirty Christmas songs. "One Night" and "How Great Thou Art."

After Elvis died, it was necessary to deify him. It isn't, after all, very becoming to grieve for a rock idol who died, as *The New York Times* once put it, "puffy and drug-wasted." But saying what and why one grieved was difficult. The South has had a lot of practice mythologizing painful and ambiguous experiences into glamorous and noble abstractions. So it was from Graceland to the Promised Land. Rex Humbard told us that Elvis found peace in Jesus, and Billy Graham assured us that Elvis was in Heaven. Billy was even looking forward to visiting him there. A disc jockey playing "How Great Thou Art" reflects at the end of the record, "And he certainly was." In Tupelo the Elvis Presley Memorial Foundation is building a $125,000 Chapel of Inspiration in his memory. Memphis will put a 50-ton bronze statue on a river bluff. Priscilla wants their daughter to remember, most of all, his humbleness. He loved his Jesus, his daughter, his lost wife. He loved his daddy. He loved the South. He was a great humanitarian. "God saw that he needed some rest and called him home to be with Him," the tombstone reads. Maybe all of this is even true. The apotheosis of Elvis demands such perfection because his death confirmed the tragic frailty, the violence, the intellectual poverty, the extravagance of emotion, the loneliness, the suffering, the sense of loss. Almost everything about his death, including the enterprising cousin who sold the casket pictures to *National Enquirer,* dismays, but nothing can detract from Elvis himself. Even this way, he is as familiar as next door, last year, the town before.

Greil Marcus wrote in his book *Mystery Train: Images of America in Rock 'n' Roll Music* that Elvis created a beautiful illusion, a fantasy that shut nothing out. The opposite was true. The fascination was the reality always showing through the illusion—the illusion of wealth and the psyche of poverty; the illusion of success and the pinch of ridicule; the illusion of invincibility and the tragedy of frailty; the illusion of complete control and the reality of inner chaos. In Faulkner's *Absalom, Absalom!* Shreve thinks that Quentin hates the South. He does not understand that Quentin is too caught in it ever to have thought of such a question, just as Elvis was and just as we were in Elvis. Elvis had all the freedom the world can offer and could escape nothing. What chance that the South could escape him, reflecting it as he did?

Southerners do not love the old Confederacy because it was a noble ideal, but because the suffering of the past occasioned by it has formed our hearts and souls, both good and evil. But we celebrate the past with cheap flags, cliché slogans, decorative license plates, decaled ash trays, and a glorious myth of a Southern "way of life" no one today ever lived. And Southerners do not love Elvis because he loved Jesus or anyone else. The Elvis trinkets, his picture on waste cans or paperweights or T-shirts or glowing in the dark from a special frame, all pay the same kind of homage as the trinkets in worship of the past. People outside the Elvis phenomenon may think such commercialization demeans the idol and the idolater. But for those who have habitually disguised the reality of their culture from even themselves, it is hard to show candidly what and why one loves. In impeccable taste. By the most sentimental people in history.

MEMPHIS TO MEMPHIS

Albert Goldman

Memphis, Tennessee has been the setting for countless legendary episodes in American music history, but as Albert Godman discovers, the city has served as an ambivaient backdrop for brief but celebrated periods of furious musical activity.

Back in June 1968, while writing a series for *New York* titled "The Blues Today," I settled down late one night in a posh suite at the Drake Hotel in Manhattan to do an interview with Jimi Hendrix. After a little preliminary palaver, Hendrix eyed me—a middle-aged Columbia University professor with long hair and granny glasses—and asked archly: "What would you do now if I whipped out the biggest joint you ever saw and started to smoke it?" Amused by his caution, I answered: "I'd tear it out of your hand and eat it!" That broke him up and he relaxed, which was the signal for his miniskirted entourage to resume their normal domestic duties, which commenced with the star's awakening at 7 P.M. and concluded the following afternoon, when he nodded out.

During the hours that followed, I watched the great psychedelic bluesman moving restlessly about in his exotic environment, suffused with the scent of burning incense and lit by flickering candles in red glasses. One moment he would pause to be sketched, the next he would listen to a reading of his latest review or scratch out a few notes on a sheet of music paper or spin a side or withdraw into his bedroom with one of his handmaidens. All the while, he was smoking dope or snorting coke or drinking Lancer wine, like a jazzman running endless changes on the same three chords. Just as I was starting to get groggy and nod out myself, Hendrix snapped me into rapt attention.

Clapping a pair of elephantine earphones on my head, he announced, "Now I'm gonna play you something really good." Dropping the needle into the groove, he smiled at me as I waited expectantly. Suddenly, my ears were filled with a brass chord that swelled so far that I imaged an I-beam thrusting endlong through the window. Then the chord was broken off by a funky bass that was in turn transfixed by a piercing guitar sound that quivered like an assegai. "Jimi," I cried, "that's the greatest lick you ever played!" He laughed and answered, "That's not me, man. That's the guitar player I learned from. That's the *king*—Albert King."

The next week I flew down to Memphis for the first time in my life to meet Albert King and research a piece on the Memphis Soul Sound. From the moment I stepped inside the Stax-Volt studios until I boarded my return flight clutching a couple of reels containing King's forthcoming album, *Blues Power,* I was enthralled by everything I discovered. I sat in an office watching Don Porter and Isaac Hayes (then a songwriter not a performer) demonstrating for my benefit all their hits. I interviewed B. B. King as he lay naked under the sheets of the Lorraine Motel. I not only interviewed Albert King but spent the first of what became many nights watching him work, on this occasion witnessing him battle B. B. King in the musical equivalent of a rigged wrestling match at the Club Paradise on South Danny Thomas Boulevard—a converted bowling alley with two artificial palms at the sides of the stage and tough billy-wielding ushers dressed like cops. That evening ended with our driving out to a speakeasy on the outskirts of town (Memphis was the wettest "dry" town in America), where we ate heartily and drank heavily with our dates, a couple of black girls who talked exclusively about black pop stars. If you had asked me for my impressions of Memphis after that trip, I would have told you that the city more than fulfilled everything I had ever imagined about the legendary home of the blues.

Ten years later I came back to Memphis to begin work on my biography of Elvis Presley. I assumed that I would have more adventures of the same kind, only this time I would get a lot deeper into the local music scene. In fact, as day after day went by and I moved from one site or interview to another, I never heard a note of music or got the sense that there was any music left in town. The famous recording studios were boarded over and the local musicians appeared to have vanished. Gradually, I came to realize that what I had experienced in the sixties had been a rare moment in the city's history. Memphis had been full of sounds for a brief time then, just as it had briefly in the previous decade when Elvis, Carl Perkins, and Jerry Lee Lewis recorded for Sun, or earlier still in the heydey of the tent-show blues queens. Those periods, however, were simply oases in what had generally been and promised to remain a musical desert.

When I finally set about composing *Elvis,* I wrote up my findings and reflections on the evolution of the blues, intending to set them side by side with an account of white gospel as the two principle traditions that had combined in the new rock 'n' roll. My sketch turned out to be too long for inclusion in the book and so it is offered here without any effort to update it because, so far as I am aware, nothing has happened since 1980 that would alter my sense of blues history.

"Memphis" and "blues" are words that lock together with the inexorableness of cause and effect. When you reflect on the legends of Beale Street and W. C. Handy or call the roll of all the famous bluesmen who have been associated with Memphis from the early days of Bukka White and Big Bill Broonzy to the post World War II generation of Howlin' Wolf and Little Walter to the last great bluesmen, B. B. King and Albert King, all the evidence appears to add up to the anticipated conclusion. In the words of a textbook—or a tourist brochure—"Memphis was one of those uniquely endowed metropolises that afford the ideal conditions for the growth and flourishing of a famous art." It is only when you come to know Memphis from personal observation and from the study of its skimpy cultural records that you begin first to question, then to modify, and finally to discard this myth.

The natural place to begin the study of the Memphis blues is Beale Street. Just pronouncing the magic name is enough to flood the imagination with beguiling images. One pictures it on a Saturday night circa 1910, crowded with plow jockeys and parlor belles, river rousters and factory frills, pimps in box-back coats and "beautiful browns in flouncy gowns." You envision blocks lined with gingerbread palaces and clapboard cribs; sporting houses filled with creoles from New Orleans and gambling halls jammed with fancy men playing cooncan rummy. Rising like an invisible but palpable cloud around this lively tableau are the sounds of Beale—the jumbling of ragtime pianos with windup Victrolas, of shouting congregations with howling bluesmen, of strolling guitar pickers with scrounging jug bands—the South's most celebrated symphony. Then, you take a walk down Beale today.

One of the saddest sights in the United States is the vestiges of what was once "Black America's Main Street." Block after block of abandoned, boarded-over brick buildings, bare ruined choirs occupied sometimes by a dismal Jewish pawnshop in whose heavily barred window the guitars, banjos and trumpets of the local blacks lie gathering dust. Beale reminds the visitor of those ruins deliberately left standing in European cities as memorials of disastrous wars lost to superior powers. Indeed, the hollow, scabrous walls of Beale make a very eloquent witness not just to the indifference and contempt for black life which is characteristic of Southern cities but also to the active hostility of the white ruling powers of this half-black metropolis, which have sought for years to wipe out the black commercial district so that it would no longer provide any distraction from the arid and lifeless cityscape which the urban renewers have imposed on all the rest of downtown Memphis.

Considered in the light of history, the ghostly appearance of Beale suggests other, less immediate associations: for one, the precise parallel between Beale's fate and that of Storyville in New Orleans. Every lover of American music knows how the legendary redlight district that was one of the spawning grounds of jazz was abolished abruptly in 1917 at the order of the U.S. Navy, which feared the corrupting effect of the tenderloin on its antiseptically uniformed personnel. What is not so well-known is that exactly the same fate befell Beale on the eve of the second World War. Generally, it is believed that Beale was either the victim of Mayor Boss Crump's moral zeal or of the deadening effects of Prohibition combined with the Depression. Nothing could be further from the truth.

E. H. Crump, who was first elected mayor in 1910, did wage a campaign to clean up the city, which was then notorious as the "Murder Capital of America." Once he got into office, however, he never raised a finger to interfere with the prostitution and gambling, the drinking and doping, that were the lifeblood of Beale. In fact, in 1916 he was turned out of office by the Tennessee Legislature for failure to enforce the State's liquor prohibition law, which antedated the Volstead Act by nearly a decade. It was this humiliating punishment that determined Crump to build a political machine so powerful that never again would he have to fear the interference of either the state or the federal authorities. So well did he succeed that until his death in 1954, he ruled Memphis with an iron hand and even decided who would be the state's governor. As a congressman, he developed strong ties with the Roosevelt Administration; generally, however, he preferred not to hold office but to rule through his puppets and minions.

Like his counterpart, Boss Pendergast of Kansas City (whose vast network of clubs and clip-joints had become the hothouse for jazz after its decline in New Orleans and Chicago), Boss Crump had no intention of allowing his machine to be deprived of the enormous bribes paid by the gamblers, bootleggers and bordello operators. What if every night the action cost some black man his life? The bodies were always spirited away to protect the reputation of the Street. (Hence the old Memphis proverb: "You never find a dead nigger on Beale.") What induced Crump to shut down Beale overnight in 1940 was a call from FDR. The former Secretary of the Navy told Crump that a new naval base was going to be built in nearby Millington; if the city wanted to profit from the federal treasury, it would have to reciprocate by locking up its cages full of man-eating whores, and pimps, gamblers and dope dealers. That phone call from the Big Boss to the local boss meant an end to high times on Beale.

Digging even deeper into the history of Memphis and the blues, one comes to an even more surprising realization: namely, that even in its palmiest days, Memphis was never anything more to the bluesman than a way station on his road north, east or west. Virtually none of the famous bluesmen whose names have been associated at one time or another with Memphis were born or reared in the city. Almost invariably they came from rural districts, especially from that great umbilicus of the blues, the Mississippi Delta. After years of developing their craft in the country and the little market towns, often through informal apprenticeships to older musicians, they drifted into Memphis because it was the only major city in the region.

They played in the streets for nickels and dimes; or perhaps they got an occasional job in a saloon or playing for a white man's party. If they were exceptionally lucky, they were spotted by a scout for a northern record company: Paramount or OKeh in the twenties, Brunswick or Victor in the thirties. Brought up to a hotel room and seated before the crude portable equipment, the bluesman cut a few sides for a few dollars. That was it. If he wanted to be better, he had to work up his nerve and go to Chicago. To think of Memphis as a city like New Orleans, Kansas City, or New York that fostered a particular music by providing abundant opportunities for work or the stimulating and educating company of hundreds of other musicians or regular access to recording studies is completely mistaken. Instead of being renowned as the home of the blues, Memphis should be notorious as the town that turned its back on the blues.

What, then, if anything, did Memphis contribute to the blues? The answer is *commercialization*. At several crucial moments in the history of the music, local musicians and entrepreneurs appeared who translated successfully this musical patois into the idioms of mass entertainment. These blues brokers, by virtue of their strategic position in the heartland of the blues, were able, like the cotton factors on Front Street, to act as middlemen for the commodity so laboriously cultivated in the Delta and the consuming public the world around. Memphis figures in the evolution of the blues, therefore, as an important, if only intermittently active, center of musical exploitation.

The first and greatest of the Memphis blues brokers was the man who bears the title "The Father of the Blues": William Christopher Handy. As Handy was not just the prototype but the archetype of all those composers and arrangers, music publishers and record producers, who have mined and minted the riches of black music for the past seventy years—including the creators of Memphis Rockabilly in the fifties and the Memphis Sound in the sixties—it is worth pausing for a moment to consider his cast of mind and mode of operation.

The first and most important thing to grasp about W. C. Handy is that he embodies to a remarkable degree the mentality of the "striver," the first generation of black bourgoisie in America. Born in a log cabin at Florence, Alabama, in 1873, the son of a former slave, Handy emerged from the same conditions of rural poverty and social ostracism that condemned millions of blacks to lives of hardship and ignominy. Handy lived up to his name, however: though his opportunities were few, he rarely let one slip through his grasp. Told as a young man that no "thick-lipped nigger" could ever play the cornet—the instrument that in the world of black minstrelsy was as much a talisman of success as was the fiddle to the first generations of aspiring Eastern European Jews—Handy became a cornet virtuoso and the leader of the Bihara Minstrels' band. Tiring of life on the road, he organized his own band and began to play dances for rich planters in the Mississippi Delta. The legend of the birth of the blues commences on a night in 1903, while Handy was dozing on a train platform in the Delta at the little town of Tutwiler. Awakened by what he describes as "the weirdest music I ever heard," Handy discovered that a "lean, loose-jointed Negro had commenced plunking a guitar beside me while I slept. His clothes were rags; his feet peeped out of his shoes. As he played, he pressed a knife on the strings of the guitar in a manner popularized by Hawaiian guitarists who used steel bars. The effect was unforgettable."

Ruminating on this strange music, Handy associated it with the old work songs of field hands, who sang:

> *Boll Weevil, where you been so long?*
> *Boll Weevil, where you been so long?*
> *You stole ma cotton, now you want my corn.*

Or the plaints of lonely river roustabouts, who cried:

> *Oh, the Kate's up the river, Stack O'Lee's in the ben',*
> *Oh, the Kate's up the river, Stack O'Lee's in the ben',*
> *An' I ain't seen ma baby since I can't tell when.*

Such rustic stuff held no charm for the sophisticated, note-reading, widely-traveled bandsman. He soon forgot the country bluesman, like a figure in a dream.

Then, one night at a dance in the Delta, Handy received an ambiguous request. Somebody handed him a note reading: "Can you play some of your native music?" Handy was not sure what the writer meant by "native." His gilt-buttoned, fancy-laced bandsmen were not like minstrels who could "fake" and "jass." He decided to call a medley of traditional Southern airs that was probably right off the racks of some musical dry goods store. When the performance concluded, Handy received another request: would he stand aside while some of the local colored boys played a few dances? Handy took the suggestion as a joke. What could these clowns do that would merit them a place on the platform where he was performing? It was all he could do to restrain his laughter when he beheld his rivals: a "long-legged chocolate boy" whose band consisted of "a battered guitar, a mandolin and a worn-out bass."

When this unpromising group got into action, the music they produced justified Handy's prejudices: "one of those over-and-over strains that seemed to have no very clear beginning and certainly no ending at all. The strumming attained a disturbing monotony, but on and on it went." Even more absurd than the music were the mannerisms of the players: they thumped their splayed feet on the floor, rolled their eyes and swayed their shoulders. What a contrast they offered to the correct military posture of Handy's men! No sooner did this interminable jig reel end, however, than a remarkable thing happened.

Silver coins began pelting down on the "darkies." Quarters, halves, even massive dollars chimed on the floor. As Handy gaped at this silver rain, he experienced a revelation. "I saw the beauty of primitive music!" he exclaims. "They had the stuff the people wanted. It touched the spot. Folks would pay for it. . . . The American people wanted rhythm and movement for their money." That moment worked a revolution in his thinking. As he put it, "That night a composer was born": for which we can read—a very deliberate and resourceful exploiter of black folk music.

By 1909, Handy was settled on Beale Street, then at the height of its fame as a *"Netzenstadt"*: a city of nets and man traps. Handy was not put off by the ubiquitous crime and violence; his job was to hustle up dates for his band, which was having trouble cutting into the market controlled by two other orchestras. At this moment, E. H. Crump was running in a three-cornered race for mayor. As his opponents had hired the better-known bands, Crump was forced to engage Handy to ballyhoo the candidacy by riding around town playing music from a bandwagon.

Handy took his assignment very seriously. He felt he had been hired to swing the Beale Street vote, and, as the "best notes get the best votes," he ought to provide his boss with a catchy campaign song. Though Crump's pious campaign promises might have been symbolized best by a hymn, something gamier was needed to capture the favor of the sporting crowd. Struggling now—exactly like the rhythm and blues producers of later times—to come up with a gimmick that would turn on the ghetto, Handy decided (like the concocters of the Memphis Sound fifty years afterwards) that the best way to tickle the fancies of his sophisticated audience of "easy riders" (pimps), "players" and "hos" was to cook up a mess of steaming grits and greens. Recollecting the music he had heard years before on the train platform in the Delta, he hied himself down to the back room of Thornton's barbershop. (Handy liked to compose in the heart of the milieu he was seeking to capture.) There he turned out the composition that has always been called "the first published blues." Actually, "The Memphis Blues" (so titled when printed in 1912 but known originally as "Mr. Crump") was not a true blues but a hybrid composition that combined features of the blues with the cakewalk.

When Handy took "Mr. Crump" to the streets, he created a sensation. Soon the song was being played night and day all over town. Though the tune had no lyrics, people would improvise their own words—salty, sassy street chants. When Handy put the best lines together, they added up to a rude rejection of Mr. Crump's self-righteous campaign rhetoric:

> *Mr. Crump won't 'low no easy riders here,*
> *Mr. Crump won't 'low no easy riders here,*
> *We don't care what Mr. Crump don' 'low,*
> *We gon' barrelhouse anyhow—*
> *Mr. Crump can go and catch hisself some air!*

In the published version, hackneyed Tin Pan Alley verses were substituted for the original words. Along with all the other precedents established by this landmark composition went the black songwriter's capitulation to the rule that pop tunes must have lily-white lyrics.

After Handy's departure for New York in 1918 (where he established a highly successful publishing business and the first black-owned record company, Black Swan), Beale Street began a slow decline. At the same time, however, the blues soared to its first great peak of popularity. Belted out on the black vaudeville stage or ground out through the flaring horn of a Victrola by a whole tribe of sonorous black mamas, led by the fabled "Empress of the Blues," Bessie Smith, the blues became—along with short skirts, roadsters and bathtub gin—one of the distinctive fads of the twenties. At the end of the decade, George Gershwin summed up the infatuation with this dark, exotic music in a single gigantic blue note, drawn with the stroke of a great caricaturist's pen as the startling two-octave clarinet glissando that opens *Rhapsody in Blue*.

Naturally, many modifications of the country blues were made to accommodate this quirky, improvisatory and, in performance, highly individualized folk song to the mass production formulas of Tin Pan Alley and vaudeville. One of the most important and far-reaching developments was the coalescence of blues with that other newly discovered black art: jazz. On virtually every Bessie Smith record, the singer is accompanied by one or more jazz players, including such famous names as Louis Armstrong and Fletcher Henderson. In this so-called "classic" period, however, it is the blues which is paramount. The jazz comes in simply as improvised accompaniment: Armstrong's cornet filling the long pauses between Bessie Smith's glacially slow phrases with bright filigree.

In the next phase of the blues, called the urban blues, the balance is reversed. Now, the musical center of gravity lies in the accompaniment, which is ideally a hard-driving, ebulliently swinging Kansas City jazz band of the type immortalized by the Count Basie Band. No longer is the singer a massive matriarch with a deep contralto voice running to gravel and growl: now he's a man mountain, like Jimmy Rushing, "Mr. Five by Five" ("He's five foot high and five foot wide") or the strapping Joe Turner—a shouter more than a singer, with a powerfully penetrating voice that rings like hard wood. The most drastic contrast is in the tempos of the two periods: the urban blues is born along so rapidly on the seething jazz current that the singer appears at times a vocal surfer riding precariously atop a surging, cresting flood of frothy rhythmic energy.

Kansas City bands accompanied blues singers by falling into short, distinctive phrases called riffs, which they repeated over and over through the performance, "setting" first one riff and then another to produce a wide range of effects, including responsorial echoes and counter-melodies (suggestive of dialogue), while always engendering the massive momentum of an organlike ostinato. These riffs were sometimes bits broken off blues lines or independent figures drawn from a large stock of conventional phrases. They were destined to play a vital part in the further development of the blues both as substitutes for melody and as background figures not just for instrumental but also for vocal accompaniments in the so-called "do-wop" groups. The growing importance of the riff, a phrase that is as much articulated rhythm as rhythmic articulation, attests to the increasing desire to make the blues "jump."

This longing was fulfilled at the end of the thirties by the emergence of the most frenzied and Dionysian of all blues: the boogie-woogie. The boogie made the blues for the second time in its history a national craze. Today, after having witnessed so many song and dance manias, it isn't difficult to account for the enormous popularity of this obsessive idiom.

All such fads have as their inciting cause an irresistible and contagious rhythm that not only drives the listener to his feet but induces in him an hypnotic and trancelike state tinged with erotic fantasy. The boogie, born and reared in the raunchy atmosphere of the "boogie house" (brothel) and the barrelhouse of the turpentine logging camp, was ideally designed to produce this effect. The relentlessly rolling bass, like Ezekiel's wheel, is enough to get anyone stoned. The powerful kinesthetic effect of the performance, which builds and builds, until it seems the whole house is rocking, is the perfect inspiration for wild dancing. But what really made the boogie an event in the unfolding of modern sensibility was its boldly erotic character, proclaimed by its name, one of those cryptic black terms, like "jazz" or "rock 'n' roll," that signify fucking. Unlike other types of erotic music, such as the tango, which evoke the sensuous or romantic aspects of sex—all those sighing, swooning violins, those predatory stalking rhythms—the boogie-woogie knows nothing about flirtation, seduction or love. It focuses exclusively on "getting down," which it mimes in dance and celebrates in song, employing earthy masculine language, sometimes leering with dirty innuendos, sometimes shouting with abandon: "Boogie my woogie till my face turns cherry red!"

To render the sex act with the utmost force and detail, the boogie employs a conventional metaphor, which generations of piano players elaborated eventually into the most extravagant feat of musical mimesis since the storm sequence in Beethoven's *Pastoral Symphony*.

The musical image of the train associates readily with all those blues verses in which railroad figures as either a symbol of release from trouble or of return to a nostalgically recollected home, but the boogie's manipulation of this image is drastically different from its use in the poetry of the blues. Instead of merely alluding to the train from time to time by suggesting its rhythm or mimicking the sound of its whistle, the boogie fastens on the train with obsessional and manic intensity, seeking by every conceivable means to conjure up the machine in all its glory. Plunging down the rails, the music summons up first the massive weight and iressistible momentum of the locomotive then it focuses upon the eccentric ball-and-sock pattern of the pistons and drive wheels, the chattering polyrhythms of the trucks on the tracks, the plaintive cries of the great whistle wailing down wind in blue notes, the huffing and chuffing of the smokestack, the dissonant clinks and chinks of the chains and couplers, piling rhythm upon rhythm. Finally, as it nears the station, the music evokes the gradual subsidence of the great beast's energies as it crawls, spent and exhausted, to a stop, signalled by a final blast of its steamy breath.

This boldly extended and superbly sustained kinesthetic conceit demands to be understood in terms of both empathy and idolatry. What it testifies to is not the black man's intimate association with machines through work (though "work" is another black euphemism for sex) or his capacity to control machines (the simpleminded notion that informs those that equate fucking a woman with driving a car). What the boogie-woogie proclaims is black man's longing to *be* a machine because he sees in its irresistible strength the ideal of his own imagined sexual prowess.

The identification of sex and mechanism, which is at the bottom of this equation of man and machine, could go no further in this period of pop music. Later, however, in the age of hard rock and heavy metal, and, later still, in the robot-ridden world of disco and rap, the concept triumphed completely. If, as T. S. Eliot observed, nothing has affected modern prosody more than the internal combustion engine, think of the effects which our industrial environment has had on pop music—and on the very constitution of our nervous system.

Once the blues had been boogied, the stage was set for the emergence of rhythm and blues, the parent of rock 'n' roll. R & B marks the end of the long ride which the blues had hitched on the jazz bandwagon. By the end of the ride, the wheels were spinning at a dizzying rate and the axles were smoking hot. The idea of making the blues jump had inspired during the war years a style of jazz that was called "jump." Jump bands were scaled-down jazz bands; they played simple riff tunes, getting on a blues phrase and riding it round and round until it assumed a feverishly spinning, hard-driving energy closely akin to the boogie. The first R & B bands were directly modeled on these jump combos. A disproportionate number of instruments—drums, bass, electric guitar, piano—were devoted to hammering out the beat, while the rest of the band, which might consist of nothing more than a pair of saxophones, would discharge all the other musical duties, from playing riffs to honking out rudimentary jazz solos. When the whole band would concentrate on the rhythm—the piano rolling a boogie bass with the left hand while clinking out triplets with the right, the drums doing a fast shuffle with an eight-to-the-bar beat on the top-hat cymbal, the horns riding the riff—the rhythm of the blues became the essence of the blues, making blues, in a phrase coined later, "beat music."

Culturally, the emergence of rhythm and blues has to be seen against the chaotic background of post-World War II America. This country went into the war dancing the Lindy to the sound of the big bands and came out of the ordeal communing in solitude with the intimate voices of romantic crooners like Frank Sinatra and Perry Como. No sooner did the war end than the swing bands, which had assumed the institutional status of big league ball teams, suddenly sickened and died from a complication of illnesses, which had commenced with the war-time draft and ended with the post-war retreat

115

into the security of home, family and TV. Jazz, which had gotten further and further "out" during the war, now became be-bop, an abstract and elliptical language completely beyond the comprehension of the common man, contemptuously tagged by the boppers as "the square from nowhere." By 1947, a good year to use as the breakthrough of R & B, American music had fallen into fractions. The various elements in the population no longer had a common language.

Black people in particular were left out in the cold. They couldn't identify with white pop music; most of them couldn't understand be-bop; they had lost most of their famous dance bands; their own best singers and musicians were intent on going over with the white public. The dilemma was resolved just as it was in 1920 when the first blues records were cut by black singers. The sensational success of these records in black communities all over the country persuaded the major companies that they had discovered a gold mine. They responded by developing the institution of the "race record," the black-oriented recording catalogued, advertised and distributed outside the normal channels of the record business. Now, in post-WWII, this old institution suddenly revived. The once-honorable but now offensive word "race" was abolished; it was replaced by the stupid redundancy "rhythm and blues." (Gospel-blues would have been much better.) As the majors were no longer interested in catering to this market, a rash of tiny independent labels sprang up to satisfy the demand.

The new "indie" operators belonged to a type familiar from the earliest days of the race record. Typically *Luftmenschen,* they worked out of their hats and off the top of their heads, baiting their hooks for fresh talent with preposterous promises of fame and wealth, chiseling their performers out of their rights and even credit for their work, and seeking always to steal a march on the competition—often by stealing one of the competition's tunes or performers. The indies were just what you would expect to find in such a hot-handed, hard-hustling, highly opportunistic business where the whole idea was to find a fresh gimmick and wrap it up fast in a cheap, thrown-together product that would return a quick buck. Though nothing that has ever been said or written about the indies would cause one to feel a moment's sympathy for them, the problems these schlock-meisters faced were of a kind that would tax the resourcefulness of even the most formidable hustler.

Established stars could not be used because they were too costly or under exclusive contract to a major label. That meant an endless talent hunt through every ghetto in the country. One ingenious solution was to arrange in each city an amateur contest with the first prize a recording contract with, say, Black Day Records. Naturally, the new "discovery," Little Retcher or Big Little, was not likely to provide much competition to Nat King Cole or Dinah Washington. Still, scores of strident-voiced waifs in the ghetto could blat out a blues line or vocalize a riff, "do-wop, do-wop," for two minutes and 58 seconds.

As for the tunes themselves, most blues lines, both musical and verbal, were in the public domain. If someone around the studio couldn't come up with a blues, there were always other ways of obtaining material. Consider, for example, the origin of the second most successful record in the entire history of R & B: *The Hucklebuck*. This crude sax solo named after a currently popular dance would probably impress most listeners today as the product of some anonymous bluessmith deep down in the urban jungle, or, to take a long shot, some very clever, chameleonlike song synthesizer in the Brill Building with a keen ear for the going thing. In fact, the author of the tune is none other than Charlie Parker, the genius of be-bop.

In 1945, Parker arrived for an important and history-making recording session at the Savoy studio in Newark. He brought with him a new blues line, which he had probably scribbled down in the cab on the way to the date. The spooky, haunting, low-riding riff, with its startling shout at the end, was titled *Now's the Time*. Though this riff tune was just the scaffolding on which Parker would raise his ingenious improvisations, it qualified in every sense as a composition. The A & R man who was running the session offered to buy the publishing rights. The price? $50. Parker made the sale on the spot, probably counting himself lucky to score the extra bread. Three years later, in 1949, Paul Williams released a jukebox version called *The Hucklebuck* (the name of a popular dance) that rode the top of the charts for thirty-two weeks and was "covered" by Tommy Dorsey, Frank Sinatra, Roy Milton and Lionel Hampton. It was the most successful R & B song of the year.

The punch line of this story is that the owner of the Savoy, the hardly scrupulous Herman Lubinsky, resisted releasing *The Hucklebuck* for a long time because he felt, quite correctly, that it was just a rip-off of the Charlie Parker original. His inability to perceive the enormous commercial potential of the piece could be paralleled by countless other instances of this same failure of vision. The truth is that the hardest task faced by the indies was discerning their audience's tastes, a job not made any easier by the fact that this public was black and the indies were almost invariably white. A great amount of atrocious music atrociously performed was recorded atrociously. (R & B was the first blues style to grow up, as it were, in public: the classic, urban, boogie, and jazz blues were all highly evolved and associated with performers of genius before they were recorded.) Eventually, R & B shook down into a number of conventionalized genres.

One of the first to achieve popularity was the hard-driving, animalistically honking tenor sax fantasia. The hero of this style was Big Jay McNeeley, who would start off playing in the conventional position, then fall to the floor, wrestling with his horn like a demon. As he reached the climax of his act, he would kick his heels at the ceiling, while wringing from the instrument the screeching and honking sounds of a trussed hog on the killing floor. This psychodrama was a great favorite with ghetto audiences and was widely copied. Doubtless it associated in many people's minds with scenes they had witnessed in church: believers falling to the floor, speaking in tongues and "slain in the spirit."

The church influence was paramount in the work of singers like Sister Rosetta Tharpe and the young Dinah Washington, the first in a long line of shouting, belting soul singers that culminates in Aretha Franklin. Though the real exploitation of gospel had to wait for Ray Charles's big breakthrough in 1955, even in the forties, R & B was starting to take on a churchy aura.

The greatest star of the early R & B, the smoothest and most accomplished performer (and the only one whose records consistently made the white-oriented pop charts), was the jivey Louis Jordan, one of those ebullient and humorous figures who have always abounded on the black musical stage, from Louis Armstrong and Fats Waller to Cab Calloway and Dizzy Gillespie. Jordan's specialty was comically phrased and jauntily accompanied vignettes of ghetto life: a teenage party doused in blue lights where everybody does the boogie *real slow* or a Saturday night fish fry down South that is broken up by a police raid.

Comedy was one of the most important elements of R & B, as it was to be of rock 'n' roll. Both the ghetto black and the white teenager were prone to view themselves as the ridiculous victims of unfortunate circumstances. Eventually, the alliance of R & B and humor would come to memorable focus in the work of Leiber and Stoller, who merged the Jewish talent for doing shtick with the blues tradition and black street jive to produce the best of all possible combinations of shticks and licks.

Though R & B was sauced with the salt and sass of the streets, it embraced just as eagerly the saccharine sweetness of the "Sepia Sinatras" and the hard-edged sentimentality of those black chanteuses with big tooshes who primp and pose before their vocal pier glasses as they dream wistfully of blue gardenias. These ladies, however, were no match for the ultimate virtuosos in the art of the lover's complaint: the juvenescent-sounding male vocal groups with ornithological names: the Orioles, Ravens, Robins, Penguins, Crows, ad infinaviary. These preening birds, always haloed with the plangency of an echoing overpass, carried sweet-talking soul to such heights of latinate extravagance and narcissism that finally their song-writers burst out spontaneously in soaring violins and erotic Latin American rhythms.

R & B was, in fine, the voice of the ghetto: the music of a whole people at a particular moment in its history. If that were all, however, it would not have leaped from the ghetto into the minds of the white kids all over the country, igniting the greatest cultural revolution in American history. To understand the real import of R & B, you have to see it in a much wider perspective as the Great Divide in the cultural history of pop America.

Up to the post-WWII period, popular culture was aimed primarily at adults and characterized by increasing urbanization and sophistication. After the war, these trends were reversed in consequence of two major demographic changes: the migration of millions of blacks from the rural South to the urban North and the maturation of the products of the post-war baby boom. The first development accounts for the character and popularity of the new R & B and its revolutionary effect on first black culture and then teen culture.

What R & B did was to turn the world of pop music on its head. Instead of aspiring to the sophistication and urbanity of swing, R & B performers gloried in earthiness and provinciality, providing their audiences with the entertainment equivalent of that "ole-time religion." Instead of working to achieve ease of execution and flawless technique, the R & B singer or instrumentalist concentrated on a primitive kind of expressionism that made technique seem irrelevant. Instead of sublimating emotions into purely musical moods, R & B offered the raw, uncut stuff that came from the gut. Love became lust, humor became ridicule, melancholy became despair, and excitement was driven to frenzy or ecstasy. As the twin values of ethnicity and expressionism deepened and became more closely entwined, the music began to cast up from the depths of black culture more and more atavistic elements, until its goal became the revelation of the deepest essence of negritude. At that point, R & B received a new and more appropriate name: soul.

Ultimately, R & B worked its way out of the ghetto to become as rock 'n' roll the music of a new generation of white youth. The medium through which this process occurred was radio; however, for radio to carry the new gospel, there had first to arise a new breed of DJs, who were the music's first evangelists. The most famous of these men was Alan Freed, a complex and controversial character who has never been properly assessed. In the movie *American Hot Wax,* for example, he is made to appear a benevolent, idealistic and paternal figure, given to confessorlike communings with his young fans. On the other hand, when you trace out the long record of violent commotions, criminal practices and self-destructive behavior that ended this man's career and life prematurely, you get the sense of a much more dissonant and hostile personality, who actively sought the martyrdom he incurred.

The essence of Freed—and of most of the early white R & B jocks—lay in the character of the "white nigger": the man who deliberately adopts the speech, dress and lifestyle of the black ghetto, partly out of enthusiasm for the vitality of the ghetto and partly out of an angry rejection of the values of the white world. If *American Hot Wax* had wanted to offer a realistic portrait of "The Father of Rock 'n' Roll," it would have found an actor who was small and Jewish-looking, with big cow-eyes, sleek black hair, a husky Negroid voice barking out the jivey language of the ghetto and a riveting intensity of personality that made his every appearance on mike or on stage an occasion for emotional tantrums. Like all the great white niggers, going back to the days of Mezz Mezzerow—the man who turned Harlem on to marijuana—Freed identified exclusively with the extravagant and way-out side of ghetto life. In championing R & B, he made himself a verbal R & B man.

Freed's overnight success—at Cleveland in 1951, after years of being a mediocre jock at various stations in Ohio—did not attest to any special personal talents but simply to the voracious but hitherto unsuspected appetite for the new music. It had now been nearly ten years—a cultural generation—since the heyday of the big bands. No powerfully exciting beat music of any description had made itself felt through the white pop broadcasting medium within the memory of the kids who comprised Freed's audience. Though much of the substance of R & B was traditional, it was radically new to these youngsters. What's more, in the uptight, play-nice atmosphere of the fifties, rock was dynamite. No wonder the music was soon associated with the dreadful menace of juvenile delinquency.

By 1954, the year that Alan Freed established himself at the center of the pop music world in New York City, R & B had become rock 'n' roll. Freed gave the music this name to cleanse it of undesirable racial overtones. (It's a sign of how naive he and his audience were that nobody understood the phrase as a euphemism for sex, long familiar from old blues lyrics.) Rock 'n' roll soon became, however, not just a new term for black music but a phrase that signalled its adoption and adaptation by an entirely new audience. The blues, which had always been so indelibly black, was about to be bleached pure white. The place of this radical transformation? Memphis, Tennessee, home of Elvis Presley.

Many people think that the young Elvis Presley walked into a recording studio one day and created rock 'n' roll. Others, better informed, know that rock existed before Elvis, at least in the form of R & B, but they believe that Elvis was the first singer to mix country music with blues to produce the style known as rockabilly. Still others, making no claim that Elvis invented any style, assume that he was simply the first rock singer to score a great popular success, sparking a national fad. All of these ideas are false, but they do define very well the achievement of another singer, who was really the first star of rock 'n' roll—Bill Haley.

Haley's story is interesting not just because it reveals the origins of rock but because it furnishes such a sharp contrast to the Presley myth. Haley, a moon-faced, klutzy-looking dude, dressed in a corny tuxedo and adorned with an absurd cowlick, is not the sort of figure that inspires a myth. The long, complicated, trial-and-error saga of the uninspired but hard-plugging, small-time entertainer is, likewise, not the kind of tale that translates easily into legend. Yet, if one follows the winding trail of the young Bill Haley across the musical landscape of America in the late forties and early fifties, you see infinitely more of the background of rock than you would even if you had been looking over Elvis Presley's shoulder the day he cut his first record.

Born in 1925, ten long years before Elvis, and reared in the Philadelphia working-class suburb of Chester—an area that produced a lot of rockers: Frankie Avalon, Fabian and The Four Aces (plus Elvis's idol, Mario Lanza)—Haley was the son of a woman who taught the piano and a man who haled from Kentucky and played the mandolin country-style. From the age of seven, Bill Haley was crazy about country music. His great ambition all through his early years was to become the country's leading yodeler. At an amateur contest in his teens, Haley met the greatest country musician of modern times, Hank Williams, and received the sort of encouragement that would thrill any young boy. At 15, Haley dropped out of school and began touring the country during the war. In 1944, a decade before Elvis cut his first record, Haley made his debut on discs with a band called The Downhomers; their record was titled *We're Recruited.*

For years Haley alternated between working at radio stations and traveling with a variety of groups and shows on the road. He toured with a little medicine show and a big country radio show, the *WLS Barn Dance,* just as Elvis was to do in later years. In the course of his travels around the country, Haley dug the boogie-woogie in New Orleans and the early R & B in Chicago. He also heard a lot of Western swing and even Dixieland jazz. Once he quit the business completely. On numerous occasions, he cut records that received no attention. Eventually, he wound up exactly where he had started: back in Chester, working at a little local station as the sports announcer and record librarian.

By 1951, Haley began to move gradually out of country music into the now mushrooming business of R & B. With his latest band, The Saddlemen, he cut a cover version of the previous year's number-nine R & B disc: *Rocket 88* (interestingly enough, the first hit recorded by Sam Phillips, the man who would give Elvis his start in the business three years later). As usual, nothing came of Haley's effort, but he kept to the same course: not just covering R & B hits but now trying to write them. In 1953, calling his band Bill Haley and the Comets, the erstwhile yodeler covered a record called *We're Gonna Rock the Joint Tonight.* On the flip side, he did a country tune, anticipating the pattern employed by Sam Phillips on all of Elvis's Sun records. Haley was just leaving Nashville, after having made a successful appearance on *Grand Old Opry,* when he learned that the new R & B record was a hit.

At this point, Haley realized the incongruity of his position. He was fronting a country and western band that was making a score in the radically different world of R & B. Being a seasoned professional, he automatically changed his image. Overnight his band discarded their ten-gallon hats and cowboy boots in favor of the tuxedos that were the working clothes of pop performers. At this point, one of Haley's songs was adopted by Allan Freed. The reason was the lyrics, which ran: "Rock, rock, rock everybody/Rock, roll, roll everybody." Haley was right on the money. His next record, *Crazy, Man, Crazy,* scored a bull's eye. As it rode up the pop charts, white rock was born.

The birth of rock out of the brain of a white country musician strikes one at first as being paradoxical: what could be further removed from the ghetto hipster than the hillbilly? In truth, there was a great gap in the two musical and cultural traditions. At the same time, however, there were numerous points of contact, similarity, and cross-influence. Even as far back as the first country musician to become a national star, Jimmie Rogers, the blues had been part of the hillbilly singer's repertoire. Later, in the thirties, when the influence of swing became as paramount as was that of rock in the sixties, Bob Wills pioneered the style known as Western Swing, whose mingling of country strings and swing rhythm dovetailed neatly with rockabilly. Finally, there was the country version of the boogie-woogie, which was called Honky Tonk and became very popular during World War II. Though the black essence did not penetrate any of these styles beyond the surface, the fact is that this essence did not penetrate rock 'n' roll any deeper. All that was required to bridge the gap from country to R & B to arrive at rock was a matching of surfaces.

Even matching surfaces, however, demands that the performer have a mastery of the idioms being combined. In the case of Bill Haley, this mastery was achieved through years of professional experience as he struggled to find the winning combination. Elvis Presley, on the other hand, scored a hit the very first time he entered the recording studio as a professional. What's more he went right on in the following years to score one hit after another, in the single greatest exhibition of chart busting that had ever been seen. As so much of his material, early and late, was derived from the early R & B style, the question arises: how did Elvis gain his mastery over this black idiom? The answer invariably given is that Elvis grew up among black people way down in the jungle of the "deep South" and that singing black was part of his birthright. To anybody who has followed Elvis's life closely from childhood to the threshold of his career, it is obvious that this customary view of his musical roots is just another portion of the Elvis myth.

The simple truth is that Elvis Presley had no significant contact at any point in his life with black people. He grew up in a white enclave in East Tupelo, lived in a white neighborhood in Tupelo proper, and divided his youth in Memphis between a white housing project and a white high school. As he was tied to his mother's apron strings until he was fifteen, there is no possibility that he had a secret life among the blacks. Once he struck off on his own and began working as a singer, he probably visited the blues bars on Beale Street, but by that point his musical sensibility had been firmly shaped by his two primary sources, the white gospel sings he attended regularly and the local black radio station to which he listened at home.

The college of musical knowledge that graduated Elvis with his degree in black arts was not some ghetto nightclub or theater or honky-tonk roadhouse. Nor was it the black church or the experience of working with black farm hands or prisoners or factory laborers—or any of the fanciful notions that fanciful fans have entertained. Indeed, this whole concept of how an artist relates to a tradition is preposterously naive. It is the cultural equivalent of saying: "You are what you eat." It is also close to saying: "All black people have a natural sense of music and dance, and if you hang out with them long enough, it will rub off on you." If this is the secret of becoming an Elvis Presley, it is a wonder that the ghetto isn't crammed with aspiring rock stars.

What Americans are reluctant to allow is the possibility that an artist can achieve something solely through the exercise of his imagination. Though lip service is often paid to the idea of imagination, what is generally understood by the term is simply fantasy. When it comes down to art that carries conviction, it is assumed there must be some model in the artist's past experience. Yet nothing is more apparent about Elvis—or the Beatles—than the fact that they approached black music not as apprentices learning a craft but as enthusiasts offering their impressions of what they had heard and admired. Elvis was not the first to do anything but be Elvis, which simply meant hurling himself on the old materials with a remarkable amalgam of energy and excitement, a good ear and a great voice, and above all, an extraordinary appearance and body language that soon made him the most imitated entertainer since Chaplin—who also had an eccentric way of moving. The most revealing statement Elvis ever made about his relationship to black music was offered in the course of a luncheonette interview with a local reporter at Charlotte, North Carolina, in 1957. Defending himself against the New York reviewers, Elvis snarled: "Them critics don't like to see nobody win doing any kind of music they don't know nuthin' about. The colored folk been singing it and playing it just the way I'm doin' now, man, for more years than I know. *Nobody paid it no mind till I goosed it up.*" That says it all.

The good days at Sun Records didn't last long, and soon Elvis was cutting his new sides in New York or Hollywood. It wasn't until the mid-sixties that Memphis finally put its name on a nationally popular style of music, the Memphis Soul Sound. Not much has been written on Stax-Volt records, but its history constitutes the last word on the theme of Memphis as the home of the blues. Founded by a white bank clerk named Stewart, who moonlighted as a country fiddler, and his sister, whose married name was Axon; financed with a second mortgage on Mrs. Axon's home; installed in an abandoned movie theater in the ghetto; and staffed almost exclusively with black personnel, none of whom were allowed to sign company checks because, as Mrs. Axon informed me, there was no need for it save their desire "to show off for their own kind," Stax-Volt became the last great plantation in the South. Opening its doors to the talent that had always sprung up in the region, it developed a whole series of new stars ranging from Otis Redding to Sam and Dave to Booker T and the MGs and Albert King. Even more important, it developed a new idiom that was the southern-black antithesis of the northern-black style made famous by Motown.

Instead of mining the angst of the ghetto and raiding the soundtrack orchestrations of Hollywood movies, Stax reached back into the history of its region and revived the ancient song of the South. Its festive brasses were reminiscent of black minstrelsy and the TOBA circuit of black vaudeville; its rhythms, like the shuffle and the heebie-jeebie (a dance that mimicked the movements of sufferers from malaria, who would stagger about and claw themselves) went back to the innocent times before World War I; its lyricism was the sweet, sensuous, relaxed singing of men and women out in the country on warm summer nights surrounded with fragrant crops and cutting the hearts out of sugary melons. It was all a prophecy of that longing to go back to the turn of the century, "where everythin's happenin'," according to a song of the day, that led in the next decade to the great ragtime revival.

Insofar as any black music was ever "made" in Memphis, it was the Memphis Soul Sound, but when I visited the studio and quizzed its creative people, like the song-writing team of Porter and Hayes, they told me flat-out that theirs was a labor not so much of invention as of recovery. "We'll go out to a stone soul picnic [not yet the title of a song]," they told me, "and sooner or later, we'll pick up something, a phrase, a lick, a line that we can build into a song." They were hip young men who recognized the value of this old-timey stuff in the current market; their challenge was to go forth like truffle hunters to find, then skillfully package, black soul. They were, in other words, the W. C. Handys of their day. With Stax-Volt, the blues had come full circle, having proceeded in six fertile decades from Memphis to Memphis.

IMAGES OF ELVIS, THE SOUTH AND AMERICA

■

(for Jerry and Adrienne)

by Van K. Brock

This piece examines the subtle complexities and irreconcilable contradictions that Elvis personified and analyzes that strange blend of myth and half-truth that informs our evaluations of him. Fascinating in its breadth and scope, this essay is a complex and detailed portrait of a paradoxical figure.

> What? A great man? I always see merely the play actor of his own ideal. (IV, 97)
>
> "I dislike him."—Why?—"I am not a match for him."—Did anyone ever answer so? (IV, 185)
>
> Frederick Nietzsche
> *Beyond Good and Evil*

One of the paradoxes of culture is that a hero is an aberration of the culture he personifies, makes visible and helps define, rather than merely the epitome of the culture. Otherwise, there is nothing to make him unique. Elvis Presley, the South, and America all illuminate each other. We should also find more than superficial similarities between Elvis and other artistic cult heroes and heroines in contemporary America, and perhaps in any time and place—artists as differ-

126

ent from Presley as, say, Sylvia Plath. If the similarities and differences are also reflected in the members of their respective cults, we should gain insights into the origins and uses of our arts and artists, and the demands we make upon them, regardless of their individual qualities or virtues. If they are alternately idolized and ridiculed, for showing the possibilities and dangers of our natures, our extremes and limits, it is no less than the Greeks did to their popular heroes and gods, in legends and plays that ranged from the most exalted tragedy to coarse comedy. But it is not my purpose here to exalt or ridicule.

Elvis has been the most universally visible, the most acclaimed and perhaps the most derided cultural hero of our time. He drew his artistic energies from a combination of his loyalty to his complex cultural origins and of his profound drive to escape the stigma of poverty and social exclusion intrinsic to them. His ambivalence and dilemma are intensified because the cultural demands that shaped his mind and his loyalties were conflicting in themselves. An understanding of his origins should not only clarify the nature of his mind and the sources of his drives, both of which were intrinsic to his symbolism; his origins should also suggest why that symbolism led to the acclaim and derision that accompanied his career. These considerations do not minimize the influence of his mother, to whom he was unusually close, or of his religion, which was also important in the shaping of his mind and emotions.

If women are often brutally degraded in rock lyrics (and their behavior in relation to men rigidly restricted), they are far less so in Presley's lyrics than in those of many others. When Elvis is sexist, he is also having fun. There is at least a slight self-mockery or posing in it. There is an immense tenderness throughout his music for women.

If he is macho, he is also feminine. There is a close balance in his projection of male strength and feminine tenderness. His voice can move from one to the other in almost any part of almost any song he sings. The stabilizing emotional strength of his mother and the stolid, unassertive acceptingness of his father will not be denied either in his music or in his image. For his fans, Elvis's mother and father are members of a kind of archetypal Holy Family, in which the "child" is of foremost importance, and they are all a part of the extended family (which includes, even after his divorce, Priscilla as well as their daughter). His affirmation of his extended family (which expands further to include his fans) in a culture in which the extended family is disappearing was an important element in his appeal.

Worship in and around Tupelo was, generally, conservative and restrained, though the modes of belief and the rituals that expressed them varied. Whether the preacher talked from a text, weaving his sermons from inspired oratory and the generously dispersed formulas of an oral tradition of pulpit oratory, or he read his sermon from a written script or from the Lesson for the Day, most white people, at least, sat attentively in their pews, dressed in their best or next best and listened solemnly, responding only in hymns or choral readings or, depending perhaps on their class, with an occasional amen, or "that's the gospel"—and reverently rather than loudly. Some women, and even a man or two, might weep silently through most of the sermon—whether for themselves, a loved one, or simply the beauty of the vision of the flawless, joyful kingdom (none could know for sure), and occasionally their sobs or sniffles would rise up to counterpoint the peaks of oratory and emotion. Clearly there were both release and relief, but not orgiastic emotion. Most whites, even among the fundamentalist denominations, were not especially demonstrative in their worship. Even their hymns were sung in a linear, rote fashion, like a teacher who reads poetry to make sure the pupils hear the meter and rhyme:

a MAZ in GRACE how SWEET the SOUND
That SAVED aa-ay WRETCH like-e MEEEE

The Presleys however were Pentecostals, and while there were a number of Pentecostal denominations, even most Christians called them Holy Rollers, a term of mild socioreligious snobbery and amused derision, and considered their expressiveness and demonstrativeness in worship a form of exhibitionism. Restrained expressions of emotion added a nice tone to the service, but excessive display disrupted it. Modern parents and psychologists might admire the Presleys and their church for allowing Elvis to run down the aisle at the age of three and imitate the preacher's vigorous singing, but most of the white Christians in Tupelo would not have approved if Gladys Presley had allowed her son to behave so freely in their church. Pentecostalism was considered the frayed edge of the fabric, a religion of last resort; and generally it was. The society in general was filled with makeshift creativity, homecrafts and various forms of singing and string musical instruments, but little bodily expression. And except for their worship, Pentecostals were more conservative even than some other fundamentalist Christians. Pictures of Gladys and Vernon Presley invariably suggested the tightness and restraint of their lives.

The acceptance of his family and the drive to escape the stigma of his poverty and social oddness—and to lift his family out of the trough of poverty—were certainly early overriding concerns for Elvis, but even that does not explain his continued intellectual and cultural passivity after success on success laid the world at his feet. Perhaps because of his enormous "success," he seems to have remained satisfied with himself and the world and its superficial diversions, until the break-up of his marriage (his first denial by someone close to him) drove him to ask difficult questions seriously for the first time, apparently, as he approached middle age. And for all of his wealth, the only resource he had for dealing with these questions was the religion of the hopeless and the poor, of emotional and intellectual escape. Though it may be easier to explain him in psychological terms, it may be more illuminative to examine (as I try to do in successive sections of this essay) his contradictions, the contradictions of his religious teaching and the contradictions and schisms in the mind of his society, for these are the forces that shaped and insulated his thinking.

I. PARADOXES

The reality of Elvis Presley is almost hopelessly confused in rhetoric, rumor, and speculation and seems all but lost in the unreality of his life and world. Newspapers echo tabloids and fan magazines, and if they inadvertently present some fact about his life, the fact may be misleading or inconsequential. His story is retold similarly enough in the books about him to suggest that the books are recapping the approved myth. But the motives given for his privacy and practices range from commercial to personal. The management of Col. Tom Parker, who is not a colonel, is credited with all of his successes, on the one hand, and blamed for all his failures on the other. Those closest to him are, even after his death, part of a multimillion dollar industry that caters to his audience image; and if they sometimes contradict the image, their testimony may be weakened by their suspect motives as well as by an apparent inability to relate facts consistently and without the use of patently sweeping generalizations or uncritical and superstitious premises.[1] If associates and friends saw a confused pattern of one who spent much of his time alone, sometimes reading and thinking, or occasionally trying to discuss his reading in the occult and science-fiction, those who listened do not always seem to know with certainty whether he was facetious, or even whether he himself knew.

His fans and critics alike almost invariably confuse their estimates of his art with their estimates of his life, and since his image was a part of both and to a large extent he lived inside it, the two are difficult to separate. Since he did not write his lyrics, though he often selected them out of a wide range of choices and sometimes altered them to his liking, it becomes even more difficult to approach his mind through his art.

The apparent range of his choices may have been greater in theory than in fact. Many of the best songwriters offered their work, but it was often written to the image, since his performance of a song assured its commercial success, just as, in his private life, his retainers apparently reflected what they thought he wanted to hear or believe, thus contributing to his own difficulty in knowing his own reality. And though his chosen range of performance might reflect his interests and taste, it also reflects his desire to appeal to the broadest possible audience.

His audience ranged from and included those who liked uncritically, if not equally, everything he did, to those who liked only certain parts of his repertoire—his rock, his ballads, his hymns—to those who rejected everything he did and reinforced the notoriety that enhanced his success. Few who accept pop at all have considered his career and not respected his achievement in some area. Fans and critics and detractors all seem to ask him to fulfill their own personal myths and needs.

If Elvis is viewed as a product of the South, even of the South understood with some accuracy, that too can be misleading, because he was much more a general American than that. The qualities of W. J. Cash's "generic Southerner" might characterize Elvis and his "generic" teen follower, but no more in the South than elsewhere: "What is ordinarily taken for realism in him is in fact only a sort of biological pragmatism—an intuitive faculty of the practical. . . . He necessarily lacks the complexity of mind, the knowledge, and, above all, the habit of skepticism essential to any generally realistic attitude. It is to say that . . . his world-construction is bound to be mainly a

[1]Red West, Sonny West, Dave Hebler, as told to Steve Dunleavy, *Elvis: What Happened?* (New York: Ballantine Books, 1977). Though "told" to Dunleavy, an Australian rock writer, by three of Elvis's fired bodyguards, the book is usually attributed to Dunleavy. The book is organized and structured to sensationalize Elvis's problems. While the book is useful, the misunderstandings, contradictions, exaggerations, suspect motives, and errors are numerous. Future references are to Dunleavy.

product of fantasy, and that his credulity is limited only by his capacity for conjuring up the unbelievable. And it is to say that he is a child-man, that the primitive stuff of humanity lies very close to the surface in him, that he likes naively to play, to expand his ego, his senses, his emotions, that he will accept what pleases him and reject what does not, and that in general he will prefer the extravagant, the flashing, and the brightly colored—"[2] In short, the outline of the "generic Southerner" (which might describe Elvis, his retainers and fans, and much of the audience for popular culture throughout America and the world) characterizes what Cash calls "one of the most complete romantics and one of the most complete hedonists ever recorded."

Whether it would have seemed less appropriate or natural for someone other than a Southerner to do what Elvis did and whether in doing it he would have been as widely cheered or blamed for it, are matters for speculation. Blacks, of course, had done it before him, but Elvis himself seemed to sense that he could never get out of his stereotype. One of Elvis's most revealing self-critical remarks—or remarks critical of his stereotyping—was that all that people saw in his movies was this Southerner always singing to dogs and children—significant because he often did not play a Southerner at all. Yet though he sometimes stripped much of the South away, from his accent, his roles, and his performances, it is true that he was wedded to the South, and especially in his best music.

One way of understanding Presley's career is to see him as a man trying to transcend his roots, while affirming them, to weave together the complex, conflicting and tortuous strands of identity that are a part of every Southerner—racial, regional, national and human—and perhaps of every American. No Southerner, at least, can make a complete integration of self without coming to terms with the anomaly he is to the world and with the awareness that his identity group has compromised or been compromised by another identity group, leaving a gulf between his and another culture, both of which are part of the complex constituency of his whole identity. However they relate to the reality, all Southerners must come to terms with two racial identities, if they are to come to terms with

[2]W. J. Cash, *The Mind of the South* (New York: Knopf, 1941), pp. 44–45. Cf. Joseph L. Morrison, *W. J. Cash: Southern Prophet* (New York: Knopf, 1967), for an appreciative perspective on the self-liberating motives of Cash's classic love-hate presentation of "the Southern mind," which Cash saw as infested by a love of romance and rhetoric. The next quotation is from p. 50.

themselves. If Presley happened on this originally by accident, courtesy of Sam Phillips of Sun Records, if at first it made him uncomfortable, it is to his credit that he accepted the necessity. If he sought to integrate the several cultures that nourished him and sometimes sought to honor them individually, as Greil Marcus points out in *Mystery Train,*[3] it should be seen as to some degree a healthy phenomenon for himself and the cultures. If the mirror he held to American culture was warped at times, it still reflected; and an important question is who or how many have held a clearer mirror to it. And if one does not believe that mimesis is the only purpose of the artist, I cannot doubt that, for Presley, whatever his motives (patriotism, narcissism, profit)—and they may have been very complex—that was a large part of his sense of his purpose as an artist.

It wasn't simply Presley's desire for the profits that made him play to almost the whole spectrum of popular music. It was his desire to be loved and honored and to pay tribute to the warring forces in himself. He began with gospel and country, acquired rhythm and blues and yearned to be a Hollywood pop crooner in the vein of Dean Martin. At his most vigorous and complex, he brought these elements together into something called rock and roll. Later, he tried to fuse them more synthetically—the Southerner, the American, the "black" spiritual yearning—with constructions like "The American Trilogy," a medley of "Dixie," the chorus of the "Battle Hymn of the Republic," and the black spiritual, "All My Trials." But the fusion kept breaking apart inside him, and ultimately out of the parts came the wide range of his music and of himself, for neither emotionally nor intellectually was he equipped to form a psyche capable of holding together their clashing tensions or eliminating the disharmonious elements from his makeup.

Elvis and the teen rebellion, as Nik Cohn has pointed out in *Rock from the Beginning,*[4] created each other and a new teen culture. The boy from Tupelo, Mississippi, without a socially respected culture, began to create his own when he was still a student at Humes High in Memphis—out of the cultural fragments lying around him: the long-hair style of early adolescence (common even then, in parts of

[3]Greil Marcus, *Mystery Train: Images of America in Rock and Roll Music* (New York: E. P. Dutton, 1975). Marcus develops the backgrounds and corollaries of the black and white musical traditions in the South that were brought together and popularized in America by Elvis, primarily as a result of the early artistic guidance of Sam Phillips, whose Sun Records label in Memphis introduced Elvis to the world.

the South, among some rural males); the outrageous dress of Beale Street he associated with both the black and the white musical styles with which he could most closely identify; the Hollywood images of Dean Martin, James Dean, and Marlon Brando that drew him, and out of which he fashioned an amused and defiant cool; and a desire, which later seemed boundless, for fame, wealth, power, and universal love and respect.

If the yearning for universal love seemed to contradict the public posture of defiance, it did not contradict the religious yearnings that had made his family life tolerable under almost intolerable poverty; it did not contradict his choice of the sentimental "I Love You Because," by means of which he originally chose to make his appeal.

But his religious yearnings were contradicted by secular yearnings. From his first movie (*Love Me Tender*) to his last concerts—and progressively in the latter—he chose songs that wooed the audience, not only in the emotional tenor of the music but in the arguments of the lyrics as well.

If Elvis accepted Sam Phillips's instincts and judgment as to what would prove popular (aside from vitality and a new sound) it was, originally, for the same desire for success—not for any idealistic or artistic wish to fuse the main traditions of popular music in the South and those in turn with the American popular impulse generally. But his impulse to combine various strands of popular music—black and white, religious and secular, regional and national—was genuine, and throughout his career he took artistic, patriotic, and religious pride in being credited with these innovative fusions.

After his success, no longer needing to be a public rebel, he reconciled his defiance with his longing for acceptance and community. When he bought his family the first house they had ever owned, in a respectable Memphis neighborhood, they and their pink Cadillac were not accepted.[5] His difficulties inherent in gaining acceptance led

[4]Nik Cohn, *Rock from the Beginning* (New York: Stein and Day, 1969), pp. 14–18, 22, 170–171, 172–173. An early overview of the rock movement by a British-born rock critic who grew up with rock and still sounds and thinks like a teddy boy who has read snatches of Nietzsche and of the existentialists. Though there is only a short chapter on Elvis, references to Elvis occur throughout the book, which apparently went to press shortly before the 1968 NBC-TV ("Comeback") Special.

[5]Jerry Hopkins, *Elvis: A Biography* (New York: Warner Books, 1971), pp. 123–124. The most complete source on Elvis up to the period shortly following his divorce. It also includes 32 pages of photographs and a complete discography (through 1970) and film list.

to his being a law to himself and pursuing a private morality within his own dependent enclave community and by displaying charitable, patriotic, and lawabiding sentiments as a public citizen. His seclusion was partly the result of Colonel Parker's strategy to avoid overexposure, to keep the commodity scarce and the demand high, but largely due to Elvis's own emotional needs.

The shy, polite boy who flaunted his independence became a liberating symbol for the emotional yearnings of millions of teenagers who felt repressed by the parents he shocked and who rewarded him with an almost instant and incredible wealth and adulation, which in turn seemed to more than justify, for most, their relatively modest expenditures on his records, concerts, photographs, movies, souvenirs, and their choice of an idol.

He seemed to come from the lowest caste in the South, the lowest region of the nation, white blues and black blues sliding in and out of each other, and his voice rose out of the diaphragm of a writhing torso to recreate the myth of America in visual image as well as sound. And the fact that he "made it" gave pride and hope to those who felt repressed, but whose lives seemed relatively futureless, although they were still suspended at what should have been the point of boundless possibility. His realization of that boundless possibility gave substance to their vague fantasies and dreams. Many tried to follow his example and a few succeeded. But for most, to the extent that he mattered to them, their following meant that he would live their lives for them; they would share vicariously the wealth and power and fame they would never have except through him.

Fan club members and followers mounted into millions, both in this country and abroad, and they became communions of saints for whom any relic was a transubstantial sacrament. I know of a boy who received his sexual initiation from a girl solely in return for a piece of gravel from Elvis's driveway, though I was not told that it was her initiation. If such individual incidents seem meaningless, the aggregate does not. For those who never saw him alive in concert, he lived in social occasions devoted to his honor. His own fan club office made regular mailings around the world; these reverential tracts were supplemented by those generated by the individual fan clubs themselves, some of which obtained glossy publication and wide circulation; and to these were added the newsstand tabloids and magazines that aggrandize the stars in their rhetoric and in their attention to the meaningless details and fabricated rumor. Add to these the endless souvenirs, photos, relics, and memorabilia spawned from every source.[6]

His common, and in many ways generous, humanity was part of the legend as it always is in those who fulfill the conditions of the American myth. His devotion to his family, friends, and fans; his polite, modest, and softspoken responses in interviews; his official public demeanor when offstage; and his acceptance of the military draft to the status of buck private, fulfilling one of the articles of the democratic myth, raised his status among his followers while crumbling the resistance of the parents and the society to whom the followers were also symbolically reconciled.

His triumph was complete. If there were still those who scoffed and doubted, he had seemingly accomplished the impossible; he had defied society by accepting certain crucial tenets and rejecting others; he had gained an almost unheard-of mass acceptance and respectability from a society while living in its midst by devising a morality of his own that was ostensibly repugnant to the society if also a realization of its buried fantasy. He established himself as a man of faith while publicly living as a moral law to himself. In Hollywood, this was to be no large matter—though a much noted one; in Memphis it was considerable, despite the example of Nashville.

In addition to his gospel songs, his religious backgrounds and sentiments and the devotion of his followers lent sanctity to his paradoxical image. In Memphis he bought, refurbished and took up residence in a mansion that was being used as a church, and he retained the name it had, Graceland. His private community was conceived of as a commune; his followers were often numbered at twelve; he called them his disciples; they lived largely inside the walls of the Presley properties, following their unquestioned leader and idol—from Graceland to his ranch, the Rising Sun, to his Hollywood home, Bel Air, and back to Graceland again. They engaged in an endless series of songs and games, which included the films he made (approximately three a year over a ten-year period—if one does not count his time in the Army), a fantasia of unending childhood, for which he received tens of millions of dollars each year.

He also picked his wife from the ranks of childhood, brought her up himself, sent her to a Catholic high school, and then to a Memphis finishing school, part of a famous chain, for her final grooming before he made her his white-gowned bride in Las Vegas. In being childlike, he was true to his religious roots, or seemed to be, and made youth a religion for the youth who made him a god. There

[6]Hopkins, pp. 147–148, 394 ff.; Dunleavy, pp. 295–302.

was a sense of immortality around him, in his ability to do as he pleased, to make toys of the machinery of adulthood and seemingly to make time stand still.

There was a time before some of them married when he and his followers lived and felt like gods who did as they pleased (though this consisted largely of boyish games) and seemed to believe their communal existence and its unfettered libidinal pleasures could go on throughout their lives: the illusion of all communes and utopias, of those who long to create their own worlds or at least the terms of their worlds. It was then, according to Red and Sonny West[7] that they most seriously thought of themselves as disciples and that Elvis began to feel that his immense fortune was evidence that the god of his childhood had singled him out to live (when his twin had died at birth) for some divine purpose, that his immense financial good fortune and his incredible power over the minds and emotions of those who had elevated him to live out their deepest fantasies were all evidence of his special powers. Even in criticizing his fantasies, they found it difficult not to somehow believe in them and, even in anger toward him, insisted on their love. One explanation is that they were still part of the industry. But despite his narcissism and outbursts of anger, he had a childlike tenderness and kindness and gentleness that inspired protectiveness and affection among those who were close to him.

The image and the myth work best when not taken too seriously, as he himself seemed to know. He poked light fun at the image, even as he increasingly clothed himself in costumes approaching sacerdotal splendor, because, perhaps, it never ceased to amaze him. The god in him (that shook his body as it rose in the tangible, invisible form of sensual sound, drove his devotees wild with agony and ecstasy, and was apotheosized in his image and person) was greater than his own ability to comprehend its nature; and if he fantasized that the mind that could not fathom the mystery of itself and of human emotion could nonetheless move inanimate matter, he nonetheless found it a little ridiculous that others would be so moved by him to anger or devotion. But as marriages and adult realities finally created ten-

[7]The rest of this account draws upon Dunleavy for details that sound true. On the question of cynicism, when Vernon Presley was "excommunicated" by the preacher for divorcing his second wife, Elvis discontinued contributions to the church. The preacher decided to reinstate Vernon, and Elvis speculated to one of his companions that he must have been talking to Jesus. Elvis's "minister" at his funeral was a Church of Christ pastor.

sions within the communal band and strained the bonds of its members, on occasions he would call them into an informal congregation and read to them from the Bible or from mystic books, making liberal commentaries on the text and on his special significance. His beliefs about his own life at times provided his criteria for the interpretation of the Bible: the Bible could not mean it was more difficult for a rich man to get into heaven than for a camel to go through the eye of a needle—because he was rich, and he was going to heaven—and if he was promiscuous, that was O.K.—because Jesus also had been sleeping with the women who followed him.

As he was both "saint" and "sinner," religious and cynical about religion, believed in everything strange or unusual (life on other planets or life after death), he was both tolerant and bigoted. He seemed to accept individuals for what they were and to some degree to recognize their qualities and worth regardless of race, creed or color, but none of this altered his beliefs about races, creeds or colors collectively. He married a Catholic, counted Jews among his close friends and employees, performed with blacks; he was generous to Catholic and Jewish charities and on more than one occasion bestowed lavish gifts on and otherwise befriended blacks and defended individual blacks against other bigots. But his former bodyguards say he made his prejudices plain to them in his talks to his inner group: Catholics were still the demons in the Bible (either a reflection of his childhood fundamentalist Protestant folklore or something he had read in one of his occult fantasy books), and Jews, collectively, were an international conspiracy. He simply considered the Jews and Catholics he knew and liked to be exceptions.

He could be incredibly tender and kind to his employees, white or black, and in a moment of anger, say cruel things about or to them, fire them and rehire them in a matter of moments, days, weeks or months. After some of his black performers objected to offensive remarks he was making on stage, he turned to an aide and privately ordered him to "Get me another nigger." But (according to Dunleavy, p. 302) the aide ignored him and the matter was dropped.

His imagination flared and ranged with his emotions, and vice-versa; if he heard a story he liked, he recounted it as fact, elaborating it imaginatively to make it more likeable. In his last three or four years, perhaps an effect of drugs and other problems as well as his ability to make his wishes commands, he seemed to have neither intellectual discipline nor discipline of his appetites. He flapped in the wind of his passions. Even his most sympathetic critics seem to agree, whether or not they say so, that the trappings of serious religious thought, like adult machines, and weapons, and human beings themselves, were hardly more than toys to the mind that could seemingly command the world to mirror its wishes.

He made more movies in less time for more money than anyone ever had or perhaps ever will, and the artistic worth of it all is generally summed up as an example of how much popular audiences can be manipulated by producers to pay for so little in return. (Or is it the audience who is manipulating the passive producers and vulnerable performers?) The real significance of his movies is in how little they contributed to him as a human being, how little he learned, and how much they reduced his achievement and put him back in his place as, to paraphrase his words, this Southerner always singing to dogs and children. If in concert he became a master performer and at his best generated a compelling unique dynamism, in his movies, except for occasional scenes, he was not extraordinary. If he commanded in one, he was a vassal in the other; if he achieved dignity in one, it was a lesser dignity, usually, in the other; if the human form was elevated in one, it was not in the other. The god whose evocations of life force tyrannized his worshippers in his concerts was dismembered in his films and made rote, harmless, and lifeless.

For a human being, given the opportunity of his already incredible wealth, to reduce so many of the best years of his life to little more than a robot in so many of his films for nothing more than money and to do no more with his money and life may be the most dramatic cry against the culture that created and affirmed him that he could have made, albeit only half-consciously.

The movies are a parody of the myth that in other ways he seemed to fulfill. A culture that can so reward a man for such mediocrity, for doing so little with his mind, and for debasing his talent to such a degree may be said to deserve these parodies. As rituals in the popular religion of America, the movies usually depict a powerless rebel against middleclass or upperclass values who eventually overcomes the social forces that have excluded or disaffected him and wins the all-American girl, after appreciating and making it big with others who have strayed, but are sorry, through the circuitous but ultimate exercise of an innate integrity from which he has been perhaps alienated by unjust circumstances.

The moral is conventional enough and on the face acceptable. But nothing much really is ever asked of him, except to stop wandering, take a job, and marry the girl. He never really needs to improve himself. His education is usually minimal; his trouble is nearly always caused by authority figures against whom his rebellion is just, or by weak friends who betray his trust; his success is nearly always based on a prowess (usually of charm, sympathy, or strength) that does not need to be supplemented by knowledge not innate or learned on the street or land. (It is, too, to a degree a parody of his own life and career. He was the living proof of the myth. His aura caused others to believe or pretend to believe that he was an expert at everything he played at—cars, karate, drugs. Complete loyalty and belief in him were expected of his disciples.) It is an adaptation of the agrarian and street myth that, in a modern society can foster only losers and hustlers. Here "street" and "salvation," blues and gospel, almost meet. If the combination made a lot of money for Elvis, it won't get most of us out of debt. It didn't make Elvis much wiser, and it certainly won't us. It is, in fact, the formula by means of which most Southerners, white and black, and many other Americans remained economically and culturally subjugated castes in America and by means of which America has remained a predominantly philistine society.

II. ASSEMBLIES OF GOD

If a whaling ship was Ishmael's Harvard and Yale, then the culture of Beale Street, the Pentecostal religion, the Grand Ole Opry, and Hollywood were Elvis Presley's. Both Beale Street and the Assemblies of God churches were pluralistic in their origins, and both contributed to the distinctive pluralistic fusion of his music and his dramatic sense as a performer. It is my purpose here, briefly, to explore the character of the Pentecostal mind as it may have influenced Elvis Presley.

Thirty years to the calendar day before Elvis was conceived in Tupelo, Mississippi, a Negro preacher, W. J. Seymour, was holding a prayer meeting in Los Angeles when, according to Walter J. Hollenweger, in his book *The Pentecostals,* "'the fire came down'"[8] and "an eight year old Negro boy" received the gift of speaking in tongues. "For three years without interruption, prayer meetings took place in the Azusa Street Mission with speaking in tongues, singing in tongues and prophecy."[9]

The revival initially met opposition even from the Holiness

---

[8]Georgia Bond, *The Life Story of the Rev. O. H. Band* (Oakgrove, Ark.: n.p., 1958), p. 281, as quoted by Hollenweger (see below), p. 22.
[9]Walter J. Hollenweger, *The Pentecostals,* trans. by R. A. Wilson (Minneapolis: Augsburg Publ. House, 1972), p. 22.

churches and evoked the amusement of papers like *The New York American* (3 December 1906), in part at least because most of the people involved were black.

FAITH GIVES QUAINT SECT
NEW LANGUAGE TO CONVERT AFRICA

VOTARIES OF ODD RELIGION NIGHTLY
SEE "MIRACLES" IN WEST SIDE ROOM[10]

Nonetheless the revival became legendary to Pentecostal denominations, both white and black, even in the South. British Pentecostal leader Alexander A. Boddy wrote: "It was something very extraordinary, that white pastors from the South were eagerly prepared to go to Los Angeles to the Negroes, to have fellowship with them and to receive through their prayers and intercessions the blessings of the Spirit. And it was still more wonderful that these white pastors went back to the South and reported to . . . their congregations that they had been together with Negroes, that they had prayed in one Spirit and received the same blessings as they."[11]

"In general," says Hollenweger, "the influence of the Negroes on the Pentecostal movement must not be underestimated."[12] If this eight-year-old black child's significance for Pentecostals, and the consequent amusement the revival elicited from the American mainstream, provided one of the legends of Elvis Presley's childhood, as Boddy's quoted remark suggests it could have done, the parallels are indeed ironic for the white Southern boy whose voice and movements—fusing the yearnings of disaffected black and white Americans with the longings of youth itself—created, almost a half century later, similar amusement and consternation in the press and society and gave rise to a movement that brought a secular form of the Pentecostal revival into a mainstream that was starved for imaginative symbols and in which little religious emotion flowed. Both phenomena were extraordinary.

His spiritual education at home and in church did not challenge many of the tenets of his secular education. But they did shape a dimension of his mind and his personal identity in ways that explain

[10]Hollenweger, p. 23.
[11]Alexander A. Boddy, *Pfingstrusse* (in the British paper *Confidence*), trans. from a German translation, Hollenweger, p. 24.
[12]Hollenweger, p. 43, n. 10.

many of the patterns and contradictions of his career and his behavior. If media stars were his models on the one hand, Pentecostal preachers were on the other. Not only were they dynamic and dramatic masters of mass persuasion; they were strong personal leaders of usually small intimate congregations who shared their intense emotional energies with one another. Furthermore, they derived their authority not from institutions, hierarchies, and books, but from their own inner spiritual resources, and they were expected to be original and innovative, even in their fundamentalist interpretations of the Bible, as proof of their divine authentication.

The paradoxes of Pentecostalism relating to the distinctions between the world and the spirit pervade Elvis Presley's life and mind. A central paradox of Pentecostalism, wherever it is manifested, is that it is an intensely personal and individualistic experience that demands to be witnessed to in a small group, but it makes responsibility to and participation in the larger institutional structure of the church or society relatively unimportant.[13] Pentecostalism and similar movements, including rock music, have appeared during the last few decades in social and religious structures traditionally unreceptive to the Pentecostal religion itself. When modern neo-Pentecostals abandon their traditional church bodies they draw a closeknit personal group of like-thinking and like-feeling intimates around them. An inward-turning spirituality rejects the necessity of cold, sterile (rational, intellectual or institutional) structures, affirms a vigorously felt faith as verification of salvation, and affirms the reality of the supernatural world or the primacy of a transrational reality. God is a personal, ongoing force in history who personally bestows a variety of gifts, including tongues, wisdom, healing, and other miraculous powers.[14] It is only one strain and source of the modern romantic cult of which Presley was a central symbol, but for Presley it was one of the most dominant influences.

The Assembly of God church that the Presley family attended was a member of the largest white Pentecostal denomination in America. The name of the denomination, The Assemblies of God, emphasized the independence of each congregation. A typical service included "easy hymns and choruses" sung in enthusiastic harmony "accompanied by a Hammond organ and a pianist who provided jazz-like rhythms and arpeggios during pauses in the tunes. The congregation

---

[13]John Stevens Kerr, *The Fire Flares Anew* (Philadelphia: Fortress Press, 1974), p. 66.
[14]Kerr, pp. 79–80.

clapped their hands in time with the tunes and ventilated their joy in spontaneous testimony."[15] Presley was aware, as others have been, of the contribution his religious background and experience made to his worldly success and has mentioned the influence and style of the Pentecostal preacher on his own. Hopkins quotes Elvis: "We used to go to these religious singin's all the time. There were these singers, perfectly fine singers, but nobody responded to them. Then there was the preachers and they cut up all over the place, jumpin' on the piano, movin' ever' which way. The audience liked 'em. I guess I learned from them" (p. 27). His worldly success strengthened rather than weakened his confidence in the validity of his general Pentecostal tenets.

The mores of his followers, moreover, reflected his own. And his ability to select what he wanted from Pentecostal doctrine and practice and to ignore what it suited him to ignore, his ability to be eclectic in music and dress and eccentric in his "fundamentalist" interpretations of the Bible, to emphasize the spiritual aspect of religion and to ignore the external aspects, were all not only in keeping with Pentecostal thinking and practice but were consistent with the expected pattern of a spiritual leader.

The more independent the congregation was, the more individualistic and important was the preacher. His originality was, to a degree, a sign of grace, and the lack of conformity to denomination was an evidence of the congregation's otherworldliness and spirituality. According to E. E. Gross, "A preacher who did not dig up some new slant on a scripture, or get some new revelation to his own heart ever stupid, unspiritual. . . . Calling a man a 'compromiser' killed his ministry far and wide."[16]

None of this should be construed as denying that Elvis's attitudes were shaped by forces other than Pentecostalism. There is no doubt that his many needs for the symbols of physical and personal power—karate, cars, motorcycles, tractors, guns, sexual conquests, bodyguards, and even God—stem in part also from the same socioeconomic roots from which the Pentecostal movement itself sprang. Neopentecostalism, the charismatic movement, and Pentecostal-like ecstatic experiences (including those exhibited by Elvis's followers as well as other variations of rock, hip, beat, and jazz) became respectable and even cool in the sixties and seventies.

[15]W. H. Durham, *Pentecostal Testimony* (June 1911), quoted in Hollenweger, pp. 24; 28, n. 34.
[16]E. E. Goss, *The Winds of God* (New York: Comet Press, 1958), p. 155, quoted by Hollenweger, pp. 31; 43, n. 20.

Rock had in common with Pentecostalism that though it was considered a rebellion of youth, it was as devoid of "social consciousness" as Presley himself, whatever his charity—which the Assemblies of God in any event always encouraged in the form of tithing. Whatever the sociopolitical identifications of many rock enthusiasts, singers, and their lyrics in the sixties and seventies, this social consciousness never affected Elvis or Pentecostalism, and it never affected rock. Rock is a search for individual and personal freedom, and even if it extends the cry for individual freedom into a cry against a present political system, if the system is changed, the new system will also be a cause for protest.

Pentecostalism, like Rock, is a Dionysian cult; offering similar ecstatic release in response to frenzied stimuli. "The occurrence of automatism among Pentecostals is apparently a stimulus for excited shouting and for further automatisms," according to William W. Wood.[17] Elvis insisted that his own movements in performance were automatisms (his words, in an interview, were: "I can't help it. I have to move around. I can't stand still. I've tried it, and I can't do it.")[18] He also needed automatisms in his audience for his best performance: his performance was responsive. (This may explain why his movies are generally considered artistic failures. Some of the better scenes in his movies are those in which he is performing for a group.)

The limits of Presley's conceptions of justice, though his sentiments for justice appeared to be genuine, are also the limits of the intellectual milieu that shaped his thinking; and these include the limits of American popular music and popular culture generally. If his songs generally present people who are going through or have been through hard times, and the speakers in his rock songs overcome or transcend adverse circumstances of love or fortune through vigorous and independent self-assertion and emotional release, those in his ballads (and these are far more numerous) usually do not overcome or transcend: they are characteristically down and out in their loves or their lives and struggling just to make it through, to the next town, a job, a woman. They are always Trying to Get to You, whether a lover or God, usually both or the one with the help of the other, in the Old Kentucky Rain. They believe, pray, love and dream their

[17]William W. Wood, *Culture and Personality Aspects of the Pentecostal Holiness Religion* (The Hague: Mouton and Co., 1965), p. 12.
[18]Elvis speaking in a recorded interview. Cf. Hopkins, p. 141: "I start playing and the movements are involuntary."

143

way; and though they never get through, the belief in the power of the wish-fulfilling magic of the right emotion sustains and gives them hope in their otherwise unyielding circumstances. The assertion is persistent enough in Presley's lyrics, and perhaps in popular music generally, to be a coherent and insistent epistemology that excludes and even denies the value of rational analysis and the critical intellect.

Presley's education taught him to believe he had a higher purpose, but to the degree that the rational intellect has a part in the determination of this purpose, his education did not equip him to cope with his experience or success. His success made him a god for the occasion and the audience that he created or that created him, a god for our times: anti-heroic, helplessly human, alienated from the humanity that deified him. Both his epistemology of passionate belief (and expression) and his metaphysics of otherworldiness (and its unconscious workings) made him satisfying to those who had little hope or little ability, background or taste for intellectual challenge and who enabled him to survive in this world only as a prisoner in his own enclave.

There is considerable evidence that Presley's enclave existence, which he felt forced upon him by the demands of his fame, was really his chosen mode of living. Once when he went out on the street in Hollywood, on a dare, to prove, as it were, that it could not be done without his creating a distraction, no one even noticed him.[19] There are plenty of places in which he could have lived a more open life had that been his desire. His manager believed firmly that decreased availability of his product would create greater demand. But beyond that, Elvis liked the image of himself as a person of such special status that he had to live in seclusion or else be always surrounded by bodyguards. Furthermore, the bodyguards provided a needed private and intimate community. His inversion of night and day—his choice to live by night and sleep by day—was dictated by preference and personal need rather than by necessity. He liked having movie houses, amusement parks, and roller rinks reserved especially for him and his friends between midnight and dawn. He was not only the king, he was the sun king: he had the symbolism woven into his garments because the need was woven into his life. In the night in which he lived and reigned, it was important to Elvis that he be the sun to his fans and those around him. And, to a large extent, he was.

[19]Hopkins, p. 347. (In 1968, while planning the NBC-TV Special.)

III. IMAGES

The mind of Elvis Presley reflects an Orphic fragmentation of social and human nature and, like Orpheus himself, is somewhat hidden in the mist and mystery he lived in. It is still guarded as the inner secret of a lucrative commercial property. Most of his closest associates who have written of him thus far seem to have had little interest in or knowledge of the books he read or of the symbols and myths in which he garmented himself in later years. Sonny and Red West and Dave Hebler (in Dunleavy, p. 166) indicate that Presley read a lot of mystical, astrological and religious literature and science fiction in addition to the Bible and technical books; but they name only one title, *Voice,* in which he apparently read a great deal and from which he read on several occasions to his paying audiences as well as to his paid followers, showing that he himself regarded its philosophy and teachings of great importance; but no author is given for the book.

I asked Ed Parker (August 16, 1978), a friend of Elvis (who is billed as Presley's mentor as well as his karate instructor and who, at that time, was promoting a book he had written about Presley), whether he knew the authors or titles of any books that Elvis read. The only title he remembered was a book called *The Hallowed Earth,* "about flying saucers." Presley was interested in, he said, and practiced things like Transcendental Meditation. I also asked Parker if he knew what, if any, significance Elvis's latter-day theme song by Strauss, "Thus Spake Zarathustra" (the theme also of the movie *2001: A Space Odyssey),* had for Elvis, or what significance Zarathustra had for Elvis, if any. Parker did not seem ever to have heard of the word *Zarathustra* (or of Zoroaster), though the name appears on many of Elvis's later albums. He indicated that as far as he knew Presley simply liked the movements and rhythms of the music, the excitement of its tempo.

Few have perceived Elvis as a person with ideas. Most observers would readily assume that the absence of evidence about the nature and source of ideas, beyond those that might be assumed from his cultural associations, is evidence enough that there were few ideas that mattered to him. (When Elvis was boarding the ship to sail to Germany for his tour of duty with the Army, he was carrying a book of sentimental love poems, *Poems that Touch the Heart,* which he showed to a reporter and described as "wonderful stuff,"[20] an opinion not unusual for a very young man, even many of those who

[20]Hopkins, p. 207.

145

have been to college.) Nonetheless, Elvis increasingly clothed himself in later years in the symbols of high myth and mysticism: the Phoenix, the Sun King, Zarathustra. Aside from the T.C.B. (Taking Care of Business) and lightning bolt symbol, he designed a T.L.C. (Tender Loving Care) monogram, both of which went on rings and necklaces of his own design. As part of the language of the cult, they show up frequently on T-shirts, in fan-club literature and on floral wreaths placed near his gravesite.

May Mann, in *The Private Elvis,* says that when Elvis was growing tired of the movies he was making he had told her he did not read books, and she had promised to send him Kahlil Gibran's *The Prophet.*

> Next time I saw Elvis he was reading everything he could get his hands on.
> "It's such an education," [Elvis said.] "I like biographies, histories, books with pictures of all the countries of the world. I'm planning a lot of travel around this old world."[21]

But elsewhere there is little indication of his having read such books. (Nor did he ever travel out of the United States, except on his Army tour of Germany.) His preference for personal reading seemed to be for what Ed Parker called "self-improvement"—what I might call sentiment, fantasy and wisdom literature. He was also interested in certain technical subjects, including medicine and pharmacology. His interests ranged from subjective and intuitive interpretations of and reflections on reality, including the purely speculative, to the factual and practical.

One might guess that the practical and factual would include car, motorcycle, and gun magazines, as well as "how-to" books on other Presley interests such as karate, as well as the "medical" books Hebler and the Wests mention. Certainly the cars and guns and karate activated Presley's fantasies and became symbols crucial to his image of himself. And if he bowdlerized the Bible to make it mean whatever he wanted, as the Wests and Hebler say, there is every reason to think he did the same with any medical text, no matter how closely he read it. Red West insists on Presley's vast knowledge of drugs, for example, and he also insists on his abuse of this knowledge.

[21]May Mann, *The Private Elvis* (New York: Kangaroo Books, Pocket Books, 1975), p. 146.

Further, like his fans, he was interested in all things extraterrestrial, whether UFOs from other galaxies, the inner mysteries of the human mind, or spirits from other dimensions. And like his fans he seems to have made no sharp distinction between noumena and mysterious phenomena. It was all otherworldly, a potpourri of fantasy and fact.

> His key is precise intuitive knowledge of who he is and what he's projecting on stage. His consistency is absolute.[22]

The pictures of Presley from earliest childhood, through adolescence and later maturity, dramatize chronologically a progress resembling that of the larval unfolding from grub to chrysalis to lunar moth. They dramatize also his strengths and weaknesses, his rise and fall, his points of maximum vigor and solidity, and his final apotheosis into the brilliance of the sun that is finally refracted only in a puffed mist, like the rainbow. The image changes on almost every page, as the artist perceives the spectrum of light changing as the sun moves or atmosphere thickens or thins.

In a gathering of Elvis fans, as on the first anniversary of his death at Graceland, one can see every stage of the spectrum reflected in facial expression, posture, movement, dress, and hair style, dramatizing the plurality of their cultural backgrounds and tastes and life styles, the specific Elvis they came to honor. But not even Elvis was ever all at once the whole spectrum that altogether he had been, though even near the end he could weave together remarkably well in the span of a single concert the diversity of a large-ranged American culture whose myth he also apotheosized—the forlorn, impoverished child, already the idol of his parents, rising through energy, work, and luck to the pinnacle of wealth and stardom without really ever forgetting where he came from or who he was. Even in the last photographs, the twisted smile on the face of the god seems to say that he knows what he is and is not and that if part of what he is is a god, there is also a part that is not.

There are two pictures that I can't keep apart in my mind, the only two in *The Illustrated Elvis* that depict any form of literature.

[22]Morgan Ames (title of article not given), *High Fidelity* (no bibliographical information given). Quoted, as epigraph to Section 2, by W. A. Harbison, *The Illustrated Elvis* (New York: Today Press, Grosset and Dunlap, 1976), no paging.

One is of the young rebel Presley in the early Graceland period, still in ordinary street dress, sitting on a couch with his arm around a girl, she absorbed in her own ecstasy while Presley is absorbed in a magazine called *Teen*. There is the face of another girl on the cover. The second picture profiles a "respectable" Elvis sitting on a couch in Graceland against a well-ordered bookcase that holds an impressive array of decorator-bound books and two decorator-framed miniatures, one of them of a camel and the other of a horse. His dress is still simple and plain, but his expression is consciously that of an idol. The books seem of dubious importance, since the picture blurs the titles, even for a magnifier. In the only other similar picture I can remember, he is reading a magazine entitled *Elvis Presley*, while his hair is being trimmed. It is included in a June 29, 1978, *Parade* feature in which Lloyd Shearer recalls the young Presley in 1955 telling him he had "made a study" or Marlon Brando and actor James Dean and "I've made a study of myself. And I know why girls, at least the young 'uns, go for us. We're sullen, we're brooding, we're something of a menace."

"'I don't understand it exactly,' he went on '. . . But I know you can't be sexy if you smile. You can't be a rebel if you grin. If you don't mind, just let me pose myself.'" Later, Shearer adds, "when I suggested that he delay signing a film contract with Paramount producer Hal Wallis and instead go on to college and cultivate the life of the mind for a few years, he looked at me with amazement.

"'I don't 'spect,'" he said, 'you ever been poor. We Presleys—we been poor as far back as I can remember.' He . . . said that when the time came for him to die, he wanted to die 'a happy millionaire.'"[23]

It is clear from these early remarks that Presley had given some original thought to his image and career and that whoever else contributed to its focus, he was his own mentor—he and Marlon Brando and James Dean and Dean Martin and Gary Cooper (others he mentioned)—and that his thinking helped to explain his studied dress and appearance since his early days at Humes High School in Memphis. It even goes back to his earliest childhood pictures—the three-year-old with the curled lips and the cocked slouched hat, the ten-year-old with the full-dress cowboy suit, hands on holsters, expression menacing, ready to draw. He was always in costume, always in performance, projecting an image. Many of his movies seemed designed to dress him like a doll. And even as he was creating the image that changed pop music and life styles and set off a worldwide cultural

[23]Parade Publications, pp. 4–9. The interview was in 1955.

explosion, he was also creating the vocabulary of rock criticism to come. The key words were *sexy, rebel,* and *menace.* Critics like Nik Cohn[24] have done no more than elaborate these into synonyms and to insist on their importance as touchstones.

The ingredients of the image were all there also. "We Presleys"—solidarity with his roots and the determination to rise above them into fabulous wealth, but to raise them with him at the same time. His independence, his politeness, his surefooted theatrical confidence, his almost flawless strategy in weaving together a mass audience into immense fame and wealth, his loyalty to his origins (his family, friends, and fans) apparently included a lack of any desire to rise above them intellectually. These are the evident ingredients of his myth and one form of the anti-intellectual myth of the popular media, of religion, politics, education, television, movies, the record industry and publishing—so much of which is based on giving the people what they want or creating tastes for performers and other products, but not alienating the customer, the voter, the parents of school children, the audience or the reader by maintaining high standards for quality and asking real questions.

It is doubtful that he would have gotten any more ideas in a high school in Tennessee where the teaching of Darwin was still forbidden by statute than he got in his fifth-grade class in Tupelo, Mississippi, where a section of each day was assigned to the study of gospel hymns, which Elvis always volunteered to sing (about all his teacher remembers of Elvis as a student). Naturally, he was amazed at the suggestion that he go to college. It is doubtful that any exciting idea of relevance for his life had come his way in school. Education as he had known it might as well have been a conspiracy against the processes of thought that would contribute to his real personal growth. No wonder society was either shocked or excited by his music.

To a larger extent than his critics like to think, we are Elvis, and, as his fans might readily claim, or more than they like to acknowledge, Elvis is America. It is not the America of Jefferson, who believed that the hunger of the mind to be free and to know the truth would vindicate his visionary democracy, or at least not yet. But some of the individualism and newness of form Emerson and Whitman thought would embody the character of this still raw nation—South, North, and West—were given a living expression by Elvis, in both his art and his life.

If the God of Thomas Jefferson, in whom America "trusts," glo-

[24]Cohn, pp. 11, 15, 17, 25.

ried in the human mind, as the crown of man, and conceived of its freedom from ignorance and prejudice as the crown of freedom, the God of Elvis—and of popular culture—has little use for that, and it is ultimately the figure of Elvis and his enormous and glittering "success" that has captured the dream of America, the possibility of the vigorous, albeit untutored, and daring individual, achieving a shortcut triumph over his limits.

Because of his social, educational and economic differences, Elvis was really never at home anywhere. In this sense, he was always a radical aberration of the society—South, North, and West—to which he gave a unified voice and a new style. When Elvis went to Nashville, after his early successes, to try out for the Grand Ole Opry and cut a "country" record, his style was about as welcome as that of a Pentecostal preacher in a Methodist pulpit. He was an alien intruder in the sanctuary of white Southern country music. Whether he left or was thrown out depends on the point of view—the antipathy was mutual. And though he reached the top before he got to Hollywood, for Elvis, the top was first Hollywood, then Las Vegas—not Nashville or New York.

"Who do you sound like?" Marian Keisker, of Sun Records in Memphis, asked the long-haired kid who came in the studio with his guitar to cut a record for his Mama's birthday. "I don't sound like nobody." She had heard that before (Hopkins, p.54). But this time, it wasn't just an echo of every singer who had more belief in his originality than originality itself. And despite the various influences she and Sam Phillips could hear in his voice—from Dean Martin and Nat King Cole to black rhythm and blues singers—he was unique. Because his yearnings were in many ways only an intensification, a focusing, of the merged yearnings of most of us to transcend our culture and ourselves, yet to be accepted by both, he was everyone and consequently no one.

His naive statement was an artistic manifesto that grew directly out of his conception of his position in the world and in the cosmos. If he felt the second class roles he was given in Hollywood were used to finance the films of the more serious actors, clearly he was a second class citizen there too and felt he was. Yet, where else in America could he possibly have felt at home? The answer was to be Las Vegas, a city that is not a society so much as a grand hotel, and he was to shuttle back and forth between it and Graceland and his road tours of America for the rest of his short life and his long American success.

IV. PERSPECTIVES

Elvis Presley might be evaluated as C. W. E. Bigsby says all popular culture is "by turns as epiphanic and apocalyptic, as evidence of social cohesion and social dislocation, as proof of subversive energy and evidence of decadence."[25] For Nik Cohn all pop is good if there is an audience for it and it makes a performer rich and famous. Stardom has intrinsic and extrinsic value, perhaps because it is outrageous. But for Cohn, pop's higher purpose is to be apocalyptic, violently expressive of subversive energy and always dislocating and revitalizing[26] those social norms Bigsby calls "a view of man (rational, puritanical, socially determined, innately moral) incompatible with an energetic emotionalism and an antinomian stance."[27] Nik Cohn is not really introducing a counterview to the notion of high and low culture; he is introducing, albeit inconsistently, criteria for distinguishing high pop from low pop.

Like Greil Marcus, Cohn would agree with Leslie Fiedler (Marcus's mentor). According to Bigsby, "What [Karl] Jaspers sees as an atomizing and automatizing force, reducing the individual to basic instincts, Leslie Fiedler . . . sees as . . . a vital rediscovery of a dimension of human existence formerly denied . . . by persistent puritanism and a bourgeois power structure intent on maintaining its control by outlawing and denigrating those elements of existence over which it has voluntarily relinquished control." Bigsby concludes that the study and criticism of popular culture for such critics "is inevitably to be seen as the advocacy of such a culture in the face of those whose apocalyptic visions are as much an expression of their own impending loss of control as of the imminent collapse of necessary structure itself."[28] The Marxist view (of critics like Theodore Adorno) is that culture heroes like Elvis get rich at the expense of fans who live in circumstances of exploitative injustice and who are tranquilized by vicariously transcending these circumstances through

[25]C. W. E. Bigsby, "The Politics of Popular Culture," in C. W. E. Bigsby, ed., *Approaches to Popular Culture* (Bowling Green, Ohio: Bowling Green University Popular Press, 1976), p. 3.
[26]Cohn, pp. 12, 18, 25. Greil Marcus, speaking at Florida State University in 1978, echoed sentiments similar to Cohn's: Rock is really good if it scares people, according to Marcus, and rock is about making plenty of money and making it fast.
[27]Bigsby, p. 2.
[28]Bigsby, p. 10.

their identification with the hero's success and fame. A counterview is that, while this may be true, for some, in "cutting across all class lines," as an Elvis fan from Northern Ireland (echoing Nik Cohn and others) says pop does, even in war-torn Belfast, pop, and especially rock, is, in Bigsby's words, "a subversive and liberating force, linking those of differing social and educational background."[29]

Clearly no one view will suffice for Elvis's fans, who are particularly sensitive to the possibility of being exploited, and they see Elvis himself as a constant victim of exploitation, thus identifying with him to the point that he embodies and transmits to them some of the values inherent in myth.

Three of the characteristics of myth observed by Levi-Strauss are particularly noteworthy to a consideration of Presley as myth. Myth establishes the precedence of the symbols of culture over society; it provides a way of moving from the "wild" to the "domesticated," "sex" to "love," "instinct" to "intelligence," in short, of "becoming human"; it provides a shareable mode "of self-awareness and awareness of the world," a "primary" (shareable) form of consciousness so that in moving from instinct to thought, existence is given order and meaning. Myths are also "common, permanent and general rather than individual, changeable, and particular"; otherwise the meaning or order that is created through them is not stable and reliable.[30]

When old myths cease to do this, when they deny the instinctual basis of the culturally desired learning objective, new myths that do not deny the life force become necessary. The validity of wildness, sexuality and instinct must be recognized by the myth or god before civilization, love and intelligence can be realized by those the myth reconciles to their own humanity. Myths and gods are also transrational forces. They may be studied and appreciated intellectually, but they act on those civilized through them as transrational symbols. Thus it is that those who merely know the myth intellectually have not really been made human through it. Consequently, they are fools to those who have. Rock is a primitive myth and primitive ritual, but to its adherents, it is experienced as a transforming power. Today, diehard rock buffs see disco enthusiasts as heretics, but disco

[29]Theodore Adorno, *Prisms* (London, 1967), pp. 109–110, quoted by Bigsby, p. 14, C. W. E. Bigsby, *Superculture: American Popular Culture and Europe* (London, 1975), pp. 23–24, quoted by Bigsby, pp. 17–18.
[30]Zev Barbu, "Popular Culture: A Sociological Approach," in C. W. E. Bigsby, ed., *Approaches to Popular Culture*, pp. 49–50.

enthusiasts see their tastes as having evolved to a more civilized stage. The debate is familiar, ironic, and, in one form or another, unending.

The person who embodies the myth and performs the ritual need not be present to be loved; but the image does need to be, and the sharing of the person (or the myth) with those who understand his (or its) primary importance is a necessity. The more primal the myth, the more important the god and the community. Thus the importance and phenomenal success of the fan clubs and fan rallies and conventions as communities or communions of the faithful. As one fan said to me in Memphis, "We are a family; we are a Presley nation." She was from New York. But in various ways, fans from Missouri, Italy, Belgium and Ireland said the same thing. I told a woman from Italy, a president of a fan club, that I did not belong to a fan club. "That is not important," she said. "What matters is that you are here." She assumed I was a fan.

The fan clubs mushroomed after Elvis's death, which, in making his presence or memory more strongly felt, increased the need to share the meaning with others. For the fan from New York, he was still a living presence. Though she had never met him personally, she said she heard him calling her by name to go to Memphis to visit his grave. Since the myth must have permanence, it cannot die. Rock critic Dave Marsh expressed his shock at Elvis's death in terms of his disappointment at not being able, later on, to share Elvis with his children.[31]

In the Middle Ages the dominant culture was religious, and the church validated the situation with the promises of spiritual peace and wealth in both this world and the next. Nowadays, the dominant culture is economic and secular, and society offers the people goods and satisfactions—"the good life" and its material rewards rather than the good life and its spiritual rewards. If for educated people the values of the Greek, the Medieval or the Renaissance thinkers and artists are still real and persuasive, for most people to-

---

[31] With David Brinkley, moderator, NBC, 17 August 1977, Marsh: "It's just that Elvis had always been there. . . . I expected him to be a part of American culture that I could share with my children," quoted by Greil Marcus, "Blue Hawaii," *Rolling Stone* (22 Sept. 1977), p. 57. In the same issue, Dave Marsh says in "Elvis in the Promised Land" (p. 58), "Elvis Presley was more than anything a spiritual leader of our generation—there is really no way to assess his importance, much less the meaning of the music he created." Marcus says of Marsh, and means also of himself, "rock is his job because it is his life" (p. 57).

day, even for religious people to a large extent, the "star" system has replaced the system of the god, the saint, and the artist. "Stars" are created by both producers and consumers to symbolize the wealth, glamor, freedom and leisure that motivate the masses. This is no less true in Marxist societies than in capitalist societies, and the "stars," in both societies, as they have presently evolved, may dissent from the system, to a tolerable degree, from within, so long as they conform to the system sufficiently to fulfill their role. In fact, where there is considerable discontent within the system, from those who do not find their needs fulfilled, the dissent can be an important part of the "star's" appeal and thus an important means by which the role is fulfilled.

Since "stars" are created by and for their audience, they must (like heroes) live out some mixture of both the fantasies and realities of the lives of their audiences, both in their life and in their art. They must repudiate in some way those things their fans find too restrictive and endorse those things the fans find comfortable or liberating, including the tastes of the audience. The demands on a ballet star and other acclaimed artists are different from those on a rock star or a movie star. Whether Mick Jagger, Rudolf Nureyev or Yevgeny Yevtushenko—they belong to one jet-set culture, have different audiences, and all protest against some element of the culture they endorse and are supported by. They create new fusions and expressive alternatives *within* the culture.

In general Elvis symbolized the youthful liberating, restorative vitality and the fusion and renewal of cultural forms called for by the advocates of popular culture; specifically he stood for the triumph of youth over age, new forms for the age and the transcendence of the limitations of class, and of educational and regional limitations. His dominant god/myth symbols (Sun King, Phoenix, Lightning Bolt) and his abodes (Graceland, the Circle G Ranch[32] and Bel Air) which augmented these symbols, reinforced his triumph over age, class and his era and asserted his superiority to time and mortality. A group of young fans displayed a sign outside Graceland, a year after his death, hand-lettered and ungrammatically ironic, saying

From Graceland
To the Promise Land—

[32]The ranch was referred to earlier as the Rising Sun and is also called the Circle G (for Graceland). Presley also had a palomino horse named Rising Sun.

We followed you here
We will follow you there.

All language is code. When young Elvis had just got through explaining to Lloyd Shearer that he *knew more* about the kind of image he wanted to project (and the language of visual imagery) than Shearer, a professional photographer, did, Shearer countered with the sincerely kind advice that Elvis should go to college and develop his mind (translate: What you really need is some class). As noted above, Elvis replied, "I don't 'spect you ever been poor. We Presleys—we've been poor since back before I can remember" ("I'm a survivor. We survivors are proud of our independence. Your colleges exist to put down people like me; they don't have anything of value for my life"). All such translations are approximate, but here two cultures were having a Chekhovian dialogue. Form is content. Both were well-trained in the forms: "high" class benevolently offering "low" class its advantages; "low" class politely asserting its own values. Education was only one route to "higher class," as Elvis knew—the two were not synonymous. (Education for this purpose would not have appealed to Presley anyway; the only value of education for him would have been to learn a trade or profession, to improve one's status materially or to learn to do something one wanted to do. He could already do it all.) Elvis was as much a master of this kind of cultural doubletalk as any member of any oppressed minority. I don't mean he wasn't sincere; he was. But he was as much in control of an interview as he was of a stage. He was on stage.

These observations do not mean that education would have had no value for Presley. The values of education are both cultural and personal, and Elvis was right to feel that those excluded are handicapped in relation to those who are included. Shearer was sincere in his advice, and it was good advice, though there may have been an element of cultural patronizing in his remarks. The problem is more complex than a simplistic explication of the dialogue suggests.

As himself, when properly rehearsed, and especially before a live audience, Elvis Presley had both musical and dramatic genius. Though his genius was evidently intuitive it was learned from and nourished by his inheritance of a complex, expressively responsive musical tradition and by his position as the only surviving child of doting parents, especially his mother. It was strongest and most natural when the audiences gave back to him what he gave to them—which is always the case with powerful charismatic leaders. Since this simultaneity of audience response was crucially important

155

to him, he was eager to learn, and, at least until merely his presence was sufficient to elicit this response, he gave totally of himself in well-practiced performances. Also, he was, largely, his own producer and director.

In his movies, however, he was walked through his parts at the rate of almost three a year, with little direction or control of the script, and the results were predictably perfunctory, for the most part. They are certainly no gauge of what he might have been as a dramatic actor, especially before a live audience, had he been rehearsed in suitable roles and been given artistic direction. In a few of his movies, he showed real talent and artistry as an actor. Otherwise, though he was able to choose his songs, he had to choose them within the limitations of the context of the film, and they had to be performed within the restricted language of those contexts.

Presley as a performer, therefore, must be evaluated in two modes; on one hand he was a creative artist who imposed his own imagination and vision onto the music, the lyrics, the stage, and the audience, giving them new dimensions, dramatically and philosophically. He projected the best of his own complex cultural character and inheritance onto the mainstream of Western popular culture, enlivening, enriching, and altering it, perhaps permanently. On the other hand, he became a pawn of his own primary commitment to the mindless, interlocking processes of mass production, stardom, and maximum profits.

The critics did their part by telling how great Elvis was, still occasionally is, and lamented the movies and the decline of the king. Their industry, their products, their careers, and their reputations were built on top of his. There was hardly space or motive for analyzing the suspicious foundations of an interlocking industry that stretched from the mass publishing houses for books or records, the national networks, and from *Time, Newsweek,* and *Rolling Stone* to the tabloids. Out of their own apparent necessity they sought and sustained an audience with little access to or interest in more elaborate understanding, the audience of least resistance to and greatest need for restricted symbols of unrestrained acclaim: stars. This is the university Elvis went to and graduated from; and what university is not simply damned proud of its best graduate!

The rock critics, the professors of rock—and Greil Marcus and Nik Cohn are among the best of them—usually stop with the assumption that the artist and the prostitute in the "star" have nothing to do with each other, that the one is sublime and the other ridiculous, that the system exploits and eventually destroys the artist who as a human being becomes caught in and ground up by the unreality and the unrelenting demands of the industry, the audience and the artist's own evolved dependence on the godlike image, like the black leather or gold lamé suit within which he suffocates. He either bears the weight and sweats it out or changes his clothes only to find the new clothes also have the weight of sacrament.

Once divinity is put on, it is difficult to take it off. The ritual must be acted out by its own intrinsic rhythm to its final scene. The calf must eventually be led to the altar to replace the priest in whose stead he is sacrificed for the purgation of the people and the renewal of the land, its life and its culture. If the calf is the priest or priestess, then he or she must be sacrificed. And if Marilyn and Janis and Jimi and Elvis do not seem to be of the same proportions as Dionysus, Orpheus or Jesus, they still perform the necessary cultural function.

Charles Bovary would say, "It is the fault of fatality," and the irony of Bovary's dullness aside, it might well be argued that the resolutions of conflicts in cultural melting pots like Greece or Europe or America inevitably put the lives of their most charismatic leaders in jeopardy so that the necessary cultural changes they pursue—instinctively, like Elvis, or knowingly, like King—for the revitalizing health of the society are all too frequently achieved only through their own violent deaths: Malcolm, Jack, Bobby—to name others who used charismatic personalities and epiphanic symbolism to seek peaceful solutions within the law. This in no way equates the qualities of these five men, but it suggests that the culture they lived in made demands on them of a similar nature and that these demands were murderous.

In this respect it should be added that rock is only one recent manifestation of radical romanticism in art and life, where self-immolation and murder have established a refrain of human sacrifice, whether at Vietnam or at home during the era in which rock has had the most impact. Dylan Thomas, Sylvia Plath, John Berryman and Anne Sexton have received their greatest acclaim from the vivisection of their psyches in public. This was not true for Thomas in England as much as in America, nor for Plath. Nowhere in Plath is there greater scorn than for the morbidly voyeuristic audience, in "Lady Lazarus." And yet she plays to and for that audience even as she scorns it. And it is that audience, in part, that made a cult around her suicide. "Dying/Is an art like everything else." And the audience waits, breathlessly, for the repetition of the "miracle," again and again. She sees it as the same audience that countenanced the death-camp gas chambers, and countenances, apparently, ever more shocking forms of purgation. This does not explain Plath's morbid psychosis any more than it explains Elvis's narcissistic genius and cravings but it suggests that the problem has a cultural basis and is not unique to any one performer. If this is true in the more elaborated mode of poetry, appealing largely to literate audiences conditioned by the nonmaterial values inherent in past traditions, it is even more true in the more sensationalist, nonelaborated codes.

Elvis was the king of rock, not only because he was the innovator, but because his emulators, in comparison, were always a bit ridiculous. They performed the ritual but seldom embodied the myth. As myth, Elvis is different things for different people, though for most of his fans, there seemed to be a ready tolerance for and acceptance of others, especially other Elvisites, regardless of background or origin. In fact, the more diverse the background, the more it verified the universal validity of Elvis and what they thought he stood for and made them stand for. Thus, the myth, whatever its content, seemed to move the individual from instinctual to civilized behavior.

There is a higher mortality rate among rock stars, perhaps, than among football players, skydivers or race drivers. If the demands of alternating between hectic road schedules and isolation were in themselves inevitably murderous, it is to Elvis's credit that he slowed and varied the tempo of his music and life despite the demands of the critics that he maintain or accelerate his pace within his concerts. Though he felt, also, the need to maintain his youth, vitality and untouchable status, his range of performance reflected a variety of cultural styles, emotions, tastes and tempos. Within the limits of pop, he constantly reached toward a golden mean that, more than anyone else, he helped define.

His education as a serious actor in serious scripts and roles would have been his best hope for achieving those extra dimensions of comprehension and respect that might have enabled him to deal more realistically with the process of growing old, would have given him better roles to play and a more elaborate language for the dialogue with death; a language of relativities, rather than the language of absolutes that is primarily offered by pop and rock.

A HOUND DOG, TO THE MANOR BORN

■

by Stanley Booth

This article originally appeared in Esquire *in February 1968, when Elvis was merely a legend in a sleepy southern town living out a story that had become wistful but not yet tragic. Booth's portrait of Elvis depicts him at that brief and quiet midpoint between his lazy Hollywood years and his hectic, sweaty decline.*

Between Memphis and Walls (you turn right a bit past a big sign saying *Church of God, Pastor C. B. Brantley,* DRINK DR PEPPER), there is a small ranch, a hundred and sixty green and gently rolling acres, a prettier spread than you'd expect to see in the poor, bleak land of North Mississippi. The owner, at thirty-three, has been a millionaire for more than a decade. He has other, more elegant homesteads, but these days he prefers the ranch. Behind the formidable chain-link fence and the eight-foot picket walls that hide his neat red-brick house, he finds a degree of privacy to share with his pretty new wife. The privacy is also shared by twenty-two purebred horses, counting colts, and nine hired hands, counting guards. (There were twelve hands, but the number was reduced recently, so the story goes around the ranch, at the request of the owner's wife.) Then, too, there are the continual visitors—the ones who are allowed inside (some driving Cadillacs given them by the owner as Christmas or birthday presents) and the ones who must stay outside, peering over or through the fences. At times, such as when the owner is out riding, the roadside is solidly lined with sight-seeing cars. Privacy—the privacy in which to enjoy his leisure time—is extremely valuable to the ranch's young owner, especially since he works less than half the year. Taxes would make more work pointless; his annual income is about five million dollars.

And yet, not too many years ago, he was living in a Federal low-rent housing project, working as a truck driver, movie usher, sometimes forced to sell his blood at ten dollars a pint. Elvis Presley, a Great American Success Story.

By the ranch's main gate, in an air-conditioned hut, sits Elvis's Uncle Travis, a small, grinning man, with hair as black and skin as dark as an Indian's. A straw cowboy hat rests on his knee. He wears black Western pants and a white shirt with *E.P.* monogrammed in black Gothic script across the front. Travis likes to reminisce about the girls he has captured and ejected from his nephew's premises. "I dragged one out from under the old pink Cadillac. She must of heard me comin' and hid under there, and all I saw was her feet stickin' out. I said, 'Come on out of there,' and she didn't move, so I reached down, took ahold of her feet, and pulled. She had a coat of motor oil a inch thick." Travis belches.

"How do they get in?"

"Slip in. Jump a fence just like a billygoat. If they can't climb over, they'll crawl under. If the gate ain't locked they'll drive right through. I had a carload slip past me up at Graceland. Hell, I didn't even go after them, I just locked the damn gate. They made the circle in front of the house, come back down the drive, and when they seen they couldn't get out, the one drivin' says, 'Please op'n the gate.' I told her 'Yes, ma'am, soon's the sheriff got there.' Made out like I was real hot, you know. She says, 'Please don't call the sheriff, my mama will kill me.' I said, 'Not till you get out of jail, I don't reckon.' She like to died. Then I started laughin', and they seen it was all right, and asked me if they could come back after while and talk. So I told them yeah, but while they was gone I got to thinkin', Why'd they have to leave, why couldn't they just stay and talk? But one of they mamas came back with them, and she told on them. I'd scared her daughter so bad she'd peed her pants."

Travis pitches his head back and laughs, displaying a strong white set of uppers. Parked in the drive is a shiny red Ford Ranchero with his name, T. J. Smith, on one door under the ranch's Circle G brand, actually a flying Circle G. I ask what the "G" stands for.

"Could be Graceland," Travis says, "or it could be his mother's name. He meant it to stand for her name." Travis's expression becomes serious when he speaks of Elvis's dead mother, his own sister. "He still keeps that old pink Cadillac he bought for her. Don't never drive it, just keeps it as a keepsake. He's got all the cars he needs. Had a Rolls-Royce up on blocks four or five years. Bought a hundred thousand dollars' worth of trucks and trailers right after he got this place. Money ain't nothing to him. Ole boy from Hernando was down here the other evenin', workin' on the fence, and Elvis drove down in one of his new pickups to take a look. Feller says, 'Shore do like that truck. Always wanted me one of them.' So Elvis says, 'You got a dollar?' Feller says, 'Yeah, I got one,' and gives it to Elvis. 'It's your truck,' Elvis says."

Next Travis tells how Priscilla, the new wife, likes Elvis to take her for rides in one of his souped-up go-karts (top speed, more than a hundred miles an hour) around the driveway at Graceland, tantalizing the squealing girls outside the fence.

Then he spits. "I sit down here, keepin' people out, seven in the mornin' till six in the evenin', five days a week, and I'm about wore out. I think I'll go in the hospital for two or three weeks, take me a rest."

"Maybe you could get a television set to watch while you're working," I suggest.

"Yeah, I believe I will get me one. Either that, or some funny books."

Just outside the gate, in a rented green Impala, are two girls who have come, so they tell me, all the way from New Zealand. "Is he home?" they ask.

"Who?"

One sneers, one ignores. "Did you talk to him? What did he say?"

I look away, trying to select a representative quote. On the roof of the house across the road a man is kneeling behind a camera, snapping pictures of the Circle G. "Let's ride up to Rosemark tomorrow and look at that mare," I tell the girls.

"Pardon?"

"That's what he said."

"What, is *that* all?"

"You should have been here yesterday. He said, 'Would somebody please bring me a Pepsi?'" Pepsi-Cola, I would have explained to the girls, is Elvis's favorite drink, just as his favorite snack is peanut-butter-and-mashed-banana sandwiches; but the Impala roars away, leaving a cloud of dust to settle on my shoes.

Sometime ago, before I saw for myself what Elvis is like, I asked a mutual acquaintance about him. "He's all right," I was told. "Pretty interesting guy to talk to."

"Really. What's the most interesting thing he's ever said to you?"

My friend sat and thought, pulling the hair on his chin. Finally he said, "Well, once he told me, 'Like your beard. How long'd it take you to grow it?' I said it took about three months, and he said, 'I'd like to grow me one sometime, but I don't think I could get away with it. Y'know?' And he sort of winked."

Another friend, whose relation to the Presley household was for a time unique, told me that Elvis is a very straight guy, who uses neither grass nor acid. In Hollywood, Elvis never goes to nightclubs or premieres. Except for work, he hardly leaves his Bel-Air mansion. "He's afraid he wouldn't know how to act," says one of his oldest friends. "And he wouldn't."

Even in Memphis, his recreational activities have been, for a millionaire, unpretentious. In the early days at Graceland (the large, white-columned estate, rather like an antebellum funeral parlor, which Elvis bought in 1957), the big kick was roller skating. After a local rink closed for the evening, Presley and his entourage would come in, skate, eat hot dogs and drink Pepsi-Cola till dawn. When skating palled, Elvis started renting the entire Fairgrounds amusement park, where he and his friends could ride the Tilt-a-Whirl, Ferris wheel, roller coaster, Dodgem cars (Elvis's favorite), and eat hot dogs and drink Pepsis till dawn. Until quite recently, Presley has been in the habit of hiring a local movie theater (the Memphian) and showing rented movies, emphasizing the films of actresses he has dated. The Memphian has no hot-dog facilities, but provides plenty of popcorn and, of course, Pepsis. Now that he is married and an expectant father, he does not get out so much at night, but the day-time is as glamorous, as exciting as ever.

On a day not long ago, when Presley happened to be staying at Graceland, the house was crowded with friends and friends of friends, all waiting for old El to wake up, come downstairs, and turn them on with his presence. People were wandering from room to room, looking for action, and there was little to be found. In the basement, a large, divided room with gold records hung in frames around the walls, creating a sort of halo effect, they were shooting pool or lounging under the Pepsi-Cola signs at the soda fountain. (When Elvis likes something, he *really* likes it.) In the living room boys and girls were sprawled, nearly unconscious with boredom, over the long white couches, among the deep snowy drifts of rug.

One girl was standing by the enormous picture window, absently pushing one button, then another, activating an electrical traverse rod, opening and closing the red velvet drapes. On a table beside the fireplace of smoky molded glass, a pink ceramic elephant was sniffing the artificial roses. Nearby, in the music room, a thin, dark-haired boy who had been lying on the cloth-of-gold couch, watching Joel McCrea on the early movie, snapped the remote-control switch, turning off the ivory television set. He yawned, stretched, went to the white, gilt-trimmed piano, sat down on the matching stool and began to play. He was not bad, playing a kind of limp, melancholy boogie, and soon there was an audience facing him, their backs to the door.

Then, all at once, through the use of perceptions which could only be described as extrasensory, everyone in the room knew that Elvis was there. And, stranger still, nobody moved. Everyone kept his cool. Out of the corner of one's eye Presley could be seen, leaning against the doorway, looking like Lash La Rue in boots, black Levis and a black silk shirt.

The piano player's back stiffens, but he is into the bag and has to boogie his way out. "What is this, amateur night?" someone mutters. Finally—it cannot have been more than a minute—the music stops. Everyone turns toward the door. Well I'll be damn. It's Elvis. What say, boy? Elvis smiles, but does not speak. In his arms he is cradling a big blue model airplane.

A few minutes later, the word—the sensation—having passed through the house, the entire company is out on the lawn, where Presley is trying to start the plane. About half the group has graduated into the currently fashionable Western clothing, and the rest are wearing the traditional pool-hustler's silks. They all watch intently as Elvis, kneeling over the plane, tries for the tenth time to make the tiny engine turn over; when it sputters and dies a groan, as of one voice, rises from the crowd.

Elvis stands, mops his brow (though of course he is not perspiring), takes a thin cigar from his shirt pocket and peels away the cellophane wrapping. When he puts the cigar between his teeth a wall of flame erupts before him. Momentarily startled, he peers into the blaze of matches and lighters offered by willing hands. With a nod he designates one of the crowd, who steps forward, shaking, ignites the cigar, and then, his moment of glory, of service to the King at an end, he retires into anonymity. "Thank ya very much," says Elvis.

They begin to seem quite insane, the meek circle proffering worship and lights, the young ladies trembling under Cadillacs, the tourists outside, standing on the roofs of cars, waiting to be blessed by even a glimpse of this young god, this slightly plump idol, whose face grows more babyish with each passing year.

But one exaggerates. They are not insane, only mistaken, believing their dumpling god to be Elvis Presley. He is not. One remembers—indeed, one could hardly forget—Elvis Presley.

The time is the early fifties, and the scene is dull. Dwight Eisenhower is President, Perry Como is the leading pop singer. The world has changed (it changed in 1945), but the change is not yet evident. Allen Ginsberg is a market researcher for a San Francisco securities company. William Burroughs is in New Orleans, cooking down codeine cough syrup. Malcolm X, paroled from Massachusetts's Charlestown Prison, is working in a Detroit furniture store. Stokely Carmichael is skinny, insolent, and eleven years old.

It is, let us say, 1953. Fred Zinnemann rehashes the past with *From Here to Eternity,* and Laslo Benedek gives us, in *The Wild One,* a taste of the future. This is a movie with good guys and bad guys, and the good guys are the ones who roar on motorcycles into a town which is small, quiet, typically American and proceed to take it apart. Their leader, Marlon Brando, will be called an anti-hero. But there is no need for the prefix. He is a new, really contemporary hero: the outcast.

Soon James Dean repeats the theme with even greater success. But Dean's career was absurdly short. "You know he was dead before you knew who he was," someone said. The outcasts of America were left without a leader.

Then, one Saturday night early in 1956 on a television variety program, a white singer drawls at the camera: "Ladies and gentlemen, I'd like to do a song now, that tells a little story, that really makes a lot of sense—*Awopbopaloobop—alopbamboom! Tutti-frutti! All rootie! Tutti-frutti! All rootie!*"

Though nearly all significant popular music was produced by Negroes, a white rhythm-and-blues singer was not entirely a new phenomenon. Bill Haley and the Comets had succeeded with such songs as "Shake, Rattle and Roll," and "Rock Around the Clock." But the pudgy Haley, in his red-plaid dinner jacket, did not project much personal appeal. This other fellow was something else.

He was not quite a hillbilly, not yet a drugstore cowboy. He was a Southern—in that word's meaning of the combination of rebellion and slow, sweet charm—version of the character Brando created in

The Wild One. Southern high-school girls, the "nice" ones, called these boys hoods. You saw them lounging on the hot concrete of a gas station on a Saturday afternoon, or coming out of a poolroom at three o'clock of a Monday afternoon, stopping for a second on the sidewalk as if they were looking for someone who was looking for a fight. You even see their sullen faces, with a toughness lanky enough to just miss being delicate, looking back at you out of old photographs of the Confederate Army. They were not named Tab or Rock, nor even Jim, Bill, Bob. They all had names like Leroy, Floyd, Elvis. All outcasts, with their contemporary costumes of duck-ass haircuts, greasy Levis, motorcycle boots, T-shirts for day and black leather jackets for evening wear. Even their unfashionably long sideburns (Elvis's were *furry*) expressed contempt for the American dream they were too poor to be part of.

No one writing about Presley should forget the daring it took to be one of these boys, and to sing. A "hood" might become a mechanic or a house painter or a bus driver or even a cop, but nobody would expect him to be a singer. If he tried it at all, he would have to have some of his own crowd playing with him; he'd have to sing some old songs his own people had sung before him; and he would have to sing them in his own way, regardless of what people might say about him.

"Mama, do you think I'm vulgar on the stage?"

"Son, you're not vulgar, but you're puttin' too much into your singin'. Keep that up and you won't live to be thirty."

"I can't help it, Mama. I just have to jump around when I sing. But it ain't vulgar. It's just the way I feel. I don't feel sexy when I'm singin'. If that was true, I'd be in some kinda institution as some kinda sex maniac."

These days, when asked about the development of his career, Elvis either ignores the question or refers it to "my manager." Generally speaking his manager is the person standing closest to him at the time. This is often Alan Fortas, officially the ranch foreman, a young man only slightly less stocky than a bull, with a history of hostility to reporters. When The Beatles visited Elvis in Hollywood, Fortas, not troubling to remember their names, addressed each of them as, "Hey, Beatle!" They always answered, too; nobody wants to displease Alan.

A more voluble source of information is Dewey Phillips. During Elvis's early career Phillips was probably as close to him as anyone except his mother, Gladys. Now retired, Phillips was then one of the most popular and influential disc jockeys in the nation. He still speaks the same hillbilly jive he used as a broadcaster.

"Nobody was picking up on the ole boy back then. He was a real bashful kid, but he liked to hang around music. They'd chased him away from the switchboard at WMPS, and he'd come hang around Q. That's WHBQ, where I was doing my show, *Red Hot and Blue*, every night. Weekends, he'd come down to Sun Records—he'd cut that record, 'My Happiness,' for his mother, paid four dollars for it himself—and Sam Phillips, president of Sun, finally gave him a session. Tried to record a ballad, but he couldn't cut it. Sam got Bill Black, the piano player, and Scotty Moore, the guitarist, to see if they could work anything out with him.

"After a lot of tries, Elvis, Bill and Scotty fixed up a couple of old songs, 'That's All Right, Mama,' and 'Blue of Kentucky' so they sounded a little different. When Elvis began to cut loose with 'That's All Right,' Sam came down and recorded these sonofaguns. One night I played the record thirty times. Fifteen times each side. When the phone calls and telegrams started to come in, I got hold of Elvis's daddy, Vernon. He said Elvis was at a movie, down at Suzore's number-two theater. 'Get him over here,' I said. And before long Elvis came running in. 'Sit down, I'm gone interview you,' I said. He said, 'Mr. Phillips, I don't know nothing about being interviewed.' 'Just don't say nothing dirty,' I told him.

"He sat down, and I said I'd let him know when we were ready to start. I had a couple of records cued up, and while they played we talked. I asked him where he went to high school, and he said 'Humes.' I wanted to get that out, because a lot of people listening had thought he was colored. Finally I said, 'All right, Elvis, thank you very much.' 'Aren't you gone interview me?' he asked. 'I already have,' I said. 'The mike's been open the whole time.' He broke out in a cold sweat."

According to Phillips, Elvis at this time considered himself a country singer. "Sam used to get him, Roy Orbison, Jerry Lee Lewis and Johnny Cash down at Sun and play Big Bill Broonzy and Arthur Crudup records for them, trying to get them on the blues thing, because he felt like that was going to be hot. One of Elvis's first public appearances was at a hillbilly jamboree at the downtown auditorium. Webb Pierce was there, and Carl Smith, Minnie Pearl, a whole houseful of hillbillies. Elvis was nervous, said he wanted me with him. But Sam and I were out at my house, drinking beer, or we had something going, and I missed the afternoon show. Elvis came looking for me, mad as hell. I asked him what he'd sung and he said, "'Old Shep' and 'That's How My Heartaches Begin.'" What happened? 'Nothing.'

"So that night I went along with him and told him to open with 'Good Rockin' Tonight' and not to sing any hillbilly songs. I introduced him and stayed onstage while he sang. He went into 'Good Rockin',' started to shake, and the place just blew apart. He was nobody, didn't even have his name on the posters, but the people wouldn't let him leave. When we finally went off we walked past Webb Pierce, who had been waiting in the wings to go on. I smiled at him and he said, 'You son of a bitch.'"

The sales of Elvis's records enabled him to get more bookings, and Dewey Phillips bought him an old Lincoln sedan for $450 so he could play out-of-town jobs. Appearing in Nashville at a convention of the Country and Western Disc Jockeys' Association, he was seen, "discovered," by talent scouts for RCA Victor. In a moviehouse matinee in Texarkana, he was discovered by Thomas Andrew Parker, a latter-day Barnum out of W. C. Fields by William Burroughs. A carnival orphan, he had worked in his uncle's "Great Parker Pony Circus," dipped candied apples, shaved ice for snow cones, operated merry-go-rounds, even put in a stretch as dog-catcher in Tampa, Florida.

Astute techniques in these businesses had enabled Parker to rise in the world to a position of some prestige. The title "Colonel" had been conferred upon him by, as he put it, "a few governors." He was managing the careers of such big name country entertainers as Hank Snow and Eddy Arnold. But in all his years as a promoter, he had never found so promotable a commodity as Presley.

He had seen Elvis at, for his purposes, just the right time. The demand for Elvis's records prompted RCA to offer $35,000 for Presley, lock, stock, and tapes. Sam Phillips accepted.

"Elvis knew he was going big time," Dewey Phillips remembers, "and he needed a manager. That was late spring of '55. He was the hottest thing in show business, and still just a scared kid. He had got his mother and daddy a nice house, they had three Cadillacs, and no phone. He asked me to be his manager. I told him I didn't know anything about managing. Then Colonel Parker came to town. He knew what he was doing. He didn't talk to Elvis. He went out to the house and told Gladys what he could do for the boy. That Parker is a shrewd moo-foo, man."

Elvis's first appearances on network television, on the Tommy and Jimmy Dorsey show in January and February 1956, changed him from a regional phenomenon into a national sensation. This might not have happened, the American public might simply have shuddered and turned away, had there not been a new group among them: teen-agers, the enemy within. When the older generation, repelled by Presley's lean, mean, sexy image, attacked him from pulpits and editorial columns, banned him from radio stations, the teenagers liked him more than ever, and went out and bought his records. Entrepreneurs could not afford to ignore Presley. As one radio producer asked, How can you argue with the country's number-one recording star? Reluctantly, almost unwillingly, show business accepted Elvis. Ed Sullivan, who only a couple of months before had condemned Presley as being "unfit for a family audience," now was obliged to pay him $50,000 for three brief appearances. However, Elvis was photographed only from the waist up, and his material was diluted by the addition of a ballad, "Love Me Tender," which oozed syrup.

Such attempts to make Elvis appear respectable were very offensive to the good ole boys back in Memphis. Steve Allen, involved in a ratings battle with Sullivan, booked Presley, but assured the audience that they would see only "clean family entertainment." Elvis appeared and sang, standing still, wearing white tie and tails, with top hat and cane, but without a guitar. Just after the show went off the air, Dewey Phillips's telephone rang, "Hello, you bastard," Dewey said.

"How'd you know who it was me?" asked Elvis.

"You better call home and get straight, boy. What you doing in that monkey suit? Where's your guitar?"

So when Elvis made his next hometown appearance (it was on July 4, 1956) he reassured his people. The occasion was a charity benefit and Colonel Parker had turned down paying engagements so that Elvis could be part of the show. His was the closing spot, and he was preceded by more than a hundred performers, including the orchestras of Bob Morris and Aaron Bluestein, the Admiral's Band of Navy Memphis, a barbershop quartette called the Confederates, Charlotte Morgan's dancing Dixie Dolls, and innumerable singers, by no means the least of which was one Helen Putnam, founder of Fat Girls Anonymous, who dedicated *A Good Man Is Hard to Find* to Elvis.

After nearly three hours, with the audience so bored that it was on the point of having a religious experience, Dewey Phillips, who was master of ceremonies, said, "All right. Here he is," and there he was, his hair hanging over his forehead, a wad of gum in his jaw.

He wore a black suit, black shoes, black shirt, red tie, and red socks, clothes with so much drape and flash that they created a new sartorial category, somewhere on the other side of corny. He sang all the old songs in the old way, from "That's All Right" to "Blue Suede Shoes" to "Heartbreak Hotel." He sang until he was dripping with sweat, and when at last he spoke, his words were a promise to his friends, a gift of defiance to his enemies: "I just want to tell y'awl not to worry—them people in New York and Hollywood are not gone change me none."

Then his voice became a growl, an act of rebellion: *You ain't nothin' but a houn' dog,* he sang, and proceeded to have sexual intercourse with the microphone.

> *They told me you was high class*
> *Well, that was just a lie—*

If the police had not been there, forming a blue wall around the stage, the audience might have eaten Elvis's body in a Eucharistic frenzy. They were his and he was theirs, their leader: it was an incandescent moment.

And at the same time it was a climactic one. For as he stood there singing defiance at his natural enemies, those with power, prestige, money, the Humes High hood, the motorcycle jockey, was gone, and in his place there was a star, with power, prestige, money. A few months from now at about three o'clock one morning, he would be standing with one of his hired companions outside the Strand Theatre on Main Street in Memphis when a couple of his high-school classmates would drive past, not going much of anywhere, just dragging Main. They would slow their car as they came alongside the Strand; they would see it was Elvis; and then, without a word, they would drive on. "A few years ago," Elvis said, "they would have spoken to me."

Elvis had tried to go on being himself. When Paramount offered him a movie contract with a clause forbidding him to ride motorcycles, he said, "I'd rather not make movies." They let him keep his motorcycles. All that was really necessary was that he stop doing his thing and start doing theirs. His thing was "Mystery Train," "Milkcow Blues Boogie." Theirs was "Love Me Tender," "Loving You," "Jailhouse Rock," "King Creole."

Then he was drafted. The Army cut his hair, took away his fancy clothes, and Elvis let them. His country had served him well and he was willing to serve his country. He is nothing if not fair-minded.

While he was stationed in Fort Hood, Texas, Elvis moved his parents to a rented house in the nearby town of Killeen. His mother, who had been doing poorly for more than a year, worsened, and on August 8, 1958, Elvis put her on a train to Methodist Hospital in Memphis. The prognosis was grave and Elvis requested the customary special leave.

It was refused. When the doctors, at Elvis's request, advised his command of the seriousness of his mother's illness, they were told in effect, "If it were anybody else, there'd be no problem. It's standard procedure. But if we let Presley go everybody will yell special privilege."

Days passed while Gladys Presley sank lower and lower. In spite of constant urging from Elvis and his doctors, the leave still was not granted. Finally, on the morning of August 12, Elvis decided that he had had enough. "If I don't get a pass by two o'clock this afternoon," he told the doctors, "I'll be home tonight."

The doctors reasoned with him, urged him to remember that he set an example for millions of other boys. But Elvis had made up his mind. A Humes High boy can be pushed only so far. The doctors could only advise the command of Elvis's plans.

So naturally, the pass came through. The Army is not that dumb. Elvis had the same rights as any other American boy.

Back in Memphis Elvis fought his way through the crowds of newsmen outside the hospital. He was in his mother's room for only a few minutes; then he came out, walked down the hall to an empty waiting room, sank into a chair and cried.

His mother had been the one, perhaps the only one, who had told him throughout his life that even though he came from poor country people, he was just as good as anyone. His success had not surprised her, nor had it changed her. Shortly after Gladys Presley was buried, her husband and son were standing on the magnificent front steps at Graceland. "Look, Daddy," Elvis sobbed, pointing to the chickens his mother had kept on the lawn of the hundred-thousand-dollar mansion. "Mama won't never feed them chickens no more."

He has never really gotten over his mother's death. He treasured for many years and may still have, in his office at Graceland, a lighted, fully decorated, artificial Christmas tree, souvenir of the last Christmas the family spent together. He had the tree cared for all the time he was in Germany, where the Army had put him safely away.

Elvis liked Germany and both he and his father found wives there. When his tour of duty was ended, he came out with sergeant's stripes. The whole thing was fictionally celebrated in *G.I. Blues*, a happy movie with a multi-million-dollar gross. One Elvis Presley film followed another: *Flaming Star, Wild in the Country, Blue Hawaii, Girls! Girls! Girls!, Kid Galahad, Follow that Dream, It Happened at the World's Fair, Fun in Acapulco, Viva Las Vegas, Kissin' Cousins, Roustabout, Girl Happy, Tickle Me, Harem Scarem, Frankie and Johnny, Paradise Hawaiian Style, Spinout, Easy Come, Easy Go, Double Trouble, Speedway, Clambake.* They all have two things in common: none lost money, none is contingent at any point upon reality.

But this is not quite true; there is one reality which they reflect. In *Fun in Acapulco*, which played on television recently, Elvis walks into a bar which is full of Mexicans, all of whom have good teeth. A mariachi band is playing. Elvis comes in on the chorus, and carries away the verse. Everyone applauds. The men smile and the girls turn on to him. They all think he's a hell of a fellow. One expects that at any moment he may produce a model plane and lead them out onto the lawn.

Elvis has fulfilled the American dream: he is young, rich, famous, adored. Hardly a day passes in Memphis without a politician wanting to name something after him. So far nothing has been found worthy of the honor. Presley has become a young man of whom his city and his country can be truly proud.

And he may not even know whether he misses the old days, the old Elvis. At Graceland, through the powder-white living room, past the gilded piano, there is a door that looks out onto the swimming pool. If you had been standing there on a recent afternoon, you would have seen Elvis, all alone for a change, riding his motorcycle around the pool, around and around and around.

THE PHYSICAL ELVIS

Despite his mythical status, or perhaps because of it, Elvis demonstrated an enormous appetite for food and drugs, which had a devastating effect on his health and in all likelihood, caused his death. The following section deals with one of the most controversial aspects of the King's life and times: his drug use.

THE KING IS DEAD! HANG THE DOCTOR!

███

by Stanley Booth

As the King's personal physician, Dr. George Nichopoulos, aka Dr. Nick, has become a permanent part of the Elvis Myth. In this article, Stanley Booth delves into the issues surrounding Dr. Nick's conduct in his unusual treatment of what surely must have been his most unusual patient.

As Dr. Nick and I drove out of Memphis, we passed one of the green and white traffic signs with a guitar pointing the way to Graceland and the likeness, sideburns clearly outlined, of Elvis Presley. Dr. Nick, driving a yellow Cadillac that Presley had given him, looked out at the cold spring rain. "For a long time," he said, "I didn't realize the full extent of the part I was playing in this thing."

We were going to Anniston, Alabama, to spend a few days with Dr. Nick's mother. It was the first chance we had found to talk since the Tennessee State Medical Examiners' hearing, several weeks earlier, where Dr. Nick had been charged with misprescribing to twenty patients, including Elvis Presley.

"One day Father Vieron came to my office," Dr. Nick said. The Reverend Nicholas Vieron, priest of the Greek Orthodox church attended by Dr. Nick and his family, has known Dr. Nick for twenty-five years. "He told me that he thought I was doing myself an injustice, I was doing my practice an injustice, my patients, my family, by being gone so much. That Elvis could have any doctor he wanted and didn't really need me all the time. That I shouldn't devote so much time to him. 'Why do you need to be there? Why can't it be somebody else on some of these tours that you go on?'

"I gave it some serious thought. This was in 1975. The tours had changed, they'd really gotten laborious. It used to be that after a performance, Elvis enjoyed having some of the fans who would hang around the hotel come up and talk to him, just to get a feeling of people in that area and what they thought of the show and to feed his ego some. This would take two or three hours. I thought it was good for him, because it occupied his time, kept him happier. But some of the bodyguards resented it, because it meant that they had to stay on duty. If he'd get ready for bed, go on and have his supper, then they could go on out to the bar and do their thing.

"So, somehow we got away from doing that, and it really got to be a drag, because a lot of that responsibility after the show—who's going to be with him and talk to him for two or three hours—a lot of times would fall on me. And this was day and night after night. My nights were just horrible. I would go to bed when he'd go to bed, and then he might sleep two or three hours and wake up wide awake, and I'd have to go in and try to get him back to sleep. Then he might sleep two or three more hours, or he might sleep four or five hours. But the average was he'd sleep two or three hours and wake up, two or three hours and wake up. It was hard for me to fit into that schedule. On a tour, I had very little time when I could go and do anything. If he woke up and I wasn't there, he'd go bananas. It got to the point where I was working eighteen or twenty hours a day, sleeping in cat naps.

"It was also causing me an awful hassle at the office. The other doctors were bitching about me being on a constant vacation. How could I expect to come home and want time off? I'd have to work double, I'd have to make up the night calls I missed. And yet it was the same sons of bitches that would derive the benefit from it. The money I got from Elvis went to them, went into office practice. I had a hell of a time with all this.

"So when Father Vieron came in that day, I'd already given it a lot of thought. But Elvis had problems when I didn't go and he'd carry somebody else. There were a couple of tours, one Vegas tour and maybe a couple of other tours, where the shows didn't go too well because he was oversedated. A lot of times when the other doctors would go, it would be hard for them to keep the medicine with them. He always wanted to keep something there by his bed in case

176

he'd wake up. He'd wake up and think he wasn't going back to sleep. He'd be half asleep, and he'd reach over and take whatever was there. Maybe three or four or five sleeping pills. The next day, try to get him up, no way to get him up. There were several times when he was a robot onstage. He'd done these songs so many times, a lot of people didn't realize it, but hell, he might not wake up till halfway through the show or after the show was over. Tell him things that he did, and he just wouldn't remember. After having gone through a few experiences with that, and some really bad ones, it was the consensus of the Colonel and the promoters that things were under better control when Elvis was with me than when he was with some other people. That they'd rather have me on the tours, and it got down to the fact that they weren't going to have any more tours at all if I wasn't going.

"I thought, 'Is it really my place to look at the business aspect of this relationship? Is it really my place to worry about what his promoters and business people are worried about, like, "Is he going to be able to make the next show? Are we going to have to cancel it? Is he going to be too groggy to do the show?"' It was a dilemma for me. It felt like this was going beyond the boundaries of doctoring, and yet it wasn't, because his welfare, his health, were involved, and it's hard to separate that aspect of it from the business aspect.

"But the kicker, my turn-on, was crowds. People wouldn't say, 'Don't you get tired of seeing the same damn show over and over again? How can you sit through the same songs all the time?' You don't hear half the songs. But you're watching these thousands of people who are mesmerized by this human being up there, and watching their expressions, their jumping up and down. The real feeling of accomplishment comes from knowing that he was able to do so much for so many. People would carry away something that would last them for weeks and months, for a lifetime."

But at the Medical Examiners' hearing, when asked what he would do if he ever again found himself in a situation like that of being Elvis Presley's physician, Dr. Nick said, "I'd get out of it, if I had the option."

Near Corinth, Mississippi, about a hundred miles from Memphis, we stopped for gasoline. With his fluorescent mane, olive complexion, and distinctive, rugged features, Dr. Nick is easy to recognize. It occurred to me that being in Mississippi this year with Dr. Nick could resemble being there some years ago with Dr. Martin Luther

King. Dr. Nick has received many threats of violence, and a bullet thought to have been intended for him struck a doctor who was sitting behind him at the Liberty Bowl football game in Memphis on Thanksgiving Day 1978, even before he had been accused in print and on television of killing Elvis Presley.

It had been raining off and on all morning. It would soon be eleven o'clock, but it still seemed early, like a winter morning just before sunrise. We bought soft drinks in cans and drove on, the wipers pushing up dirty trickles of mist.

Before we left Memphis, Dr. Nick had said, "Ask me anything." I asked him how he got to know Elvis Presley. He remembered the first time he treated Presley, who was at the time newly married and staying at his ranch near Walls, Mississippi. On a Saturday afternoon early in 1967, George Klein, a friend of Presley whose fiancee, a nurse, worked for Dr. Nick, called Dr. Nick to the ranch to attend Presley. "He had a movie to start Monday, and he'd been real active the last couple of days riding his horses," Dr. Nick said. "The movie was going to have a lot of action in it, and he was having a difficult time walking because of the saddle sores and blisters he had received. He thought that there might be some way that he could get an immediate cure so he could go on out there. I don't know if he thought I was a faith healer, or what."

Dr. Nick convinced Presley to postpone making the movie for a few days and helped him to notify Colonel Parker and the film company of the delay. Then Dr. Nick left, but he was called back to the ranch twice that afternoon, once to answer a question of Presley's "that he could have asked me over the telephone," and once again even though Presley "didn't have any problem. He just wanted to talk. I don't remember what the talk was about. That was the first encounter. I didn't realize at that encounter that this was the way he was. That this was going to be a way of life. But it was typical of him; throughout our relationship, there would be times that he could handle something over the telephone, but he'd rather for you to come out and talk to him about it. He'd want me to fly out to California. He'd make up some ridiculous problem. There wasn't anything wrong, he just wanted somebody else to talk to.

"Things got a lot easier for me when he moved to Memphis. After his first major illness, he felt more secure here from a medical standpoint than he did seeing different people on the west coast. His first major illness was that an acupuncturist out there was not giving him acupuncture. He'd have a syringe with with Novocain, Demerol,

178

and Cortisone that he would inject, and he'd tell Elvis this was acupuncture. We discovered this when we had to put Elvis in the hospital in '73. We almost lost him then.

"From that time till the time he died, except for a few skirmishes we had, he became very dependent on my opinion. He wouldn't feel like he was show-ready unless he was involved in a certain program. We'd start going through the routine of what we needed to do about his weight, what we needed to do to build up his endurance. We needed to be sure that he'd seen his dentist, that he'd gotten his ingrown toenails clipped so he didn't get in trouble onstage. We had to be sure we had things like a nasal douche, a little glass cup that we'd put salt water in to clean out his sinuses. We had Ace bandages and adhesive tape in case he pulled a groin muscle. He was always having trouble with a sprained ankle, and we took ankle corsets, made sure we had two or three. Sometimes he'd be on such a strict diet that somebody would go to these hotels a day or two ahead of time and prepare his special diet food for him. On a couple of tours he didn't eat anything but diet jelly. He'd get the hots about something like that, some fad. At the time, it was terrible. We wanted him to lose weight, but he's got to have the energy to perform, and it's hard to build up physical endurance without eating properly.

"Actually we had better control over his diet on the road than we did at home. At home we had the problem of everybody mothering him—scared if they don't carry up a dozen ham and biscuits, fix six eggs and a pound of bacon, that the poor little boy won't get enough to eat or else he's gonna get mad at them and they're gonna get fired because they didn't fix the usual thing. A lot of times I'd go by at mealtimes just to eat part of his food, so he wouldn't eat too much.

"When he started spending nearly all of his time here, it was a sort of a daily thing. On the way home, I'd stop by and see how he was and kill two or three hours there, then get my ass chewed out when I got home. Where had I been?"

"What made you inclined to stop by there on a daily basis?"

"He'd get his feelings hurt if I didn't. I just enjoyed talking to him. I'd get busy and say I'll go by there tomorrow instead of today, and then tomorrow I'd be busy too and still wouldn't go by there, and the next thing I knew I'd get flak, like, 'Why are you mad at Elvis?' People that he liked, he just liked to be around them, and if you weren't around him, he'd want to know why you weren't.

"We'd usually have sort of a family gathering, have supper all together and break bread. His father would be around, Priscilla was around for a while, some of the guys who were working there. Then that was put to a halt. I'm not sure whether it was Priscilla's doing or a joint thing between Priscilla and Mr. Presley. A lot of guys would go there just to freeload, and Priscilla was into this thing that she wanted some privacy with him. She didn't want to have somebody around every minute of the day. But he couldn't be satisfied unless he had five or ten people around all the time."

"How did he take Priscilla's leaving? Was he crushed by it?"

"He was hurt I think mainly because of the circumstances. That she got involved with her karate instructor, and he's the one who pushed her into that. I think he was more mad at Mike Stone than at Priscilla. He thought that they were friends and that Mike stabbed him in the back. Yet on the other hand he was gone so much of the time touring, he was with other women, and he had such a guilty conscience about being gone so much and doing so many things that he was doing, that he encouraged her to get involved with other activities and other people. That way he wouldn't feel so guilty.

"He seemed to have to have female companionship. Not on a sexual basis, just female companionship. Because he missed his mother so much—because of his not having that relationship, mother to son, he enjoyed relationships like the one with Mrs. Cocke, the nurse. It was a kind of maternal relationship."

"Did Elvis get along with his father?"

"He had a lot of respect for his father. He and his father didn't see eye to eye about a lot of business things that they did together. He kind of let his father run his business, give him something to do. Elvis was always spending more than he was taking in, and it was always driving his father crazy. If Elvis spent all the money in his bank account, he figured he could do another tour and make more.

"I remember one time that we were talking about how rough our parents had it back in the Depression, how they had a hard time making ends meet. We talked about the number of hours our parents worked, and how little they got out of it, and he told this story about his daddy. Once when they were living in Mississippi, they'd gone without food for a couple of days, and Vernon went to some grocery store or food market and stole some food, and he got caught and went to jail for several days. Elvis made me promise that I'd never say anything about that. He said, 'Nobody knows about this. I don't want anybody ever to know this, it would really hurt my daddy if people knew.' Right after Elvis died, it was in one of those damn—*Midnite,* or the *Enquirer*—a lead story, 'Elvis's Father in Jail.' That was when everybody was selling everything they could get."

"When you met Elvis, he was already depending on sleeping pills to go to sleep?"

"Since he started in the movie business, he was taking at least two or three sleeping pills, sedatives, nearly every night. Take it on down to the last few years, on the road, it was so important to him to get rest and sleep so he could be perfect for the next day. He felt like people had to travel so far and pay so much money to see his shows, he wanted everything to be perfect."

"Did the problem you had controlling the amount of medication Elvis took worsen as time went on?"

"No, it never really worsened, in the sense that there was a perpetual problem of taking more and more all the time. It was an episodic thing. There were times when he'd get by with almost nothing, times when he'd take a normal amount, other times that he'd take more—I'm talking about sleep medicines or tranquilizers—depending on what he was going through. There were times when he wanted to sit up and just read. He wouldn't take anything for sleep. He'd sit up and read for two or three days and not take any kind of medicine other than maybe a decongestant or his vitamins. This to me is not an addict.

"They talk about the importance of records of what was done, when the same person was doing the same thing day in and day out. You know this one person as well as you know yourself. You know what you've been through with him. You know if he's having a bad night, if the speakers were bad and he's upset about it, or some song didn't go off right, or the guitar player's string broke, or something created in his mind a bad show. It was always worse in his mind than it was in anybody else's. He was such a perfectionist that I would know when it was going to be hard for him to sleep and hard for me to sleep because I'd be busy all night long trying to get him to sleep. Instead of seeing him every three or four hours, I'm going to be in there every two hours. There have been many nights when I fell asleep across the foot of the bed waiting for him to go to sleep."

"He was seriously against coke, grass, things like that?"

"I don't think I ever saw anybody using drugs on the plane or in the hotel—smoking grass, snorting, or anything. He just wouldn't have it around him, especially when we were working. If he even heard of somebody that was doing something, he'd eat 'em out."

"Do you think he was happy, in the sense of being satisfied with where he had been and where he was going, when you knew him?"

"I think he was happy, up to that point, but he had greater expectations—things that he wanted to accomplish. He in no way had fulfilled his hunger for either knowledge or improving himself as a performer in films or on the stage as a singer. He had a lot that he hadn't touched.

"He had some problems with his health. His blood pressure was a little elevated. He was most of the time overweight, he had problems with his colon that contributed somewhat to his protruding abdomen, he had some liver problems we thought were related to his Tylenol intake. He had some back problems and neck problems. He was a compulsive water drinker. He had to have a gallon of ice water with him all the time. A lot of his puffiness was—he'd take in more than he could get rid of. I never could figure out why he drank so much water. It's a psychological hangup for some people. A psychiatrist could tell you about it.

"He liked the short cuts to everything. He always thought there had to be a quicker way to do everything than the logical, practical way. He was talking one time about how nice it would be if he could go to sleep for a few days and then wake up and lose all his excess weight. He said, 'Why don't you do that? Just keep me asleep for a week or two weeks or something, and let me lose some weight, and then wake me up?' I said, 'It's just not practical, Elvis. Your bowels still have to function, this has to go on, that has to go on. We can't do that.'

"So he goes out to Vegas and talks Dr. Gahnin into doing it. He was out there three weeks, kept him knocked out asleep, had him on some sort of papaya juice diet, and he came back all bloated up, he was taking in more drinking papaya juice than he was taking in on a normal diet. That really clobbered his colon. You need physical activity for your colon to function properly. His was already nonfunctioning because of his laxative abuse, and all he did was sleep for three weeks."

"Why would he abuse laxatives?"

"He abused laxatives because he stayed so constipated. A lot of things contributed to it. Finally his colon, just like a muscle that you don't use, lost its ability to contract. The normal colon is about this big around," Dr. Nick said, gesturing with his doubled fists together. "Elvis's colon was about the size of your leg. You can imagine how much stuff was in it. Whether it was gas or water or shit or whatever, it occupied space. He thought he had control over things. He thought when he'd lose control that he could regain it any time he wanted to."

"Did you try to get him to be easier on himself, more natural?"

"We talked about it many times, and he'd try something else, follow some other routine until the newness wore off, and then he'd go right back to the same old routine that he'd always done."

"Was his death totally unexpected to you? Did you have any kind of previous indication?"

"No, his death was completely unexpected. Several of us had seen Elvis close to death's door before. We always worried about it. In town, one of the aides was supposed to sleep upstairs in the room next to his in case he got up in the middle of the night, so they could go in and check on him. But unfortunately, the night of his death, the aide was Ricky Stanley, and he was drugged out on something and instead of being upstairs he was downstairs. That morning, Elvis had called down to Ricky to go get him something, he had trouble going to sleep, but they couldn't get Ricky up. Elvis's aunt and the maids had gone down to try to get Ricky up, and he's completely in another world. So Elvis called my office, eight o'clock in the morning, and I wasn't there yet. But Tish Henley, the nurse who lived at Graceland, was there, and Elvis talked to her. Tish told her husband where there were a couple of sleeping pills, to put them in an envelope and give them to Elvis's aunt, and Elvis sent his aunt over to Tish's house, and she carried them back over there to him.

"At the time when I was trying to resuscitate Elvis, in the ambulance, I was so out of it, what was going on—I should have realized that he'd been dead for several hours at that time. Except that when I got there, Joe Esposito told me that Elvis had breathed. If he had just breathed, then there might still be some hope. What had happened was that when they moved Elvis, turned him over, he sort of sighed. He had fallen straight forward like he was kneeling on the floor, but with his head down."

According to the police report, Elvis Presley was found at about 2:30 P.M. on August 16, 1977, face down on the red shag carpet of his bathroom floor, "slumped over in front of the commode. . . . his arms and legs were stiff, and there was a discoloration in his face." The bathroom adjoined Presley's bedroom in the white-columned mansion at Graceland, the thirteen-acre estate in Whitehaven, Tennessee, where he had spent most of his life since the early days of the career that had taken him out of poverty and made him the highest paid entertainer and possibly the most famous human being of his time.

A Memphis Fire Department ambulance and Dr. Nick were called. Dr. Nick arrived and boarded the ambulance as it was leaving Graceland to take Presley to Baptist Memorial Hospital, ten minutes away in Memphis. On the way there and in the emergency room,

183

cardio-pulmonary resuscitation attempts were made without effect. At 3:30 P.M., Dr. Nick pronounced Elvis Presley dead.

In the state of Tennessee, when someone is found dead, the local medical examiner must investigate. Dr. Jerry Francisco, the Shelby County (Memphis) Medical Examiner, was informed of Presley's death by Dr. Eric Muirhead, chief pathologist at Baptist Hospital. Dr. Nick had returned to Graceland and received consent for an autopsy from Elvis's father, Vernon Presley. The fact of Elvis Presley's death had been made public, and a crowd had gathered at Baptist Hospital, creating a traffic jam outside the emergency room. Francisco agreed that the autopsy should be performed at the Baptist Hospital morgue rather than across the street at the Medical Examiner's morgue.

The preliminary, or gross, autopsy was completed before eight o'clock that night. In a press conference afterwards, Dr. Francisco made the "provisional diagnosis" that Presley had died of cardiac arrhythmia: his heart had lost its regular beat and then stopped. To determine the precise cause of the attack, Francisco said, "may take several days, it may take several weeks. It may never be discovered." Francisco also said that the preliminary autopsy had revealed no evidence of drug abuse. The Medical Examiner's office reported to the Homicide Division of the Memphis Police Department that Presley had died a natural death.

A few days before, a book had appeared, titled *Elvis: What Happened?* Written by three former bodyguards of Presley and a writer for the tabloid press, the book told of Presley's desire to have his wife's lover killed, described his "fascination with human corpses," and called him "a walking drugstore." The book also told of Presley's "having a fit of the giggles" at the 1964 funeral of Memphis radio announcer Dewey Phillips, causing some people to doubt its overall accuracy, since Phillips died in 1968. Still, Presley's sudden death, coming at the same time as the allegations of his drug abuse, caused many to speculate, in spite of the Medical Examiner's statements, that he had died from a drug overdose.

On October 21, 1977, Dr. Francisco, after having reviewed Presley's complete autopsy report and other data including reports from four toxicology laboratories, issued his final opinion. Francisco said that Presley died of hypertensive heart disease resulting in cardiac arrhythmia, and that the death had not been caused by drugs. The next day, the Memphis *Commercial Appeal* carried a story listing ten drugs said to have been found in autopsy samples of Presley's blood at Bio-Science Laboratories in Van Nuys, California. The story was titled, "Near Toxic Level of Drugs Reported in Presley's Blood."

For over twenty years, Elvis Presley had been famous, but he had not been well known. The details of his private life, of passionate interest to many, were known to very few. These few—the "Memphis Mafia," employees who were friends or relatives of Presley—had surrounded him during his life, basking in the warm glow of his affection and generosity, guarding his privacy with almost total silence. *Elvis: What Happened?*, the three fired bodyguards' lament, had broken the stillness, but with Presley's death and the revelation that he had left almost his entire estate to his daughter, there were among the Mafia few indeed who did not take part in a Babel of Elvis memories. Almost everyone had a story to tell or at least a book to sell.

The books included *My Life with Elvis,* by a secretary; *A Presley Speaks,* by an uncle; *The Life of Elvis,* by a cousin; *I Called Him Babe,* by a nurse; *Elvis, We Love You Tender,* by Presley's stepmother and brothers; *Inside Elvis,* by a karate instructor; and *Elvis: Portrait of a Friend,* by one of Elvis's numerous best friends. The movies would come later.

The books told and retold the story of Elvis Aron Presley, the Depression-born son of a Mississippi sharecropper Vernon, who, with his eighth-grade education, misspelled the Biblical name Aaron on his son's birth certificate. Elvis's twin brother, Jesse Garon, born dead, was much discussed, and to it many attributed the unusual affection between Elvis and his mother, the former Gladys Smith, whose actual middle name was Love. "She worshipped that child," a friend was often quoted, "from the day he was borned to the day she died."

The little shotgun house, built by his father and grandfather, where Elvis was born; the single room where Elvis and his family first lived in Memphis; the housing project where they lived during Elvis's years as an outsider at Humes High School; all have become standard parts of the legend. So have the Crown Electric Company, where Elvis worked for forty dollars a week after his graduation from school, and the Sun Recording Company, where Elvis paid four dollars to record on an acetate disc two songs, "My Happiness" and "That's When Your Heartaches Begin," as a present for his mother. Sam Phillips, the owner of Sun, heard Elvis, gave him the chance to make a record for release, and the rest is history, the kind of history that sells.

The first Elvis Presley record was released in 1954; his first movies were released in 1957; the next year, as the career for which she alone had prepared her son was just getting started, Gladys Presley died. Though Elvis made three films a year for ten years after her death, he did not appear in public concert again for over twelve years. He kept for the rest of his life a pink Cadillac that he bought for his mother and kept for many years the tree from their last Christmas together.

There are some interesting photographs of Elvis and Gladys—one of Elvis kissing Gladys while holding a pair of jockey shorts to her bosom, another showing Elvis holding Gladys's head, a handful of her hair, looking into her eyes, curling his lip in a smile, but not a smile, an *earnest* look . . .

What must Elvis have seen, looking into Gladys's eyes? God visited Gladys Presley with the mysteries of birth and death, and the life of Elvis was the result, the realization, of her awe-filled vision. It was her image of him, idealized beyond reason, that the public—his public—accepted.

> He is dressed like a prince, the diamonds glitter, the cape waves; he is tall and athletic, and in the cunning play of lights (all that pale blue and crimson) he seems as unreal as the ghost of a Greek god, the original perfect male. Who cares if he's made up? if the lights are deceiving? if the tune of "Thus Spake Zarathustra" makes you fall for the trick? The fact remains that he *is,* that he floats through countless dreams, and that whatever he was, or wherever he is going, he is now, at this moment, the living symbol of freedom and light.
>
> —W. A. Harbinson, *The Illustrated Elvis*

Elvis was buried—after ghouls tried to steal his body from the mausoleum where it was first interred—at Graceland beside his mother. "What has died," stated one of the hundreds of editorials about the death of Elvis Presley, "is the adolescence of an entire generation. It is the memory of several million people's first intimation of freedom that was in the white hearse."

The anniversary of his death promises to become a holiday like Christmas or the Fourth of July, when each year more Elvis products are served up. One year after Presley's death, a Canadian writer, in a piece called "The Last Days of Elvis," listed eleven drugs found in Presley's body by the University of Utah Center for Human Toxicology and quoted a pharmaceutical guide regarding contraindications and the dangers of drug interactions. The story contained allegations of a conspiracy of silence including the Memphis police, the *Commercial Appeal,* and Presley's doctors, none of whom were named.

About a year later, the book *Elvis: Portrait of a Friend* was published. It was produced by an ex-employee of Presley named Marty Lacker and his wife Patsy with the help of an editor of veterinary publications. The book contained chapter titles like "The Doctor as Pusher" and "Prescription for Death" and left no doubt that the death-dealing doctor was Dr. Nick.

George Constantine Nichopoulos was born in 1927 in Ridgway, Pennsylvania. His parents, Constantine George (Gus) and Persephone Nichopoulos, both came from villages in Greece. At sixteen or seventeen, Gus came to New York City and worked as a bus boy. In 1925, on a six-month return visit to Greece, he met and became engaged to Persephone Bobotsiares. In January, 1927, after working with a cousin in a restaurant in Ridgway and saving his money, Gus married Persephone in Greece and brought her to Pennsylvania, where, in October, their son was born.

In 1928, with the help of Persephone's brother in Greenville, South Carolina, Gus started running a restaurant in Anniston, Alabama. When he retired, more than forty years later, Anniston celebrated Gus Nichopoulos Day. There are not many Greeks in Anniston, a handsome town of about 45,000 people, on rolling hills in eastern Alabama, and the Nichopoulos family was in many ways exemplary. Since Anniston has no Greek Orthodox church, the Nichopouloses regularly attended a local Episcopal church. Gus, who died in June, 1979, had been a Shriner, a 32nd Degree Mason, an Elk, a Rotarian, a State Farm Valued Customer, a greatly beloved citizen. Persephone still lives in the white frame house where she and Gus reared their son, who came to be called Nick, and his sister Vangie, six years younger.

Nick walked a few blocks to the Woodstock Grammar School and then to Anniston High School. His parents allowed him to play football only if he studied music, and there are photographs of him standing on the front lawn at home, wearing short pants, holding his violin under his chin. He is a dark, serious, little boy. From the time Nick was quite small, he worked in his parents' restaurant. He was a first-string fullback and halfback on the Anniston Bulldogs football team. He became an Eagle Scout. He couldn't decide whether he wanted to be a priest, own a restaurant, or be a doctor.

In 1946, Nick graduated from high school and joined the Army, which put him to work for eighteen months in a hospital in Munich. When he got out of the Army, he entered the pre-medical course of study at the University of the South in Sewannee, Tennessee, graduating in 1951. That fall, he entered medical school at Vanderbilt University but left after one year to study for a Ph.D. at the University of Tennessee in Memphis. While going to school in Memphis, Nick met Edna Sanidas, whose father also owned a restaurant. Nick and Edna were married in 1954. The next year, their son Dean was born. In 1956, Nick went back to Vanderbilt Medical School, and in 1959 he graduated with an M.D. degree.

In 1963, after serving his internship at St. Thomas's Hospital in Nashville, Dr. Nick brought his family (now there were also two daughters, Chrissie and Elaine) to Memphis and started working in a partnership called the Medical Group. He had worked there four years when he met Elvis Presley.

After he pronounced Presley dead, Dr. Nick stepped out of the emergency room into the room where Presley employees Billy Smith, Joe Esposito, Charlie Hodge, David Stanley, and Al Strada were waiting. Billy, Presley's cousin, had been as close to Presley as any friend Presley ever had. "Dr. Nick started to speak to me and he couldn't talk," Billy told me at the Medical Examiner's hearing. "That's how much Elvis's death hurt him. Dr. Nick loved Elvis. He did everything he could to help Elvis. How can anyone think Dr. Nick would hurt Elvis?"

Ten days after Presley died, the *Commercial Appeal* published an exclusive interview with Dr. Nick. In it Dr. Nick said, "I spent many hours a day thinking about different things to do to help him . . . It's going to take some time to lose some of those thoughts and I think everybody's lost . . . We keep thinking that he's here someplace. It's hard to accept."

A year later, Dr. Nick talked briefly about Presley on a local television show, but otherwise he said no more. While friends and relatives of Presley, no longer on his payroll, signed contracts for books and movies, Dr. Nick, almost alone, kept silent. Priscilla did not speak, but she had been left well off by the divorce. There had been around Elvis Presley a hierarchy of silence, and Dr. Nick was very near its top.

Meanwhile the Elvis memories, finding an audience, began to resemble the music business, sometimes described as a self-devouring organism that vomits itself back up. In New York City, Charles Thompson, a Memphis-born television producer, was reading about Presley. *20/20,* the ABC television news program for which

Thompson works, was new and had to have some hot stories if it were to compete with its opposite number, CBS television's popular *Sixty Minutes*.

Thompson had worked as a field producer at CBS, leaving when ABC beckoned partly because he and CBS had not seen eye to eye on a story about Billy Carter's supposed violations of federal energy regulations. Thompson had wanted to do the story, but the powers at CBS had thought there was no story, or none worth putting on television. It wasn't Thompson's first such disagreement with an employer. In 1970, when Thompson was working for a television station in Jacksonville, Florida, he did a story on pollution that accused the station itself of polluting and got himself fired.

Thompson had graduated from high school in Memphis, studied journalism at Memphis State University, worked at the *Commercial Appeal*. In the middle nineteen-sixties, Thompson did two tours with the Navy in Vietnam, serving as liaison with the Marines, calling in air strikes. He saw a good bit of action, and when he came back home had troubling nightmares of mangled bodies, burning children, and seemed to see the dark side of issues.

When Thompson learned, the day it happened, that Presley had died, he expected, so he said later, that "by night they would say it was drugs." He was surprised when they didn't, but when he read the Elvis books, among them Marty Lacker's accusation of Dr. Nick, his expectations were at last fulfilled. Thompson's reportorial sixth sense told him, This is Good, this is a Story. King Dies of Drugs from Court Physician is *Good*. The King Is Dead! Hang the Doctor! Still, Thompson admits that he came to Memphis for "a top-to-bottom investigation on Elvis" with nothing more than a hunch. "I didn't have *anything*," he has said.

In looking through the Presley file at the *Commercial Appeal*, Thompson came upon the Bio-Science toxicology report which had been quoted in the "Near Toxic" story. Thompson says that he showed the report to a doctor at Baptist Hospital, who said, according to Thompson, "Jesus Christ, it's obvious. The son of a bitch died of drugs."

At least one doctor at Baptist Hospital says that Thompson showed him the report. He told Thompson that in his opinion, Presley's drug problems had been primarily with laxatives and steroids. The doctor advised Thompson, should he have questions about Presley and drugs, to call Dr. Nick. In July of 1979, by his own count, Thompson tried three times to question Dr. Nick, who would not

189

talk to him. Armed with that fact and the toxicology report, Thompson told the doctor who had suggested that he talk with Dr. Nick: "I think I've got a homicide."

Thompson brought James Cole, his brother-in-law, who like Thompson had worked for the *Commercial Appeal,* in to help research the story. Cole learned that a routine audit of prescription records in Memphis was going to be conducted by the Tennessee Healing Arts Board and telephoned the Board's office in Nashville, the state capitol, "to find out what was going on." He talked with Jack Fosbinder, the Board's chief investigator, who told him that an audit of the first six months of 1979 was in progress. Cole told Fosbinder, so he has said, "We suspect Elvis may have died a drug death. Maybe you should look back into 1977."

In August of 1979, after Charles Thompson's three failed attempts, Thompson's New York colleague, ABC television news performer Geraldo Rivera, came to Memphis to talk to Dr. Nick and failed six times. The *20/20* team had no such trouble talking with the state Health Related Boards' investigators. On September 6, Thompson, Rivera, and Cole came to Dr. Nick's office after a meeting with the investigators, who had told them that Dr. Nick was about to have formal charges brought against him. On this, his seventh try, Rivera succeeded.

In the interview, Rivera asked Dr. Nick various questions about Presley, leading up to the big charge: "The records indicate that, especially in the last year of his life, you prescribed certain medications to Elvis Presley in quite extraordinarily large amounts. Why?"

"I can't comment on that," Dr. Nick said, "and I don't believe that it's true."

"The records we have, Doctor—and I'll say this as gently as I possibly can—indicate that from January 20, 1977 until August 16, 1977, the day he died, you prescribed to Elvis Presley, and the prescriptions were all signed by you—over five thousand schedule two narcotics and/or amphetamines. That comes out to something like twenty-five per day."

"I don't believe that."

"Well, is it something that you'd like to refresh your recollection on, or is it something you deny?"

"I deny it."

While all this television business was happening, I knew nothing about it. I had my own worries. They led me to Dr. Nick. On March 24, 1978, I had fallen from a granite boulder on a north Georgia mountainside, breaking my back, bruising my brain, learning more about pain than I cared to know, finally developing a drug dependence only slightly less grand than that of the late (and no wonder) Howard Hughes.

After a year I tried to stop taking the drugs my doctors prescribed. I tried twice and twice had *grand mal* seizures, full-scale epileptic brain-fries, blind, rigid, foaming at the mouth, fighting off unseen enemies, screaming, turning into a hydrophobic wolf. A neurologist tested the electrical impulses emanating from my head, told me they were abnormal, and advised me to have my brain injected with radioactive dyes, which I declined to do.

About this time, I was at a friend's house and happened to mention that one night soon I was going to be dead before I was asleep. My friend, a patient of Dr. Nick, advised me to make an appointment to see him. On July 5, 1979, I told Dr. Nick all the above.

"This is interesting," he said, "but what do you want from me?"

"I've been given this room full of drugs," I said. "I don't want to go on taking drugs and I don't want to be epileptic. What are my chances?"

I filled a bottle, bled, coughed, inhaled, exhaled, held still, bent over, dressed, and waited, sitting on a metal table in a cold little room. Dr. Nick came in, shook his head and said, "Looks like you've lived through a nightmare."

I've survived, I thought. It was news to me. Dr. Nick sent me into his office to wait for him. On the wall beside the door there was a large photograph of Elvis Presley, signed and with the inscription, "To my good friend and physician, Dr. Nick." The office was thick with things that were obviously gifts from Dr. Nick's patients. Among them were many small frog figures, so that the office looked like a Greek gift shop being taken over by swamp life.

Dr. Nick came in. We talked about diet and exercise. I hadn't drunk a glass of milk in years and hadn't exercised since running for a helicopter at Altamont. I mentioned that I had worried my family, and Dr. Nick said he would call and reassure them. He gave me no drugs, sent me to no specialists, but he let me know that I was going to be all right. I was a bit dazed, trying to get used to the idea.

On September 13, 1979, the ABC television network presented the *20/20* show titled, "The Elvis Cover-Up." One of its most characteristic touches was an interview with a retired pharmacist from Baptist Hospital, where Presley's stepbrother, Ricky Stanley, picked up a prescription of Dilaudid for Presley from Dr. Nick the night before Presley died. The pharmacist said that having sold Presley the fatal dose weighed mightily on his conscience. No one bothered to tell the man that no Dilaudid was found in Presley's body.

After "The Elvis Cover-Up" was shown, I saw Dr. Nick socially two or three times. He had been presented with a list of charges by the Board of Medical Examiners—not pathologists but doctors who, to help maintain professional standards in the state, examine the practices of other doctors—but he didn't seem terribly worried. I kept telling him that if there was another side to his story, he'd better tell it.

"The lawyers don't want the Medical Examiners to get the idea that we want to try this thing in the media," Dr. Nick said. His accusers had no such reluctance.

On January 13, 1980, Dr. Nick's hearing before the Board of Medical Examiners began. Because of Tennessee's "sunshine law" requiring that proceedings of this kind be held in public, the hearing took place in the five hundred-seat City Council Chamber in the Memphis City Hall. Public interest in the case was believed to be great, and attendance was expected to be heavy, but it had not been thought necessary to hire the Mid-South Coliseum.

Whatever else the hearing may have been, it was a physical ordeal. The weather was seasonable for January, cold and sometimes wet. The sessions lasted from Monday through Saturday, starting each morning at 8:30 and adjourning usually ten hours later.

The audience, smaller than anticipated, averaged about a hundred people. It included Elvis fans of many descriptions, from old ladies in E.P. baseball jackets to a pair of effete, young, male twins who had come from Ohio to see Dr. Nick swing. Also in the audience were Dr. Nick's immediate family and many of his friends, among them his priest, Fr. Vieron. There were reporters, print and broadcast, local and international, and the photographers were like ants at a picnic. ABC television's numerous lights, cameras, sound recorders, and crew, including Charles Thompson, James Cole, and Geraldo Rivera, were a constant presence, on hand to take postcards of the hanging.

Behind the Chamber's wooden railing sat the state's attorneys and interrogators, Dr. Nick and his lawyers, the five Medical Examiners, and the referee, or hearing officer. Police in plain clothes stood against the rear wall, staring at the audience.

The start of the hearing was delayed by the glare of the television lights. As the Medical Examiners shielded their eyes, the hearing officer insisted that the lights be moved: "We're going to be here for a week, and we can't have everybody go blind."

192

The charges against Dr. Nick were: first, gross incompetence, ignorance, or negligence; second, unprofessional, dishonorable, or unethical conduct; and last, dispensing, prescribing, or distributing controlled substances "not in good faith" to relieve suffering or to effect a cure. On the first day of the hearing, the state's attorneys called ten of the twenty patients of Dr. Nick listed in the charges to testify. Tennessee has no statute protecting the privacy of exchanges between doctors and patients; Dr. Nick's patients had to testify or go to jail. The patients—among them an investment banker, a record promoter, a landscape gardener, a restaurant cashier, a doctor's wife, and two ex-heroin addicts—were questioned before the public and the press concerning their most intimate problems, which included alcoholism, insomnia, divorces, abortions, obesity, cancer, and bereavement. After each patient's name in the charges there was a list of prescriptions from Dr. Nick, each list showing a decline in the amount of medicine prescribed. Contrary to the usual pattern in malpractice by over-prescribing, Dr. Nick made no charges for prescriptions and saw his patients often, giving frequent physical examinations. Every patient who testified praised Dr. Nick.

After the patients had testified, the state called Dr. Nick himself to the witness stand. His lawyers insisted that he should not be forced to testify for his accusers; that he would take the stand and submit to cross-examination, but as a part of his defense, not the state's prosecution. The hearing officer took the position that the hearing was not a criminal court, and that no statute prevented the state from calling Dr. Nick. The first day ended with Dr. Nick's lawyers intending to seek a ruling on the question in chancery court.

But on Tuesday, the second morning of the hearing, the defense relented. A chancery court suit might take years; so Dr. Nick, wanting to settle the larger issue, took the stand. He discussed his prescribing practices, talking about each patient in the charges. Count number fifteen, Elvis Presley, received the most attention.

Responding to questions from the state's attorneys and the Medical Examiners, Dr. Nick described the progress of his relationship with Elvis Presley. He told of his efforts, with the help of Memphis alcohol and drug abuse specialists David Knott and Robert Fink, to save Presley's life and restore him to health after his nearly fatal overmedication by the fake acupuncturist in Los Angeles. After Presley learned that Drs. Knott and Fink, who had been called in by Dr. Nick, were psychiatrists, he refused to see them.

Keeping drugs from other doctors away from Presley was a continuing problem, Dr. Nick said. He attempted to consult with other doctors who saw Presley, "trying to get some continuity in his treatment," but Presley, without telling Dr. Nick, saw doctors in other towns, some of whom sent him medications by mail. Presley employees were instructed by Dr. Nick to turn over to him all medicines from other doctors so they could be discarded or replaced with placebos.

In 1973, following Presley's "acupuncture" treatments, Dr. Nick said, "I thought he was addicted. I do not think he was an addict." Although he made extensive use of placebos in treating Presley, Dr. Nick said, Presley "had a lot of chronic problems . . . degenerative changes in his back and in his neck . . . that you couldn't treat with placebos." Still, there were times when Presley could not be persuaded to take any medicine at all. Before a Las Vegas opening that Presley considered most important, he refused to take even antihistamines, saying, "This one's on my own."

On "The Elvis Cover-Up" program, Geraldo Rivera had accused Dr. Nick of prescribing five thousand drug doses to Presley in the last six months of his life. The Board's revised list of charges made it twelve thousand drug doses in Presley's last eighteen months. Perhaps the single most important point in Dr. Nick's testimony was his statement that the drugs were not for Presley alone but for the entire company, as many as a hundred people, who worked with Presley on the road. Presley appeared with a male vocal group, a female vocal group, a rock and roll rhythm section, and a large orchestra with strings. Dr. Nick, after learning from a few tours' experience what he was likely to need, came prepared to care for everyone from the equipment handlers to the flute player, including the record producer with the transplanted kidney.

"I carried three suitcases full of equipment," Dr. Nick said. "I had everything you'd expect to find in a pharmacy—all kinds of antibiotics for people who were allergic to penicillin, I had expectorants, I had decongestants, I had just what you can imagine you'd use every day in your office. I carried a laryngoscope, I carried some long forceps in case he aspirated, I carried these little bags for breathing, I carried suture material, adhesive tapes, splints, everything that you would expect a first aid stand to have someplace, plus what a physician would have."

The suitcases were kept locked and in Dr. Nick's possession. When he was away, a nurse kept the suitcases and dispensed drugs only according to Dr. Nick's specific orders. Twice during the last six months of Presley's life, Dr. Nick's car was broken into, and drugs for tours were stolen and had to be replaced. The Memphis Police Department had been notified both times.

The drugs were bought in Elvis Presley's name because otherwise Vernon Presley, his son's bookkeeper, wouldn't have paid for them. A long-time acquaintance of the Presleys has said, "Vernon would cringe when somebody spent money. You could actually see him cringe." Dr. Nick wrote prescriptions in his own name before a vacation trip to Hawaii with Presley, some of his associates, and their families because "I knew that if I had charged him for the medication that I was taking along, his father would blow a gasket." Presley gave away fleets of cars, fortunes in jewelry, houses, hundreds of thousands of dollars, but his father could never stop pinching pennies. It was all part of the unique dilemma of being Elvis Presley's physician.

Dr. Nick acknowledged the absence of written records of Presley's treatment, saying, "The reason some of these things were not kept in the office and some of them were not written down someplace else was that people were always perusing his charts. It was difficult to have any confidentiality with his records, whether it be in my office or the hospital or wherever. I certainly wish now there were records. That would certainly be helpful. I think that if he hadn't died, the end result as far as his improvement during this period of time is answer in itself."

Dr. Nick said that he had received with Presley's help a bank loan to pay for his house, and that he was repaying the loan with interest. He had never charged Presley for visits to Graceland. Speaking of the *per diem* fee Presley paid the Medical Group for Dr. Nick's time on the road, Dr. Nick said, with cold understatement, "It's difficult to pay for services that last eighteen hours a day."

"My objective was to help him," Dr. Nick said, "because I thought that he helped so many people—not physically helped people, or monetarily helped people, but—to keep him rolling and to go to his show and see what reward all these people got out of his shows—it's an experience that you'd have to go through, it's like having your first child."

In spite of Dr. Nick's talk of rewards, the state's firm assumption seemed to be that Presley was, as Geraldo Rivera had suggested on *20/20,* "just another victim of self-destructive over-indulgence" who had "followed in the melancholy rock and roll tradition of Janis Joplin, Jimi Hendrix, and Jim Morrison." The idea of Presley following in the tradition of Joplin, Hendrix, and Morrison is one that defies chronology, sociology, musical history, and common sense, but neither "The Elvis Cover-Up" nor the hearing was designed for the purpose of furthering common sense.

On the second day of Dr. Nick's testimony, there was a bomb threat. Dr. Nick's years of effort to help Elvis Presley had earned him threats and accusations, cost him many thousands of dollars in legal fees, and brought shame to his family. "You killed Elvis!" people driving past Dr. Nick's house yell at him, or his wife, or his children.

The Medical Examiners didn't appear to sleep while he testified, as some of them seemed to do at times when other witnesses testified, but Dr. Nick's testimony had the effect of making the witnesses for his defense anti-climactic.

The first of the three doctors who were the state's expert witnesses was a pharmacologist who had never treated any patients; the next said that drug addiction should be cured in two or three weeks, and the last testified that he refused to treat patients who smoke. None of them had any firsthand knowledge of Dr. Nick's patients. Each of the experts perused the charges, saying where he thought Dr. Nick had gone wrong.

Then the defense began. It was late Wednesday afternoon. The party had been going on for three days. There was time this afternoon for the defense to present only two witnesses. Both were ex-girl friends, one of Presley, the other of Presley employee Joe Esposito. Both were good-looking, and though they verified important matters—Dr. Nick's treating Presley with placebos and intercepting drugs from other physicians—they seemed to be comic relief.

On Thursday the defense called sixteen witnesses. Among them were doctors, members of the Presley staff, Health Related Boards investigators, a coordinator from the Medical Group, and a patient. The patient, a department store executive, told how Dr. Nick helped him overcome the addiction to narcotics he developed while hospitalized for months following an automobile accident. The coordinator testified that the Medical Group had fifteen thousand patients, thirty-five hundred of whom were Dr. Nick's. The twenty patients listed in the charges represented one half of one per cent of Dr. Nick's patients. By choosing at random and comparing six of Dr. Nick's full working days at the Medical Group, it was shown that he prescribed controlled substances to only one out of every twenty patients.

The Health Boards investigators admitted meeting and exchanging information with the *20/20* staff before the charges were delivered to Dr. Nick. One of the investigators testified that the recommendation for the state to file charges against Dr. Nick was made without consulting even one licensed physician. Later, James Cole would admit that he gave the investigators the tip on the Presley "drug death" in the first place.

The Presley employees testified that Dr. Nick cared for all the people who worked with Presley, not just Presley himself. They verified that Dr. Nick gave Presley no medication in an uncontrolled manner, that Presley at times left town to get drugs he couldn't get from Dr. Nick, and that Dr. Nick had instructed them to intercept all drugs coming to Presley from other sources.

Dr. Nick had testified that in 1975 he had arranged for a nurse to live at Graceland "so we could better control and dispense medications." The nurse, Tish Henley, testified that she often took away from Presley medications that did not come from Dr. Nick, and that she sometimes, under Dr. Nick's orders, gave Presley placebos. At no time was dispensing drugs left up to her discretion. After tours, she said, copious amounts of leftover drugs were destroyed.

Some doctors to whom Dr. Nick had referred Presley testified that Presley had showed no signs of narcotic or hypnotic abuse. Dr. Nick was said to show a remarkable interest in patients he referred to other doctors. Dr. Lawrence Wruble, a gastro-intestinal specialist, said that at one point he and Dr. Nick had told Presley to stop doing two shows a night in Las Vegas or they would stop being his doctors, and from that time Presley did only one show. Wruble spoke highly of Dr. Nick's care and concern for Presley. Dr. Walter Hoffman, a cardiologist at the Medical Group who has known Dr. Nick since he was a graduate student, said that Dr. Nick has a unique quality of being "more empathetic than any practitioner I have ever known."

During the hearing's first days, the audience had been divided between Dr. Nick's supporters and detractors. By Thursday afternoon, the troops were tired. Some of us had settled down to being simply reporters with battle fatigue. When the hearing stopped for the day, I had a question for Geraldo Rivera, who was sitting amidst his crew beside an empty seat in the Chamber. After "The Elvis Cover-Up" story, Rivera had done a follow-up in which he said that if Presley's autopsy report were released, the information in it—

"'. . . would send at least one doctor to jail,' yeah, I remember," he said.

"Were you talking about Dr. Nick?"

"Yes, but I didn't understand. I didn't know about all his other patients. I didn't believe Elvis was getting drugs in the mail. I'm beginning to see another side of Dr. Nick. He was definitely no scriptwriter. He made mistakes with Elvis, but I think he's a good man. I just feel bad about his family. I see them looking at me, and I can tell what they're thinking."

"It's obvious they hate your guts," I said pleasantly.

On Friday morning, Dr. Jerry Francisco, the Shelby County Medical Examiner, took the stand and repeated his conclusion that Elvis Presley died of cardiac arrhythmia brought on by high blood pressure and hardening of the arteries. Presley's heart had been twice the normal size for a man of his age and weight, his coronary arteries had been occluded, and he had a long history of hypertension.

Dr. Francisco said that the amounts of drugs in Presley's body did not, even in combination, indicate the likelihood of a drug overdose. The circumstances of his death also indicated that drugs were not at fault. If Presley had taken an oral overdose of drugs shortly after 8:00 A.M. on the day he died, he might have been in a coma by 2:30 P.M., the time he was found, but he would hardly have been stiff and blue, dead for several hours. The typical victim of an oral drug overdose dies a lingering death in a comfortable position, not pitched forward on a bathroom floor.

Dr. Francisco was followed by Dr. Bryan Finkle, an English toxicologist, now Director of the University of Utah Center for Human Toxicology. Dr. Finkle, who has worked in forensic toxicology at New Scotland Yard, testified that the concentration of drugs found in Presley's body was not sufficient to affect Presley's respiration or the amount of oxygen in his blood. Dr. Finkle said that although he had been quoted on "The Elvis Cover-Up" program as saying that drugs may have made "a significant contribution" to Presley's death, he had not been informed, when a member of the *20/20* staff telephoned him, that he was being interviewed or that his statements "would be construed in such a fashion."

Dr. David Stafford, a toxicologist at the University of Tennessee Center for the Health Sciences, said that he had tested Presley's autopsy samples for thirty or forty drugs and had found nothing consistent with the diagnosis of a toxic drug dose.

The last defense witness, not a doctor, testified that Dr. Nick, by caring enough to seek an opinion from a second surgeon, had saved the leg of his old maid aunt.

After lunch on the last day of testimony, portions of "The Elvis Cover-Up" program were shown to the Examiners, and the lawyers for both sides made their closing statements. The defense said that the collaboration between ABC television and the state's investigators concerning Dr. Nick "allowed the media to punish him unmercifully—without any justice—from September 13, 1979, through January 18, 1980." It was pointed out that Dr. Nick profited from no one's drug dependence, that even patients who took advantage of his trust to obtain drugs had, over the length of time in the charges, been withdrawn from drugs. Dr. Nick had at times, for a variety of reasons, kept incomplete records, but that situation had been corrected before the charges against him had been filed. Dr. Nick, the defense said, "is a fine, compassionate, sensitive physician" who said to his patients, "'I'm going to help you. Remember I'm not perfect, but I'm going to exercise my judgment,' and that is what he did."

The prosecution said that regardless of Dr. Nick's good faith and intentions, we live by standards, and Dr. Nick had violated the standards of his profession. He prescribed too many drugs, in inappropriate amounts, for too long a time. The Examiners were called on to revoke Dr. Nick's license "until such time as the Board can be sure that his practice is consistent with good medical practice."

On Saturday, January 19, 1980, the Board voted on the charges against Dr. Nick. Of the first two charges—gross incompetence, ignorance, or negligence; unprofessional, dishonorable, or unethical conduct—the Board unanimously found Dr. Nick innocent. But he had violated certain relatively minor regulations. He had discarded, without keeping records, drugs whose fate must be recorded. He had also allowed certain patients to receive too many drugs, even though in the long run he had withdrawn his patients from drugs. The Medical Examiners found Dr. Nick guilty on ten of the charges of improper prescribing in the complaint.

One patient to whom Dr. Nick was found guilty of improper prescribing was Elvis Presley. However, one of the Examiners said that the guilty verdict was only for faulty record-keeping and commented that he had found "no evidence that Dr. Nichopoulos was negligent in his care of this patient." Another of the Examiners said, "I think we have to consider the extraordinary circumstances under which he was operating. He was under the gun. I think he exercised considerable restraint in trying to control the medication. There are very extenuating circumstances, and I certainly agree that there was no involvement by Dr. Nichopoulos in any way in the death of Elvis Presley."

The Board suspended for three months Dr. Nick's license to practice medicine, and he was put on probation for three years. The sentence, after "The Elvis Cover-Up" allegations, seemed to some people absurdly light. To others, it seemed unnecessary chastistement of an excellent physician.

At least, Dr. Nick thought, he had run the gauntlet, it was over. He had told what he had done, the Medical Examiners had made their ruling, and it was a relief to have the matter settled at last.

So Dr. Nick thought until he realized that the matter wasn't settled at all. No one had gone to great lengths in reporting the testimonies of Dr. Nick or the witnesses for his defense, but in March, 1980, *Memphis,* the local slick-paper magazine, published an article called "The Elvis Expose: How ABC Unearthed the Story, the *Real* Story." It said that Dr. Nick at the hearing had described Presley as a "ranting drug addict." Without irony it quoted Charles Thompson as saying, "They haven't said anything that disagrees with our first report ('The Elvis Cover-Up') last September." It took no notice at all of the testimonies that the drugs Dr. Nick ordered in Presley's name were not all for him. This is not surprising, since the writer of the article, Tom Martin, a Federal Express employee who writes in his spare time, attended the hearing only on Friday and Saturday mornings and was not present to hear any of the other testimony. It was as if Dr. Nick and the other defense witnesses had never spoken.

The article described matter-of-factly Thompson's personal inclination to believe that Presley died of drugs, James Cole's telling the Health Related Boards' chief investigator about Presley's "drug death," and presented the ABC team in much the same light that they, in one of their various motions to have Presley's autopsy report released, had shone on themselves: ". . . we think that we behaved toward Dr. Nick with the highest courtesy and consideration. We are confident of the truth, honesty, and fairness of what we have broadcast and believe there are no grounds for charges of unfairness, false portrayal, prejudice, exploitation, or sensationalism."

Except for the Greek newspapers, calendars, and bric-a-brac, Dr. Nick's mother's house in Anniston, Alabama, is exactly like my grandparents' old house in south Georgia, down to the African violets in the breakfast room. Being there is like my idea of Greek Orthodox Heaven: nobody forces you to do anything, and there is so much delicious Greek food that you don't have a chance to get hungry.

We arrived on a Friday; Saturday afternoon we took a break from Mrs. Nichopoulos's wonderful cooking and ate sandwiches from Anniston's Golden Rule Barbecue. After lunch we went to the Highland Cemetery to visit the grave of Dr. Nick's father, who died in June, 1979, before "The Elvis Cover-Up" scandal broke. Dr. Nick had told me that one strong bond between him and Presley had been the respect they both had for their parents. I was sure Dr. Nick was glad that his father hadn't died suffering with him the humiliations of the last year.

Later, in the late afternoon at the house Dr. Nick had left to find his future, he reminisced further about the days when he had spent so much time taking care of Presley: "I'd spend two or three hours a night taking care of his eyes. Elvis had glaucoma. He used to dye his eyelashes, and I think that may have had something to do with it. And he'd get these bacterial infections on his skin—you know, Elvis didn't bathe."

"No," I said, "I didn't."

"He'd take sponge baths, but he wouldn't get wet. He took these pills from Sweden that are supposed to purify your body."

I remembered Billy Smith, Presley's cousin, testifying at the hearing that on the morning of the day Presley died, after they had played racquetball, Presley had cleaned up, and Smith had dried his hair. It was nothing unusual to Presley or to Billy Smith, but I wondered whether many people would ever understand the strange life of Elvis Presley, the sharecropper's millionaire son, the Pauper who became the Prince. He may have been uneducated, he may have been uncultured, his favorite food may have been Pepsi-Cola and peanut butter and mashed banana sandwiches, but he was still the King, and the King didn't open jars, or dry his own hair, or take baths like the common folk. Not even Mick Jagger keeps a cousin on hand to dry his hair, but Mick Jagger's mother never worshiped him or cared for him as lovingly as Gladys Presley had cared for Elvis.

Elvis had been the King, and now he was just a dead junkie, and to many people, the fault was all Dr. Nick's.

The next day, when we left for Memphis, it was misting in Anniston, with just a few raindrops. As we drove, the rain stopped, the afternoon grew warm, the sky was clear and blue. We opened the sun roof and listened to tapes of Elvis singing. Then the weather changed again, and by the time we reached Memphis it was cold, and the sky was overcast, gray and bleak.

On May 16, 1980, the Shelby County Grand Jury indicted Dr. Nick on fourteen counts of illegally prescribing. Each count is punishable by a prison sentence of two to ten years and a fine of as much as $20,000. Dr. Nick is free on bond and awaiting trial.

A local official, a friend of both Presley and Dr. Nick, told me, "They'll ruin him. It's not that they *could* do it; they're *doing* it. The prosecutors don't care what good he's done. They'll put him in jail if they can, and if they can't, they'll bankrupt him. They'll get him on a technicality or keep indicting him on slightly different charges until they break him."

"It's like a medieval ducking trail by ordeal," said a doctor who also knew both Presley and Dr. Nick. "If Dr. Nick drowns, he's innocent."

THE FUN YEARS

■

by Albert Goldman

The following is a chapter from Albert Goldman's controversial biography
Elvis. *His gritty and detailed portrait of Elvis as a drug-crazed sex fiend
shocked and enraged countless fans and critics and undoubtedly will continue
to do so.*

When Elvis Presley returned to America after his years in the
army, he was a changed man. His mother's death, his father's remar-
riage, his own sufferings in the service, as well as the prolonged
interruption of his career and his anxiety about its revival, had
eroded the great self-confidence he displayed in his early years. His
first TV appearances, particularly his queer showing on *Frank Sinatra's Welcome Home Party for Elvis Presley,* testify to the change in the
man that underlay the change in the image.

The first signal that something important had happened to Elvis
was sexual. The Elvis who had appeared in the Dorsey, Berle, and
Sullivan shows, who had starred in *Loving You* and *Jailhouse Rock,*
was butch. He had a chunky, clunky aura as he stood four-square
before the camera and blasted out his soul with total indifference to
public opinion. Even his legendary shyness, cunningly exploited in
those scenes in *Loving You* in which he plays opposite the sophisticated sexy Lisbeth Scott (who has a wonderful time toying with this

202

enfant terrible, alternatively seducing and mocking him), comes across as a kind of strength, the coiled-up power of a boy whose manner warns: "Don't get me started or you'll be sorry!"

After the army, Elvis appears very delicate and vulnerable, as if he were recovering from major surgery. He wrings his hands as he talks. He has become extremely wary. With his preposterous Little Richard conk, his limp wrist, girlish grin and wobbly knees, which now turn out instead of in, he looks outrageously gay. When he confronts the much smaller but more masculine Sinatra, Elvis's body language flashes, "I surrender, dear."

Nor is this sudden loss of his former virility merely a deceiving appeareance: It is paralleled by many more significant changes in Elvis's manner of conducting his life and career. Instead of partying with his peers, the young actors and actresses of the Jimmy Dean clique, Elvis locks himself up now in a house with six stooges and never goes out to play. Instead of falling in love with a beautiful film star, he herds hundreds of anonymous groupies through his bedroom. Instead of being basically a sympathetic character with some ugly traits, he becomes an arrogant punk who closely resembles the character he portrayed in *Jailhouse Rock.* As for his career, he abandons all control over it and submits himself completely to the machinations of Colonel Parker and his cronies in Hollywood. All these changes attest to a profound metamorphosis in the character of Elvis Presley. Though they first become manifest when he is discharged from the service, we must search for their source in that deadly wound Elvis suffered when his mother died.

Gladys was as much the source of Elvis's self-confidence as she was the cause of his extreme dependency. She was also his only confidante and his moral governor. Once Gladys died, Elvis found himself desperately alone and naked. His first instinct was to retreat from the world and wall himself round with people who were devoted to him, body and soul. His second impulse was to drown his sorrows in an endless round of parties and games that would keep him perpetually distracted from his real state of mind. His ultimate resolution was the most fateful: It was to sever the link between his past and present by totally inverting the relations between his life and his image. Instead of being an innocent and naive kid who impersonated publicly a wild and orgiastic figure, Elvis would now play in public the All-American Boy, while off camera he indulged himself in an endless debauch of sex and drugs.

The inception of Elvis's new life-style was a two-week furlough that he took in the summer of 1959 in Paris with several of his boys.

203

Settling down at the posh Hotel Prince de Galles, he swiftly discovered an old-time nightclub on the Champs Elysées called the Lido, which had a chorus line bearing the legendary title, The Bluebelle Girls; in other words, the descendants of those turn-of-the-century chorus girls who had swarmed over the original Prince de Galles or Prince of Wales, the future Edward VII. Elvis, wearing for the first time his elegant dress blues and looking like a latter-day version of the Student Prince, instinctively fell into the pattern of his renowned and royal predecessor. Every night he ate dinner at the club; then, after the first show, he swept up the entire chorus line and carried it back to his hotel, where they partied extravagantly, until the phone would ring and the manager of the club would beg Elvis to return the girls so that the supper show could commence. Elvis would witness that show as well and afterward return to his suite with the girls, with whom he toyed till dawn.

When Elvis returned to Hollywood, he showed no sign at first of adopting this orgiastic pattern so close to home. He was still a little inhibited, still exhibiting traces of his mother's morality. Then, one night, a random occurrence initiated a chain of events that concluded with Elvis finding himself once again in a position to indulge his appetite for orgiastic parties. The decisive event was being asked to leave the Beverly Wilshire Hotel for precisely the same reasons that had led to Elvis's expulsions from hotels in Germany: extreme rowdiness.

On this particular night Elvis and the Guys were involved in one of those childish games in which he spent so much of his spare time in the early years: a water battle with squirt guns. What made the battle characteristic of Elvis was the violence with which he drove it, that innate violence that always made him take everything to the limits and beyond, never feeling that he had had enough of any game until limbs broke and blood flowed and screams of pain accompanied the pleasure.

First, one of the boys had slipped on the wet kitchen floor and gashed himself deeply on a broken bottle. Then, Red, Joe and Sonny grabbed Elvis and threw him on the floor. As Sonny held Elvis's legs and Joe his midriff, Red rubbed his palm back and forth over Elvis's nose, driving him completely crazy. When he had brought Elvis to the ultimate peak of rage, Red shouted, "Let go!" At that moment, Red and Sonny leaped up and ran for their lives. Joe, seeking to do the same, slipped and fell on the floor. Instantly, Elvis was on top of him, kicking him like a log as he rolled across the floor. Then, Elvis seized a guitar and, swinging it like an axe, hit Joe a stunning blow on the elbow. Joe screamed in pain and lay there watching his arm inflate like a balloon. Red and Sonny, who had circled back, realized now that the fight had gotten out of hand. They made a dash through a fire escape door and took off down the hall with Elvis in hot pursuit. When Elvis saw he couldn't catch up, he threw the guitar with all his might after the fleeing figures.

At that moment, an elderly lady who lived on the floor opened her door. Just as she was about to step out into the hall—whoosh!—a guitar flew by her nose, almost hitting her. Jumping back, she slammed the door and picked up the phone to call the manager. A few minutes later this worthy was upstairs demanding to know what was going on and inspecting with a horror-struck countenance the damage to the rooms. Next day, Elvis and his boys were asked to leave.

The Colonel decided at this point that it didn't make sense to confine these rambunctious boys to a hotel. They needed more space to stretch out—and they needed to be kept away from the little old ladies of this world. The solution to the problem was obviously a good-sized private house in some secluded spot. A short search turned up a unique residence in Bel Air that had formerly belonged to Ali Khan. It was a doughnut-shaped structure, ringed around a fifty-foot patio edged with shrubbery. Situated on the side of a winding hillside road called Perugia Way, the house overlooks the greens of the Bel Air Country Club. Carpeted with thick white shag, filled with expensive California-style furnishings and staffed by a black cook and houseman, this flying saucer was the perfect playpen for a wealthy young playboy. Soon it became legendary as the headquarters of the Memphis Mafia, the most intently partying group of bachelors in the history of Hollywood.

The Presley parties are invariably depicted as tedious get-togethers whose only singularity lay in the disproportion of men to women. Though literally thousands of young women were guests at these parties over the years, those who got beyond the formalities would not have been eager to recount their adventures for the benefit of the press. Nor would any reporter or editor who valued his job in Hollywood have been willing to publish such scandalous tales. Though one hears a great deal about the outrageous violations of privacy suffered by the stars, if we are to judge by the example of Elvis Presley, in his day one of Hollywood's greatest stars—and one about whose private life curiosity reached unprecedented proportions—there are few limits to what a celebrity can do and escape exposure in the film colony.

The parties, which swiftly became the focal point of Elvis's life, would commence every night after supper, at about ten. The basic idea was to fill the house with attractive young women who had been especially selected to conform to Elvis's exacting criteria. Elvis's tastes in women were just as fixed and unvarying as his tastes in food. It was only natural that a man who could subsist for six months at a time on a steady diet of burnt bacon, mashed potatoes, sauerkraut and sliced tomatoes would want one and only one kind of girl. The interesting question is: What is the female equivalent of the aforesaid diet?

Elvis liked small, kittenish girls who were built to his ideal proportions. They were to be no higher than five feet two and weigh no more than one hundred ten pounds. The prime areas of erotic interest were the ass and legs. Hair coloring, complexion, facial features were not important, though beauty was, naturally, desirable. What was critical was that the girls be as young as possible, certainly no older than eighteen, and that they be not too far removed from the condition of virginity. Married women were out of the question and a woman who had borne a child was a complete turn-off for Elvis Presley. As for clothing, Elvis liked to see a pretty girl dressed all in white. When she undressed, he was hoping to see that she wore white underpants. White panties were Elvis's erotic fetish.

All the Guys became at Elvis's urging quite accomplished procurers. Their readiest source of supply was the studios where Elvis worked. Most Presley pictures had party scenes that called for as many as a score of pretty young girls. The moment the first call for such extras went out, the Guys were busy among the applicants, like cooks in the morning market, making their selections for the Boss. After the studios, there were many other sources for Presley chicks: talent agencies, nightclubs, theaters, stores—Hollywood is full of pretty young girls, many of whom will do anything to advance their careers. All one of the boys had to do was mention that Elvis Presley was having a party that night at his home in Bel Air and the prey was winging toward the net.

Once the parties became an institution in Hollywood, a lot of girls started trying to crash the gate. On a typical evening, the whole street and the parking area before the house would be swarming with scores of young women who behaved very much like the crowd seeking admission to a popular discotheque. Like the patrons of a disco, they came in all sorts of costumes from simple cotton dresses to sweater and pants outfits to stylish frocks topped with fur jackets. Parking their cars along this once-quiet street, they would stand, lean or sit all over the property, chattering and gossiping and looking each other over carefully. The focus of everyone's attention was the heavy brown door to the house, which was opened from time to time by one of the boys, who would admit the girls he knew and tell the others to "try later." As at Studio 54, the decision as to how many and which girls to admit depended entirely on the demands of the party going on inside the house. Some of the more determined girls would remain standing in front of the door until two in the morning.

Once a girl was admitted to the house, she would be ushered about with great politeness by one of Elvis's man mountains. Her first impression was invariably one of great luxury and style. As you entered the house, for example, you could look straight through the foyer to the patio, which was romantically illuminated at night and filled with the splashing of a fountain at its center, where a statue emptied endless jugs from its shoulder. Sinking into the deep-pile carpet and following her guide as he turned to the left, she would enter first the living room, which was dominated by a fireplace above which hung a painting, actually a painted photograph, of Elvis, Gladys and Vernon in front of Graceland. The next room around the circle was the den; here the parties were always held. Loud rock music would be playing from an illuminated jukebox filled with Elvis's favorite records; a wet bar at the far side of the room would be piled high with refreshments suitable for a Sweet Sixteen party—soft drinks, potato chips, pretzels, cookies—and in the middle of the room a TV set, whose back was concealed by a folding mirrored-glass screen, would be playing with its sound turned off.

Facing the television, on a huge built-in sofa, the King would be enthroned with his feet up on a cocktail table. Flanked by a couple of his men and surrounded by a bevy of young women, he would be watching TV. No matter who arrived, even if she were the most famous or beautiful star in Hollywood, Elvis would not rise to greet her. "Get her coat . . . find out what she wants to drink." With such bossman orders, Elvis would beckon Tuesday Weld, Joan Blackman or Connie Stevens into the circle around him.

Elvis had a very sarcastic and vulgar sense of humor that would emerge when he settled down at ease and removed the phony mask of southern gentlemanliness that he wore in public. From years of listening to the local wits in his hometown—that type of southern joker who responds to every situation with a proverbial line and a snap of his extended fore- and midfinger—Elvis had developed quite a patter of Memphis jive. As the aspiring young extras and starlets sitting at his feet constantly looked back and forth from the silent video screen to the immaculately groomed and carefully dressed star, they would treated to an endless stream of witticisms.

Watching Jerry Lewis caper on the screen, Elvis would sneer and drawl: "That's about as funny as a turd in a punch bowl." Or perhaps he'd say "as funny as a Smitty on a hearse." (A Smitty was the Memphis name for a device designed to make a teenager's motor roar.) Every time Elvis got off one of these gags, the Guys would roar with laughter. Their response would encourage Elvis to continue his bizarre commentary, which soon blurred into what must have sounded to the girls like a code:

"He's stronger than Tarzan's armpits. . . . He's been there since Hitler was a corporal. . . . He's wilder than a peach orchard boar. . . . Tell 'em where the cow et the cabbage! . . . That cat's lower than a whale. . . . Cute as a bug's ear. . . . So uptight you couldn't drive a straw up his ass with a ten-pound sledge!" Watching two guys back off from each other in a western, Elvis might crack: "He's scared and the other's *glad* of it!" Or if someone said, "If only so and so were to happen, then . . ." Elvis might retort scornfully, "If my aunt had nuts, she'd be my uncle!" The moment the laugh died, the whole party would fall silent and return to the basic activity, which was watching Elvis watch TV.

As there were perhaps forty or fifty girls in the house and only eight men, it would have been natural for the Guys to start hitting on some of these chicks. This was a practice that was sternly forbidden. Elvis considered any such advances highly improper, an act of *lèse majesté,* until he had exercised his prerogative to make the first choice. Allowing Elvis what was called "the pick of the litter" was an obligatory act of deference. To behave differently would be to invite some terrible explosion.

Elvis's temper and his overbearing manner had gotten much worse during his years in the army. The boys who had known Elvis for long said that the army had made him "mean." His ugly traits were greatly exaggerated by the presence of women. When girls were around, Elvis felt obliged to play the big shot, the boss. He would put one of his little cigars in his mouth, his Hav-a-Tampa Jewels or Rum Crooks, and hold it there a moment. If one of the boys didn't jump up and give him a light, Elvis would explode. "Goddamn it to hell! Am I gonna sit here all night like this, or is one of you lardasses gonna gimme a light?" That sort of behavior was supposed to impress the girls. Elvis didn't stop at just being overbearing. Sometimes he would humiliate his men so grossly that even these faithful flunkies were compelled to rebel.

Sonny West recalls a night when Tuesday Weld came to visit Elvis, bringing along a very attractive friend named Kay. As Elvis and Tuesday got deep into conversation, Sonny started promoting Kay, while preparing a drink at the bar. In the middle of Sonny's pitch, Elvis pops up suddenly between them, stares provocatively at the girl and says admiringly, "You're really pretty!" Then, he flits off to continue talking to Tuesday. Sonny resumes his efforts to woo the young woman and is starting to make progress when Elvis appears again, gives the girl one of his patented heavy-lidded stares and murmurs, "My man!" Just as Sonny is recovering from this fresh intrusion, Elvis swings back for a third pass at the target. This time, he gives the girl a little peck. When she doesn't object, he kisses her firmly on the mouth. She kisses him back. Sonny gives up in disgust and retreats to the other side of the room, where Alan Fortas and Gene Smith are watching the scene.

"He's smooth as silk," rumbles the admiring Fortas. "Yeah, he shot me right outta the saddle," concedes Sonny. Gene leans in confidingly at this point and, nodding his head toward the two women, he says: "Sonny, if you had your pick, which would you take?" Sonny replies without hesitating, "Tuesday—she's got some body on her!"

Elvis, who is always scanning the room, spots Gene and Sonny with their heads together. Instantly, he assumes that they're bad-mouthing him. Jumping up and walking over to the boys, he says, "What the hell are you two whispering about?" Sonny is dumb-founded. He's too embarrassed to repeat the conversation. His confusion confirms Elvis in his conviction that he was the topic of conversation. "If you don't tell me," he warns Sonny, "you're in big trouble." Sonny, exasperated, hurt, angry, looks at Elvis and exclaims: "Man, you have *changed!* I *quit!*"

In a flash, Elvis grabs a Coke bottle. Sonny barks, "You're not gonna hit me with no goddamn bottle!" Elvis backs down and relinquishes the bottle, but he can't control his anger. The moment Sonny starts walking out of the room, Elvis plants himself in the big boy's path. "You're not quittin'," snarls Elvis, "'cause you're *fired!*" "Call it anything you want!" shouts Sonny. "I'm gettin' outta here!" Nobody could talk back to Elvis and get away with it. Flashing red, Elvis swings from the floor and hits Sonny squarely on the jaw.

If Elvis had been on a movie set, where he was always punching guys out, Sonny would have flown halfway across the room, smashed into a wall and come sliding down onto the floor like a stiff. Instead, he simply twisted his head with the blow and then turned back to stare at Elvis in shock and pain. As the tears started coming to his eyes, Sonny gasped: "I never thought you would hit me, Elvis!" Then, he turned and left the room.

It was the only time in Sonny's life that he didn't return a punch. If he had struck back, he would have knocked Elvis into the middle of next week. It never crossed Sonny's mind, though, to defend himself. Nobody ever hit Elvis. Though he abused them, humiliated them, hit them with his hands or kicked them with his feet or even drew weapons and threatened their lives, *nobody ever struck back at Elvis Presley.*

Sonny went to his room and packed. He called his girl and told her that he had quit his job. When he came to the front door, he found Elvis standing there alone. "You got any money, Sonny?" he asked. Sonny said he was okay. Elvis handed him a check, which he had had one of the boys draw. "Can one of the Guys take you someplace?" asked Elvis. "No, I called a cab," replied Sonny. When he pulled away from the house in the cab, Sonny saw Elvis standing in the doorway.

The other disaster that could ruin a party was a girl who dared to talk back or challenge the "Boss." Elvis had strict rules for feminine behavior. As long as women deferred to him, he was gallant to them. If, though, they "got down on his level," as the Guys put it, then Elvis was freed of the obligation to play the gentleman's role and was allowed to teach the girl her "lesson." One night, for example, the sophisticated daughter of a famous movie star came up to the house. Appalled, most likely, by the court of the Hillbilly King, she made the mistake of getting into an argument with Elvis. Galvanized by a terrible flash of rage, he leaped to his feet, seized the young woman by the hair, dragged her stumbling head over heels across a marble coffee table and into the next room, where he planted a very vigorous kick in her ass and ordered one of the boys to throw her out in the street.

Another night, while he was entertaining a young actress, Elvis got so enraged at something she said that he picked up a watermelon and threw it at her, hitting her a mighty thump on the ass. Throwing things like a hysterical woman was one of Elvis's more dangerous habits. One night, many years later, when he was having supper, Joanie Esposito, Joe Esposito's wife, said something that infuriated Elvis. Instinctively, he hurled the knife that was in his hand straight at her face. If Sonny West hadn't flung up his hand to block the knife, Elvis might have knocked out one of Joanie's eyes.

In 1963, Elvis did inflict a disfiguring injury on a young woman in this manner. She had demanded that one of the boys playing pool with Elvis move his car so that she could leave the party. Elvis was so enraged by the woman's insistence that he hurled his pool cue at her, striking her on the breast. The cue paralyzed a nerve in the breast, causing it to sag permanently. The most interesting fact about the story is that no compensation was offered the woman and none was sought. As always, Elvis walked away from his misdeed without any apology or desire to make amends. As far as he was concerned, the fault was all the woman's who had provoked him.

Assuming the party was not spoiled by some "fool" or some "bitch," the final phase, about 2:00 A.M., after the late movie, would consist of the "slipaway." Elvis would finally rise and make his way past the bar to the adjoining room, which was the master bedroom. This was the signal for all the Guys to take off the wraps. Like beggars at a royal feast, they were free now to enjoy the scraps. All the girls who had been passed over by the boss were fair game. If the boys could score, they carried their girls off to the other bedrooms. If they were failures, as was poor Lamar so often, they were delegated "night duty," which meant they lay down fully clothed in the living room to snatch some sleep before they were roused before dawn to carry home Elvis's girls.

"Girls" is the word because Elvis almost invariably retreated to his bedroom with two or three young women in tow. His preference for groups rather than for one-to-one encounters had hardened now into a habit. Most young men with such tastes are assumed to be prodigiously virile studs whose sexual appetites are so enormous that they cannot be satisfied by a single woman. This was certainly not the case with Elvis Presley. Generally speaking, he never had normal sexual relations with these girls. The reason? Elvis was a pervert, a voyeur.

What he sought as his erotic goal was a group of girls who would agree to strip down to their panties and wrestle with each other while Elvis stared out his eyes with a rocklike hard-on pressing up against his underwear. He accounted for this obsession by recalling an incident from his childhood: a moment when he had seen two little girls tumbling together on the ground with their dresses rising to show their crotches. In fact, with the fine focus characteristic of his kind, what Elvis described as his ultimate fulfillment was not the sight of the girls or even the crotch but the vision of black pubic hairs protruding around the edges of white panties. Out of all the sexual excitements in the world, this one teasing image represented the ultimate in arousal to Elvis Presley.

The panties were not just a tease, like the fan dancer's fan or the bubble-dancer's bubble. They were also a protective shield. Elvis could not tolerate the sight of a completely naked woman. If one of the gorgeous showgirls or actresses who filled his bed night after night were to disrobe completely in his presence, he would protest: "You have a beautiful body but I would feel better if you put something on." Elvis was just as loath to show his own body. As a rule no woman ever saw him undressed. His shyness focused on his penis, which he called "Little Elvis" and went to great lengths to hide. Instead of pissing in a urinal, for example, he would always go inside a stall, like a woman. He was not modest but ashamed. Like most country boys of his time, he was uncircumcised. A sensitive adolescent at heart, he saw his beauty disfigured by an ugly hillbilly pecker.

He complained also that when he engaged in intercourse, the foreskin, pulled back and forth in the grip of the vulva, would fray and tear, sometimes emerging bloody. There was an obvious solution to this vexing problem, but Elvis could not bear the thought of a knife cutting into Little Elvis. (Vernon was much braver. In his last years, when he became involved with a young woman, he submitted to the dread operation in the hopes of reviving his deadened dick. Perhaps that was what he meant when he once told Elvis: "You'll never be half the man your father was.")

In addition to being an orgiast and a voyeur, Elvis was also a lifelong masturbator. Every month one of the boys would be dispatched to those extended newsstands off Hollywood Boulevard to buy the boss all the latest "fuck books." The man might spend as much as forty dollars obtaining enough material to satisfy his master's appetites. Elvis would take a different magazine to bed with him every night and jerk off looking at the pictures.

If Elvis became sufficiently aroused by the spectacle of the girls wrestling, he might go down on a girl or dry hump her. Gene Smith recalls Elvis changing clothes after a date and looking like he sprayed his Jockey briefs full of whipped cream. If Elvis were feeling particularly daring, he might allow a girl to jack him off. One of the familiar tales of the Presley circle concerns the night Elvis went to bed with a famous Hollywood sex kitten. When this aggressive young woman—who had slept with half the men in the movie industry in the effort to advance her career and who had learned through that ordeal as much about men as any old hooker—divined where Elvis was at, she not only jerked him off with great skill but, when he ejaculated, she caught the semen in her hand and rubbed it all over her face like cold cream. Those two moves put Elvis completely in her hands.

If Elvis did have intercourse with an unfamiliar woman, he would never allow himself to ejaculate inside her. He was terrified of an unwanted pregnancy or a paternity suit—or so he averred. The Guys interpreted his anxiety as the product of some episode in his early years, when Elvis had gotten a girl pregnant. An exaggerated fear of knocking a girl up, however, is also characteristic of young men, especially adolescents, who suffer from sexual anxiety and are afflicted with other sexual problems, like premature ejaculation. Though Elvis Presley was always girl crazy, this obsession can sort very well in a young man with a deep underlying fear of women, of marriage and of begetting children: all signs of masculine maturity.

These sexual predilections explain also how it was possible to go through so many women without ever once contracting venereal disease, the universal fate of the swinger. That Elvis escaped all the dangers of the game was owing not to good luck but to the most extraordinary self-control: a lock-hold on his sexual behavior that must have been powered by uncontrollable sexual phobias.

Looking at half-naked girls grappling with each other or jerking off while ogling the centerfold of *Playboy* were by no means the full extent of Elvis's voyeurism. As soon as he moved into the house on Perugia Way, he made provision for indulging his letch on the sly. He observed that the closet of his bedroom had a common wall with an adjacent bedroom. In the neighboring room, the wall was lined with floor-to-ceiling bookcases. Elvis and the boys removed a portion of the wall between the shelves and installed in the space a two way mirror. Now, they were in a position to view everything that happened in the bedroom from a secure location in the closet. The only problem was that normally nothing was happening in this room. Elvis quickly solved this problem by ordering a couple of the boys to get girls into the room and have intercourse with them while he watched with the other Guys.

This sport had only one danger: With so many guys crowded in the closet chortling and whispering about the "action" they were watching, there was the distinct possibility that the sound would carry through the wall and alarm one of the girls who was being exploited. Again, Elvis came up with the answer: Whenever one of the boys was about to get down with a girl, he must make a point of turning on the radio in the room. He could say that it was more romantic that way or there was such beautiful music on such and such a station. Girls would go for crap like that and the sound of music would mask the mumbling behind the wall. Eventually, however, it was agreed by all hands that the little window they had opened was not adequate for the proper enjoyment of the show. In the next house the boys occupied, they installed a mirror that was as big as a suburban picture window.

Elvis's second house in Bel Air offered a total change in atmosphere from his first. Instead of an architectural whimsy, redolent of a sheik's tent, the new mansion on Bellagio Road was a classic 1920s movie star's mansion. Modeled upon an Italian villa of the Renaissance, the exterior boasted statues in niches, a steeply landscaped terrace and an old-fashioned swimming pool off to one side. The decor was baronial: a grand entrance foyer paved with marble and adorned with a sculptured fountain, an imposing open staircase to the second floor, an ornamented fireplace rivaling that at Pickfair.

People who have special appetites are very quick to spot novel ways of fulfilling them. No sooner had Elvis moved into this old mansion than he noticed a peculiarity in the dressing room that adjoined the swimming pool. Rather than waste time describing the vision that inspired this latest and grandest peephole, let's examine the finished product.

First, you have to imagine the King and his lusty men bidding a momentary good-bye to a covey of beautiful young women whom they have urged to change into bathing suits so they can all enjoy a dip in the pool. The moment the girls go clattering down the steps beside the pool to the dressing room cut into the sloping hillside, Elvis and the Guys dash around to the side of the pool where there is a little louvered door at ground level that looks like a utility hatch. Opening this door, they crawl into a dark low space which they have laboriously excavated by hand from the foundation of the building. The dirt floor is covered with blankets because there is no room to stand. One wall of the room is a huge plate-glass window that looks directly into the women's side of the locker room. To the women, of course, this huge window appears as a mirror.

Lying on their sides and trying to breathe as shallowly as possible—heavy breathing fogs up the glass and spoils the view—Elvis and the Guys fall to studying the girls as they undress. Though it is often said that voyeurism is a scaredy-cat perversion, this new four-by-eight-foot window was, as the boys discovered, a great test of nerve. As long as the girls removed their clothes or made their toilettes from a distance, the peek effect was perfect. When a girl walked up close to the mirror and stared directly into it—while holding up, perhaps, one breast and then the other for examination—the more timid guys, like Lamar, would be terrified. It was hard to believe that this girl, just inches from your face, couldn't see you lurking there in the darkness.

Eventually, Elvis got anxious about this king-sized window and ordered it removed for transport to Graceland. There the boys sought high and low for a suitable place to install it, but the old house was very ill-suited to such contrivances. Finally, the mirror was stored in the attic, along with many other abandoned toys and devices for recreation. Meantime, the house on Bellagio Road received a new inhabitant who was destined to compensate Elvis for the loss of his old toy by sending the girls screaming around the house every night in a manner that was positively provoking.

Scatter was the ideal frat house mascot. A forty-pound, three-foot-tall chimpanzee, he had been trained by his first owner, a Memphis cartoonist who used him on his local TV show, to wear clothes, drink whiskey and raise hell with women. When Elvis first brought the beast out to Hollywood, he was enthralled with his antics. Elvis would treat him like a baby, carrying him around on his shoulders, showing him off for company and even changing his diapers. What tickled the Guys most about Scatter was the fact that he was so damn horny. Just let a girl step in the house and old Scatter would be hot on her tail. He would lift up her skirt and stick his head up toward her crotch. He would follow women to the bathroom or try to get inside while they were on the toilet. He would also chug-a-lug a few drinks at the bar, and then turn around on his stool and start whacking off in some girl's face.

Elvis was always thinking of fresh ways to use Scatter as a device for driving people crazy. He would have the chimp dressed up in his cute little middy suit and tennis sneakers. Then Scatter would be enthroned in the back seat of the Rolls-Royce Silver Cloud and driven about by one of the Guys wearing a chauffeur's cap. That night Elvis would scream with laughter as the chauffeur, generally Alan Fortas (who has a somewhat simian build), would recount the stories of how this motorist almost ran off the road staring at the chimp or how that old lady looked shocked or a cop on a corner did a triple-take as the car went by. What really bugged Elvis was that they could never find one of those trick cars, like they have in the circus, that can be driven from the rear by a hidden operator, while the ape sits up front turning the driving wheel. To roll down Hollywood Boulevard of an afternoon with Scatter at the wheel of a big costly Cad, casting Ubangi-lipped looks to right and left with a driver's cap on his head and his long funky fingers wrapped around the wheel—oh, God! Wouldn't that be heaven!

Short of the ultimate thrill, however, there were lots of other tricks you could play with the chimp. One of his most celebrated exploits was the time he got loose at the Goldwyn Studio and climbed up the drainpipe to the second-floor office of the boss, Sam Goldwyn. When Scatter came swinging through the window, Goldwyn's secretary screamed in horror and fled from the room. Scatter kept on going until he was in the Big Man's private office. Before the astonished movie mogul could utter a word, the ape had leaped on his desk and was cavorting among his contracts, pub shots and pictures of his grandchildren. Fortunately, the animal was well diapered so he couldn't do anything totally outrageous.

The best fun Elvis had with Scatter was always some stunt involving sex. It was as if Elvis were using the beast as his proxy, as the perpetrator of all those crazy sex pranks that he would have liked to have played but didn't dare. There was a little stripper, for example, who was a regular at the Presley parties. Elvis would entice this girl to come up to the house; then he would persuade her to get down on the floor and wrestle with Scatter. She wasn't much bigger than the chimp. If you didn't look too carefully, you would swear that the horny ape and the hot little chick were getting it on. That killed Elvis.

Another time when one of the Guys went upstairs with a young woman who was an aspiring songwriter, Elvis got Alan and Sonny to slip Scatter into the bedroom after the couple had started balling. Scatter outdid himself on this occasion, eliciting from the girl some of the loudest and most piercing screams of his entire career. Sad to say, the Guy was so outraged that he picked up the beast and hurled it about ten feet down the hall.

Poor Scatter! He soon suffered the fate of all Master Elvis's other toys. He lost his charm and was shipped back to Graceland, where he was installed at the back of the house in an air-conditioned cage. Neglected after all the attention he had received for years, he pined and dropped and turned vicious. Late in the sixties, he bit a maid who was feeding him. Two days later, he was found dead in his cage.

About the time Scatter died, the steady advance of electronic technology provided Elvis at last with the perfect toy for a man who was an orgiast, a voyeur and a masturbator. It was the first Sony videotape machine for "home use." Once Elvis got this machine, he was enabled to seek relief from the monotonous routine of acting in films by getting behind the camera and functioning as a director. He soon found some cooperative young women and set to work turning out an endless series of bedroom follies. What he was after in these films was what he had been after all his life in sexual encounters: a chance to watch while beautiful young women grappled with each other and simulated lesbian sex. Naturally, no one but Elvis was permitted to view these hot reels. Once, however, one of the Guys found the opportunity while Elvis was away from home to view some of the forbidden footage. What he saw shocked him profoundly. The two girls, naked save for white panties, who flashed on the screen were intimates of the Presley circle. They were giggling and wrestling and taking turns diving into each other's crotches. At the end of the film, Elvis suddenly popped up before the camera with a full erection and a very smooth jack-off motion.

Eventually, Elvis made a great auto-da-fé of his private videotapes. Yet some of the tapes escaped destruction. They are allegedly being peddled in Los Angeles at high but not exorbitant prices: five hundred dollars for a five-minute quickie and fifteen hundred dollars for a long-playing orgy. In that great black market that consists of bootleg Elvis records, TV out-takes and other scraps from the cutting room floor, these home movies must be the most sought-after items. As biographical documents, their value is also enormous. What could be more basic to the study of a great sex hero than a filmed record of his sex life? Perhaps that is what Elvis meant when he said that some day he wanted to write an autobiography entitled *Through My Eyes.*

Eventually, Elvis discovered a curious genre of soft-core pornography that appealed to him even more than his private videotapes or the hardcore Danish stuff that came on the American market in the late sixties. As this type of pornography pleased him more than any other, we are justified in regarding it as the clue to his basic sexual fantasies. Interestingly, these were of a highly hostile yet not conventionally sadistic variety. The films Elvis relished are called in the trade "cat films." Their subject is women fighting. The typical film opens up on a shot of a couple of tough, coarse-looking broads sitting on a sofa and having a violent quarrel about a man. Suddenly, one of the women reaches over and slaps the other's face. The second woman retaliates by grabbing her opponent's hair. Then, they really get into it like a couple of cats, screaming and clawing. Inevitably, their legs go up and the viewer gets a flash of their panties, which was the part that most excited Elvis. By the end of the film, the women have reduced each other to wrecks.

As it's impossible to watch two people fighting without identifying with one or the other, these films offered Elvis Presley the opportunity to experience vicariously the pleasure of beating up a woman while at the same time protecting himself psychologically from the shame or guilt that would have been entailed if it were a man with whom he was identifying, a man who would obviously be a stand-in for himself. That Elvis's basic relations with women took the form of push and shove is clear from his behavior during his teenage pajama parties. That there was an angry hard-on behind these little games we should not have known but for the cat films. His excitement in viewing these films suggests not just his fundamental hostility toward women, which is pretty clear from his stage act, but also the source of that hostility.

The typical woman in a cat film is a hefty, older woman of a type that Elvis could easily have associated unconsciously with Gladys. If this sounds improbable, bear in mind that nothing is more basic to a mama's boy than deeply buried hatred for the woman who has enslaved him and frustrated him and imprisoned him psychologically for a lifetime, including all the years after her death. To take a celebrated example of this phenomenon, the literary world's most famous mama's boy is Marcel Proust. After his beloved mother's death, Proust donated the furniture of her house to a male brothel he patronized, and he arranged to have rats, animals that he associated with his mother, trapped, caged and then impaled on long needles while the illustrious author watched their death agonies with fascination. It would be a very naive observer of the relations between Elvis and his mother who did not suspect that beneath the surface of obsessive love there did not lurk, as a kind of psychic counterpoise, an opposite and no less powerful emotion, which finding no outlet in relation to its proper object had necessarily to be worked off on some substitute target.

One cannot relinquish the subject of Elvis Presley's sex life without considering the widespread suspicion that he was latently or actively homosexual. Perhaps the most perceptive way of viewing this issue is to stress the fact that Elvis was above all an adolescent sex hero. Adolescence is a period of imperfect sexual differentiation, a fact that was once proclaimed by our very language: the word "girl," meaning in the vocabulary of Chaucer a young person of either sex. What Elvis projected through this epoch-making act was not just the enormous sexual excitement of puberty but its androgynous quality. Much of Elvis's power over young girls came not just from the fact that he embodied their erotic fantasies but that he likewise projected frankly feminine traits with which they could identify. This AC/DC quality became in time characteristic of rock stars in general, commencing with Mick Jagger and the Beatles (who had such ravishingly girlish falsettos) and going on to include Jim Morrison, David Bowie, Elton John and many figures of the punk pantheon. It's also worth noting that "punk" in its original meaning, as prison jargon, signifies the passive homosexual lover of a tough, typically older convict. (The subliminal meaning of Elvis's role in *Jailhouse Rock* is that he is Hunk Houghton's punk.) Indeed, it has always been a tradition of the rock world that the young studs who are the stars should have managers who are homosexuals and who "style" their boys in accordance with their own ideas of what is cute and kissy. Such was Brian Epstein with his punk, John Lennon. Though Elvis was not homosexual, his image was "rough trade."

When you dig down to the sexual roots of an Elvis Presley, you detect a profound sexual ambivalence. Elvis plays the strutting, overbearing macho in public; but in private he loves nothing better than to rough-house with teenage girls with whom he exchanges beauty secrets. His basic erotic image is a crotch covered with white panties and showing a bit of pubic hair—an image no different essentially from male to female. Eventually, as we shall see, he staged orgies in which the star was an aggressive lesbian who not only wrestled with other girls but dominated them sexually, just as an aggressive man might dominate a submissive woman—while Elvis got his kicks by watching. The inference is irresistible, therefore, that at bottom Elvis identified with a strong, aggressive woman rather than a strong, aggressive man. As his mother was precisely such a woman, threatening to bash in his father's head with a heavy skillet while calling him "steercottled," it makes sense to conclude that Elvis was his mother's son in sex as in everything else.

The flourishing of Elvis's perverse sex appetites in the sixties is paralleled by the sudden escalation in his consumption of drugs during this period. Prior to 1960, there is no evidence that Elvis was habituated to any sort of drug but benzedrine or amphetamine compounds. These pep pills had been part of his life since his first days on the road, and his use of them had continued straight through the period of his service in the army. Once he got back to Hollywood, however, he suddenly began consuming a whole range of drugs that produce narcotic and hypnotic as well as stimulant effects. How he first discovered and familiarized himself with these drugs is unknown; but, considering his later practices, it is very likely that he owed his introduction to these dangerous pills to the doctors to whom he complained of his inability to sleep.

Elvis was always an insomniac; now, under the stress of making movies and overstimulated by the constant use of Dexies to get him going after nights with little or no sleep, he must have quickly approached that manic, round-the-clock sleeplessness that is typical of the speed freak. To one who believed that the solution to any problem of mind or body was a drug, nothing would appear more logical as an antidote to uppers than the use of downers. So, it is not surprising to learn that as soon as he became established at the Beverly Wilshire, he came to an understanding with a druggist at the Milton F. Kveis Pharmacy in the lobby. This man began to supply Elvis with unlimited quantities of drugs without prescriptions at the price of one dollar a pill.

Soon Elvis was buying seven or eight thousand dollars' worth of pills at a time and paying for them by check. No less great than the volume was the variety of drugs that Elvis and the Guys began to experiment with at this time. They were into Dexamyl, Quaalude, Percodan, Demerol, Seconal, Tuinal, Valium, Nembutal and Placidyl. One of the reasons there were so many different drugs is that Elvis discovered in this period what was to be, along with the Bible, his favorite book for the rest of his life: *The Physician's Desk Reference*. This bulky volume, with its exhaustive enumeration of every pill in the pharmacopoeia, accompanied by a full clinical description and a very tantalizing picture, became Elvis's favorite study. With his prodigious appetite for pleasure and his quick, retentive memory, he had both the motive and the means to explore all the resources of the legal drug world. So obsessed did he become with this theme that he even made a sly public confession. In an interview in *Parade* in November 1962, he is quoted as saying, "I've got very simple pleasures. I like to read medical books. One time in high school I thought I'd become a doctor."

Elvis's way of playing doctor soon produced near-fatal results. Gene Smith recalls driving back to Memphis at this time in a Dodge mobile home that Elvis used instead of taking the train. Smith was so overstimulated from being awake for three days and two nights on speed that he could not fall asleep. He complained to Elvis, who quickly upped with the cure: a 100-milligram dose of Demerol, a synthetic opiate. Smith popped the tiny white pill and waited for the anticipated relief. For another forty-five minutes he stared at the highway with his mind still racing the van. Finally, good old Doc Presley gave the insomniac another 100-milligram pill. Smith retired to the back of the van and lay down on one of the beds.

An hour later, Billy Smith, who was riding up front with Elvis, who was driving, went to the rear to check on his cousin. He found Gene laid out cold, barely breathing and with a heartbeat so slow and faint that it seemed he must be near death. Billy had only recently been the one who discovered Junior Smith dead in his bed, probably the victim of an overdose. Now he realized that he was witnessing the same thing happening all over again. He rushed into the front of the van and warned Elvis. "Pull off!" he shouted, "I think there's something the matter with Gene!" "What do you mean?" demanded Elvis, steering the bulky vehicle off the road. "I shouted as loud as I could in his ear, and he didn't move a muscle," cried Billy. "I think he's dead!"

Bringing the van to a lumbering, lunging halt, Elvis scrambled into the back compartment, followed by Billy and Joe Esposito. After trying everything they knew to rouse the comatose drug victim, they hauled him out onto the highway. It was a freezing cold night. The unconscious man was clad only in jeans and a T-shirt. For three hours, the boys took turns dragging the limp body back and forth along the road. Finally, the drugged boy began to come out of his stupor. If Gene Smith had been allowed to lie in his bunk a couple of hours more, Elvis and the Guys would have brought him home dead.

This was by no means the only time when Elvis's reckless dispensing of drugs nearly caused a death among his friends and lovers. Like all heavy drug users, Elvis was keen on having everyone around him doing what he was doing. This pattern of imposing his addictions on his entourage is readily explainable by two of his basic character traits. On the one hand, he loved to wield authority, to be the boss and force others to do his bidding. On the other hand, like most drug abusers, he suffered from a vague sense of guilt that he sought to dissipate by telling himself that everyone was doing just what he was doing. Polypharmacy loves company.

It needs no saying that in forcing all this junk down other people's throats, Elvis was imposing on their trust and naivete. Ultimately, what he was doing was exploiting their attachment to him to gather them into the embrace of his own profoundly self-destructive lifestyle. Though Elvis figures in the Myth as a refulgent Lifegiver, a priestly figure dressed in white and dispensing love and vitality to the world gathered at his feet, in his private aspect he was precisely the opposite figure to that projected by the Myth. No less glamorous, possibly even more beautiful and seductive than the Lifegiver, in his private world he was that ancient figure of Hebrew legend, the *Maloch HaMovet*—the Angel of Death.

It is worth remarking in this connection that though Elvis turned square in his public image after the army years, he never altered in the direction of his private development, which carried him swiftly down the well-worn grooves of the drug underworld. Though he made his peace with the establishment and danced to the Colonel's tune on the day shift, at night he was still the same old cat, perpetually on the prowl, sniffing his way along the trail that led to ever more bizarre sexual perversions, drug addictions and spiritual and mental delusions and hallucinations.

Elvis Presley is therefore that classic American figure: the totally bifurcated personality. Always professing his undying love and loyalty to Ma, Country, and Corn Pone, always an unregenerate southern redneck who stopped just short of the Klan and the John Birch Society, he was also the first great figure in that devolution of American society that has led to the narcissistic, anarchistic, junked-up heroes of the world of rock and punk. A Faustian figure, like most of our American mythmen, he registers both poles of the American schiz with perfect clarity. What makes him so appalling and alarming—but, again, so *echt Amerikan*—is his incredible innocence and self-righteousness, his stunning incapacity to recognize or even sense subliminally the total contradiction that informs his being. Accustomed to living in two worlds simultaneously, the day world of the squares and the night world of the cats, he embraces disjunction as the natural and inevitable condition of human existence. It is this Janus-like existential stance that makes him appear so often an enigma. Yet, though he lacks a middle term that could unite the opposite and opposing halves of his soul, he makes perfect sense as a totally responsive being who found himself alive at a time when the national values pointed in divergent directions and who reacted by rushing off in both directions at once.

THE
MORTAL
ELVIS

These are glimpses inside the King's castle, Graceland. We often forget that underneath the trappings of myth and fantasy, there was a genuine human being who must have been as baffled as anyone at the events of his life. It is impossible to conceive of what constitutes everyday reality for an individual so far removed from it, and if Elvis's version of it sometimes seemed strange, perhaps it was only an appropriately illogical response to a positively surreal situation. Beyond that, all we can do is wonder if our own responses would have been much different.

SELECTIONS FROM
ELVIS AND ME

■

by Priscilla Beaulieu Presley
with Sandra Harmon

In a field where firsthand accounts are often mere exercises in self-promotion or greed, Priscilla Presley's chronicle of events stands out as an articulate and reliable source. In this excerpt we get the perspective of a real insider, a portrait of the King at home.

EVERYTHING WASN'T NEARLY as promising as I led my parents to believe. Elvis and I couldn't really be happy together because he was so unhappy with his career. At first glance, he had it made: He was the highest-paid actor in Hollywood with a three-picture-a-year contract, at a phenomenal salary, plus fifty percent of the profits. But in reality, his brilliant career had lost its luster. By 1965 the public had access to Elvis solely through his films and records. He hadn't appeared on television since his special with Frank Sinatra in 1960, and he hadn't performed in a live concert since the spring of 1961.

The sales of his records indicated that his massive popularity was slipping. His singles were no longer automatically Top Ten hits, and he hadn't enjoyed a Number One record since the spring of 1962.

He blamed his fading popularity on his humdrum movies. He loathed their stock plots and short shooting schedules, but whenever he complained to the Colonel, Colonel reminded him that they were making millions, that the fact that his last two serious films, *Flaming Star* and *Wild in the Country*, were box-office failures proved that his fans wanted to see him only in musicals.

He could have demanded better, more substantial scripts but he didn't. Part of the reason was the lavish life-style he had established and become accustomed to. The main reason, however, was his inability to stand up to the Colonel. In Elvis's personal life, there were no stops in letting anyone know how or what he felt. But when it came time to stand up to Colonel Parker, he backed off. Elvis detested the business side of his career. He would sign a contract without even reading it.

He was an artist to whom the act of creation was everything. He and the Colonel had an unwritten agreement: Elvis would handle the artistic end and the Colonel would take care of business matters. This resulted in the Colonel locking Elvis into one bad picture after another. The Colonel's view was, if they were a success in the past, why change the trend?

Elvis was also becoming disillusioned with his music. Although he'd never had a lesson in his life, he was brilliant musically, and he loved all kinds of music—gospel, opera, rhythm and blues, country, and rock. The only kind of music he wasn't terribly fond of was jazz.

For years Elvis had stayed on top of the record charts because he had been given a good selection of songs to choose from, and he'd had free rein to record them in his own style, his own way, and had not yet become disillusioned with the music industry.

In the studio, Elvis worked well with people he felt comfortable with, and he knew exactly what sound he wanted. He handpicked his musicians and backup singers, and if he liked their sound, his own voice would reach new heights. He loved blending voices, and he marveled at the range of the tenor and bass singers. During a session, he'd stop recording, walk over to the backup singers, and harmonize the songs with them, laughing and joking and daring each one to go higher or lower, seeing if he could keep in their range. Most of the time, when he was vocally in shape, he could, and did.

When he was excited about the material, he loved recording sessions. He liked to work as a team—with his voice, the backup singers, and the instruments all recorded at the same volume. He didn't want his voice out front alone. He liked the impact of the whole group. It was his sound, and it was a fabulous sound until one day Colonel said there were complaints from fans and from RCA that they couldn't hear Elvis well enough. Whether or not this was true, he suggested Elvis's voice be brought out more.

This is one of the few times Elvis bucked heads with him, stating, "I've been singing that way all of my life. What do a few heads in RCA know about music? I'll sing the songs the way I hear them."

The recording engineer, however, worked not for Elvis but for RCA, and he began pulling back the group.

"The old man's tampering with my soundtracks," he complained to Red West and me in the back of the limo on our way to the Memphian one evening. "I don't have a chance in hell. RCA's listening to him. Fans aren't gonna want to hear my goddamn voice out front. Hell, that's what my style was all about. You could hardly understand me. Made you want to listen. And the songs that are hits today—you can hardly make out what they're singin'. The man should stick to his deals, keep out of my goddamn affairs."

Elvis could handle only so much and then he'd lose heart. He'd put up with the horrendous movies, but now they were tampering with his songs.

Colonel did not intentionally plot to make Elvis sound bad, or to get artistic control. His only interest was in getting out the product so the money could keep coming in. But when he started crossing over the line from business negotiations into Elvis's artistry, Elvis slowly began going downhill.

I wanted desperately to help him, but I wasn't sure how. In my innocence, I kept trying to convince him to argue with the Colonel. But he would only get angry, saying I didn't know what I was talking about.

I didn't understand his difficulty in revealing his weaknesses to me. Only later did I realize how important it was to Elvis to always appear in control in front of me. Whenever I stated my own opinions too strongly, especially if they differed from his, he'd remind me that his was the stronger sex, and as a woman, I had my place. He liked to say that it was intended for woman to be on the left side of man, close to his heart, where she gives him strength through her support.

His role with me was that of lover and father, and with neither could he let down his guard and become fallible or truly intimate. I longed for that, and as a woman, I needed it.

There were nights when he slept restlessly, beset by worries and fears. I lay silently beside him, anxious about what he might be thinking and whether there was a place in his life for me. Lost in our separate miseries, we were unable to give each other strength or support. He was controlled by his inability to take responsibility for his own life and for compromising his own standards—and I was controlled by him, compromising mine.

When things were bad, Elvis called Vernon and they talked for hours about their problems. He told his daddy he was lonely and depressed and no one understood him. When I overheard these words, I continued to take it personally, again thinking that I was failing him.

I would put on my brightest smile, my prettiest dress—and my phoniest personality—and try to rouse his spirits. When I couldn't get him out of the dumps, he would shut himself up all day in his room. This left me devastated. Afraid of saying or doing the wrong thing, I suppressed my real feelings and eventually developed an ulcer.

The more frustrations increased, the more pressure he felt and this resulted in his manifesting physical illnesses. Specifically to handle depression, he was now prescribed antidepressants. His enormously creative gifts were being squandered and he couldn't face it.

Although Colonel Parker knew about his state of mind, he had a long-standing agreement with Elvis that he'd stay out of his personal life. Instead of confronting Elvis, he tried to get the guys to report to him. It was a very touchy situation, and the boys were skeptical. Colonel used to have Sonny West and Jerry Schilling drive him back and forth to Palm Springs on weekends. During the long drive he casually tried to pump them for information. They had to be very careful. If they said the wrong thing, they would be put in a position of having betrayed Elvis.

It was especially hard on Joe Esposito who, as foreman of the group, spent a lot of time with the Colonel. When Elvis began canceling meetings, or acting strangely on the set, Colonel would say, "What's going on with Elvis, Joe? He looks like he's in bad shape. We can't let him be seen like this."

Joe was torn between his loyalties to Colonel and to Elvis. He cared about Elvis and respected his wishes, but he understood that the Colonel made the deals and had to deliver "the product": Elvis.

When Colonel made Joe responsible for reporting to him on Elvis's "mental and emotional state," a euphemistic phrase for drug use, Elvis found out and said, "I don't want any sons of bitches here telling Colonel what I do or what goes on in this household." He fired Joe on the spot. Six months later he forgave him and took him back. It was typical of Elvis to blow off steam and then forgive all.

From the time I first arrived at Graceland I began to notice a gradual change in Elvis's personality. In the early days of our relationship he seemed to be more in command of his emotions.

He was a man capable of enjoying life to the fullest, especially during our own special times. We loved to stroll about in the early evenings just before dark. Usually we'd end up at his father's home and stay and watch television, father and son relaxing, puffing on cigars, discussing the state of the world.

Frequently the subject was Vernon's intention to trade in his car, an elaborate Cadillac Elvis had given him, for a 1950 Olds he felt far more comfortable driving. Vernon loved old cars and trucks, trading them every few months, delighted with each new deal.

Walking back home with Elvis, we'd speak of fate—how it had brought us together, how we were meant for each other, how God worked in strange ways, uniting two people from different parts of the world.

I loved it when he'd talk like this. He'd plan our lives, saying how he was destined to be with me and could never be with anyone else. In this loving atmosphere I found I could open up and express my opinions freely.

I look back now and realize that our love affair was dependent on how his career was going. During protracted periods of noncreativity, his temper often flared.

Once we were going through a stack of demo records for an RCA soundtrack album and his distaste for each song grew increasingly apparent. Before a record was halfway through, he was on to the next, getting more and more discouraged. Finally he found one that held his attention and asked me what I thought. Remembering that first incident in Vegas, I truly felt our relationship had developed to where he would want my honest opinion. "I don't really like it," I said.

"What do you mean, you don't like it?"

"I don't know—there's just something about it, a catchiness that's missing."

To my horror, a chair came hurtling toward me.

I moved out of the way just in time, but there were stacks of records piled on it and one flew off and hit me in the face.

Within seconds he had me in his arms, apologizing frantically. It was said that he inherited his temper from his parents. I'd heard stories about how, when Gladys was furious, she'd grab a frying pan and fling it at Vernon, and I'd already observed Vernon's harsh words firsthand. This genetic trait was inherent in Elvis's temperament.

You could sense the vibration when he was angry. The tension in the room mounted to flash point, and no one wanted to be around for the explosion. Yet, if anyone decided to leave, they automatically became the target for his rage, me included. Like the time he came storming downstairs because his black suit—which he had worn only the day before—hadn't been returned from the cleaners.

"Why isn't it back yet, Cilla?" he screamed. "Where the hell is my goddamn suit?"

He had two other suits identical to the one at the cleaners, but he wanted *that* one.

When he was angry, it was like the roar of thunder. No one could challenge his biting words; we could only wait until the storm passed. When he calmed down, he made excuses—he hadn't had enough sleep, he'd had too much sleep, or he hadn't had his morning coffee yet.

Sometimes he lashed out just to drive home a point. If he thought it would teach us a lesson, he'd blow some minor grievance out of all proportion, and even as he was yelling he might wink at someone nearby. Then, ten minutes later, he'd be fine, leaving us bewildered and emotionally depleted. There were also times he would leave us emotionally uplifted. He was truly a master at manipulating people.

ELVIS WAS FILLED with complexities and contradictions. We would spend an evening discussing the spiritual life and then watch horror films.

One evening while watching the classic horror movie *Diabolique,* Elvis leaned over and asked if I was in a daring mood.

"Sure." I didn't know what he was up to, but adventure excited me.

"I'm going to take you somewhere that will scare the *fire* out of you—it did me the first time I went there."

After the film he took my hand and we all piled into the limo. Elvis instructed the driver, "Take us to the Memphis morgue."

"What!"

I didn't believe what I had just heard.

"Yeah, there's this guy who oversees the place. I went there once before. I was roaming around the rooms, looking at bodies, and we ran into each other. It scared the shit out of us both."

"You mean we're going *inside?*"

"Well, we're not supposed to, but I got ways."

"Okay, I'm game."

His fame was his passkey. It was eerie walking through the halls and viewing each room. They were still, solemn, dimly lit. I clutched at Elvis's hand. At first I didn't want to look, but he assured me the bodies were at peace and that once I looked, it wouldn't be so bad.

We wandered from room to room. I was amazed at how easy it was to become accustomed to this unusual sight. It was serene, almost as if we were in church.

We were doing fine until I looked on a table and saw an infant who appeared to be two or three months old. We both gazed in silence.

"Oh Sattnin," I said, "he's so little, so innocent. What could have happened? There's no scars." Tears were streaming down my face.

"I don't know," he said softly. "Sometimes God works in strange ways. I guess it was just meant for the little fellow to be with Him."

We both took the infant's hand and Elvis said a prayer. A few minutes later, we stood over a middle-aged woman who had just been embalmed. I looked away.

"This is good for you," he said. "You have to see things like this sometimes. This is the hard cold fact—reality. When you look at a body, you realize how temporary it all is, how it could end in a matter of minutes."

The spiritual side of Elvis was a dominant part of his nature. As a small boy growing up in Tupelo, Mississippi, he and his family attended church regularly at the First Assembly of God. He was raised on hellfire-and-brimstone preaching that put the fear of God in you and music that led to the Pearly Gates. Elvis, Vernon, and Gladys would join in with the congregation and choir, and it was then that music first rocked Elvis's soul. He was capable of spiritual healing; one touch of his hands to my temples and the most painful headaches disappeared.

He always kept the Bible on his bedside table and read it often. Now, faced with an ever-deepening despair, he began looking to other philosophical books for answers and guidance. He read the works of Kahlil Gibran. One book in particular, *The Prophet,* inspired him. He also read *Siddhartha* by Hermann Hesse and *The Impersonal Life* by Joseph Benner. He became so enamored of these books that he passed them out to friends, fellow actors, and fans. They appealed to his religious nature and he loved bringing people together "in the spirit of one underlying force—Almighty God."

When his mother, Gladys, was alive, Elvis had one person to answer to, whom he respected and who constantly reminded him of his values and his roots. It was Gladys who kept Elvis aware of the difference between right and wrong, of the evils of temptation, and of the danger of life in the fast lane.

"Mama," he'd say. "I want you and Daddy in Hollywood with me. There's a lot of fast-talkin' businessmen there, makin' a lot of decisions, fancy talk I don't understand."

In the early days, Vernon and Gladys accompanied Elvis on most of his major appearances around the South and visits to Hollywood when he made his first films. It was Gladys's common sense that counteracted Elvis's insecurities in his youth.

Since Gladys's death, there were no boundaries for Elvis. She was the force that kept him in line. Now that she was gone, he was continually in conflict between his own personal ethics and the temptations that surrounded him.

By the mid-sixties he was holding Bible readings in the den of our Bel Air home. I sat next to him one evening as he read passages with great force. Facing us were several of his young female admirers wearing the lowest-cut blouses and the shortest miniskirts. They all listened attentively, disciples enraptured in the presence of "their" lord. The sermon stretched to hours, followed by a question-and-answer period during which they vied for his attention.

Sitting at his feet was an attractive, well-endowed young girl wearing a blouse unbuttoned to her navel. Leaning over seductively, she asked in honeyed tones, "Elvis, do you think the woman at the well was a virgin?" With me right beside him, he avoided taking in the fleshy spectacle obviously exposed for his benefit.

"Well, honey," he said, "that's somethin' you'll have to come to a conclusion on yourself. As for me, I personally think Jesus was attracted to her, but that's my opinion. I'm not sayin' it's fact."

I watched Elvis and the girl talking, feeling undermined and angry. How stupid, I thought. Can't he see what she's doing? It's so obvious.

He drew in a deep breath and said, "I like your perfume, honey. What's it called?"

"Chanel Number Five," she answered.

Chanel Number Five? That's what *I* was wearing! Why didn't he notice it on me? I slowly rose and walked into my dressing room adjacent to the den. Determined to snare his attention, I changed into his favorite outfit—a tight-fitting black sheath he had picked out himself.

Returning a few minutes later, I took my place beside him, but he was wrapped up in preaching to his devotees and had totally overlooked my absence. To make matters worse, he didn't even notice my change of costume. I managed to conceal my distress behind a fake smile and an attentive gaze, but I couldn't help noticing that he was responding to them with an occasional wink or smile.

I asked questions like they did, but my heart wasn't in it; I knew they all wanted to take my place. "That's it," I thought. "If I'm not appreciated, loved, or wanted, I'll end it. That will make it easier for everyone."

I got up and went back to our room. Picking up a half-full bottle of Placidyls, I devised a plan to create a dramatic effect that, in my mind, would win his attention. I stared at them, thinking, What if I choke to death? I decided to take two pills to start. That way I could take a quick shower, redo my makeup, put on my prettiest camisole, and still have time to position myself dramatically on the bed before I consumed the rest of the bottle.

I swallowed the pills and started to prepare myself for the end. In tears, I thought of leaving him a note, writing down everything I'd never been able to say. I'd tell him how I wished that it could have been just the two of us again, as it had been during the long hours we'd spent together in his room in Germany. I'd confess that I was jealous of any woman who caught his attention and that I hated the times when there was only silence between us, even though he'd said he had things on his mind. I'd tell him how I feared his violent temper, which robbed me of my freedom of expression; and how I wished that he'd have tried to understand me as I'd desperately tried to understand him.

Maybe he's missed me by now, I thought. I ran to the door and pressed my ear against it. I heard him laughing. He was having a great time. They all were.

I found that I was disgusted with all of it. I wouldn't go in there now if he begged me, I told myself. I was too tired anyway.

But I wasn't too tired to remember how I wanted to be found. I lay down on the bed with my long jet black hair spread over the white pillows, my lips moist with gloss. In my naive fantasy he'd take my listless body in his arms and tell me how much he loved me, kissing me passionately back to life.

I forced down one more pill, lay perfectly still in the position I wanted to be discovered, and waited for what seemed like hours for sleep to overtake me. But the longer I lay there, the less sleepy I became. The more I heard Elvis's laughter, the angrier I got. My adrenaline-charged fury was overriding the effect of the pills. Soon I began to feel foolish.

Then I heard Elvis say good night to everyone as he approached the room. I grabbed the nearest book and lay it at my side, as though

233

I'd been reading and had fallen asleep. I heard him come in, quietly walk over to the bed, and pick up the book. He whispered the title, *The Listener*. I could imagine him smiling, pleased as always when I read philosophical books. He stood over me for a second, probably thinking how sweet I looked and how tired I must have been to retire so early.

Then he covered me snugly with blankets and bent down to kiss my carefully-parted lips. All my anger and jealousy vanished. I realized how even a little of his attention could make me happy.

IN APRIL OF 1964, Larry Geller was hired to replace Elvis's barber, Sal Orfice. Little did we know that their relationship would not only cause a drastic change in Elvis, but it would create tension, jealousy, and fear within the group.

I was in Memphis when he first met Larry, but I learned all about him through our nightly phone conversations. Elvis's enthusiasm over his newfound friend was infectious.

"You're not going to believe this guy, Sattnin," he said. "Larry knows more about the spiritual world than all the preachers and Catholic priests and religious fanatics put together. We have discussions that last hours, just talkin' and talkin' about the great masters and my purpose for being here. I'm invitin' him to Graceland. He'll enlighten your spiritual development."

When Larry and his wife, Stevie Geller, joined us, I was surprised to find them both young and attractive. He was kind and mellow. She was sweet and quiet and kept to herself.

However, many in the group, myself included, were suspicious of them. We were all threatened by Elvis's involvement with Larry. It was keeping him from us. It seemed as if Elvis was always off alone reading esoteric books or deep in discussion with Larry about God's master plan for the universe.

Elvis discovered there were many great masters besides Jesus. There were Buddha, Muhammad, Moses, and others, each "chosen by God to serve a purpose." What I was now witnessing in Elvis was the emergence of that part of his nature that was thirsting for answers to all the fundamental questions of life.

He asked Larry why, out of all the people in the universe, he had been chosen to influence so many millions of souls. Granted this unique position, how could he contribute to save a world burdened with hunger, disease, and poverty? Why was there so much human suffering in the first place? And why wasn't he happy, when he had more than anyone could want? He felt he was missing something in life. Through Larry's insight, he hoped to find the path that would lead him to the answers.

He was eager for all of us—especially me—to absorb all the knowledge he was consuming. Happy to share everything, just as he had with his Bible discussions in L.A., he read to us for hours and handed out books he thought would interest us. He announced that in order for us to be perfect soul mates, I'd have to join him in his search for the answers to the universe. To help me, he gave me several large books, including Vera Stanley Adler's *The Initiation of the World.*

He suggested I attend the lectures of the metaphysical philosopher and author Manley P. Hall. I did. I found the lectures difficult to understand and painful to endure, but I managed to survive with the hope that "this too shall pass."

Then he became interested in Cheiro's *Book of Numbers,* which defined people's personality traits and characteristics according to the day of the month on which they were born. To find out who was compatible with whom, Elvis added up the numbers in the birthdays of everyone within the group. I waited in terror, praying that my number would be a six, seven, or eight, so I would be compatible with Elvis, who was an eight. Fortunately, my number linked with his.

Although I was striving to be his soul mate and subtly becoming more aware of myself as a spiritual being, my heart longed for the very temptations he was fighting to conquer.

While I patiently waited at home at Graceland for his returns, planning romantic interludes, he was attempting to overcome worldly temptations and believed he was going through a cleansing period, physically and spiritually. Any sexual temptations were against everything he was striving for, and he did not wish to betray me, the girl waiting for him at home who was preparing to be his wife.

He felt guilty and confused about his natural reaction to female advances and I believe that this was his greatest fear when it came to marriage. He loved me and deeply wanted to be faithful to me but never felt certain that he could resist temptation. It was a persistent battle, and it even got to the point where he felt he had to resist me.

"Cilla," he said one night before we went to bed, "you're going

235

to have to be pretty understanding these next few weeks, or however long it takes. I feel that I have to withdraw myself from the temptations of sex."

"But why? And why with me?"

He was quite solemn. "We have to control our desires so they don't control us. If we can control sex, then we can master all other desires."

When we were in bed, he took his usual dose of sleeping pills, handed me mine, and then, fighting off drowsiness from the pills, pored over his metaphysical books.

As his soul mate I was expected to search for answers as fervently as he did, but I just couldn't bear reading the ponderous tracts that surrounded us in bed every night. Usually within five minutes of opening one, I'd be sound asleep. Annoyed at my obvious disinterest, he woke me to share an insightful passage. If I voiced the slightest protest, he'd say, "Things will never work out between us, Cilla, because you don't show any interest in me or my philosophies." Then, pointedly: "There are a lot of women out there who would share these things with me."

Faced with this threat, I forced myself to sit up and try to read the passage. The print swam before my eyes in one big blur.

I wanted to share romantic, not religious, inspirations with him. I tried to cuddle as close to him as I could, feeling the warmth of his body. He told me to sit up and listen, and he read yet another passage, repeating it several times to make sure I grasped its significance. I could bear it no longer. I lost control and started screaming.

"I can't stand it! I don't want to hear any more! I'm sick and tired of your voice going on and *on*! It's—driving—me—crazy!" I was hysterical, pulling at my hair like a wild woman.

"What do you see?" I demanded. "*Tell* me, what do you see?"

He stared up at me, his eyes half-closed. "A madwoman, a goddamn raving madwoman," he answered, slurring his words because of the sleeping pills.

I fell on my knees beside him, crying, "No, Elvis, not a madwoman, a woman who needs to make love to and to feel desired by her man. Elvis, you can have your books and me too. Please don't make me beg," I cried. "I really need you and want you."

By the time I'd finished my tirade, all I could hear was the faint sound of religious music playing on the radio. I looked up at him. He had fallen into a deep sleep.

ONE LAST NIGHT OF FUN

███

by Albert Goldman

Elvis's death has long been the source of much debate, speculation, and commentary. The loneliness and indignity of his passing may seem all too human, but as a cultural icon, death was Elvis's boldest and most brilliant statement. The following is Albert Goldman's account, rich in clinical detail, of the King's last hours.

ON AUGUST 15, 1977, Elvis Presley was preparing to depart on a twelve-day tour that would begin at Portland, Maine, and take him to Utica, Syracuse, and Uniondale, New York; Hartford, Connecticut; Lexington, Kentucky; Roanoke, Virginia; Fayetteville and Asheville, North Carolina; and home to Memphis for two final shows. Elvis awoke about four in the afternoon and called for his extra-strong, almost syrupy coffee. He ate no solid food because he was fasting to reduce his weight. As always his awakening was a slow and difficult process, a laborious reversing of the physical and mental machinery slowed virtually to a stop by massive doses of barbiturates and opiates. Eventually, he got out of bed and went into the bathroom to make that long and elaborate toilet that was designed to restore him, like a man taking rejuvenation treatments, to the image of youthful beauty and vigor.

By early evening, he had gone so far as to step out of doors, a thing he did rarely in his last years, where he watched Lisa Marie riding merrily about the back of the house in the specially built electric golf cart that was her favorite toy. The child had been sent to Graceland for a long visit by Priscilla, who was eager to cheer up Elvis and distract him from his worries about the book. For this last night at home, Elvis had planned one of his favorite treats: He had ordered that the Ridgeway Theater be reserved after the last show and that a print be obtained of his favorite recent movie, *MacArthur*. Doubtless he looked forward to the scene in which the great general, brought home in disgrace from Korea, stands up in the American Senate and delivers his eloquent farewell address, a speech that Elvis had memorized twenty years before and recited so many times since. Yes, Elvis was perfectly capable of seeing now a parallel between his own fate and that of his hero, MacArthur. They had both served their country with genius and devotion; they had both been acclaimed the greatest heroes of their time; and now Elvis, like MacArthur, was being humiliated unjustly by people who owed their lives to him. No wonder he was calling for this film again at this moment. It spoke to his condition.

As it turned out, Elvis was deprived of this last night at the movies. The projectionist said he could not work late, and no one else could be found to take his place. Casting about for something else to do, Elvis decided abruptly to see his dentist, Dr. Lester Hofman. Calling the dentist at his home after supper, Elvis explained that he was about to leave on tour and needed some last-minute treatment. Dr. Hofman, who had known Elvis for years and who drove a Cadillac that he had received from Elvis, made light of the inconvenience. He agreed to open his office for an appointment that night at ten-thirty.

Though Dr. Hofman did fill, according to his own account, an upper right first bicuspid and an upper left molar that evening, it is doubtful that Elvis's motive in suddenly seeing the dentist was purely medical. As the prescription records compiled after Elvis's death indicate, on this day Dr. George Nichopoulos prescribed for his famous patient the following drugs:

Amytal: 100 three-gram capsules and 12 half-gram ampules. Amytal is a barbiturate which in high doses has a pronounced hypnotic effect. As it is not manufactured in ampules, the compiler of this record may have confused Amytal with Amytal Sodium, which *is* packaged in half-gram ampules and sold in boxes of six. Amytal Sodium is a very powerful drug whose proper medical application is in the treatment of grave disorders, such as convulsions, meningitis, tetanus or strychnine poisoning.

Quāāludes: 150 300-milligram tablets. Ludes are one of the most widely abused drugs in the world. Called "wall bangers" by the kids, they produce the slurred speech and loss of muscular control that were such conspicuous features of Elvis Presley's behavior in later years.

Dexedrine: 100 five-milligram tablets. These little golden "hearts" are the most familiar form of speed.

Biphetamine: 100 twenty-milligram spansules. This is the familiar "Black Beauty," a powerful amphetamine that is surpassed in effect only by the injectable varieties of speed, like Methedrine.

Percodan: 100 tablets. Percodan is another drug that has been used by heads for many years. Unlike the other preparations on this list, Percodan is a compound of five different drugs that act in concert to relieve pain. The principal ingredient, oxycodone, is a narcotic with effects similar to morphine.

Dilaudid: Fifty four-milligram tablets and twenty ccs of two-milligram solution. Elvis was furnished with the drug in both oral and injectable form. The solution was provided in a multiple-dose vial rather than in a fixed-dose ampule, thus allowing him to inject far more than the normal dosage.

Stockpiling drugs in this manner on the eve of a tour was standard practice with Dr. Nichopoulos. The reason was simply that doctors cannot write prescriptions in any state but the one in which they are licensed to practice medicine. As this tour was of less than two weeks duration, the list indicates clearly not only what drugs Elvis was taking but the rate at which he was consuming them under Dr. Nichopoulos's supervision.[1] Actually, of course, Elvis had access to drugs from many other sources, as no junkie ever recognizes the concept, enough. Hence, the sudden inspiration to go to the dentist this night, otherwise a rather odd substitute for an evening at the movies.

Elvis left Graceland for his dental appointment about ten in the evening. He was wearing a blue jogging suit with the letters DEA (Drug Enforcement Administration) blazoned across the back. He was accompanied by Ginger, Charlie Hodge and Billy Smith. As he drove out of the Music Gate for the last time behind the wheel of his Stutz Blackhawk, he was hailed by a handful of fans. One of

[1] Dr. Nichopoulos argued at a medical board hearing after Elvis's death that these drugs were intended for the whole touring group but were prescribed for Elvis so that he would receive the bill.

them snapped a picture that shows an obese and gross-looking Elvis wearing his trademark shades and with the hood of his suit pulled over his head.

Arriving at Dr. Hofman's office on Estate Drive in a prosperous neighborhood in East Memphis, Elvis appeared to be in high spirits. "Isn't this an ugly girl here?" he jested as he introduced the beautiful Ginger to Dr. Hofman. Then, as she sat in the waiting room and the two Guys trailed off somewhere, Elvis closeted himself with the dentist.

Dr. Hofman recalled later that Elvis inquired about the dentist's wife, Sterling, and boasted of his new Ferrari. When the session ended, Dr. Hofman made a request. "Listen," he said, "next time you're going out to California, I'd like to come. It would be a nice surprise if I could drop in on my daughter out there." "Sure," answered Elvis, "there's always room on the plane—you know that!"

When Elvis got back to Graceland, it was nearly twelve-thirty. A small crowd of fans was still hovering around the gate. One of them was Robert Call from Pierceton, Indiana, who had come to Memphis with his wife and four-year-old daughter, Abby, expressly for the purpose of taking pictures of the family against the backdrop of Graceland. As Elvis pulled up to the gate, Mrs. Call had the little girl in her arms. She raised the child to Elvis's car window. Automatically he grinned and waved his hand. At that instant, Robert Call, using a twenty-dollar Instamatic with a flash cube, snapped the last picture of all the millions of pictures that were taken of Elvis Presley.

Back at the house, Elvis showed unwonted energy in calling the men on duty up to his room and making inquiries about the arrangements for the tour. He was told that every concert was sold out. The Colonel was already at Portland, Maine, with the advance party. The musicians were leaving after dark from Los Angeles on the Jet Star, which would be captained by Milo High. Everything was in order, as always. Everybody was taking care of business. Elvis, for his part, had come up with a list of five or six new songs that he wanted to try out on this tour. He asked Dick Grob, the former Palm Springs cop who was now working the security detail, to see if he could find the lead sheets for the songs. As Elvis and Grob continued their conversation, the topic of the recent press reports concerning Elvis's health and the shocking revelations in *Elvis—What Happened?* came up.

Elvis was going to face the public for the first time on this tour knowing that many of them had read this book and were examining him for signs of drug addiction. He certainly didn't look very well. Though he had been fasting for the past two days, he weighed 255 pounds. His weight troubled him so much that he had even told Ginger that they should go to a fat farm, an idea that would never even have crossed his mind in the old days. Still, he was confident he could deal with the public. The trick was simply to give them the kind of show that would make all the ugly rumors look ridiculous. "Dick," Elvis said, winding up the conversation, "we'll just show them how wrong they are. We'll make this one the best ever."

At two-thirty in the morning, Elvis called Tish Henley—Dr. Nichopolous's head nurse, who lived with her husband in a trailer behind Graceland—and told her that Ginger was suffering from menstrual pain. Nurse Henley testified at a hearing after Elvis's death that she dispensed one tablet of Dilaudid. Ginger recollects nothing about suffering menstrual cramps on this evening or receiving any medication. The little white pill went straight down the throat of Elvis Presley. Scoring had such a good effect upon him that he was inspired once more to take up his favorite theme: his forthcoming wedding to Ginger.

Calling her into his office, where he had been watching TV, he started building chapels in the air. He said they should be married in a church of pyramidal design. (Charlie Hodge had gotten on a pyramid kick and persuaded Elvis that such spaces concentrated precious spiritual energies.) Though the wedding was going to be Elvis's production, he said that he wanted the occasion to reflect Ginger's tastes as well. For example, he wanted to know what color she preferred for the limousines. Before she could answer, he told her that he had some original ideas about organizing the security forces so that they wouldn't mar the appearance of the event. Then, at last, he came around to the theme that obsessed him most of all: Ginger's bridal gown.

Priscilla had offended Elvis with her gown. Impelled by her crazy pinch-penny attitude toward money, she had bought an inexpensive gown and fitted it with a train herself. Elvis wanted Ginger to have the most magnificent gown imaginable. There were certain features he described with such vividness that Ginger has never been able to forget them. He told her: "Your dress is already being made. I want you to have small rosebuds with gold sparkles that will shine in the light. I want you to wear glass slippers, like Cinderella. I . . ." "But, Elvis!" broke in Ginger (who, as we have seen, was of a common-sensical turn of mind), "they don't even have my measurements!"

241

Elvis smiled knowingly at this remark. "Well," he said, "they'll just have to come here and give you a fitting." Oh, he was high that night!

Finally, he disclosed the most thrilling idea of them all. He was considering announcing their engagement from the stage here in Memphis on August 27, the last night of the tour. Ginger was breathless when she heard these words. As she listened for further revelations, she was surprised to see Elvis leap up and pace excitedly back and forth in the room. Now he started explaining who was going to be present at the ceremony. There would be many famous people and public officials: mayors, governors, congressmen. Unlike the last time when he had been married by a judge of the Nevada State Supreme Court, this time he was determined to be married by a judge of the national Supreme Court. As that image flashed through his hopped-up brain, he exclaimed—"God! *It's gonna blow all this stuff sideways!*" Ginger couldn't imagine to what he was alluding, though he repeated the statement several times, like a man relishing a marvelous thought. Obviously what he had in mind was the ultimate riposte to the West-Hebler book.

Here these guys were saying that he's a junkie freak, an evil dude who lays around stoned out of his gourd blasting away at TV sets with pistols. *Then,* he steps out in front of his own people in his own hometown and tells them: "I'm getting married! Here's my fiancée!" Wow! Elvis Presley getting married! That announcement would blow any story in the world off the front page and set every woman in the country blithering and gossiping and crying like a baby. Then, as the capper to the whole scam, he would be surrounded at the wedding by public officials and police officials and all the straightest, strictest, law 'n' order ole daddies in the country, with a Supreme Court judge standing up there like Judge Stone pronouncing the vows. After a snow job like that one, who would ever believe that he was a junkie? Ha! Elvis hadn't spent a quarter of a century with Colonel Parker without learning a thing or two about manipulating public opinion.

As Elvis raved on that night, probably feeling the tongue-loosening effects of those big Black Beauties, he thrilled Ginger time and again with the sweet and sentimental things that he said. Just the other day, he told her, he had been talking with his father. Poor Vernon! He was so ill. Nowadays, the doctor didn't allow Vernon to walk more than fifty feet at a time. His health was very precarious. Yet, he was so happy with his new companion, a former nurse named Sandy Miller. Elvis and Vernon had been talking about Elvis's relationship with Ginger. "Does she do little things for you, son?" Vernon had asked. Elvis assured him that Ginger did. Then, they had drifted to the differences in age between Elvis and Ginger. Elvis was old enough to be his fiancée's father. Vernon had assured Elvis that this was no problem; in fact, if anything, the shoe was on the other foot. "What could a thirty-year-old woman do for you?" asked Vernon, adding before Elvis could reply, "What could a sixty-year-old woman do for me?" Gladys would have been sixty-three now, if she had lived; but Elvis let the remark pass. Then, his father had looked at Elvis and said something that when Elvis repeated it to Ginger thrilled her more than anything else he had ever said since the day he proposed. "You know what my father said to me?" Elvis confided with a radiant smile. "He said he had never seen me so happy as a man. I looked so happy to him, he said, that I reminded him now of that little boy he put overalls on back in Tupelo."

After this long and ebullient conversation, which had been practically a monologue by Elvis, he was certainly in no mood to walk in the next room and fall to sleep. In fact, he felt like going out and blowing off steam! Though it was four in the morning, the night was still young for Elvis. He picked up a phone and called Billy Smith at his mobile home out in the backyard. He told Billy to wake up his wife, Jo, and join him at once at the racquetball court; they would all play for an hour and have some fun. As soon as Elvis hung up, he started changing into his exercise suit and urging Ginger to do the same.

The racquetball court behind the house at Graceland is a monument to Elvis's last and most costly folly. Originally, he was interested in the game by Dr. Nichopoulos, who urged Elvis to take it up as a means of conditioning his body. The spectacle of the physician encouraging his patient to exercise and then in the same breath agreeing to give him enough drugs to stun an elephant is one of many ironies implicit in this grotesque doctor-patient relationship. The building, a windowless cast-concrete structure of severe modern design, resembles from the outside an industrial structure or a coastal defense bunker. On the inside, it is a two-story gym. The approach is from the rear door of the house by means of a curved and covered walkway. Entering the building, you find yourself in a large space that resembles a lounge, with a bar to the right and to the left a piano, pinball machine, jukebox and sofa. At the rear of this chamber is a sunken observation area with a long sofa that permits visitors to view the action on the court through a glass wall. Up the curving stairs that rise beside the bar is a second floor that suggests a health club, with a Jacuzzi whirlpool, steam room, showers and dressing rooms. A balcony at the back of this floor offers an overhead view of the action below on the court.

It was about four in the morning when Elvis emerged from the house, wearing a striped exercise suit and accompanied by Ginger, who was similarly dressed. Pointing off in the distance, he indicated where her future painting studio would stand. Then, entering the new building, he walked out on the court and began to play with Billy. As Ginger and Jo sat in the downstairs observation pit, Elvis and Billy banged the ball around the court. Elvis was still in high good humor, performing trick shots and showing off for Ginger's benefit. Every time he made an eccentric move, he would turn around to see if Ginger were watching; then, he would do something even more nonsensical. Unfortunately, the ludes, which he had taken a little earlier, were showing their effect; soon his coordination began to deteriorate. Finally, he took a mighty swing at a ball and struck himself painfully in the shin. At that point, he limped off the court and came back behind the glass wall to sit beside Ginger.

Once Elvis had recovered himself, he got up and went to the piano, where he started playing and singing an old country weeper, revived by Willie Nelson, "Blue Eyes Crying in the Rain." Then he mounted an electric exercycle. By the time the foursome left the building, it was about six and the sun was rising. Elvis and Ginger went upstairs, but he was still extremely restless. He had ordered the bed turned down much earlier in the evening. Mary Jenkins had removed the spread and laid back the sheet invitingly. Ginger threw herself on the bed at once, without even troubling to get out of her clothes. Elvis changed into a pair of blue pajamas and switched on the big TV facing the bed. He picked up a book on psychic energy but found that he was still not inclined to sleep. At six-thirty he called downstairs for his sleeping medication, and Rickey Stanley brought upstairs some Dilaudid that he had obtained the day before by presenting one of Dr. Nick's prescriptions to the pharmacist at the Baptist Memorial Hospital.

Around eight in the morning, Ginger was awakened by Elvis calling downstairs for more sleeping medication. She assumed that he was nervous about the tour, as he often was on the day of departure. Rickey brought up a standard packet of sleeping pills that included Quääludes, Seconal, Tuinal, Amytal, Valium and a couple of Demerol tablets; eight pills in all, a fatal dose for a normal human being but precisely what Elvis took every morning before retiring.

This morning, apparently, he feared that he would not experience the desired effect because just fifteen minutes after Rickey left his room, Elvis was on the phone to Dr. Nick's office, where he found Nurse Henley. He explained that he was going to have a trying day, what with Lisa going back to California and his own departure imminent: It was vital that he receive some extra sleeping medication so that he would be equal to the day's demands. She agreed to help him.

She called her husband, who was still at home, and instructed him to take from the bag of medications that was kept in the trailer two Valmid tablets and a "Placidyl placebo." Valmid is a nonbarbiturate hypnotic, and two of these elongated pale blue pulvules are a standard prescription for insomnia. Placidyl is another sleeping pill. Dr. Nichopoulos dispensed this drug in staggering quantities to anyone in the Presley organization who complained of sleeplessness. (Marty Lacker has testified that between January 1971 and October 1976, he received from Dr. Nick 6,464 doses of Placidyl, plus numerous other drugs.) The drugs were given to Aunt Delta, who brought them up to the bedroom and handed them to Elvis. Receiving these pills was the last act anyone in the group witnessed Elvis perform, save for Ginger.

Groggy and nearly asleep, she saw Elvis pick up another book, this one on the interesting topic of the Shroud of Turin, and start to go into the bathroom. "Precious, I'm gonna go in the bathroom and read for a while," he explained. "Okay," she sighed, "but don't fall asleep." He smiled at her and answered, "I won't."

What happened during the next six hours can only be inferred from the position of Elvis's body when it was found and from the results of the post-mortem examination. According to Dr. Norman Weissman, a pathologist at Bio-Science Laboratory at Van Nuys, California, Elvis's body contained at death fourteen different drugs, three of which may have been produced by metabolism or interaction among the other eleven. The drugs found and their sources are as follows:

Codeine—(at a concentration ten times higher than the toxic level)
Morphine—possible metabolic of codeine
Methaqualone—Quāālude (above toxic level)
Diazepam, diazepam metabolite—Valium
Ethinamate—Valmid
Ethchlorvynol—Placidyl
Amobarbital—Amytal
Pentobarbital—Nembutal
Phenobarbital—Carbrital

245

Meperidine—Demerol
Amitriptyline—Elavil (antidepressant)
Nortriptyline—Aventyl (antidepressant)
Phenyltoloxamine—Sinutab (decongestant)

This list suggests a pretty busy night. If one were not familiar with Elvis's astonishing pattern of drug abuse, the simultaneous consumption of so many drugs would suggest a grave crisis or a bad breakdown. Actually, the volume was probably only a little greater than was customary for Elvis. The enormous quantity of codeine, for example, is easily accounted for by the enormous tolerance of opiates which Elvis had developed after so many years of addiction. Far from seeing these drugs as evidence of suicidal despair, one should regard them as evidence of reckless overconfidence. If Elvis's last night were any different from other nights that preceded it, the difference would have to be ascribed to higher not lower spirits. Elvis died as he had lived, pleasuring himself bountifully and anticipating future triumphs.

Around two in the afternoon, Ginger awoke in the big bed, still wearing her exercise suit. It didn't surprise her that Elvis was not at her side. For all she knew, he had gone downstairs or even left the house. The only thing that occupied her mind was the thought that within a matter of hours she would be leaving to go on the tour. Suddenly, it occurred to her to call up David Stanley's girlfriend, Cindy Mies, and find out if she were going, too. The girls chatted briefly, and Ginger learned that Cindy had been invited to make the trip. That pleased Ginger because she would have another young woman to keep her company. Then, she called her mother to say that she was coming home directly. Only after she had been on the phone for a quarter of an hour did it occur to her that Elvis might still be in the bathroom.

Getting out of bed she crossed the room and knocked on the door. "Elvis?" she called. Getting no response, she knocked again and again. Unlike Linda Thompson, who would have barged right in to check on Elvis, Ginger was reluctant to violate his privacy. Finally, she opened the door and peeped inside. What she saw was Elvis doubled up face down on the floor, with his buttocks elevated, in the fetal position. Clearly, he had been sitting in the black leather and chrome chair reading and had toppled forward onto the floor. The book was still lying on the chair. In falling, his head had struck a hair dryer that someone had left on the floor. If it had been anyone else Ginger had found in this condition, she might have been alarmed. With Elvis, this kind of thing was normal. He was always dropping off abruptly from the effects of his sleeping potions and landing head first in the most unlikely places. Ginger hated to see him in these grotesque positions, but there wasn't any reason to panic.

Walking over to him, Ginger called, "Elvis!" Then, suddenly, she began to feel alarmed. The thought crossed her mind that he might have struck his head in the fall and injured himself. She reached down and touched him. He was as cold as ice. Again, this was typical. Sleeping for hours without stirring in a room whose temperature had been forced down twenty degrees by a powerful air conditioner, Elvis often felt icy to the touch. Finally, Ginger knelt down and turned Elvis's head around so she could see his face. Now, for the first time, she was gripped by terror. Elvis's face had become a grotesque mask, purple with engorged blood, his teeth set in his lolling tongue. Trembling, she raised one of his closed eyelids. The eye was blood red and motionless. The thought that Elvis was dead never once entered Ginger's mind. She was certain that he had collapsed from the medication and struck his head on the floor. He had injured himself. But he was certainly still alive.

Standing up again, she reached for the phone next to the toilet. She pressed the button for the kitchen and heard the voice of the cook, Pauline. "Who's on duty?" Ginger asked anxiously. When she heard it was Al Strada, she said, "Would you tell Al to come up here really quick?" Then, she started out of the room to meet Al coming up the stairs.

Now she was convinced that something was terribly wrong, but the thought of death had still not forced itself into her mind. Al came running up the steps, where Ginger met him as she came down. "I think something's really wrong with Elvis!" she blurted out. "Come and look at him!" Al didn't speak a word. He took one look at Elvis; then he said, "Let me get Joe up here." Picking up the phone, he called downstairs. Joe had just arrived at the house to supervise the departure for the tour. He charged up the stairs and came hustling into the bathroom.

Having been through this business so many times before, Joe knew exactly what to do. First, he turned Elvis over on his back. As he did so, he heard a sighing sound that convinced him that Elvis was still breathing. Turning the body over, however, produced a grotesque sight. The legs remained rigidly flexed at the knees. It looked as though Elvis were trying to touch his chin with his kneecaps. Ginger had never heard of rigor mortis. She stood there marveling at the odd position of her lover's legs. Joe reacted very differently. He leaped up and grabbed the phone. Punching into an outside line, he tapped out the emergency number. Talking rapidly to the dispatcher, he explained that someone was having great difficulty breathing at 3764 Elvis Presley Boulevard. He told the dispatcher to tell the ambulance driver to come straight through the gates and drive up to the front door of the house. The name of the victim was never mentioned.

A minute later, Unit Six of the Memphis fire department emergency division got the call. Charles Crosby and Ulysses Jones started racing toward Graceland at 2:33 P.M. Though all they had was the address, they knew it was Graceland. In fact, they had an idea who it was they were supposed to succor. Once before they had been summoned to the house to rescue Vernon Presley, who was succumbing to a heart attack. They had rushed the old man to the hospital and saved his life. Trained paramedics, the men were prepared to find the same situation and apply the same remedy: CPR (cardiopulmonary resuscitation).

Meantime, at the house, Joe was down on his knees giving Elvis mouth to mouth resuscitation or, alternately, pounding on his chest, while Al Strada stood at the phone making call after call for help. The first person called was Dr. Nick, who was at Doctors' Hospital, five miles distant. The operator informed Strada that she would page the doctor by beeper. She advised him to keep a phone line open. Then Strada called Dr. Perry Holmes, a local physician in Whitehaven, whom they used sometimes for minor complaints. Learning that Dr. Holmes was also out of the office, Strada slammed down the phone. Moments later, Dr. Holmes's associate, Dr. James Campbell, was told of the call by his receptionist. He called Graceland and got Aunt Delta. She told him that her nephew was experiencing some difficulty breathing. She asked the doctor if he could come to the house immediately. He suggested that they bring Elvis to his office.

By this time, everyone at Graceland was crowding into the bathroom in a vain effort to save Elvis. Charlie Hodge arrived and started shouting, "Breathe, Elvis, breathe!" Aunt Delta fell on her knees to continue the mouth-to-mouth resuscitation. Then Vernon, desperately infirm and barely able to climb the stairs, came gasping into the room. At the first sight of Elvis, he started wailing: "Son, don't die! Son, don't leave!" Ginger was wandering around in a daze when she heard Lisa's voice, as the child climbed the stairs to the second floor. As Ginger rushed to the bedroom door to intercept her, Lisa yelled, "What's wrong?" "Nothing!" cried Ginger, reaching down to seize the child. "Something's wrong with Daddy and I'm going to find out!" shouted the little girl. Then she darted around the other end of the landing to enter the bathroom from the opposite side. "Al!" shouted Ginger, "Lisa's trying to get in!" Strada swiftly threw the lock on the bathroom door.

Suddenly, the two paramedics burst upon the scene, having dashed up the stairs unheard by the people in the bathroom. Pushing away the dozen people who had squeezed into the room, the firemen looked down and saw a man who was so disfigured that neither of them recognized the most famous man in Memphis. Ulysses Jones recalls that this totally unfamiliar-looking man was "clothed in pajamas—a yellow top and blue bottoms. From his shoulders up, his skin was dark blue. Around his neck, which seemed fat and bloated, was a very large gold medallion. His sideburns were grey. I knelt down and checked the pulse and shined a light in his eyes. There was no reaction. No pulse. No flicker from the eyes. He was cold, unusually cold. The people around me were weeping. 'Is there anything you can do?' they cried. I couldn't give them an answer. Suddenly a young man [David Stanley] blurted out, 'I think he ODed.' It was the second time that an overdose was mentioned. The first time was at the door of the house where a guard had said, 'He's upstairs and I think it's an OD.' I inserted an airway tube into his throat and gave the nearest man a squeeze bag for pumping air into his lungs." The other paramedic, Charles Crosby, recalls: "It took five of us to lift him onto a stretcher. He must have weighed two hundred fifty pounds. The pajama top was unbuttoned all the way down, and I could see the great big rolls of fat on his belly. It looked like he had been dead for at least an hour."

As the men jockeyed the stretcher around the corners and down the stairs, feeble, emaciated old Vernon tried to follow, crying and calling: "Son, I'm coming. . . . I'll be there. . . . I'll be meetin' you there!" Two of the Guys had to forcibly restrain Vernon, who could have dropped dead of a heart attack at any moment.

Just as the ambulance was preparing to roll down the driveway, Dr. Nick came racing up to the house. He had spoken to Joe just after the paramedics had arrived and been told that Elvis was still breathing. Now, he climbed into the ambulance and started massaging Elvis's heart. At 2:48 the ambulance cleared the gates of Graceland and took off at speeds that reached eighty m.p.h. for Baptist Memorial Hospital. All through the incredibly swift seven-minute trip, Nichopoulos kept shouting: "Breathe, Elvis . . . come on, breathe for me!" Said Jones: "All the way to the hospital, the doctor had this look of sheer disbelief that this could have happened to Elvis."

At the hospital's communications center, a call was received now from the speeding ambulance: "Have a white male, approximately forty, under CPR, no response." Immediately, a summons sounded from every loudspeaker in the building: "Harvey Team report to E.R. [Emergency Room] . . . Harvey Team report to E.R. . . . Harvey Team report to E.R." Harvey Teams are groups of emergency specialists who literally come running the moment the arrival of a critically injured or dying patient is announced.

Elvis was borne into Trauma Room Number One, a small operating theater, and laid out naked on a surgical table. Instantly, his body was covered with monitoring electrodes, as the doctors and technicians struggled to revive him with oxygen, mechanical respiration and injections of powerful stimulants. For nearly half an hour they worked on him but all their labors were in vain. Finally, they abandoned the effort and classified the case as a DOA: dead on arrival.

All this while, Joe Esposito, David Stanley and Maurice Elliott, the vice president of the hospital and its principal public relations officer, waited for word in an adjoining emergency room. Finally, at three P.M., the door to Room Number One opened and out came Dr. Nick, with his head hanging. Looking up at Joe Esposito, the white-haired Nichopoulos said, "There is nothing we can do . . . we tried." Then, as his eyes began to water, he herded everyone out of the room, turning to close it behind him as if he were sealing up a tomb. Ten minutes later a nurse emerged carrying a bag which contained Elvis's necklace, rings, bracelet and pajamas. She gave the bag to Nichopoulos. Now, it was his painful duty to break the news to the family. This was not just a task that was hard to perform for emotional reasons: There was a distinct possibility that the news might kill Vernon Presley. Nichopoulos persuaded the two paramedics who brought Elvis into the hospital to drive him back to Graceland and stand by until it was clear that Vernon would survive the shock of his son's death.

Once the ambulance had left Graceland, Vernon, Sandy, Aunt Delta, Aunt Nashville, and some members of the staff drifted into Minnie Mae's room where they began to pray for Elvis. Ginger had felt she should ride in the ambulance with Elvis to the hospital, but before she could gather up her resolution to go, the door slammed shut. Suddenly, she felt that she had been shut out of his life. "I never felt so alone in my life," she recalls. Then Aunt Nashville put her arms around Ginger and sought to comfort her. "He's going to be all right," she soothed. "He's got so much to live for." Ginger felt so much better at this moment that she was impelled to comfort someone else. She thought of Lisa and went upstairs to find the child. Entering the little girl's room, Ginger said, "Lisa, your daddy's gonna be okay." Lisa was easily persuaded that there was nothing to fear. Soon she was chasing merrily from room to room, playing with Amber.

Now Ginger went downstairs and while she was standing in the parlor, Dr. Nick walked into the house flanked by the two paramedics. He didn't say a thing. The moment Vernon, who was seated in a chair, caught sight of the bag in the doctor's hand, he fell backward, crying, "Oh, no, no! I know he's gone!" Nichopoulos was virtually speechless. "I'm sorry," he murmured, but his words were drowned out by the wail that went up from everyone in the house. Screams, cries, moans and curses filled the air. Suddenly, people started running aimlessly in every direction. Little Lisa was beside herself, crying, "My daddy is gone! I can't believe my daddy is gone!" Before anyone could reach her, she dashed halfway up the stairs toward her room. Then she darted back down again and ran into the kitchen. A second later she came tearing back into the drawing room. Vernon was sobbing and shaking in every limb. Nichopoulos got the old man to his feet and led him slowly into the kitchen. Ginger recalls staring out the back window toward the pasture. "It was like all the leaves were dying," she recalls. "It was weird . . . like everything died." She kept saying to herself, "No, no!" Finally, Dr. Nick came back into the parlor and signed to the paramedics that they could leave. Then, he picked up a phone and called Maurice Elliott. It was time that the announcement be made to the public.

By the time Maurice Elliott got the go-ahead from Dr. Nichopoulos, the hospital had been laid under siege by the press corps. Word of the crisis had spread from the reporters who routinely monitor police and fire emergency calls. Then the rumors had begun to fly. Elliott had stalled the press, saying that Elvis was having difficulty breathing. Now, at last, he could disclose the truth. Joe Esposito, who had been closeted during this time in Elliott's office, making calls to the Colonel and Tom Huelett of Concerts West, was asked if he would like to make the announcement. He said he couldn't face the press. It now became Maurice Elliott's duty. He called in the reporters and told them that Elvis had been pronounced dead at three-thirty, apparently from heart failure. He stressed, however, that nothing official would be forthcoming until that evening, when a press conference would be called to release the results of an autopsy.

The autopsy is a traditional ritual of royalty. At the French court, whenever a member of the ruling family died, the other members would assemble in the bedchamber, just as they would for a birth, to witness the court physician dissect the body, each organ being plopped into a fine silver bowl. The reason for this practice lay in the fear of poisoning, which, strange to say, was precisely what Vernon Presley believed was the cause of Elvis's death. Actually, Vernon knew as well as anyone in the inner circle that his son was a confirmed drug addict. The staff of Baptist Memorial Hospital knew a great deal about Elvis's addiction because he had gone there several times to kick his habit, his most recent stay being in April. Their knowledge was shared undoubtedly by the Memphis Medical Examiner, Dr. Jerry Francisco, whose responsibility it was now to establish the cause of this sudden death in a relatively young man.

Within an hour of Elvis's death, his body was brought into the hospital morgue, where an unusually large number of people were present, including as many as eight pathologists. Though autopsies are usually conducted by one forensic pathologist and an assistant, in this case the combination of curiosity coupled with the desire to have every detail witnessed and verified as a protection against charges of carelessness or unprofessional conduct produced an extraordinary multiplication of medical men, as it did also of laboratory reports and independent analyses of the findings. It is one of the great ironies of Elvis Presley's life that his death, which was the subject of intense scientific scrutiny, should have been enveloped in the same cloud of mystery that long enshrouded his birth.

Elvis's body was laid out on a stainless steel table, equipped with a sink and drains, under a battery of powerful lights similar to those used in operating rooms. The autopsy was conducted by Dr. Eric Muirhead, chief of the department of pathology. Dressed in a gown with a plastic protective apron and flanked by his assistant, notebook in hand, the pathologist commenced the process by examining carefully the surface of the body, which he would have found pitted with countless needle marks. Under the skin he would have found traces of the hematomas produced by earlier injections. Once every detail of the surface had been noted, the internal examination commenced.

The procedure is to make a Y incision: two long cuts from the shoulders down to the belly button and then a single incision down the abdomen to the pubis. The skin is then lifted back and secured so that the pathologist can examine the underlying tissues and muscles. Next the rib cage is cut with a saw so that the chest plate can be removed, exposing the heart and lungs. Each major organ is examined, removed and weighed. Slices of the liver and kidneys are taken and put into bottles filled with preservatives for microscopic examination and chemical analysis in the toxicology laboratory: Elvis's heart was found to be enlarged, his arteries somewhat clogged and his liver—the organ most affected by drug abuse—so diseased that it looked exactly like pâté de foie gras.

After opening the stomach and examining its contents (which would normally have included some half-dissolved pills[2]) samples are taken of the blood, blood serum, urine, spinal fluid and bowel contents. The final task is the examination of the brain. The scalp is cut and pulled both backward over the nape of the neck and forward over the face to expose the surface of the skull. The entire top of the head is then cut off with a power saw, which sends puffs of dust into the atmosphere, against which the operators protect themselves by donning face masks. When the top of the skull is lifted off like a bowl, the brain beneath is examined and then scooped out for sampling and sectioning.

When every part and organ of the body has been exhaustively examined, the three-hour procedure terminates with the remains of the brain being put back inside the skull and the internal organs gathered in a bag and stuffed back inside the body cavity, which is then stitched up. Encased in a paper shroud, the corpse of Elvis Presley was now ready for the embalmer and the cosmetician.

At the same time that Elvis was being cut up in Memphis, he was being repackaged in New York. Colonel Parker received Joe Esposito's announcement that Elvis was dead in his hotel suite at Portland, Maine. After a brief conversation, the Colonel slumped for a few minutes in his chair. Then he called Vernon Presley at Graceland. Colonel told Vernon that it was vital they act immediately to protect their own and Lisa Marie's interests. What concerned the Colonel especially was the prospect of a wild exploitation of Elvis's name and image by a horde of unauthorized souvenir and paraphernalia manufacturers and merchants.

As soon as the Colonel received Vernon's permission to carry on, the canny old man put into effect a long-meditated plan. Getting in

---

[2] The gut-paralyzing effect of opiates greatly retards digestion, which is one of the reasons why drugs ingested by mouth are so slow to produce their effects in addicts.

touch that very afternoon with Harry "The Bear" Geissler, president of Factors, Inc., a merchandising company whose hottest item was a Farrah Fawcett-Majors T-shirt, the Colonel commenced the negotiations that concluded two weeks later with Factors obtaining exclusive rights to the Presley merchandising in exchange for a $150,000 guarantee and a sizable royalty on every item sold. Colonel chose Geissler, it has been said, because Factors had once been forced to pay one hundred thousand dollars in damages as a merchandising bootlegger. Operating on the principle that it takes one to know one, the Colonel reasoned that Geissler, whose contract obliged him to prosecute bootleggers, would be the ideal man to police the Presley market.[3]

It is highly significant that the contract with Factors was negotiated by Colonel Parker not on behalf of the Presley Estate but with his company, Boxcar, Inc. The deal Colonel made with Vernon Presley provided for two fifty-fifty splits: half of the income received by Boxcar would be paid to Colonel Parker as manager; the other half would be divided equally between Boxcar and the Estate. The upshot of this arrangement was that Colonel and his men obtained *seventy-five percent* of the merchandising income. Another oddity of the deal was the ten percent off-the-top commission given to William Morris, an immense sum of money that Colonel characterized later as a "finder's fee."

At eight o'clock the night of Elvis's death, the medical examiner and Dr. Nichopoulos held a press conference to disclose the gross findings of the autopsy. Dr. Francisco said that the death appeared to have been caused by "cardiac arrythmia," or, in plain English, an erratic heartbeat. Asked to elaborate, the coroner averred: "There was severe cardiovascular disease present. He had a history of mild hypertension and some coronary artery disease. These two diseases may be responsible for cardiac arrhythmia, but the precise cause was not determined. Basically, it was a natural death. It may take several days, it may take several weeks to determine the cause of death. The precise cause of death may never be discovered." Strike "discovered" and substitute "disclosed," and this statement becomes a prophetic utterance.

---

[3] Two months after Colonel signed with Geissler, the FBI received a tip that Factors had defrauded three of its licensors of a substantial sum in royalties. The company pled guilty to three counts of mail fraud.

THE METAPHYSICAL ELVIS

Elvis was, is, and will always remain a creature of our subconscious desires. His longevity as a cultural icon is largely due to his flexibility—his willingness to take the shape of what we most wanted to see. Whether our fantasies were psychic, sexual, cosmic, financial, or religious, Elvis accommodated all of us to extremes while remaining purely himself. These pieces are a celebration of that unique quality—Elvisness—in all its strange beauty.

ENCOUNTER ON THE ROAD TO MEMPHIS

by Dr. Raymond Moody, Jr.

The following is an excerpt from Dr. Moody's book Elvis After Life, *a fascinating look at individuals who have apparently had psychic encounters with Elvis from beyond the grave. Moody's straightforward and rational examination of a phenomenon that is scoffed at and frequently joked about makes for absorbing and thought-provoking reading.*

I FIRST HEARD OF Jack Matthews's amazing encounter with Elvis Presley from Bill Grady, the manager of an auto parts business in a sleepy little town in Alabama. I had gone there to lecture, and I had mentioned my interest in this topic casually during the presentation. Afterwards, Bill came up and in a helpful and engaging fashion mentioned that he knew of a story which might intrigue me. Bill said that an acquaintance of his, a long-haul truck driver named Jack Matthews, once claimed to have seen Elvis on a highway after Elvis's death and had even, he believed, claimed to have given the singer a ride. Bill wondered if perhaps I might be interested in talking with Jack, who lived about eighty miles away in another Alabama town. I replied that I certainly would be interested, and Bill invited me to drop by his store the next morning. We could find out how to get in touch with Jack from the address file in his shop, he said.

I arrived at the shop at nine o'clock A.M. the next day. Bill smiled from behind the big oak counter and, reaching out to hand me a slip of paper on which was printed Jack's address and phone number, he invited me to sit with him for a while and have a cup of coffee.

As we drank our coffee, Bill told me that he wasn't sure that Jack would talk to me, that he was a loner who pretty much kept to himself. Bill also told me that Jack had had some health problems lately—stomach and lung trouble, he said, from drinking and smoking too much—but that I might be able to get through to him if I mentioned to Jack that Bill had told me about him.

When I got back home, I immediately started trying to contact Jack by telephone. The next four weeks were a frustrating time as I attempted again and again, without any success, to reach him. I left several messages with his mother, but he never returned my calls. Finally I forgot about Jack, assuming that he wasn't comfortable with talking to me.

One morning about 8 A.M. as I was sitting in my office, the phone rang. A sleepy, somewhat hoarse voice said, "Dr. Moody, this is Jack Matthews." Delighted, I explained to Jack that I am a psychiatrist who has a special interest in unusual experiences concerning Elvis and that Bill Grady had outlined to me the strange tale that he had heard Jack tell. Would Jack be willing, I asked him, to meet me sometime and tell me what had happened to him? Jack wanted to know what I thought about such things, whether I was going to label him a "nut" or a "liar." I replied that in the course of my study I had met many psychologically normal people who had reported incredible happenings involving Elvis Presley and that although I had no idea whether these happenings were actually "real" or not, I was convinced that the people who had told them to me were being sincere with me.

Jack sighed an audible sigh of relief. He told me that he had wanted to tell his story to someone who would listen sympathetically. He agreed to talk to me sometime soon.

About three weeks later, I got another call from Jack. In about two days, he told me, he would be coming through Tennessee. He asked if I could meet him at a truck stop near a certain town. He would probably get there about five in the afternoon, or perhaps a little later, he said. I told him I would be there. He would recognize me, I told him, by my tape recorder and my brown jacket.

On the appointed day, I arrived at the truck stop at about 4:15 P.M. Five o'clock came, and then six, and then seven, and Jack didn't show up. I had almost decided to give up waiting when, about twenty minutes before eight, I saw a tall, thin, somewhat grizzled-looking trucker walk in the front door and look around nervously. When my eyes caught his across the room, he nodded and walked toward me. He wore blue jeans, a blue plaid flannel shirt and leather cowboy boots. I noticed that he was carrying a red plaid wool jacket draped over his right arm. He had about a two-days' growth of beard.

As he reached the booth where I was sitting, he spoke to me. "Sorry I'm late, Dr. Moody. Had some trouble on the road a hundred miles back, and it's been raining hard besides." I looked out the window at the rain that had been pouring down for about an hour.

Jack sat down and we ordered dinner. As we ate, we learned about each other. Jack told me from the beginning that he had been under treatment for alcoholism and that he had been in the hospital three times to dry out. It was working now and he hadn't had a drink for almost a year. He had the sunken, soulful eyes of an alcoholic, I thought to myself.

After dinner, he lit up a cigarette. I suggested we talk about his experience with Elvis Presley.

This was back in 1980. The date was December 20th. I remember it exactly because not only did it shake me up so bad but also this was two days before my mother's birthday, which is December 22nd. It was real important for me to get back home to Alabama for my mother's birthday. I was hauling a load to Memphis from out west and I had been worrying that if something went wrong with the truck I might not make it home in time for her birthday. I planned to unload in Memphis on the 21st and to drive home that night. All the family was coming on her birthday, but we were going to be there by ourselves on Christmas Day.

I was worried about my mother because she had been in the hospital two months before with heart trouble, and I was afraid that this might be her last birthday. I still live at home with her. I was married for five years but my wife left me in 1978 and I have been living at home with my mother ever since.

Anyway, I was running behind that night and it was dark. It was about nine-thirty at night. I was about a hundred miles west of Memphis. I knew that road well and I was planning to go on into Memphis that night. Now, one strange thing about this to me was that I hardly ever have picked up hitchhikers. Once, about six years before, I had picked up a guy in Nevada, and he turned out to be crazy and started yelling at me. He pulled a knife on me, but I knocked it out of his hand and pushed him out of the cab onto the side of the road.

I am an independent trucker but since that time I don't pick up hitchhikers. You never can tell who's going to get in the truck with you these days when you stop to pick up a hitchhiker.

But that night of December 20th was different. I had stopped for fuel. I was nervous and I got out of the truck to walk around and stretch for a while to calm my nerves. I drank two cups of coffee. The lights around the station where I had stopped were bright floodlights, but this was out in the country and the other side of the road across from the station was dark. There were trees across the road, a clump of trees. I looked over there and I thought I saw a light in the woods. Not a light like a flashlight but more a patch of light, like a glow coming from in the woods.

I wondered what it was. I wondered at first if I was seeing a bright cloud through the trees, but I never could tell where the light was coming from. I stood there by the road gazing at that smudge of light and trying to focus my eyes on it. Then all of a sudden I saw a fellow walk sort of in front of the light. He walked along the other side of the road toward the highway. I noticed he was wearing an overcoat and was carrying a bundle under his arm.

I guessed he had been walking along the road and passed in front of the light, but I just guessed that because by the time I saw him he was walking along the road. He may have walked out of the woods for all I know. I really don't know where he came from. I was just guessing that he had been walking along the road before I saw him, but I really don't know.

When I first saw him I didn't see his legs. He was walking behind some low bushes and I just saw from his head down to his hips. Anyway, he seemed to notice me and walked out toward the street. As he did I walked on across the road. There was no traffic on that road at the time.

I got right up to him, almost to the other side of the road from the station and I said, "Where you headed?" I felt sort of sorry for him. Why, I don't know. He looked worried. I didn't think he heard me. I had been speaking quietly and he didn't answer, so I said it again, louder. "Where you headed?"

This time he looked at me and said, "Memphis."

I said, "Going to Memphis for the holidays?"

He said, "Yeah, I'm going home to see my momma and daddy."

I noticed that he had a Tennessee accent and a deep voice. I couldn't see his face well because he had a big hat or maybe a hood over his head. I wondered why he was walking along the road a hundred miles from Memphis, so I said, "How are you traveling?"

He said, "I'm going over to the highway to try to hitch a ride."

Then he walked on and went out of my sight down the road. I went back to the station, got in my truck and turned around and drove back toward the highway. Where the station was was maybe half a mile on that road off the highway and I hadn't gone a quarter of a mile until I saw him again, walking along beside the pavement on the left side of the road carrying that bundle under his arm.

Before I had a chance to think better of it I had stopped my truck on the road beside him. I opened up the window and leaned my head and shoulders out of the cab and I said, "I'm going to Memphis. I'll give you a ride."

He thanked me and crossed the road in front of the cab and got in, and I drove on and got back onto the highway for Memphis. As soon as he got in, I could tell he was a real polite man. He kept calling me "sir." Every little thing was "Yes, sir" this or "No, sir" that. I thought this must be a real fine man with good upbringing.

Well, I was real tired for the rest of the run into Memphis, but with the coffee in me I stayed awake, and so my rider and I were batting the breeze. I don't remember what all we talked about. I remember there was some talk about music we both liked. He told me that he was looking forward to seeing his mother and father. I could tell he felt about his mother about like I feel about mine. I could tell they were real close, as my mother and I are. He told me he had some presents for his parents in the package he was carrying. He also told me that he had been a truck driver for a while and he knew a lot about cars. He said he had several Cadillacs, but I didn't believe him. I thought he was just a poor boy trying to look big. I just let that one go and didn't say anything else to him about it. I thought it was pretty weird that a man with several Cadillacs would be hitching a ride home from out in the middle of nowhere.

We got along real well, though. I told him that I had been having trouble with alcohol. He seemed very understanding and told me that he had had trouble with pain killers and sleeping pills, so he knew how I felt.

All this time, it had been dark in the cab so I hadn't gotten a real good look at his face. I can't say for sure how old he seemed to be. I assumed maybe thirty or thirty-five, maybe younger. I don't know.

A few miles outside of Memphis, though, it began to brighten up from all the lights along the road and I could see him better. I could tell he looked familiar. I was sure I had seen him before. I asked him where he wanted to be let off, and he told me the address, which was Elvis Presley Boulevard. He said that he would get off as close to there as I was going. I had never gotten around to introducing myself and I wanted to know who he was, too, so I said, "My name is Jack Matthews." I glanced over at him for a second.

Just as I looked at him, he turned toward me and looked straight into my eyes and he said, "I'm Elvis Presley, sir."

I froze and I was stiff as a board. Sweat popped out on my forehead and my palms and I couldn't talk. I sort of stammered and I said something like, "You've got to be kidding." The next mile or so I was scared and I couldn't say a word. I can't say how I was able to drive that truck in the state I was in.

It was Elvis Presley, all right. Or his ghost. He looked just like he did in his heyday. I was quaking in my boots.

Finally he said that he wanted to get out at a certain road and I stopped the truck. I had seen a ghost, and my heart was pounding.

I never had been to Graceland at that time, but about two weeks later I got up my nerve and I went back to Memphis and went over to Graceland. It was real close, it turned out, to the spot where I had let him off.

Well, that's my story. I wasn't drinking at the time this happened. I had been on the wagon for about a week when this happened, and I swear I hadn't touched a drop that night. I hadn't taken any kind of drugs at all."

After Jack had finished telling his story, I spent another hour asking him questions. I wanted to know whether he had been an Elvis Presley fan before the night of December 20th, 1980. He replied that he had liked Elvis all right, but that he much preferred country music to rock 'n' roll. His favorite singers were Willie Nelson and Waylon Jennings, he told me.

I remarked to Jack that it had struck me as I had listened to him that there were several parallels between his own life and character and that of Elvis Presley. In the first place, it is well known that Elvis was very closely attached to his mother, and it was obvious that Jack had a very similar bond to his mother. Both of them had been truck drivers, both liked cars, both of them had been divorced, both of them had trouble with substance abuse. Also, it seemed significant to me that when Jack met up with the apparition of Elvis on that lonely country road, Elvis's expressed concern was the same as had been weighing heavily on Jack's mind just before the encounter, namely, getting home to his family for a reunion.

Jack listened thoughtfully as I spoke, and he said that he was surprised at the similarities and parallels that I had just pointed out, and that he hadn't thought of it in quite that way. He asked me if I knew any psychological or medical reason for what had happened to him that night.

"In all honesty, Jack," I answered, "I really don't know. But if you want me to tell you one possible explanation that comes to my mind, I will, as long as you understand that I'm not trying to dismiss your experience out of hand and that I am just telling you this explanation as a possibility, not as a certainty."

"Shoot," he said.

My mind raced back over what I had learned in medical school, in my subsequent residency training, and in practice about a condition which sometimes occurs in alcoholics when they abruptly stop drinking, as Jack had told me he did "about a week" before the bizarre incident on the road to Memphis. I began to speak slowly to the kind trucker who was sitting across the table from me.

"Jack," I asked, "have you ever heard of delirium tremens, the D.T.'s?"

"Yeah," he replied. "They told me about that every time I went into the hospital for alcoholism. It's where you see pink rats after you go off alcohol. I've never had it, but several of the fellows who were in the hospital with me did, and they told me about it, too."

I told him that sometimes, a few days after an alcoholic stops drinking suddenly, he will start to have vivid hallucinations. He will see things that aren't there. He will sweat, and he'll shake and tremble. People who are going through the D.T.'s aren't able to sleep and they are very restless and frightened at times.

Jack was paying close attention as I talked. I paused and watched him take a sip of his coffee and another puff of his cigarette.

"Several of those things that happen in D.T.'s were happening to you that night." I went on. "You told me that you were 'nervous' when you stopped at the station. You were obviously pretty restless then, too, and walking around. Later on, you said that you broke out in a sweat and that you were frozen with fear. All this happened about a week, you said, after you had stopped drinking."

I paused, and as I did Jack stared soberly and reflectively off into the distance. He appeared to be lost in thought. As we sat there in silence I began to wonder if it was even possible that a man undergoing active delirium tremens would nonetheless be able to drive a huge truck one hundred miles without incident, as Jack apparently had done. Just offhand, it seemed unlikely, yet as soon as I had put the question to myself I remembered something that had happened several years before which put my mind at more ease. One night, when I was working in the emergency room, a man—coincidentally, also a trucker—had come in severely ill with impending D.T.'s. He was an alcoholic, and he told me that he had been driving along the highway in his truck from another state when the hallucinations began. He began to hallucinate dead bodies and large, grotesque animals lying alongside and on the surface of the road. Even in this condition, however, he managed to make it all the way back home—a long distance—to come to the hospital in his own town for help. I had my answer: It *was* possible for a person who was undergoing alcohol withdrawal and hallucinations to maneuver a truck along the highway.

Jack interrupted my reverie; his words jolted me back to the reality of a booth in a restaurant in a truck stop in rural Tennessee.

"All that you say is true, Dr. Moody," Jack said. "It's true. And I had the shakes real bad, too, that night. I didn't tell you because I had forgotten about it. Now I remember. I was shaking real bad that night."

"Well," I said, "the fact that you were shaking is even more evidence that you were going through alcohol withdrawal. It is possible that the experience of seeing Elvis was a hallucination, if you were going through D.T.'s."

"So I might have just imagined the whole thing?" Jack asked.

"Who knows?" I answered. "Maybe it was part real and part hallucination. Maybe there really was a hitchhiker who really rode with you for a hundred miles, and you just hallucinated the last part about him being Elvis Presley . . . like a dream."

Jack looked uncertain. "I don't know, Doc," he said.

"I don't know, either, Jack."

We both laughed.

By then it was getting late. Jack wanted to get farther down the road that night before stopping to sleep, and the rain had let up. I walked him out to his truck, where we shook hands and Jack turned and climbed into his truck. He rolled down the window and looked at me; a friendly grin covered his face. By now the engine of the truck was chugging and roaring.

"To think. That whole thing might have happened because of my drinking, he said, raising his voice against the noise of the engine.

"Yeah," I said. "It's possible. But there's another possibility, too."

"What's that, Dr. Moody?" he asked.

"Maybe you really did see the ghost of Elvis Presley!" I shouted.

We both laughed again, and I stood there watching as the big tractor-trailer truck, its lights flashing, pulled away into the cool Tennessee mountain night.

Although delirium (which results, in effect, from a chemical disturbance in the function of the brain) may well have entered into Jack's experience, we can hardly assume that it accounts for the whole picture. There must have been deep-seated psychological factors as well, which also helped shape the content and the emotional tone of his encounter with Elvis. This is illustrated by the story of Bess Carpenter, in whose case delirium also appears to have played a prominent role. Here, though, the emotional context of her vision, and the role it seemed to play in her life when it happened, were quite different.

It alarmed and saddened Bess when she learned, in 1979, that she was pregnant. She wasn't married and had no prospects. The man whose child she was carrying lived far away, and she had broken up with him. She had no intention of letting him know about her pregnancy. She never seriously considered having an abortion, and there was no one to support her emotionally during her pregnancy. Elvis Presley had been her idol since she was fourteen years old. In her moment of greatest despair, she feels, he was there to help her.

"When I found out about the pregnancy, I was horrified. I wanted to die, which was unthinkable because I had two kids from my marriage to raise. I wasn't about to leave them wondering about why their mother had committed suicide. When I told my parents, they freaked out. I'll never forget it. It was on a Sunday, after church. I thought I could catch them in a forgiving mood if I told them then. No soap.

I hope you understand that I wasn't myself then. I got a divorce in 1977, with two kids. For two years I was hell-bent on self-destruction. It was depression, I guess. Believe me, when you are depressed you can do anything. So I ran around with a guy who was a bad seed. When I found out I was pregnant, I worried about it for two months before I told my parents. By then it was too late to get an abortion, which I wouldn't have done anyway.

My parents couldn't fathom a thirty-four-year-old divorcée with two kids and a Christian upbringing getting pregnant out of wedlock. They disowned me and wouldn't have a thing to do with me. I was absolutely alone during this time, let me assure you.

Well, I have a thing about Elvis. He was my dream man from the time I was fourteen. At my fifteenth birthday party, my girlfriends gave me a cake that had "ELVIS and BESS" written in pink icing on the top of it. Our names were enclosed in a heart. I love Elvis. I don't mind telling you.

It nearly killed me when he died. My divorce had come through a month before and I was just beginning to cheer up. The way I heard about it wasn't the happiest circumstance, either. I was eating dinner in a bar and grill on my way home from work when it came on television. When the news came over the tube, the place fell into a hush. There were some groans and sobs. This one drunk guy sitting at the bar mumbled something about being glad that Elvis was gone, and three people were on him right away, calling him unprintable names. What a creep. I could have hit him myself and probably would have if those three other guys hadn't shoved him out of there fast. My mother always used to tell me that if you accomplish something worthwhile in life, there will always be people around who want to bring you down. They will criticize people who've done great things to try to get the attention off their own inadequacies. I guess this guy was a prime example.

Anyway, I cried about Elvis on and off for weeks. I still cry about it sometimes. I went to Memphis for the funeral. Loaded the kids in the car and drove all night to get there.

The saddest part of my pregnancy in 1979 was going to the obstetrician's office and seeing other women there with their husbands. Naturally, I read a lot about pregnancy. My last pregnancy had been eight years before. Some of these articles talked about natural childbirth, the role of the father in the delivery, and so on. That really upset me. I was a wreck. I wished there was someone like that to be there for me.

I remember the date of this experience about Elvis Presley exactly. Naturally, it was November 4th, 1979. That was the day Todd was born. It wasn't one of those middle of the night things. He was born in the afternoon: 2:15 P.M. I went into labor that morning. I called my neighbor, Pat, and she took me to the hospital. My parents had told me they didn't want anything to do with it, so I didn't call them. Then, the next day when they found out from Pat, they were upset. "Why didn't you call us?" they said. My mother took to the bed for a week, she was so upset I hadn't called. There's no accounting for people.

When they wheeled me into the delivery room, they put this mask on me and I breathed the anesthetic. I was conscious the whole time, but I had a weird experience. The doctors and nurses were all around me in these white gowns, looking at me. Right there among them, Elvis Presley appeared. He smiled and winked at me. He said, "Relax, Bess, it's O.K. I'll be here with you." It looked just like him. I stared into his face, then I would blink or look away, but when I looked back he was still there. The others had on surgical masks but Elvis didn't. It was his voice, too. I'm certain of it. When you hear Elvis Presley's voice speaking to you, there can't be any doubt whose voice it is.

I stared into his face the whole time. He was so sweet. He stood there the whole time. Then, when the baby came, it was he who said, "It's a boy!" For an Elvis Presley fan, there can't be a bigger thrill than hearing Elvis himself telling you you have a new baby.

All the commotion started then. Doctors and nurses were running here and there, checking the baby and sewing me up and I sort of lost Elvis in the crowd. I didn't see him anymore after that. They wheeled me out of the delivery room and I tried to tell my doctor that Elvis had been there with me. The doctor didn't say anything but the nurses chuckled and said I was dreaming. But I wasn't dreaming. It wasn't like a dream. I'm not sure it was real, either. I still wonder what it was. Was Elvis there with me in the delivery room, or wasn't he? Whatever, I feel like he came through for me when I was feeling so low. I don't know for sure if it was real or not. I guess when I meet him in Heaven, I'll ask him and find out for sure. For now, I don't know. It's really like something he would do, no matter how it turns out. Either way, I appreciate Elvis."

The simplest explanation for Bess's experience is that it resulted psychologically from her deep yearning to have someone there to support and to be with her during a particularly troubled time in her life. Her parents had turned away from her, and she had no husband, so she turned to an important figure in her life: Elvis Presley. Because she was delirious due to the effects of the anesthetic, she hallucinated Elvis. Whatever the actual mechanism of what happened, however, her experience had a positive emotional effect on her. What would have otherwise been a dreary episode in her life was turned into an occasion of joy and hope.

CHAPTER 15 FROM
WHITE NOISE

███████

by Don DeLillo

The following is a brief selection from Don DeLillo's 1985 novel, White
Noise. *Like much of DeLillo's work, this chapter's comic absurdity has a
subtle hint of menace and its cadences are poetic. He brilliantly captures the
academic vernacular of two professors lecturing in counterpoint on the similarities between Elvis and Hitler.*

I put on my dark glasses, composed my face and walked into the
room. There were twenty-five or thirty young men and women,
many in fall colors, seated in armchairs and sofas and on the beige
broadloom. Murray walked among them, speaking, his right hand
trembling in a stylized way. When he saw me, he smiled sheepishly.
I stood against the wall, attempting to loom, my arms folded under
the black gown.

Murray was in the midst of a thoughtful monologue.

"Did his mother know that Elvis would die young? She talked
about assassins. She talked about the life. The life of a star of this
type and magnitude. Isn't the life structured to cut you down early?
This is the point, isn't it? There are rules, guidelines. If you don't
have the grace and wit to die early, you are forced to vanish, to hide
as if in shame and apology. She worried about his sleepwalking. She
thought he might go out a window. I have a feeling about mothers.
Mothers really do know. The folklore is correct."

"Hitler adored his mother," I said.

A surge of attention, unspoken, identifiable only in a certain convergence of stillness, an inward tensing. Murray kept moving, of course, but a bit more deliberately, picking his way between the chairs, the people seated on the floor. I stood against the wall, arms folded.

"Elvis and Gladys liked to nuzzle and pet," he said. "They slept in the same bed until he began to approach physical maturity. They talked baby talk to each other all the time."

"Hitler was a lazy kid. His report card was full of unsatisfactorys. But Klara loved him, spoiled him, gave him the attention his father failed to give him. She was a quiet woman, modest and religious, and a good cook and housekeeper."

"Gladys walked Elvis to school and back every day. She defended him in little street rumbles, lashed out at any kid who tried to bully him."

"Hitler fantasized. He took piano lessons, made sketches of museums and villas. He sat around the house a lot. Klara tolerated this. He was the first of her children to survive infancy. Three others had died."

"Elvis confided in Gladys. He brought his girlfriends around to meet her."

"Hitler wrote a poem to his mother. His mother and his niece were the women with the greatest hold on his mind."

"When Elvis went into the army, Gladys became ill and depressed. She sensed something, maybe as much about herself as about him. Her psychic apparatus was flashing all the wrong signals. Foreboding and gloom."

"There's not much doubt that Hitler was what we call a mama's boy."

A note-taking young man murmured absently, *"Muttersöhnchen."* I regarded him warily. Then, on an impulse, I abandoned my stance at the wall and began to pace the room like Murray, occasionally pausing to gesture, to listen, to gaze out a window or up at the ceiling.

"Elvis could hardly bear to let Gladys out of his sight when her condition grew worse. He kept a vigil at the hospital."

"When his mother became severely ill, Hitler put a bed in the kitchen to be closer to her. He cooked and cleaned."

"Elvis fell apart with grief when Gladys died. He fondled and petted her in the casket. He talked baby talk to her until she was in the ground."

"Klara's funeral cost three hundred and seventy kronen. Hitler wept at the grave and fell into a period of depression and self-pity. He felt an intense loneliness. He'd lost not only his beloved mother but also his sense of home and hearth."

"It seems fairly certain that Gladys's death caused a fundamental shift at the center of the King's world view. She'd been his anchor, his sense of security. He began to withdraw from the real world, to enter the state of his own dying."

"For the rest of his life, Hitler could not bear to be anywhere near Christmas decorations because his mother died near a Christmas tree."

"Elvis made death threats, received death threats. He took mortuary tours and became interested in UFOs. He began to study the *Bardo Thödol,* commonly known as *The Tibetan Book of the Dead.* This is a guide to dying and being reborn."

"Years later, in the grip of self-myth and deep remoteness, Hitler kept a portrait of his mother in his spartan quarters at Obersalzberg. He began to hear a buzzing in his left ear."

Murray and I passed each other near the center of the room, almost colliding. Alfonse Stompanato entered, followed by several students, perhaps drawn by some magnetic wave of excitation, some frenzy in the air. He settled his surly bulk in a chair as Murray and I circled each other and headed off in opposite directions, avoiding an exchange of looks.

"Elvis fulfilled the terms of the contract. Excess, deterioration, self-destructiveness, grotesque behavior, a physical bloating and a series of insults to the brain, self-delivered. His place in legend is secure. He bought off the skeptics by dying early, horribly, unnecessarily. No one could deny him now. His mother probably saw it all, as on a nineteen-inch screen, years before her own death."

Murray, happily deferring to me, went to a corner of the room and sat on the floor, leaving me to pace and gesture alone, secure in my professional aura of power, madness and death.

"Hitler called himself the lonely wanderer out of nothingness. He sucked on lozenges, spoke to people in endless monologues, free-associating, as if the language came from some vastness beyond the world and he was simply the medium of revelation. It's interesting to wonder if he looked back from the *führerbunker,* beneath the burning city, to the early days of his power. Did he think of the small groups of tourists who visited the little settlement where his mother was born and where he'd spent summers with his cousins, riding in ox carts and making kites? They came to honor the site, Klara's birthplace. They entered the farmhouse, poked around tentatively.

Adolescent boys climbed on the roof. In time the numbers began to increase. They took pictures, slipped small items into their pockets. Then crowds came, mobs of people overrunning the courtyard and singing patriotic songs, painting swastikas on the walls, on the flanks of farm animals. Crowds came to his mountain villa, so many people he had to stay indoors. They picked up pebbles where he'd walked and took them home as souvenirs, Crowds came to hear him speak, crowds erotically charged, the masses he once called his only bride. He closed his eyes, clenched his fists as he spoke, twisted his sweat-drenched body, remade his voice as a thrilling weapon. 'Sex murders,' someone called these speeches. Crowds came to be hypnotized by the voice, the party anthems, the torchlight parades."

I stared at the carpet and counted silently to seven.

"But wait. How familiar this all seems, how close to ordinary. Crowds come, get worked up, touch and press—people eager to be transported. Isn't this ordinary? We *know* all this. There must have been something different about those crowds. What was it? Let me whisper the terrible word, from the Old English, from the Old German, from the Old Norse. *Death*. Many of those crowds were assembled in the name of death. They were there to attend tributes to the dead. Processions, songs, speeches, dialogues with the dead, recitations of the names of the dead. They were there to see pyres and flaming wheels, thousands of flags dipped in salute, thousands of uniformed mourners. There were ranks and squadrons, elaborate backdrops, blood banners and black dress uniforms. Crowds came to form a shield against their own dying. To become a crowd is to keep out death. To break off from the crowd is to risk death as an individual, to face dying alone. Crowds came for this reason above all others. They were there to be a crowd."

Murray sat across the room. His eyes showed a deep gratitude. I had been generous with the power and madness at my disposal, allowing my subject to be associated with an infinitely lesser figure, a fellow who sat in La-Z-Boy chairs and shot out TVs. It was not a small matter. We all had an aura to maintain, and in sharing mine with a friend I was risking the very things that made me untouchable.

People gathered round, students and staff, and in the mild din of half heard remarks and orbiting voices I realized we were now a crowd. Not that I needed a crowd around me now. Least of all now. Death was strictly a professional matter here. I was comfortable with it, I was on top of it. Murray made his way to my side and escorted me from the room, parting the crowd with his fluttering hand.

ELVIS IN DEATH

███████

by Nick Tosches

Elvis in Death was first published in German, in American Dreams *(Zurich: U. Bar Verlag, 1984), and appears here in English for the first time. In this essay, Tosches approaches the Elvis phenomenon with a keen eye, a savage wit, and a healthy skepticism, providing fresh perspective on our continuing obsession with Elvis.*

On Tuesday, August 16, 1977, I was sitting at home, which at the time was in Nashville, lost, as was my wont, in lazy midday broodings of dirty lucre and dirtier deeds. The telephone rang, and I picked it up. It was my buddy Al Bianculli, a song-plugger at Combine, the publishing company owned by Bob Beckham and Kris Kristofferson. Al was, and is, one of the greatest admirers of Elvis Presley's whom I have ever known, and there was actual distress in his voice as he spoke to me that day.

"Hey," he said, "you're not going to believe this. Elvis is dead. He O.D.'d."

He told me that Beckham's son-in-law Chip Young, who played guitar on some of Elvis's recordings, had been set to leave for Memphis that morning for a session that Elvis had scheduled at Graceland. A mysterious call had informed Chip that the session had been canceled. Then, at noon, a second call had informed him that Elvis had been canceled.

Less than twenty minutes after I hung up the phone, the news was being tolled forth with morbid excitement by every radio and television station in America. Elvis Aron Presley was dead, at the age of forty-two. I shall never forget the thundering storm clouds that darkened the Tennessee sky that afternoon, as if the Four Last Things, descending to Memphis, had rented the day in brandishment of their sovereignty.

So that was his end. I was nonplussed. I had not known Elvis Presley as a man. I had never even met him. I started then to realize that, on some level of faint illogic, I had never truly thought of him as a creature of flesh and blood but rather as an absurd effulgence of hoi polloi mythology, an all-American demigod who dwelt, enthroned between Superman and the Lone Ranger, in the blue heaven of the popular imagination. He had been so distant from reality—even the pope was more visible, more likely to grant an interview—that he seemed unreal, thus immortal. But now, less than two hundred miles from where I sat, a pathologist prepared to make a large Y-shaped incision in Elvis Presley's thorax and eviscerate the quite mortal organs from his cold remains.

Five days later, traveling east, I saw a sign outside a Baptist church on Highway 178 in Orangeburg, South Carolina. All That Hip Shaking Killed Elvis, it gloatingly declared. Snazzy dressers, too, those Baptists, I reflected.

By then, of course, the world knew that hip shaking had nothing to do with it. Traces of thirteen different drugs were found in Elvis's system—grim corroboration of the sensational allegations that had been published less than a month before in an ill-written paperback called *Elvis: What Happened?* But that stupid, malicious sign, posted as it was in the shadow of the great wooden cross that stood before the church, set me to thinking about the matter of Elvis's fame and the nature of his death.

It was an immense fame. In his own lifetime, his name was as immediately recognizable and as legendary as the names of Jesus, Caesar, Charlemagne, Shakespeare, Napoléon, and Einstein. And like those other names, his will live on. Yet what was his achievement, the source of his fame's enduring power? He won no wars, created no masterpieces (I hope that none among us will argue the depths of "Heartbreak Hotel" against those of *Coriolanus;* those days are over), made no great discoveries.

Elvis was, simply and supremely, a singer. Although he was, in the early days, popularly given credit for having invented rock 'n' roll, this was, of course, not remotely true. Rock 'n' roll was not invented. It evolved in the years immediately following World War II. While Elvis was still a blossoming schoolboy, rock 'n' roll, as fine as any that would ever be heard, was being made by Wynonie Harris, Amos Milburn, Fats Domino, and other less-known black recording artists. It cannot even be said in truth that Elvis was the first white rock 'n' roll star. Bill Haley's "Crazy, Man, Crazy" was on the pop charts when Elvis, paying four dollars to cut an acetate souvenir disc, made the first visit to Sam Phillips's Memphis Recording Service, on a Saturday afternoon in 1953.

No, Elvis did not invent rock 'n' roll. But he was its avatar, the embodiment of its spirit and might. He was more than a star. He possessed the souls of his followers. Virgins burned for him, and boys strove to recast themselves in his image. He had charisma, in the true and Greek New Testament sense of that word, meaning, divine grace. It was that grace, that mysterious, innocent power, that raised Elvis, the singer with no song of his own, the praiser of abject mediocrity (proclaiming at the height of his fame, in 1957, that Pat Boone had "undoubtedly the finest voice out now"), from the merely mundane to the profoundly ineffable. He could have started a religion. In a way, he did.

The years 1956 to 1960 were the golden lustrum of his reign, when he was the god of teenage America. By the mid-sixties, when he descended to the likes of "Bossa Nova Baby" and "Do the Clam," he had become an embarrassment of sorts, a gaudy anachronism in a day of more momentous and sensitive pretentions. Though he regained respect at the end of that decade—and that new respect grew in direct proportion to the increasing abandonment of the "new age" meatball mentality of the 1960s—he never again regained the magnificent success that had been his. His records in the seventies rose to the tops of the C&W and Easy Listening charts, but there were no more Top Ten pop hits for the king of rock 'n' roll, who had begun to recede into dark solitude and deathward ways, the curse at blessing's end. But through all those years, though his following waxed and dwindled, the cult never died.

This cult was almost of a religious sort. In the extreme, there were fanatics—mostly adult, middle-class males—who forsook their own identities and were born again in Elvis. These men, a few of whom I had the quite singular pleasure of meeting, lived vicariously through their idol, surrounding themselves with icons and sacred Presleyana, immersing themselves in the facts of his life, listening endlessly to the sound of his voice, until that life and that voice became more meaningful than their own. They presented him with

274

gifts, expensive guitars and such, and with vows of undying fealty, that his acceptance of these things might bring them, the adorer and the adored, closer and more intimately together. This odd religiosity was evident, in lesser degrees of fervency, throughout the saner majority of Presleyans. Like pilgrims to the Holy Land, they arrived in endless numbers at the two-leaved gate of Graceland, cherishing ever after the handfuls of gravel they picked up from his driveway. Small pieces of his clothing, such as those RCA packaged in a 1971 record album, were also treasured, not unlike *brandea,* the pieces of cloth, blessed by the remains of Saint Peter, that were sold to Christians in the early Middle Ages. This was more than the frivolous devotion of fans to their idol. It was worship. And there falls the shadow of that Baptist cross.

The Crucifixion is the heart of Christianity, the center of its mystery and power, without which Christianity most probably would have died out along with Mithraism and the other cults of the late Roman Empire. It is also the heart of another, related mystery, the mystery of popular idolatry.

When one man idolizes another, the hate and envy in his heart are as great as the love and respect of his outward homage. The idol, whom the idolator would, but never can, be, is both the object of his adoration and the cause of his effacement and insignificance. So overwhelmed is the being of the idolator by that of the idol that only the latter's supreme sacrifice, martyrdom, can justify and sanctify their relationship. Popular culture especially thrives on the self-killed. Fanatical fantasizers love to feel that Jean Harlow, James Dean, Marilyn Monroe, Jim Morrison died for them, Christ-like, on the cross of reciprocal love. (We have now even entered an age when idolators take a more active part in the process of martyrdom and canonization. Thus, John Lennon being blown away by a "fan.") As it has been said, the biggst mistake Bob Dylan made in his career was not to die in that motorcycle crash.

And so Elvis, who had fallen from grace, who had not had a Top Forty album in nearly five years, was redeemed. His old records sold as fast as RCA, with pressing plants running overtime, could ship them. "It don't mean a damned thing," Colonel Parker was rumored to have remarked about Elvis's death. "It's just like when he was away in the Army." As sales rose on the third day, the excitement—and it was excitement, of a decidedly perverse and hysterical sort, to be sure—waxed more and more ecstatic. Mourners lost their lives, crushed in the frenzied funerary convergence on Memphis. The cemetery tomb, to which the dead king had been delivered by a Cadillac hearse the color of the Resurrection raiment, was defiled by thieves in search of grisly spoils; and the body was reinterred within the hallowed, guarded walls of Graceland.

Like the fourth-century impresario who hauled Saint Stephen's coffin through Christendom, a holy huckster toured the South in Elvis's limousine, allowing believers to sit in it for a fee and to have their pictures taken in it for an additional charge. (When I encountered him that fall at the Tennessee State Fair Grounds, he was also doing a brisk business selling photocopies of Elvis's autopsy report and death certificate.)

Morbid "tribute records" (ah, euphemy!) flooded forth in waves of formaldehyde and glucose. One of these was Billy Joe Burnette's "Welcome Home, Elvis." Sung as if by his twin brother, Jesse Garon, who died at birth, the song warmly welcomed Elvis to the hereafter, where mama was "waitin' for ya, Elvis. Yeah, she's right over there. And soon our daddy will take our hand, and we'll be a happy family once again." Eventually, there was a record called "The Shroud of Memphis," celebrating the miraculous retention of Elvis's divine image à la the Turin winding sheet.

Sleazy weekly tabloids like the *Midnight Globe* and the *National Examiner* promulgated Elvitic apocrypha. Among other things, there was foretold the coming of Baby Elvis, who was to be born to a Midwestern virgin who claimed that she had been supernaturally impregnated by the spirit of the king. There were stories that Elvis was not really dead, that he had faked his own death. (These stories bore a striking likeness to the Crucifixion theory put forth in Hugh Schonfield's 1966 best-seller, *The Passover Plot,* and, more recently, in *Holy Blood, Holy Grail.* The ill-wishing cynicism of our time seems to be equaled by its gullibility.)

The Nashville entrepreneur Shelby Singleton cashed in on the fantastic notion that Elvis had not truly departed. He released an album, *Reborn,* by a masked Elvis imitator called Orion. Publicized as the risen Elvis, Orion was reputed to be a prophet who could make the blind see and the lame walk. Unfortunate cripples attended his concerts in the hope of being cured, and fanatics bought his records—there were in time six Orion albums—as if they were buying Elvis's own.

The ultimate Elvitic text came in the form of Ilona Panta's *Elvis Presley: King of Kings.* The insinuation that Elvis was none other than the Son of God was also made in *The Truth About Elvis,* written by Jess Stearn with Larry Geller. The equivalent of *The Day Christ Died* arrived in Neal and Janice Gregory's obsessive chronicle *When Elvis*

Died. Members of the Presley family also turned to the typewriter. There were books by Elvis's uncle Vester and by his stepmother, Dee.

Then came the carrion birds, those in whom hate and envy are more than just the mere and natural concomitants of love and respect. Though such creatures hate omnivorously, their cowardice prevents them from preying on the living. For them, Elvis's corpse was the feast of the aeon. The popular press, its eulogizing done, cawed forth scandalous tales of drug abuse, violence, madness, and perversion. It is distressing that of the many books about Elvis published since his death, the most successful has been *Elvis* by Albert Goldman. To behold Goldman, a miserable little wad of failed manhood, gnawing in abject rancor at the crotch of a dead hero is to be reminded of the depths of moral penury to which a man can be driven by self-loathing and greed. The fact that his ghoulish grovelings have made him rich does not speak well for the rest of us.

Veneration had become desecration. When there was no more blood left to drink and no flesh left to eat, the feast was done.

Now it is 1984. Seven years have passed since that hot summer day when the storm clouds passed over Tennessee. The long, mad spectacle of Elvis Presley's death is ended; but the Elvis cult is as strong as ever it was.

The cult's principal shrine is Graceland, the Memphis mansion where Elvis lived since 1957 and where, on that August morning twenty years later, he died. There, in the Meditation Garden, beneath a stone cross and a stone Christ, Elvis lies near his mother, Gladys, who alone of all her sex was loved by the king.

No other tomb in America is the object of so many pilgrimages as Graceland. Even the grave of her most beloved martyr, John F. Kennedy, is ill attended in comparison. Day in and day out, they stream through the gates, their eyes wide, their cameras strung round their necks: middle-aged women in print dresses, their lizard-skinned husbands in tow; children too young to know for sure why they are there, led by parents who were his disciples, drifting now between lust and menopause, youth and their own, less noticed, place in the ground; skeptics and zealots; lunatics and the dull, ordinary grist of democracy. They come from everywhere to gawk in fascination at the grave of the American dream, to walk where Elvis walked, to touch what he touched, and to send postcards of death to their loved ones back home.

The faithful bring flowers and tokens of their undying love. Housewives stand transfixed and dolorous before the tomb, like the women who kneel lost in prayer for hours at the sarcophagus of Pope Paul VI beneath the Vatican Basilica. Like those prayerful women, they seem to be petitioning for divine intercession. Elvis was the supreme son, sacrificed on the altar cloth of maternal love and laid to rest by his mother's side. He was their son, the son of all motherhood. He died for them, they seem to feel.

Younger women lavish the grave with less motherly affection. Some of them place love letters on the tomb, or floral displays bearing romantic sentiments. They knew him only in their fantasies while he lived. What mattered death to a love that had never been real? He died for them, too, of course. He died for everyone and everything, but for the drugs that had killed him.

Teenage boys enamored of death in their innocence, children of a later rock 'n' roll culture, approach the grave with delectation. Like Jim Morrison's numbered stone in Paris, it is for them a symbol of self-destruction, one of the sacred monuments of the rock 'n' roll church of death.

Some of the older males regard the grave as if it holds a kindred spirit, a good old boy like themselves, but one who got lucky and who paid for that luck with his life, just as they would doubtless have ended up paying if they had been lucky, for such are the ways of the Holy Spirit that wields the sword that moves them.

Other men seem merely to be satisfying themselves with the fact that lies in the dirt at their feet—the fact that they are alive and Elvis is dead, his fame and wealth and wet young girls gone with the breeze that is yet theirs to savor.

"How many towns in every kingdom hath superstition enriched!" exclaimed Robert Burton on the subject of holy shrines. Like much else in his *Anatomy of Melancholy,* this remark is no less trenchant today than it was in the early part of the seventeenth century. Burton surely would have been stirred by the instance of Graceland.

The Graceland mansion was built in 1939 on 500 acres belonging to the Moore family. Though it was popularly believed in later years that Elvis gave Graceland its name, the estate had been christened by its original owner, Dr. Moore, in honor of his aunt Grace. By the time that Elvis purchased Graceland, in early 1957, the estate had been whittled down to its present size of thirteen and a half acres.

Graceland is now owned and operated by Elvis Presley Enterprises, Inc., a division of the Elvis Presley Residuary Trust, all the assets of which will soon belong to Elvis's daughter and sole heir, Lisa Marie Presley.

Officially opened on June 7, 1982, Graceland attracted more than

520,000 people in its first year of business. (The prices of admission are $6 for adults and $4 for children.) Designated as a historical landmark by the Tennessee State Historical Society, Graceland has grown into one of the major tourist attractions in America. It has transformed the city of Memphis into a vacationers' mecca, enriching the municipal treasury and local economy with a steady flow of millions of tourist dollars. In death Elvis is worth far more to his hometown than he was in life.

Crass commercialism has always flourished around the major religious shrines of the world. Thriving souvenir shops surround Saint Peter's Square in Rome, and similar commerce constitutes the only big business in the remote Pyrenean town of Lourdes. As far back as the eighth century, when the decomposing bodies of the early Christian saints and martyrs were torn apart to satisfy the international demand for holy relics, such merchandizing was an immense and very lucrative industry. (In his book *Western Society and the Church in the Middle Ages,* Richard W. Southern states, "If we were able to draw up statistics of imports into England in the tenth century, relics would certainly come high on the list.") It is by means of such items that common men have always sought to bring themselves closer to the supernatural. Today as in antiquity, relics, icons, religious medals, and the like are superstitiously used to ensure good fortune and ward off bad luck. The medieval farmer who believed that his possession of a blessed relic would result in better crops and the modern automobile driver who feels that a Saint Christopher medal will help to protect him from accidents are in essence subscribing to the same magic.

No marketplace of necrolatry can compare with that which has burgeoned on Elvis Presley Boulevard, directly across from Graceland. (Ironically, this shopping center is situated on eleven acres of land purchased by Elvis in the 1960s. This property and the Graceland estate were his only landholdings at the time of his death.) Here, in a number of jerry-built stores, one may purchase all manner of Elvis Presley mementos, souvenirs, and bric-à-brac. Vendors offer everything from T-shirts and license plates to crucifixlike pendants and plaster-of-paris devotional statues. There is no telling just how much money is spent at this vast and tawdry bazaar of kitsch. One store alone, the Graceland Souvenir Shop, did more than $1,000,000 in business in 1983. Much of the merchandise sold in the great mall of death is developed and designed by Elvis Presley Enterprises, Inc., which profits directly from its sale. I was told by one of the adminis-

279

trators that more than a million postcards are sold at Graceland each year and that graven images of the king are in general the most popular merchandise.

Though a court ruling has now disentitled him to share in the large profits of Elvis Presley Enterprises, Inc., Colonel Parker's original appraisal has proved to be accurate: "It don't mean a damned thing. It's just like when he was away in the Army." Death has not hampered the marketing of Elvis. If anything, it has enhanced it. Elvis is more salable in death than he ever was in life. The Graceland shrine is more than just a monument to him. It is a monument to the majesty of the almighty American dollar. It is a temple of eternal revenue, a place where the thronging populace of the middle classes can dream the dream of kings and taste the miraculous glory of he who died for them—providing, of course, that they have the price of admission. There are no free dreams.

However we choose to look at Elvis Presley—as a saint, a savior, or a monstrosity; as the apotheosis of America's fatal and garish yearning; or as the final god in the pantheon of the West—we can be sure that the likes of him will not soon pass this way again. America heeds the call from his grave, where Jesus, Gladys, and Elvis form a new Trinity—the Lord, the mother, and the sacrificial son of the dream. It heeds that call as it heeds no other.

One thing is certain. In an age bereft of magic, Elvis was the last great mystery, the secret of which lay unrevealed even to himself. That he failed, fatally, to comprehend that mystery gives the rest of us little hope of ever doing so. After all, the greatest and truest mysteries are those without explanations.

THE ELVIS JUNKYARD

by Tubbs Gillis

This article first appeared in the New Age periodical Magical Blend. *Tubbs Gillis, aka Jerry Snider, uses the junkyard metaphor to examine the cultural debris that surrounded Elvis in life and overshadows him in death. This is a celebration of the strange, weird, tacky but ultimately lovable side of Elvis and his fans. Beneath the humor and whimsy of this piece lie some valuable insights into the Elvis phenomenon and its continuing impact on popular culture.*

Don't look now, but there's a great big hole where Elvis used to be. Only it doesn't look like a hole anymore; it looks more like a mountain. You see, that hole's become sort of like a landfill at the dump; it starts out as a hole but people start throwing all their junk in there, and pretty soon it looks more like a mountain than a hole. Only the hole's still there; now it's just got itself a mountain on top—a mountain of junk. I don't mean to say that everything we've put in our Elvis-hole is junk. I mean, you go to the junkyard and allow yourself the time to make a leisurely examination, and you can find yourself some real good stuff, but most of it's garbage. Still, it's *our* garbage, and that makes it sort of endearing in a way. I mean, you take your dump, and what does it represent? The damn thing's filled with all the stuff we've liked well enough to use till we've used it up. The same thing's true for our Elvis-fill. It's got a lot of junk, and it's got a lot of good stuff in there, too. And, like all the bottles and cans at the dump, it's got the fingerprints of our culture all over it. Let's face it, if you were a Buck Rogers era archaeologist digging around in ancient cultures, where would you look for clues? You could look in the stores, but that doesn't tell you what we actually bought, just what was available. You could look in the libraries, and that might tell you about our knowledge and what we thought about things, but the written word is second-hand and information can be made to look like something it's not. You could dig around in the cemeteries and see how we looked as specimens, but by this time all our frills and furbelows have been devoured by the worms. No, I'll tell you, if you want to know about a particular time and a particular society, the best place to dig is in its garbage. And that's what we're going to do. We're going to roll up our sleeves and have a go at all this Elvis-fill that started getting dumped in that Elvis-hole when his death was reported in August, 1977. And we're going to have a good time doing it, because that's what rock 'n' roll is all about. That's the way Elvis would have wanted it.

> *When I look out into your eyes out there;*
> *When I look out into your faces*
> *You know what I see?*
> *I see a little bit of Elvis in each and every one of you out there*
> *And let me tell you, well . . .*
> *Elvis is everywhere*
> *Elvis is everything; Elvis is everybody.*
> *Elvis is still the King.*

By the way, that snippet of song above is by Mojo Nixon. I just threw it in because it's catchy, and I'll throw it in some more as we go along. It's sort of our Elvis-fill national anthem.

So, got your sleeves rolled up? Me, too. You'll notice that the smell's not too bad—sort of an odor of reheated grease. So, we're all set. For our textbooks today we're using *Is Elvis Alive?* by Gail Brewer-Giorgio which is published by Tudor Publishing Co., and *Elvis After Life,* by Raymond A. Moody, Jr., M.D. which is published by Peachtree Publications. If you want a copy visit your book store. I've only got two, and I ain't giving mine away.

Before we get to going, I want to give out a few pointers to you beginning Elvis-fill archaeologists. First of all, you'll notice that we've only got a gunny sack each, and I can tell you we're going to

282

find a lot of stuff—a lot more than will fit in a gunny sack. So just put the important stuff in the bag. That's it. Start digging.

Something's bound to turn up at any time. Until then I'll provide you a few Elvis facts. Elvis was born January 8, 1935 in Tupelo, Mississippi. A lot of people don't know it, but he had a twin that died at birth. He grew up poor, fantasized about being Captain Marvel, and drove a truck for a living before becoming the idol of millions. His favorite sandwich was peanut butter and banana, and he ended up his career dressing a lot like Liberace. Elvis was, and is, a big star. Great Britain has a fan club with 20,000 members, and there are over 200 fan clubs in the U.S., some with 3,000 members each. When a West German poll asked 2,100 teenagers who they'd like to emulate, Elvis grabbed eight per cent of the vote.

One billion of the King's records have been sold, and, between drug busts and digging up Al Capone's vault, Geraldo Rivera figured out that that was enough records so that "every family on the face of the planet could own an Elvis album." Elvis's Memphis mansion, Graceland, draws some 2,000 visitors a day—over 700,000 annually—and pulls in nine million dollars a year as a tourist attraction.

Some say Elvis died in August of 1977, but dead or not, a lot of folks think he's still around. Some say he really did die and is with us in spirit. Others say he never did die and that he's with us in flesh. Still others say he was carted aboard a flying saucer, and he's with us in ectoplasm. That's probably the top layer you'll find in your digging today. Wait a minute! I was wrong. It seems Roy over there has made the first find. What have you got, Roy?

Roy's found himself a clipping about the Postage Stamp Controversy. It's got the by-line of Leah Garchik on it. And it says here that a lot of people are foaming at the mouth for an Elvis stamp, only they can't seem to get together on it. Seems there's several different groups fighting for the stamp: one faction wants a stamp of Elvis pictured in his prime; another group—Garchik calls it the fat faction—wants Elvis to look the way he did about the time of his death, only they say they need a larger stamp for that. There's also a group that wants the stamp to carry an anti-drug message. Of course if Elvis isn't really dead it's a moot point, because the postal service only makes stamps honoring dead heros. I tell you what, Roy, put it in the bag if you want; it *is* the first find. But I say wait until they print the stamp.

Has anybody else . . .

Look! Wanda Lou's made a real find. Of course all that digging around has sort of knocked the stuffing out of her bouffant, but I don't need to remind you that the search for knowledge is not without its perils. What have you got there, Wanda Lou? It looks like a whole sack stuffed with tabloids, newspapers and magazines. Let's see what we've got.

Here's sightings of Elvis from readers of the *Weekly World News* who've spotted the King in auto races in Minnesota, fishing in upstate New York, walking along the beach in Maine, shopping in a department store in Texas, sipping wine in California . . . That Elvis, he really gets around.

> *Elvis is everywhere, man!*
> *He's in everything.*
> *He's in everybody*
> *Elvis is in your jeans.*
> *He's in your cheeseburgers*
> *Elvis is in NuttyBuddys.*
> *Elvis is in your Mom.*
> *He's in everybody.*
> *He's in the young, the old, the fat, the skinny,*
> *The white, the black, the brown, and the*
> *blue.*
> *People got Elvis in them too.*

Now, here's a good one. We've got a *Rainbow Earth Dwelling Society Newsletter* that says Elvis was well aware of a previous life on a blue planet orbiting a blue sun in the Pleiades Dogstar system. You say you think that's a bit far-fetched, Wanda Lou? Maybe. But need I remind you that Elvis's father, Vernon, reported that, on the night Elvis was born, he (Vernon, not Elvis) went out into the backyard and was astonished to see the heavens ringed in blue light? Apparently Vernon forgot all about this and didn't mention it until years later, but when he did . . . well, Elvis perked right up. You see, Elvis had a thing for the color blue, and not just some wimpy favorite color attitude. No, Elvis thought blue had real significance—supernatural significance. So who's to say? I mean you've got to admit that Elvis moves in strange and mysterious ways. Take this clipping, for example. It quotes an unemployed auto mechanic in Detroit who says, "I fell asleep for a minute in my easy chair, worrying about me and my family's future. When I woke up I thought that movie *Blue Hawaii* was on TV. . . . But then I realized my TV was off and Elvis was in my fish tank." Anyway, Elvis told this guy to buy a farm in South Dakota, which he did, and it turned his life around.

Now, some people are surprised by stories like this, and don't like them at all. They say such stories are eerie. But Elvis would understand. Elvis had a real appreciation for eeriness. For one thing, he liked to hang out at a Memphis funeral parlor at night after it closed. Sometimes he even took his buddies with him. And you remember that twin I mentioned earlier? Well, Elvis felt real close to that twin. He somehow felt that when that twin died its spirit just kind of passed on through to Elvis, and that sort of gave Elvis twice the helping of everything everybody else has—twice the energy, twice the talent, and twice the heartaches. All of this gave Elvis a real respect for the unseen world. And Elvis did a lot of studying into that world, too.

In *Is Elvis Alive?* Gail Brewer-Giorgio provides a complete rundown on Elvis's spiritual studies. I quote: "As many Elvis historians have written, Elvis Presley was both a student and a believer in such concepts as parapsychology, numerology, the occult, psychic phenomena, mysticism and religions. . . . He was fascinated with the inner workings of the human mind and the human body. . . . Books that taught self-enlightenment became favorites." His particular favorite, though, was numerology. Seems he had this book, *Cheiro's Book of Numbers,* that he carried around with him everywhere. He charted everything by the numbers: important events, concert tours, and, according to Gail Brewer-Giorgio, maybe even his own faked death. She figured that if Elvis did everything by the numbers, why then he'd probably "un-Elvis" himself by the numbers too. So, she added up the date on his tombstone—8-16-77—and discovered that they ciphered up to 2001. Now, if you're a real Elvis fan, you know that in his later years "2001" became the King's theme song.

It says here that Elvis studied yoga, and was supposedly an ace student. Seems he once faked out a band he was traveling with by having a friend of his pretend to shoot him, and then Elvis pretended to die. Well, he used this yoga stuff to affect his heart and breath, and those rubes really thought he was a goner! Some sense of humor, huh?

But anyway, back to Wanda Lou's find. . . . Here's a June, 1979 issue of *People* magazine. They've got an article here saying that Merle Haggard thinks that Elvis's death may have been faked. Of course a lot of people think that, but a lot of people just aren't Merle Haggard. You know what I mean? Say, for example, that you wanted a serious opinion about something from someone you could trust, who would you ask? Some stranger off the street or Merle Haggard?

285

And here's a TV Guide. It's from the week that they showed that Bobby-comes-back-from-the-dead-in-a-shower sequence on *Dallas*. That was a good one. Priscilla Presley was in that one. Some say that episode of *Dallas* is a clue to the truth about Elvis. They say that, like Bobby, Elvis didn't really die, and Priscilla got on *Dallas* just so she could tell us that she still takes showers with the King. I doubt that. Still, you've got to admire Priscilla. Boy! Can she act or what?

Elvis is in everybody out there.
Everybody's got Elvis in them
Everybody except one person that is . . .
Yeah . . . except one person—the evil opposite of Elvis—the anti-Elvis!
Anti-Elvis has got no Elvis in him, let me tell you.
Michael J. Fox has no Elvis in him.
And Elvis is in Joan Rivers, but he's trying to get out, man!
He's trying to get out.
Listen up Joannie baby!
Elvis is everywhere
Elvis is everybody
Elvis is still the King
What I want you to see, is that the Big E
Is inside of you and me.

That pretty much does it for this particular find. Most of the rest of this stuff looks pretty much the same. You got your *Star*. You got your *Tattler*. You got your *Weekly World News* . . . Here's an interesting item. They've got an explanation here in the *Weekly World News* for why everybody, everywhere seems to be sighting Elvis in different places at the same time. Seems Elvis got kidnapped by some spacebrothers who ran him through the Xerox and faxed him back to earth. The gist of it is that all those Elvis impersonators out there may not be impersonators after all. They may be Elvis clones.

Man, there's a lot of unexplained phenomena out there in the world
A lot of people say, "What the heck is going on!" Let me tell you.
Who built the pyramids? ELVIS
Who built Stonehenge? ELVIS
Yeah. . . . You see a man walking down the street pushing shopping carts,

And you think they're talking to Allah or talking to themselves
No. They're talking to Elvis.
You know what's going on at that Bermuda Triangle?
Elvis needs boats! Elvis needs boats!
Elvis, Elvis, Elvis, Elvis, Elvis, Elvis, Elvis, Elvis, Elvis needs boats
Ah! The sailing Elvis. Captain Elvis. Commodore Elvis, it is.
You know man, people from outer space come up to me,
They don't look like Dr. Spock.
They don't look like Klingons and all that Star Trek jive.
They look like Elvis. Elvis!
Everybody in outer space looks like Elvis 'cause Elvis is a perfect
    being!

Now here's something different. This one's got real scientific appeal. It's an article by John Leland and Beth Eiles published in the September, 1988 *Spin* magazine: "On a recent expedition in south-central Africa, a German archaeologist, Dr. Otto Rhode, unearthed what he determined to be a Neanderthal skull, a relic from the Stone Age. Using modeling clay to reconstruct the skull's original facial structure, Rhode and Dr. Jacob Springer were surprised by the appearance of clean, chiseled features uncharacteristic of the Age, and by a pair of black muttonchop sideburns. At a press conference in Emsdetter, West Germany, Dr. Rhode told reporters, 'If the American rock singer Elvis Presley isn't it direct descendant of this Neanderthal Man, then I don't know who it could be.'"

We're all moving to perfect peace and harmony towards Elvisness.
Soon all will become Elvis.
Everything, everywhere will be Elvis.
Why do you think they call it evolution anyway?
It's really Elvislution!
Elvislution . . .
Elvis is everywhere
Elvis is everything
Elvis is everybody
Elvis is still the King
Man 'o man what I want you to see
Is that the Big E's inside you and me.

Looks like Travis has found himself a bottle of pills. You'll probably find a lot of those out here today. Elvis took lots of pills. Oh, I know a lot of you think that's disgraceful; that it tarnishes the King's memory and all, but remember: Elvis wasn't bad, he was just bad-off. I mean, yes, he took drugs, but you've got to remember they were *prescription* drugs. In *Is Elvis Alive*, Gail Brewer-Georgio shows Elvis in a whole new light in this regard. You see, Elvis didn't abuse drugs; he used them. Elvis wasn't a junky; he was more like a doctor—learned, well read, and medicated to a tee. So, if all those pill bottles bother you . . . well, just think of him as Dr. Elvis. I mean, you know Elvis would want you to just say no. Richard Nixon wouldn't have appointed no junky as a special agent of the Bureau of Narcotics and Dangerous Drugs, but in 1970 he did appoint Elvis. So, don't worry yourselves over those bottles. Elvis got headaches just like the rest of us.

> *Elvis is everywhere*
> *Elvis is everything; Elvis is everybody.*
> *Elvis is still the King.*
> *Man, oh man, what I want you to see,*
> *Is that the Big E*
> *Is inside of you and me.*

Billy Bob seems to have dug himself up a Captain Marvel Jr. comic. You go ahead and put that in your sack, Billy Bob. You remember I told you that Elvis used to fantasize as a kid about being Captain Marvel Jr. Well, take a close look. See the resemblance? The King really did become Captain Marvel: he's got the stance; he's got the forelock and, near the end in Vegas, he even had the cape. *Is Elvis Alive?* quotes a remark the King made in 1971: "When I was a boy, I was the hero of the comic books and movies. I grew up believing in a dream. Now I live it out."

Hank's got his arms full. Didn't even recognize him at first. Does everybody see this? Hank's dug himself up some of those black velvet paintings you see hanging in cafes and gift shops across the country. One's got Elvis on it. The other's got Jesus. I guess I don't need to point out that Elvis has become a Christlike figure for many. Now you take these black velvet paintings . . . I mean, who are they of? They're of Elvis and they're of Jesus. Obviously this black velvet stuff is religious art. I mean, you don't see Whoopi Goldberg painted on black velvet. You see Elvis painted on black velvet and you see Jesus painted on black velvet, and anybody who paints anyone else on black velvet is a subversive. Period!

To firm up this point I'll direct your attention to our other guide-book for today, *Elvis After Life* by Doctor Ray Moody, Jr. Dr.

Moody figured that there might be a lot of pertinent stuff in this Elvis-fill of ours that would be of interest to shrinks and those with shrink-like interests. In fact, Dr. Moody spent nine whole years digging through this Elvis-fill trying to make heads or tales out of it, and he found that there were *hundreds* of people who had psychic experiences involving Elvis Presley. Dr. Moody says that what we see going on with Elvis isn't really much different than the kinds of things that go on when a close loved-one dies. Basically, the two things that are different is that the *Weekly World News* don't come into our homes and tell everybody at the supermarket how crazy you act in your grief. And the other thing, of course, is that Elvis was loved by so many people. So, when Elvis dies and comes back to visit some greengrocer in Mississippi everybody laughs, but when your grandaddy dies and your grandma tells you she saw him floating around the house in a sheet, well . . . everybody's got the good manners to just sort of ignore it, even if they don't understand. But with Elvis we mourn on a grand scale, and, as most of you know, whenever we do anything on a grand scale good manners seem to be the first thing to go.

Another thing Dr. Moody found out was that our relationships with celebrities are just as screwed up as our relationships with each other, except that we sort of blow up celebrities larger than life. The fact that we don't really know them makes this a lot easier. I mean you spend ten years around your Uncle Harry watching him pick his teeth and stick his hands down his pants, and you just can't help but doubt the proposition that old Harry was created in God's image. But then you *know* Uncle Harry. You just *think* you know Elvis. And what's even more important is that Elvis doesn't know you. I mean, let's face it, Uncle Harry has his doubts about *you,* too. But not Elvis. Elvis loves everybody. So, you see, it ain't surprising that Elvis is looking more and more like a religious figure these days.

> *That's right ladies and gentlemen*
> *The time has come. The time has come*
> *To talk to that little bit of Elvis inside of you. Talk to it.*
> *Call it up. Say Elvis heal me.*
> *Save me Elvis. Make me be born again in the perfect*
> *Elvis light*

Of course, you got to admit that Elvis is not your god-the-father type; he's more god-the-big-brother. I mean, if you found yourself in Elvis heaven, what would you expect to find? Angels flying around playing harps, or Harley races and rock 'n' roll? And I'll tell you another thing: everybody in Elvis Heaven is 30 years old, and in good shape. I know this because in *Elvis After Life,* everybody that saw Elvis-the-ghost says he looked to be about thirty years old and in his prime. That's good news for the overindulgers among us. I mean look at Elvis—he was a mess, and he died at 42 years old. But it's no big deal because now he's going to be thirty for eternity. That sort of makes Elvis the Patron Saint of overindulgers, and we need a saint. So far, about the best we could manage was St. Jude, but you've got to admit that as the saint of hopeless causes, Jude must be stretched pretty thin. I mean, if you were Jude and had all these hopeless causes to take care of, where would you put the drunks and the pill poppers? To the back of the line, right? But not Elvis. He wouldn't send you to the back of the line. Elvis knew what it was like to be a hound dog man.

So, maybe it's a good thing we got this Elvis-the-miracle-worker notion fixed in our heads. I say, if Elvis can provide a little comfort to those in need, then what's the harm? Still, it only makes sense to be *selective.* You take this Elvis-fill, for example. Everything in here means something to somebody, but you put it all together and it don't mean diddly 'till you sort it out. Not everything's significant. Now you take those little slips of paper people have been finding all day. You know the ones . . . all those little scraps of paper with the letters E-L-V-I-S moved around so that now it's not E-L-V-I-S but L-I-V-E-S. Now some say that this is significant, but I would point out that we're not talking backwards spelling here, we're talking anagrams. There's a difference. Elvis spelled backwards is Sivle. What the hell is that? I mean, you spell dog backwards and it's significant—why I don't know, but it is. Trust me. You spell Elvis backward and you get Sivle. I fail to see the significance of that.

You want significance? How about this, from *Elvis After Life:* Elvis's face has appeared miraculously on a pantry door in Massachusetts, and it's not painted on, either. It's in the grain of the wood. And apparently it just sort of popped up one night when two fans were having cake and ice cream to celebrate the King's birthday. The way Polly Tyson sees it (she's the one who owns the house with the Elvis-pantry) is that it's just Elvis's way of comforting her in his absence. And Polly needed that comfort because when she first found out about Elvis's death at the mall, well . . . she took it pretty hard. But now all she's got to do for Elvissurance is sit down at her kitchen table and look at the pantry door. Of course Elvis is significant to a lot of people, and not everybody's got a pantry door, but the same message has been made in different ways. In *Elvis After Life* we read about this ex-girlfriend of Elvis who ended up with one of Elvis's jackets. Well, after Elvis died, that jacket started jumping off the hanger and before long was doing calisthenics all by itself in the closet. Now, needless to say, this was disconcerting, but finally Elvis came to her in a dream and told her all those jacket-calisthenics were just his way of telling her that life goes on. There's another account of this little girl who, right before her death, told her mother and father "Look. Elvis is coming." Some of Dr. Moody's stories are touching like that one, and some are just bizarre like the story of this fellow and his wife who set up a computer in the basement and programmed in a bunch of Elvis quotes. Now he and his wife spend most of their time down in the cellar "talking to Elvis." My favorite quote in the whole book doesn't need any explanation: "Ruth Ann, this is weird. . . . Why in the world would my Elvis records melt on the day he died?"

So, in the course of our digging here today, I think you get some notion of the magnitude of this Elvis-fill. But so far all the finds have been recent. Has anybody found anything older? I mean, after all, the Elvis myth didn't just start the day he died. Looks like Wanda Lou's found herself a golden oldie. I mean she not only dug, she tunneled. You're a mess, Wanda Lou.

Well, let's see what we got? It's a *Life* magazine with Elvis's face on the cover, and it's an oldie, too—1956. 'Fifty six was the year that Elvis burst upon our national attention. And even if Ed Sullivan didn't let us see his hips, we heard the songs: Heartbreak Hotel, Hound Dog, Love Me Tender, and Blue Suede Shoes.

Elvis wasn't the only thing shaking and shimmying in 1956. While half of America was fat and happy, the other half . . . well, if they were fat it was because potatoes were cheap, and as for being happy . . . the Montgomery boycotts that year proved they were not. It wasn't until November 13 of that year that the United States Supreme Court declared segregation on busses and streetcars was unconstitutional.

And if there was a whole lot of shaking going on in the back seats of America's busses in 1956, well . . . our ship of state had its tensions, too. In 1956 Secretary of State John Foster Dulles gave his historic "Brink of War" speech in which he said, "The ability to get to the verge without getting into war is the necessary art."

Still, even if there was tension, there was also smiling Ike Eisenhower who sat Buddha-like in the White House and reassured the majority of the nation that the good old fashioned American values were still intact. And though undoubtedly Elvis was a threat for some people in Ike's golf-course-vision of America, he was not too much of a threat. After all, Elvis symbolized the bedrock moral values of America as well as anyone. He was the American success story, the poor boy who made good; he was deeply religious, generous to his friends and fans and, holy of holies in 1956, he was "good to his mother." In short, he was a suitable subject for a Norman Rockwell cover for the *Saturday Evening Post*—so long as we didn't see his hips. It was his mid-section (his naughty bits) that was the cause for the blushing of America in 1956. It seems our national hormones had come to a roiling boil, and we didn't know what to do with them. Consider this: in 1956 we not only had Elvis-the-Pelvis, we also had the publication of *Peyton Place*. Things were steaming up. Who knows, maybe 1956 was the year that the sexual revolution started, and maybe that's what all this Elvis-fill represents: innocence and loss of innocence and innocence regained. I mean, 1956 was also the year that the original Ringling Brothers and Barnum and Bailey Circus performed its last show.

You've got to admit, you hear a lot of people bellyaching and moaning over our culture's lost innocence. But I think they got it all wrong. I mean they're the very ones who told us not to spend so much time listening to Elvis. They're the ones who told us to be serious. And they must have got on Elvis's case too, because by the time he'd gotten to be a big star and couldn't belch in public anymore, he got serious, too—real serious.

One thing's certain. It's not 1956 anymore. The sexual revolution, like Elvis, seems to have come and gone. And we are—like we were always told we should be—real serious about life. Of course, you can get too serious. Then things start to change. In 1956 we shook ourselves out of our seriousness with Elvis. Well, Elvis is gone. He's either dead or in hiding, and all we've got left is the music and the memories, and the myth. Only now, we're all real serious all over again. Elvis knows we need him. Why else do you think he decided to team up with the space brothers and start showing up at dog shows all over the country, and in people's dreams, and on their pantry doors? If you ask me, Elvis just thought we were getting way too serious, and he's putting on a show for us just like he always did, and for the same reason. Elvis wants us all to lighten up.

Well, the sun's going down, and it's time to take what we got and go home. I know a lot of you have been digging all day, and found lots of stuff but didn't think it was significant, so you threw it out and now you ain't got nothing. Don't feel bad. I mean, this Elvis-fill is a pretty big undertaking. I tell you what: there's another fill not too far from here that's just getting started. It's not too full yet, and it might be easier to negotiate. If you're interested, just go down the back road about three miles and ask for the John Lennon-fill.

> *Man, oh man, what I want you to see*
> *Is that the Big E*
> *Is inside of you and me.* ★

★*Lyrics to "Elvis Is Everywhere" by Mojo Nixon courtesy of Enigma Records, published by Muffin-Stuffin Music, La Rana Music. BMI coyright © 1987.*

ELVIS BOUND

███████

by W. P. Kinsella

This short story, which originally appeared in Kinsella's Red Wolf, Red Wolf, *speaks to the question of how we come to terms with the lingering image of Elvis, what it means to us, and why. What is perhaps most appealing about this story is the way in which Kinsella captures that subtle flavor of strangeness that surrounds all our dealings with Elvis.*

We drove up Highway 26 from Charleston and picked up Interstate 40 near Asheville, North Carolina. We'll visit Tyler's grandmother in Knoxville, then spend a few days at the Grand Ole Opry before heading on to Memphis. This is our first genuine family holiday in the middle of the summer, up until now I've been playing for, or managing, a baseball team all the years I've been married.

The kids are in the back seat of our brand new stationwagon; they're pounding around and singing "We are marching to Mehhem-fuss, as we have done before," though none of them has ever been to Memphis.

A visit to Graceland, Elvis's homestead, is going to be the highlight of the trip for everyone but me. Somehow I've had enough of Elvis, and it don't matter how excited Tyler and the kids get, I'm not about to be impressed. I couldn't be impressed now if I wanted to; I've made too much fun of everything about Elvis. It's even got to be kind of fun, them lined up on one side and me on the other.

"I hear they have three of Elvis's pubic hairs in a golden dish with a crystal dome over top of it," I say to Tyler. "They've got an old Egyptian attendant with a turban on his head, who, for an extra dollar will let you look at them hairs just a laying there like curly cracks in the golden plate."

"Oh, Dad," says our oldest girl who's fourteen, easily shocked, and would, as she says, "expire from embarrassment," if she knew even part of the story I'm about to tell.

"What's a pubic hair?" says Austin, our youngest, who's named after the city in Texas, 'cause that's where I was managin' the year he was born. You think I didn't have a fight on my hands over that name? Tyler, she was hell-bound on namin' the boy Elvis.

Tyler finally gave in, not because she backed down one inch, but because she'd had her way when it came to naming the girls. The oldest's Priscilla, and then Lisa Marie is ten. Lisa Marie is just dyin' to see the airplane with her name on it that they rolled up on the lawn across the street from Elvis's mansion.

I sneak a look over at Tyler and it's hard for me to realize that she's lived almost half her life as my wife. Nobody gave our marriage the chance of a snowball in hell. Consequently we didn't get interferred with much. The only person who caused us grief was Elvis Presley. Elvis damn near broke up our marriage until I found his weakness and got the best of him.

Tyler was sixteen and waitin' tables in a Sambo's in Baton Rouge when I met her. We were married within a month, against everybody's advice—my folks, my manager, my friends on the team, and Tyler's probation officer. She'd been sort of a juvenile delinquent; never raised, just dragged up by a mama who OD'd on something when Tyler was ten. She'd spent time in foster homes and orphanages, lived on the street for a year, and was workin' her second shift on graveyard hours at Sambo's when I met her. Tyler never held what her mama did against her. I remember maybe the second night we were together cuddled up in the front seat of my car in the darkest corner of Sambo's parking lot waiting for her to go on duty at midnight when I said something about how awful her childhood must have been. She snuggled into my neck and said, "It was just that Mama never met a soft-hearted ballplayer." And I guess it was at that moment I knew I loved her, and that ain't ever changed, or ever will, in spite of what Elvis tried to do to us.

"I did everything but turn tricks," Tyler told me early on,

"though a couple of guys I lived with at times sure wanted me to. I don't know why I didn't. Some of my best friends on the street were whores. I guess it was just that they never seemed to have a pot to piss in or a window to throw it out of, in spite of all the tricks they turned. All that money just passed through their hands . . ."

Tyler had her initials tattooed on the back of her left hand, T.P., for Tyler Presley. And she has another tattoo, a little blue rose just below her left collarbone. I been lovin' Tyler for almost fifteen years now, and I still get hard as a baseball bat when I see that little tattoo. If it wasn't on there good I'd have licked it off years ago.

Tyler is dark skinned with lazy blue eyes that never seem to get all the way open. She looks like there are little weights forcing her lids down. She's got small, even teeth, and crow-coloured hair that glints with greens and purples in some light.

Let me explain about that name Presley. It's not that she's a relative . . . well?

Ty-lah was the way she pronounced her name when I met her. Her voice lost some of its softness over the years as we've kicked around from Baltimore, to Indianapolis, to Oakland, to Cincinnati, to Syracuse during my thirteen-year, undistinguished career, up and down from Triple A to the Big Show a dozen times with half a dozen teams, as a utility infielder. I spent three years managin' in the minors, then a former teammate who happened to make six or seven million dollars during his career offered to take me into his business. We bought a nice home in Charleston and I look out for his interests in South Carolina and Georgia.

So my baseball career paid off in the long run. Some of my teammates called me Hoover, because of the way I vacuumed up ground balls. But the sad truth was I never could hit the curve, and the last couple of seasons I couldn't hit the fastball either. Then this new breed of shortstop came along, guys like Ozzie Smith, Alfredo Griffin, Spike Owen; they cover more ground than I ever dreamed of. So I became dispensable and got out-righted. I managed. I got invited into business. This is my summer to really get to know my kids.

I've noticed, just in the few months since we settled permanently in Charleston, that Tyler's speech has softened again—she's a chameleon, able to adapt. Her voice hardened, became clipped and curt the summer we were in Boston, in Omaha a nasal twang crept into her voice.

Tyler was born in '57 at the height of the Elvis craze. Her mama was a 16-year-old rock and roll groupie. Her family name was Clowers, but she named the baby girl she bore nine months after an Elvis Presley concert in New Orleans, Tyler Presley.

Tyler lived some of the time with her grandmother, some of the time in foster homes; she spent part of her childhood bein' dragged around the country by her mother, who, to put it kindly, never got her life together. Not that Elvis Presley was to blame for what happened to her; if it wasn't him it would have been somebody else. The way I see it a certain percentage of teenage girls are destined to be Rock groupies or Baseball Sadies. The glitter of the costumes, the thrill of the uniforms, the aura cast by men in the public eye, draw these girls in.

"Trouble is," Tyler said to me once, "men in the public glare are electric—like bug lights—their victims are zapped and left for dead."

The only picture Tyler has of her mother is one taken a year before she died. She was one of those women who must have been very beautiful as a girl, but who aged rapidly. In the photo she has sunken cheeks and suspicious eyes, a coyote leanness brought on by years of too much whisky and too little sleep.

"I knew it wasn't him. I know fantasy from reality," Mama said to me just a week before she killed herself. "But tellin' that story gave me somethin' nice to think about all those months I was expectin' you. He, your daddy, was a boy in a leather jacket, with a nose that had been broken. I'd stayed around after the concert until the hall was empty and the doors were locked and there was nothin' but me and blowing newspapers in the parking lot. I hitched a ride. He was drivin' a 1953 Chev Bel-Air with blue terrycloth seat covers. He had a pack of Winstons laying on the dash and a pair of foam-rubber dice dangling below the mirror. I helped myself to a cigarette the minute I got into the car. I slid right over beside him. The car radio was on loud to a rock and roll station and Elvis was singing *Don't Be Cruel*. That's all I know about your daddy, Hon. I was hitchhiking a ride after the Elvis Concert. He stopped for me. I never gave him a chance."

In the back of the stationwagon our kids are singing again, and our sheepdog, Col. Tom is barking.

"Y'all settle down," says Tyler. But she and I smile at each other, and that glance says—as long as the sounds are happy and don't break our ear drums, everything's okay.

Priscilla fancies herself a songwriter. And, putting a daddy's pride aside, she may well be. She plays the guitar and puts on concerts for us. She begins to plunk away. Tyler turns down the volume on the tapedeck where Elvis was crooning *In the Ghetto*.

I just dropped by to see
If you would talk with me

Prissy has a mournful country twang in her voice. "A good front porch picker and singer," is how Tyler describes her.

I was too wild to see
There was no tellin' me
Now, there's no tellin' you

A creditable lyric. Prissy sings her own compositions at school talent shows.

"She must have inherited her talent from her grandaddy,' whispers Tyler, as she bares her teeth in what I know is both a secret and a sexy smile.

This Elvis business, whatever the truth of it may be, has been the plague of our life together. Elvis Presley was like a religion to Tyler's mama. She followed him around the country, sometimes dragging Tyler with her. Once a lawyer fellow got to talkin' to Tyler's mama and he wanted to start an action on her behalf, an action to make sure Elvis acknowledged his child and provided for them both. He said he wouldn't need to take nothin' to court but photographs of Tyler and maybe Tyler herself. He said Tyler looked more like Elvis than Elvis. But Tyler's mama wouldn't hear of it. "I'd never want to cause Him a moment's grief," is what she claimed she said to the lawyer. In those days Tyler still believed Elvis was her father, was some kind of god that was one day gonna come down off the stage or screen and sweep her and her mama up and carry them off.

"I grew up believin' in Santa Claus, the Easter Bunny, the Tooth Fairy, and Elvis Presley."

Like children who are indoctrinated early and often in the mythologies of religion, and who grow up feeling guilt and unease when they come to realize religion is no more substantial than, say, the Tooth Fairy, so Tyler, as the child of Elvis's most devoted disciple, was affected. Her obsession with Elvis nearly destroyed our marriage.

I suppose it would have helped if I had been an Elvis fan. But I wasn't; though I did have big, blue-black sideburns when we met. I've just never liked Elvis much. I was raised on old time country music. I always took it as an insult that the same people who wouldn't touch rock and roll with surgical gloves accepted Elvis just because he was a good ole' Southern boy from Mississippi, and they

298

took that pig-sticking music of his to heart just as if it was country. Being five years older than Tyler and comin' from a family that still played Jimmy Rodgers blue yodels and train songs, and owned every record Hank Williams ever made, I just didn't get taken in by the Elvis craze, or Chubby Checker, or the Beatles, or whatever came after them.

But when you're in love you don't think too much about what kind of upbringing your sweetheart has had, or what her hangups are. At least I didn't. Tyler wasn't living much of anywhere when I met her, but within three days she was moved into my little apartment. The place was supposed to be furnished but about all I'd brought with me was a lot of dirty socks and a case of Bud for the refrigerator. I gave Tyler two hundred dollars and said, "Do your best to make this little box a home." And she did—with curtains and bright yellow dishes, throw rugs and a Leroy Nieman reproduction of a reproduction of a ballplayer swinging at a bad pitch. And! A life-sized poster of Elvis on the wall right beside our bed, and there was a little pink light covered with a frilly shade. The light turned Elvis's white jacket pinkish, actually seemed to make his sequins glitter, and cast a nasty aura around his head, making it look as if he were winking.

The first time Tyler reached up her arm and turned on that light was just as I was lickin' my way down her belly: I had discovered that she could be induced to make the damndest pleasurable noises and I was all set for some enjoyable listening. I damn near died of shock.

"Shhhh, Love," she said. "Ain't that the prettiest thing you ever did see? Between you an' it I'm straight on my way to heaven."

"I don't want that patsy watchin' us," I said, and decided then and there I'd been mistaken about Tyler. Too many hangups, I told myself.

"Oh, Baby," Tyler said, "close your eyes and make me cry the way you did last night."

And I did. She was new to me. She went wild when we made love. I like noisy women. All the time we made love Tyler sobbed and shrieked and carried on like some girls do at a concert.

I brought up the business of Elvis in our bedroom a couple more times, but Tyler just said things like, "It don't do no harm and it makes me as horny every night as if you just came home from a ten-day road trip."

"I think it's sick," I said. "You grew up thinkin' that weirdo was your father."

"But I know he ain't," argued Tyler.

"What if I wanted to drool over a picture of Marilyn Monroe while I was gettin' it on with you? Wouldn't that piss you off?"

"Not if I knew you loved me best. And I do love you," said Tyler.

I'd always let the subject drop, but I seethed inside, and more than once I considered finding me a woman who didn't need to stare at Elvis Presley to get her rocks off. But then Priscilla came along, and when I looked at her wizened up little face why I fell in love without even trying.

I mean what was I supposed to do? There was nobody I could talk to. Young ballplayers aren't supposed to have to worry about anything except their statistics. My manager that summer was one of those guys who had read too many books by Dale Carnegie; he used your name in every sentence of every conversation, and liked to slap his players on the back a lot and deal only in positive emotions. In other words he was a twit. He'd say things like "That was a hell of a hit you made in the second inning last night, Ben. It was a good pitch and you just overpowered the ball. I really like the way you're swinging, Ben, and the way you contribute to our offense. However, Ben, I think we should talk about the ball you misplayed in the seventh . . .'

Even though he encouraged communication, actually wanted us to talk over our personal problems with him, I just couldn't imagine myself saying to him. "Skip, my sex life is driving me crazy. My old lady stares at a life-sized poster of Elvis Presley all the time we're fucking."

I got out a sheet of Tyler's notepaper one night, and got as far as writing, 'Dear Ann Landers,' before I tore it up.

It's difficult to compete when your wife is in love with Elvis Presley.

"I wouldn't mind as much if you got off on John Wayne, Mickey Mantle, James Coburn, somebody with balls," I told her over and over again. "Fucking Elvis couldn't get it up with a block and tackle. He just lies around Graceland with his Memphis Mafia, all good-ole'-boys, if you notice, and gets fatter. I hear he's gonna be spokesman for Butterball Turkeys. It takes one to know one."

But nothin' I said made any difference to Tyler. That languid poster of Elvis continued to live right beside our bed. Tyler still insisted that the "adoration light" as I called it, remain on while we made love.

I remember once after my team had been on a road trip to Tucson

300

for a five game series, I was just wild for Tyler when I got back. The team bus dropped me off a block from our apartment. Tyler was curled up on the sofa watching TV when I came in. I just took her hand, pulled her to her feet and marched her right to the bedroom. She hardly had time to put her cigarette out and was still exhaling smoke when we got to the bedroom door. Still, even though I was kissing her like she had diamonds hid in her mouth, she reached behind me and turned on the adoration light as I was laying her down on the bed: Elvis in a white rhinestone jacket and black slacks, reclining on a chaise lounge, looking sleepy and greasy, his lips slightly parted in what might have been the beginning of a sensual smile, or what might have been a sneer of contempt for all the foolish, wet-crotched women who got excited by his pose. Elvis, I thought, probably got it up for cocked revolvers, and seven-foot black basketball players from Uganda.

Tyler undid her blouse and rather than taking it off just tossed it open to show off her round, freckled breasts: to me a few clothes are more erotic than pure nakedness. I undid her jeans and pulled them down. The first time I ever undressed Tyler, in that little apartment in Baton Rouge, when I helped pull her jeans and panties down, I said, "Throw your fucking panties away. If you're gonna be my old lady, you don't wear panties. When I look at you I want to know your cunt is right beneath the denim." Tyler tossed her panties to the furthest corner of the room. When I was inside her I scuffled around until I found her jeans and placed them crotch up on the pillow beside her head. "While we're fucking I like to bury my face in your denim crotch, the best of both worlds, fucking you and tasting you at the same time." What I said totally surprised me, for I'd only met Tyler a few hours before. Baton Rouge was a sweet place for a young ballplayer that summer, and I'd averaged at least three women a week when we were in town. But I knew Tyler was the one. And she is. Except for a long time there was this Elvis thing.

This Elvis thing. I mean I wouldn't touch the psychology of it with a ten foot pole. I'm not a scholar. I don't suppose I've ever read a book I wasn't required to. I was raised in Kentucky. My daddy was a foreman at a strip mine. We had a couple of spotted hounds under the back porch, a pickup truck and a pitcher's mound in the back yard. I never could pitch though, and Daddy took to hittin' me grounders in that uneven sloping yard.

"If y'all can field in among them gopher holes and jack-grass plants, it'll be easy for you on a regular field," Daddy said, and he'd spit tobacco juice so it flowed with the wind, and whack me another twister.

I don't suppose I knew any psychology, except what's dished up like butter on grits, on the Sunday Night Movie, until one year when I was with the Oakland A's. We'd lost fifteen in a row, and our team batting average during the slump was .188. Charlie O. called in a psychologist to find out what the trouble was with us.

I guess that psychologist was pretty tired by the time he got to me. I was either the 24th or 25th man on the roster. If somebody had to go it was either me or the mop-up reliever, the guy they brought in when the score was 9–1 in the seventh inning. That kind of reliever is known as Whale Shit and he gets left in no matter what kind of trouble he gets into. I was what's called a Puffball, a defensive infielder who couldn't hit his age, let alone his weight.

"Well, Ben, suppose you start by telling me how you feel about your teammates and management," the psychologist said. Another Dale Carnegie groupie. That opened lots of doors. I knew most of the guys were complaining about the food on the road, the way the press wrote about us, the things Charlie O. said about us. Not very exciting stuff.

"Call me Ian," the psychologist said. He was a skinny guy about my age, dressed in an A's jersey and baggy jeans. I figured him for a guy who would trade the remaining years of his sex life to start three games at second base and get one hit off Catfish Hunter. Since Charley O. was known in baseball circles as Cheap Charlie I knew this guy wasn't getting paid. He was probably doing it because he got his rocks off by being around professional ballplayers.

"I've got personal problems," I said. Actually I was batting 1 for 3 during the slump and hadn't made any errors in the field. Ian smiled and then looked serious. He was finally going to get some stuff he could sink his teeth into. He'd told a couple of guys that they were trying to get back at their own fathers by annoying Charlie O. And what better way to annoy Charlie O. than by not hitting or fielding or hustling.

"My old lady's in love with Elvis Presley," I said. Then I explained everything about Tyler and Elvis and the adoration light, and how it pissed me off that Elvis was getting credit for all my hard work in bed.

"It's not as if Tyler is empty headed," I said. "I'd have got shorn of her soon enough if that was the case. She's smart. Smarter'n me, I have to admit." Soon after we were married it became apparent

302

that Tyler knew how to handle money. Over the years she's checked every deal my agent wanted to make. I never brought in big bucks, like some players, but Tyler saw to it that we've always been comfortable; she vetoed some deals, found some of her own, even. "A lot of guys want a stupid wife," I explained to Ian. "'I want a wife whose only question is "Which place you want to put your cock, Sugar?" My old lady keeps her mouth shut and her legs spread; the way it ought to be,' are the kind of things my teammates have said to me."

Ian talked for about an hour, so long that the Whale Shit, relieved, went out for a beer and missed his appointment. He talked about complexes, libido, unconscious and collective unconscious, and somebody named Ed, all of which meant as much to me as stock market quotations. But finally he said something that made sense. "Ben, what would you do if it was the real Elvis Presley there in your bedroom, and not just a paper doll? Would you bust his chops, or what?"

I had to smile at the silliness of it all. I mean there's been an Elvis tape or record playing in our house every waking hour for the past fifteen years. When Austin had pneumonia a year ago, was in the hospital and we were afraid he was dying, the only special thing he wanted was to hear *In the Ghetto*. Well Prissy plucked on her guitar and we sang it to him, her in her high, sweet, bluegrass voice, me in my hound dog bass that is only occasionally on key. That damn kid was like a wilted flower sponged with water. Hearin' that song did the same for him as a visit from Jerry Falwell might for some of the bonehead Baptist kids in the ward with him.

"I'd be better off if he *was* real," I told the psychologist. "I don't know if I'd bust his chops or not. But I'd be able to do something. Once, right after we were married, I took down the poster while Tyler was out. Tore it up and put it out with the trash. Tyler never said a word to me. She just looked hurt, her bottom lip turned down, and her chin kind of trembled. I guess as soon as I headed for the ballpark she split for the record store. When I got home after the game Tyler was sittin' on the sofa bare as a jay bird from the waist up. Soon as I led her into the bedroom I saw that there was a brand new non-flyspecked poster of Elvis on the wall. What with Tyler touchin' me the way she's so good at, already crooning in her throat as she kissed on me, I didn't have the inclination to complain about Elvis."

"Why don't *you* pretend a little," Ian said to me. "Pretend it's the real live Elvis Presley dropped into your bedroom to watch. Find out how you'd act."

Elvis was already dead by then. But not for long. His death didn't cause Tyler and the kids as much grief as I would have expected. She did put a black wreath on our doorknob. And her and Prissy sent flowers to Graceland.

"It ain't as if we was close family," she said to me. But I look at her and I wonder. She looks so much like Him. Maybe the only smart thing her mama ever did was lie about who Tyler's father really was. All she had to do was look in the mirror to see what her obsession had done to her. Maybe she figured Tyler deserved better. "I've got him there in the posters and records and pictures and statues. He ain't ever gonna change. He'll never get any older, and that's even kinda nice. And I can always listen to his records and tapes." I was touched by what she said, by how strong she was. I even stopped badmouthing Elvis for a month or so.

This will be Tyler's second trip to Graceland. She went down from Austin on a bus tour to celebrate the fifth or sixth anniversary of Elvis's death. She came back laden with geegaws and souvenirs. She brought me a black baseball cap with GRACELAND in fluorescent green letters across the crown. She brought postcards of Graceland viewed from land, sea, and air. She bought records from a store called EP's LP's. Prissy still has the bag they came in hangin' on the wall of her room. And there were these really gross photographs of the Meditation Garden where Elvis and all his family are buried. The place is decorated with plastic flowers and there's blue religious crosses, tall as a man, look like they're made of toilet brush bristles. And there's plastic wreaths bigger than you see at the Kentucky Derby, and little photographs imbedded in the lawn. And they named the street in front of Graceland, Elvis Presley Boulevard. Crass. Gross. Grotesque. But I'm the only one seems to think that way.

That psychologist didn't help the A's win a pennant. The team eventually pulled out of the slump on its own and finished the season with about the record a submediocre team deserved. Ian, the psychologist, didn't help me as a baseball player. I got sent to the minors in mid-August and didn't see the Bigs again until the next spring when I was 25th man on the Minnesota Twins roster. But some of the things he suggested helped me with the Elvis problem.

I wasn't entirely sure what I was gonna do the next time Tyler and I made love, but I had a sneakin' hunch. I kissed down Tyler's belly, licked her inner thighs, parted her lips with my tongue, found her little clit ripe as a grape, already soaked with her particular honey. I moved my tongue in slow, massaging circles, fast as a butterfly, then slow again. Tyler groaned, stiffened her legs as she came the first time, gripping the bed clothes, crooning her love. "Baby, Baby," she cried deep in her throat. Then she actually cried out loud, gasping for breath, sobbing. As always the more passionate she became the noisier she got. As she thrashed beneath my mouth rapidly reaching a second climax, I opened my eyes and stared up over Tyler's belly between the flattened mounds of her breasts. Her mouth was open her lips swollen with passion. BUT! She had her head turned and was staring at the pink-haloed poster of Elvis. It wasn't me between her thighs giving her pleasure. It was fat Elvis in his rhinestone jacket, his oily hair greasing her thighs.

I leapt off the bed so suddenly Tyler screamed and half sat up.

"I got you, you son of a bitch," I yelled. "I knew you been spying on us. But now I got you. I'm gonna show you what we do to fucking voyeurs."

"Y'all gone crazy or what?" said Tyler. She was sitting up, one hand over each tittie, as if I'd really caught someone spying on us.

"That's right. That's exactly what I've gone. I've gone fucking crazy."

I stepped across the room, naked as the day I was born, my shadow crossing Elvis's shadow. I picked up a baseball bat, a favourite of mine that I'd been taping and sanding early in the evening.

"All right, motherfucker, you're gonna need about three million dollars worth of dental work when I get through with you," I roared.

"Ben!" Tyler cried.

The poster was a new one, made out of some kind of embossed paper—it was almost 3-D, with Elvis's features raised, his sideburns crinkly, his jacket was silky and sequins glittered like sandpaper. He was as real as somebody dead can be.

I raised the bat.

"That's right, beg, you motherfucker. If you don't say the right words in the right order, I am gonna be known as the man who killed Elvis Presley with a baseball bat."

"Ben, you're gonna wake the kids," said Tyler in a desperate attempt to distract me.

"That's better," I said to Elvis. "You fuckin' well better be sorry. You better fuckin' apologize for all the grief you've caused me."

"Ben!" Tyler's eyes were wide.

"All right, I won't kill you," I said, lowering the bat. "But you can't buy me either. No sir. I caught you redhanded, peeping tom, and you're gonna suffer for it."

305

"Ben?" said Tyler, pulling a sheet up around her neck, her brow furrowed. "You feelin' all right, Ben?"

She started to get out of bed.

"Stay put!" I said. "I'll take care of this sleazy creep."

I got the roll of tape from the chair when I'd been fancying up my bat. I stripped off a piece the length of my arm span, the tape making that stickety-click sound as it unpeeled from the roll. The poster was fixed to the wall by its corners, so I was able to get my hand behind it in the middle. I ran the tape across the back then whipped it across the front so a black bar held Elvis' fat arms pinned to his side. I circled him three more times with the tape. Then I tied his legs at the ankles the same way.

"I should blindfold the son of a bitch," I said to Tyler. "Hah! Imagine that. He'd have to lie there and listen and sniff the air. He'd look like one of those photographs in the newspaper when they put a black bar across someone's eyes to hide their identity."

"Ben, I think this is crazy."

"Not any crazier than you starin' at this fat-assed freak while we make love. If we're gonna stay together, he stays tied up. He can watch us, and you can watch him. But I'm the one in control. He's trussed up like a turkey goin' to market and he's goin' to stay that way."

And he has.

"What am I gonna tell the girls when they come in here during the day," Tyler said.

"You'll think of somethin.' Tell'em Grandpa Elvis likes to be tied up."

There's a good chance we conceived Austin that night. Didn't we have a time though. Every once in a while I'd holler over at Elvis, "See what I'm gonna do to her now you sleazebag."

Elvis has stayed bound all these years. And him being that way keeps us both real happy. He travels with us too. Tonight, after the kids are asleep in their adjoining room at the motel, why we'll unzip Elvis from the full-length suit carrier he rides in, and prop him up somewhere where Tyler can see him good. And I'll say something like, "You reckon our sex life would be any better if some fat-assed ole' rock and roll singer with a greasy curl on his forehead had sneaked in here and was a watchin' us?"

"I suspect it just might perk things up a bit, if you know what I mean. What do you figure you'd do if you caught a fellow like that spying on us?" Tyler grins as sexy and evil a grin as any woman ought to be allowed.

"Why I'd capture him, tie him up and make him watch."

"Would you now?" and Tyler smiles again.

I look down to where's she's cuddled up beside me on the car seat, her nose just a touchin' on my bicep. I love her as much as I ever have or ever will, and fourteen years have gone by like an hour.

'We are marching to Meh–hem–fuss,' sing the kids. Col. Tom barks.

CAST OF CHARACTERS

———

Colonel Tom Parker—Elvis's agent and manager for more than twenty years, Parker illegally immigrated to the United States in 1929 and worked in odd jobs in carnivals and circuses and eventually as a promoter and manager. He was managing Hank Snow and Eddy Arnold when he signed with Elvis in 1956 for a 25% fee. Beneath his carefully cultivated cigar-chomping Good Old Boy image, he was a canny businessman and entrepreneur. Under Parker's direction, Elvis was hustled and sold like a carnival act, a strategy that soon made Elvis one of the highest-paid performers in the world. While it is clear that Parker's ruthless dollar-driven promotion played a major role in Elvis's success, it is also apparent that these same practices led to many decisions that betrayed both Elvis and his audience. After Elvis's death, lawsuits against him by Elvis's family involving fraud, Parker was forced to sever all business ties with Elvis's estate.

Gladys Love Smith Presley—Elvis's mother. Born April 12, 1912, she married Vernon Presley on June 17, 1933. Elvis, born on January 8, 1935, was her only child. A twin, Jesse Garon Presley, died at birth. As Vernon Presley was frequently out of work, she worked as a seamstress and a nurse's aide to help support the family. She lived with Elvis and her husband all her life; except for his time in the army, Elvis never left home in any sense. By all accounts, Elvis and his mother had a very close relationship, and her death on August 14, 1958, devastated him.

Vernon Presley—Elvis's father. Born April 19, 1916, the seventeen-year-old Vernon married twenty-one-year-old Gladys Smith in 1933. The couple lived in Tupelo, where Vernon worked as a sharecropper and a truck driver. In 1938 he spent nine months in jail for forgery, having altered the amount on a check made out to him. In 1948 he moved the family to Memphis. Frequently unemployed, he stopped working altogether when Elvis's singing began to pay the bills. After Gladys's death in 1958, he accompanied his son to Germany while Elvis served there in the army, and in 1960 he married Dee Stanley. They were divorced in 1977, shortly after Elvis's death. He died at 63 on June 26, 1979.

Priscilla Beaulieu Presley—Elvis's wife (1967–73). Born May 24, 1945, Priscilla first met Elvis in Germany in 1959. She was fourteen years old, the stepdaughter of a U.S. Air Force captain also stationed in Germany. When Elvis returned to Memphis in 1960, he invited Priscilla to spend Christmas with him and his family at Graceland. Following that visit, he invited her to live at Graceland and finish her education in Memphis. She obtained permission from her mother and stepfather, and in 1962 she moved in, with Elvis's father and stepmother acting as her guardians and chaperons. Priscilla and Elvis married on May 1, 1967, in Las Vegas and their daughter, Lisa Marie Presley, was born nine months later. Priscilla and Elvis remained together until 1972; they got divorced in 1973.

Lisa Marie Presley—Elvis's only child. Born February 1, 1968, exactly nine months to the date after her parents' marriage, in Baptist Memorial Hospital, where nine years later her father would be pronounced DOA. After her parents' divorce, she lived with her mother but often visited Elvis at Graceland, and she was visiting there when he died in 1977. She is the sole heir to Elvis's estate, which will be held in trust until 1998.

Sam Phillips—Record producer. Sam Phillips was born January 5, 1923, and began his career as a technician and DJ at radio stations in Alabama and Tennessee. In 1950 he founded the Memphis Recording Service, which primarily recorded black musicians, among them the legendary Howlin' Wolf, B.B. King, and Bobby Bland, whose recordings were leased out to R&B labels such as

Chess and RPM, which were based in Chicago and Los Angeles respectively. In 1952 he started his own record label, Sun Records, and began to record such artists as Junior Parker, Rufus Thomas, and Jackie Brenston, whose "Rocket 88" became a minor hit and has since been hailed as the first real rock 'n' roll record. Phillips, one of the very few white people actively involved in the creation and promotion of black music, was aware that if this music could be introduced to white audiences via a white performer, the result could be massively popular. He heard in Elvis the potential to cross the racial barriers of popular music, and his instincts, as history has proved, were correct. Elvis's success and eventual departure to RCA Records helped Phillips develop and expose the talents of such artists as Jerry Lee Lewis, Johnny Cash, Carl Perkins, and Roy Orbison. In addition to his prescient vision of the potential of the artists and the music he helped develop, Phillips's skills as a producer should also be noted. The Sun Sound that made the records he produced famous was as much a result of his sparse arrangements and technical skill as it was of the abilities of the artists themselves. The Sun Sound is best represented by the following records: *The Sun Story* (Rhino RNDA 71103) and *The Complete Sun Sessions* (RCA 6414-1-R).

Scotty Moore—The guitarist on Elvis's Sun and early RCA recordings, Moore played an essential role in creating the sound that made Elvis's early recordings so distinctive. His work on recordings such as "Baby, Let's Play House," "Good Rockin' Tonight," "Mystery Train," and "Heartbreak Hotel" influenced generations of guitarists, and the sparse phrasing and slap-back echo effects that characterized his playing remains the definitive 1950s rock 'n' roll guitar sound. Moore was also Elvis's first manager; for a brief period of time in 1954 he received 10% of his earnings for his services in securing bookings for the band. Moore and bass player Bill Black appeared in several of Elvis's early films but left in 1957 in a dispute over wages. Moore also appeared with Elvis in 1968 as part of the NBC-TV special "Elvis."

LOCATIONS

— — —

Graceland—3764 Elvis Presley Boulevard, Memphis. Located in the Memphis suburb of Whitehaven on what is now Elvis Presley Boulevard, this two-story mansion was Elvis's home for twenty years. He purchased it in 1957 for $100,000, and he continued to keep Graceland as his primary residence for the rest of his life. It was in the upstairs bathroom off the master bedroom that Elvis Presley died on August 16, 1977. His remains are buried in a family plot behind the house.

Humes High School—659 North Manassas Street, Memphis. High school Elvis attended from 1948 to 1953, during which time it was attended only by white students. Elvis sang in the school variety show in April 1953, performing "Keep Them Cold Icy Fingers Off of Me," receiving enough applause to earn an encore, for which he performed "'Til I Waltz Again with You." According to his yearbook, Elvis majored in shop, history, and English. The yearbook photograph shows him sporting not only a case of acne but the long greasy hair and sideburns that would become his trademarks before long.

Sun Studio—706 Union Avenue, Memphis. Site of Elvis's first re-

311

cordings ("That's All Right," "Good Rockin' Tonight," etc.). The studio was founded in 1952 by Sam Phillips, who recorded legendary blues artists such as Howlin' Wolf, B.B. King, and Bobby Bland and leased the recordings to R&B labels such as Modern, RPM and Chess. The physical space itself is unimpressive, but it represents an epiphany in American musical history where time, space, and social forces culminated in a brief moment to produce a revolution in popular music. After years of sitting empty, the studio is once again open for tours as well as for recording.

Memphis, Tennessee—Although he was not born here, Elvis lived here most of his life and has always been closely associated with the city. Elvis's family came to Memphis from Tupelo, Mississippi, in 1948, and it was here that Elvis first established himself as an artist. In the fifties, Memphis was a vital urban center and a major hub of musical activity. Long after his passing, Elvis is still very much in evidence in Memphis. Graceland, Sun Studio, and other Elvis-related tourist attractions form a substantial part of their tourist trade, and local DJ's still refer to him as "our boy Elvis."

Tupelo, Mississippi—Elvis's birthplace. He was born in a tiny one-room shotgun shack that still stands today and is open for tours. Nearby is the Elvis Presley Memorial Chapel, a park, and a community center. Elvis and his family left Tupelo in 1948 and made their home in Memphis, where Elvis remained for most of his life. Elvis, always conscious of the mythical character of his existence, often visited his birthplace later in life as a reminder of his roots.

Las Vegas, Nevada—It is ironic that this city, so closely associated with Elvis in his later years, was the scene of one of his bitterest failures. In 1956, just as his career began to gain momentum in the wake of some widely viewed national television appearances, Elvis, Scotty, and Bill got a gig at the New Frontier Hotel in Las Vegas. Elvis found himself playing to a dining room filled with the parents of the screaming teenagers who usually made up his audience, and they were not amused. Thirteen years would pass until Elvis attempted another frontal assault on the glitzy desert town, and this time he was hailed as a conquering hero. Vegas was the site of Elvis and Priscilla's wedding at the Aladdin Hotel in 1967. And finally, Las Vegas is the setting of many a tale of food binges, chandelier and television shootings, and videotaped adventures with showgirls. Vegas and Elvis will be forever intertwined in our hearts as symbols of all things big, loud, sparkling, and open all night.

SELECTED LISTENING LIST

■

A full exploration of Elvis Presley's recorded music is a study in itself, and the following is simply a brief list of recordings intended to familiarize the reader with a small amount of representative material. It is hoped that this will be helpful in directing the reader toward those recordings that will give him or her a feel for the various styles that Elvis helped define. Despite the critical line adopted by many critics and listeners today, Elvis made a good deal of compelling and exciting music throughout his lifetime, and listeners who choose to ignore his later recordings will miss out on some fine work. While it cannot be denied that the early rockabilly and rock 'n' roll recordings occupy a special place in the hearts of most listeners, the reader is urged to approach a listening study of Elvis with an open mind.

As a general rule, recordings presented in their original monaural format are preferable to those in electronically produced stereo. This recommendation is made not only out of considerations of historical accuracy but because the mono recordings simply sound better, the processed stereo adds a great deal of clutter and noise to recordings that are often fairly raucous to begin with. Listeners brought up on these fake stereo records, which were common up until just a few years ago, will be surprised at how warm and clear Elvis's early recordings sound and may be shocked to discover that not all early rock 'n' roll records were made with a thick wall of echo and reverberation between the performer and the listener. Above all, the listener should remember that these recordings are worthwhile in any form or condition; their charm and energy transcends any medium. These recordings should not be seen simply as historical artifacts or nostalgic souvenirs. This music, at its best, is as fresh and vibrant today as it ever was.

The Complete Sun Sessions (RCA 6414-1-R) This is the definitive collection of Elvis's Sun sides, the music that started all the fuss. This two-record set includes the master takes—the recordings that were eventually pressed as singles—as well as outtakes, false starts, and alternate takes. Also included is some of the chatter, laughter, and instructions from producer Sam Phillips between takes, giving the listener a fascinating fly-on-the-wall perspective of history in the making. *The Master Takes:* "That's All Right," "Blue Moon of Kentucky," "Good Rockin' Tonight," "I Don't Care if the Sun Don't Shine," "Milkcow Blues Boogie," "You're a Heartbreaker," "Baby, Let's Play House," "I'm Left, You're Right, She's Gone," "Mystery Train," "I Forgot to Remember to Forget," "I Love You Because," "Blue Moon," "Tomorrow Night," "I'll Never Let You Go (Little Darlin')," "Just Because," "Tryin' to Get to You." *The Outtakes:* "Harbor Lights," "I Love You Because," "That's All Right," "Blue Moon of Kentucky," "I Don't Care if the Sun Don't Shine," "I'm Left, You're Right, She's Gone," (My Baby's Gone)," "I'll Never Let You Go (Little Darlin')," "When It Rains, It Really Pours." *Alternate Takes:* "I Love You Because" —takes 3, 4, 5, "I'm Left, You're Right, She's Gone (My Baby's Gone)"—takes 7, 8, 10, 11, 12, 13.

Elvis: The Hillbilly Cat (Music Works PB-3602) Representing the first official release of material that had previously appeared only in bootleg form, this record gives the listener a good indication of what an Elvis concert, or radio show, sounded like in 1955. Songs: "That's All Right," "Blue Moon of Kentucky," "Good Rockin' Tonight," "I Got a Woman."

His Hand in Mine (RCA LPM 2328) Elvis's musical roots in blues and country music are well known and plainly evident in much of his music. The influence of gospel music, however, is less often acknowledged. Although gospel has never achieved the popular status of other forms, Elvis, along with the Jordanaires, proves that this music can be every bit as exhilarating as the best rock 'n' roll. Songs: "His Hand in Mine," "I'm Gonna Walk Dem Golden Stairs," "In My Father's House," "Milky White Way," "Known Only to Him," "I Believe in the Man in the Sky," "Joshua Fit the Battle," "He Knows Just What I Need," "Swing Down, Sweet Chariot," "Mansion over the Hilltop," "If We Never Meet Again," "Working on the Building."

The Top Ten Hits (RCA 6383-R) This two-record set pretty well covers all the popular singles released during Elvis's career. This is the music that Elvis is best remembered for, and assembled in this way, it makes for an impressive body of work. All the material that appears on these records is widely available elsewhere; this particular collection is recommended only for convenience and because it avoids most of the less interesting material. The *Elvis's Gold Records* series (Volumes 1–5) is also a perfectly acceptable compilation of much the same work, although Volume 4 of that series can safely be omitted. (Volume 5 is discussed later in this list.) Songs: "Heartbreak Hotel," "I Want You, I Need You, I Love You," "Hound Dog," "Don't Be Cruel," "Love Me Tender," "Love Me," "Too Much," "All Shook Up," "Teddy Bear," "Jailhouse Rock," "Don't," "I Beg of You," "Wear My Ring Around Your Neck," "Hard Headed Woman," "One Night," "I Got Stung," "A Fool Such As I," "I Need Your Love Tonight," "A Big Hunk o' Love," "Stuck on You," "It's Now or Never," "Are You Lonesome Tonight?," "Surrender," "I Feel So Bad," "Little Sister," "(Marie's the Name) His Latest Flame," "Can't Help Falling in Love," "Good Luck Charm," "She's Not You," "Return to Sender," "(You're the) Devil in Disguise," "Bossa Nova Baby," "Crying in the Chapel," "In the Ghetto," "Suspicious Minds," "Don't Cry, Daddy," "The Wonder of You," "Burning Love."

Reconsider, Baby (RCA AFL1-5418) A celebration of Elvis's blues side, this collection assembles some lesser known blues-oriented material and offers an alternate take of "One Night" with its original, slightly more licentious lyrics. This collection could have been much larger; Elvis recorded far more than one album's worth of blues, but it is nevertheless an excellent effort. Songs: "Reconsider, Baby," "Tomorrow Night," "So Glad You're Mine," "One Night," "When It Rains, It Really Pours," "My Baby Left Me," "Ain't That Loving You Baby," "I Feel So Bad," "Down in the Alley," "Hi-Heel Sneakers," "Stranger in My Own Home Town," "Merry Christmas Baby."

From Elvis in Memphis (RCA LSP 4155) This release, unlike many others, was conceived and recorded as an album rather than as a collection of recordings from different sources. Recorded at American Studios in Memphis in 1969, this is Elvis riding the crest of his post-Hollywood "comeback," and the music captures the spirit of this renewed vitality. Songs: "Wearin' that Loved on Look," "Only the Strong Survive," "I'll Hold You in My Heart," "Long Black Limousine," "It Keeps Right on a-Hurtin'," "I'm Movin' On," "Power of My Love," "Gentle on My Mind," "After Loving You," "True Love Travels on a Gravel Road," "Any Day Now," "In the Ghetto."

Elvis's Gold Records, Volume 5 (AFL1-4941) This collection of singles from 1968 to 1977 represents a few high points in what many consider to be unproductive years for Elvis. While the string and brass arrangements on these songs may not be to everyone's taste, the melodies are engaging, and the vocal work (featuring J. D. Sumner and the Stamps, the Imperials Quartet, the Sweet Inspirations, Kathy Westmoreland, and Myrna Smith) is superb. Songs: "Suspicious Minds," "Kentucky Rain," "In the Ghetto," "Clean Up Your Own Backyard," "If I Can Dream," "Burning Love," "If You Talk in Your Sleep," "For the Heart," "Moody Blue," "Way Down."

ELVIS GOES TO HOLLYWOOD

When Elvis Presley signed a seven-year movie contract with Hal B. Wallis in 1956, he probably never imagined he'd spend most of the next decade either in the army or in Hollywood making movies that would become synonymous with mediocrity. On the contrary, he had ambitions to be a serious actor—the next James Dean—ambitions he shared with almost every other young actor of his day. Elvis was a movie fanatic, from his teen years when he sought shelter in the darkness of Memphis's Suzore No. 2 while WHBQ played his first record on the air to his later years when he would rent entire movie theaters for private screenings of favorites such as *Dr. Strangelove* and *Patton*. Elvis loved movies, and like millions of other American teenagers he was in awe of actors such as Dean and Marlon Brando, whose performances wordlessly articulated the boredom, frustration, and moral inertia of their times. Elvis was a natural performer, obviously photogenic, and he loved movies. For Elvis, signing a film contract was the fulfillment of a dream, and he was eager to meet the challenges of a different medium and prove himself a capable actor. Elvis had the look, the drive, and the ambition to become a credible actor. In short, he had everything. Everything except a good movie, that is.

There are a number of reasons for this. For one thing, Elvis was still regarded as somewhat of a freak at this point in time, a bizarre but profitable phenomenon. His entire career at this point was based on his proved ability to draw huge numbers of young people, mostly girls, to his performances and to sell vast numbers of records. The last thing Tom Parker, Hal Wallis, and the rest of the money men cared about was whether Elvis had any acting ability. The fact that Elvis willingly placed his trust in the hands of such people makes the story even more pathetic. Elvis was signed to a film contract for the sole purpose of exploiting his phenomenal popularity to fill seats in theaters. Elvis was not signed to make great films. Even at the outset, the films were regarded by their producers as mere vehicles for displaying Elvis the singer and teen idol, not Elvis the actor. Elvis often declared at this stage of his career that he had no interest whatsoever in singing in a motion picture; he desperately wanted a chance to play a dramatic role that would rely solely on his ability as an actor, not on his singing or his popularity with teenagers. It would be several years before he gave up this hope entirely.

This scenario was, sadly, fairly typical of Elvis's career. The deal makers and corporate entities behind Elvis often showed their contempt for Elvis and his audience by releasing inferior material and endlessly repackaging his work in an attempt to capitalize on the quick buck. While we should recognize that the profit motive was always an essential aspect of the Elvis Presley phenomenon, we should also note that it did not always serve Elvis or his audience well. We know from interviews he gave at the time how excited and enthusiastic Elvis was about signing his first movie contract; his humble determination to prove himself worthy of the challenge practically screams from every pore.

No one bothered to ask him how he felt a few years later when he found himself singing to animals and little children in yet another bland travelogue. We can only imagine Elvis's disappointment when he finally understood that nobody cared whether he was the next James Dean. We can only imagine the sad, sinking feeling he must have had when he woke up and realized he'd come all the way to Hollywood just to make Elvis Movies.

There is little to be gained, however, by maligning or ridiculing these films. Their formula plots, their poor production values and weak soundtracks are well known and well documented; these films are famous for being bad. Perhaps the worst thing about them was how these films transformed our image of Elvis. They turned the King of rock 'n' roll into a grinning buffoon. They even altered his appearance; his lean face became round and puffy, and his celebrated hair mutated into a heavily lacquered bouffant until he resembled a moderately realistic store-window mannequin. It is remarkable that Elvis made so many of these films, apparently without objection. More remarkable still is that he was able to recover from the slump in his career that these films helped create and to resume a performing and recording career.

Whether Elvis was capable of a credible film performance is a question that still lingers. The evidence seems to point in different directions. To be sure, his early films occasionally revealed glimpses of Elvis performing his roles with the same bemused and casual indifference that made his concerts so captivating. His punk-turned-rock-star character in *Jailhouse Rock* is a good example of this, and perhaps the reason it works so well is that Elvis is simply playing himself, with a wry undertone of self-parody. He operates along the same lines in *Loving You* and *King Creole,* although somewhat less successfully, probably because the characters he plays in those films lack the violent and aggressive traits that make his *Jailhouse Rock* character so intriguing.

The conventional wisdom regarding Elvis's career in general has been that his pre-army work (1955–58) was brilliant and his post-army work (1960–77) was worthless. As is usually the case, the conventional wisdom is valid up to a point and perhaps is more accurately applied to Elvis's film career than to his musical career. Perhaps the general preference for the early films merely stems from the fact that fifties B movies hold more charm for us than sixties B movies. Or possibly it's because Elvis, a creature of the fifties, seems more comfortable in the decade he helped define than in the one that followed. There is something slightly disturbing about the singin' swingin' psychedelic Elvis of *Easy Come, Easy Go* or *Live a Little, Love a Little.* Ultimately, there may be a more concrete reason behind partiality toward the pre-army work: the Elvis films of the fifties had better scripts, longer shooting schedules, a younger and thinner Elvis, and usually contained a certain amount of actual rock 'n' roll music. Although these forces never converged to produce a single work that could reasonably be called fine filmmaking, they certainly produced some fine cinematic moments, such as the performance of "Got a Lot o' Livin' to Do," at the end of *Loving You,* or Vince Everett's (Elvis's) sneering put-down of a party of socialites in *Jailhouse Rock*. These are the moments in which we're reminded that we've lost something; a world without Elvis is not quite as much fun as it was with him.

Elvis's films may not be masterpieces of cinema but they're all we've got, and it's too late for him to win an Oscar anyway. The Elvis scholar travels a road marked with disappointment and embarrassment as well as gratifying rewards and unexpected surprises, and Elvis Movies contain plenty of both. You may find these films corny and comical; go ahead and laugh. Elvis wouldn't have minded; he thought they were pretty funny, too. The world may not need more Elvis Movies, but we can always use more laughs.

SELECTED VIEWING LIST

All of Elvis's thirty-one feature films as well as several excellent documentaries and concert films are now available on video. The following is a selected list of some of the better material available and is intended solely as an introductory guide. Due to the scarcity of performance footage from the fifties, the documentaries often contain much of the same material. The list below is designed to avoid repetition as much as possible while directing the reader to those sources that present the material the most coherently and completely.

Loving You (Warner Home Video 1957) The plot more or less follows Elvis's own story, as he plays Deke Rivers, a truck driver who becomes wildly successful as a rock 'n' roll singer, driving girls wild and parents crazy with his suggestive gyrations. This film, made in 1956, is a clear indication of the extent to which myth was built-in to Elvis's persona. In his first year of fame, Elvis already was firmly established as an American archetype. This film is also unusual in its self-conscious and frankly cynical portrayal of the manipulative managers and image makers behind Elvis. Lizabeth Scott's character is a sort of female Col. Tom Parker, and Elvis plays the bewildered Noble Savage, representing the first and most earnest self-impersonation he ever did. *Loving You* has probably the best soundtrack of any of his films, which in light of some of the musical atrocities that were committed to provide cheap filler and merchandising for later films, is hardly in itself a recommendation. However, this film does have an authentic rock 'n' roll soundtrack, and Elvis's lip-synched performances of the songs provide some of the film's best moments. Scotty Moore, Bill Black, and the Jordanaires all appear in the film, as do Gladys and Vernon Presley (as audience members in the film's final production number). A great supporting cast, gorgeous Technicolor, and Elvis's hair at its longest, greasiest best make *Loving You* one of the most watchable and entertaining of Elvis's films.

Jailhouse Rock (MGM/UA 1957) In this, arguably his best film, Elvis plays an angry young punk who kills a man in a barroom fight. He is sent to prison, where he becomes an angry young prisoner and is flogged for participating in a food fight. When he gets out of jail, he quickly becomes an angry young rock star and stays angry for pretty much the whole film, until the end when he gets punched in the throat and loses his voice. When he recovers, he's not so angry, and he falls in love. The plot is not quite as silly as it sounds, and watching Elvis sneer and snarl his way through this film is actually a great deal of fun. Elvis demonstrates a real affinity for bad-guy roles, even though this film betrays its initial promise by softening him up at the end. Photographed in black and white, this film has a genuinely stark and gritty quality that is unique among Elvis films. "Jailhouse Rock," "(You're So Square) Baby, I Don't Care," and the gospel-tinged "I Want to Be Free" are among the songs Elvis performs in the film's less angry moments. Highly recommended.

King Creole (CBS/Fox 1958) Based on Harold Robbins's novel *A Stone for Danny Fisher* and directed by *Casablanca* director Michael Curtiz, this film has a strong cast and an absorbing plot. The love triangle places the young and innocent Dolores Hart up against the older and considerably less chaste Carolyn Jones in a struggle not only for Elvis's affections but for his soul, as he battles both his conscience and his desires. Walter Matthau puts in an excellent performance as gangster Maxie Fields, and Vic Morrow is terrific as a young hoodlum. The sleazy New Orleans nightclub settings are perfect for Elvis's performances of "Hard Headed Woman," "New Orleans," and the classic "Trouble."

Viva Las Vegas (MGM/UA 1964) While the Beatles were busy invading North America in 1963 and '64, Elvis was busy go-go dancing with Ann-Margret in *Viva Las Vegas* and that pretty well says it all. By this time, rock 'n' roll had passed him by and Elvis had lapsed into a pattern of formula films and forgettable music, but this time out he had Ann-Margret along, and it makes all the difference in the world. There is no need to explain or apologize for the plot of this film; it is best to simply ignore it, and outside of a passable rendition of Ray Charles's "What'd I Say," the music is uninspired. Nevertheless, the film succeeds on its own level, and the legendary chemistry between Elvis and Ann-Margret is, for once, more than just promotional jive.

Charro! (Warner Home Video 1969) In one of the last films he would ever make, Elvis tried to break free from his image as a cardboard matinee idol. Despite the success of his 1968 TV special and his return to live performances, this film is clearly a case of too little, too late. While *Charro!* attempts to emulate the spaghetti-western style of Clint Eastwood's and Sergio Leone's films, it lacks the stark atmosphere and visual beauty that made their work memorable. Nevertheless, this film is worth a look, if only for its novelty value and the curious experience of seeing Elvis with facial hair.

This Is Elvis (Warner Home Video 1981) Although sometimes confusing and annoying in its occasional use of the docudrama format, this film remains the best overview of Elvis's life and career and contains as good a compilation of TV clips, home movies, and concert footage as can be found in any one source. While the film is narrated by an Elvis imitator (Ral Donner), it is the film footage itself that tells the real story—of a brilliant performer who is bewildered, trapped, and consumed by his own success. The film sometimes undermines the inherent poignancy of Elvis's story with a cloying sentimentality, but perhaps that too is part of the myth. *This Is Elvis* is highly recommended, particularly as an introduction or a general overview.

One Night with You (Astral Video 1968) This fabled 1968 comeback special is a pure joy to watch; Elvis is thinner than ever, his hair restored to its former glory, and his voice has acquired a raunchy edge only hinted at in his earlier recordings. This film shows Elvis paying a rare tribute to the music that made him famous. In later years his performances of the rock 'n' roll songs of the fifties seemed halfhearted, despite their continuing popularity among audiences and critics alike. Rock 'n' roll may have been our favorite Elvis music, but it certainly was not his, and he often condensed these tunes into two or three medleys and buried them under the orchestral arrangements of which he grew so fond. For this film, however, the arrangement consists merely of a few guitars, with the rhythm slapped out on a guitar case. The music is stripped down to its essential elements—simple and repetitive lyrics, driving rhythm, and a fast and loose delivery. Bob Dylan spoke of how hearing Elvis for the first time was like "busting out of jail," and that's exactly how this music sounds. This music is about freedom, and it's about Elvis facing himself and his audience for the first time in nine years.

That's the Way It Is (MGM/UA 1970) Filmed in the summer of 1970, this documentary gives a good indication of what a Las Vegas Elvis show looked and sounded like. We get to see Elvis backstage and in rehearsal, and he comes across as a restless, tortured soul who seems at ease only when he is performing. While the film's direction is often intrusive, featuring some dizzying zooms and psychedelic camera effects, it does a fairly good job of capturing the essence of a Las Vegas Elvis show in all its sweaty, tacky glory. It is also valuable in its attention to Elvis's audience: the aging teenagers of the fifties making an awkward transition from the sixties to the seventies. Perhaps not an ideal portrait of Elvis and his generation, but a legitimate one. The music may not appeal to all, and in general the rock 'n' roll sides are given a fairly shabby treatment, but Elvis's voice remains, as always, extraordinary.

Elvis '56. (Cinemax 1987) Narrated by Levon Helm, this documentary is a gold mine of stills, film clips, and home movies of Elvis in his prime. In a way, it all seems so innocent; the shaky, flickering, grainy images of young Elvis seem slightly naive. It's almost impossible to look back and see how it must have looked to us then. To see this Elvis on film is to see a ghost, a promise of eternal youth, raw pure energy. This Elvis will have no regrets or worries. He wears the gleeful smirk of someone who has just got away with the scam of the century. He is clearly bewildered by the female reaction to his movements, but he likes it nonetheless and retains his sense of humor about it. While he doesn't understand this power he has, he is becoming aware of it; he begins to test its limits. What is it about this particular image of Elvis that remains so fascinating? It is, after all, only an image, and maybe as such it's not any more accurate or essential than the Elvis of the sixties or seventies. It may be mere innocence itself that we find so entrancing; an innocence that couldn't—and didn't—last. This is the Elvis that will live forever, the Elvis in whom we see everything we want and cannot have.

FILMOGRAPHY

■

The following is a list of basic information on the thirty-one feature films and two documentaries made about Elvis during his lifetime, as well as a selected list of television specials. See the Elvis Goes to Hollywood and the Selected Viewing List for a critical analysis. All the films listed are available on video (through MGM/UA Home Video or CBS/Fox). For more complete credits and plot summaries, the reader is referred to the following: *Starring Elvis* by James W. Bowser (Dell, 1977) or *Elvis in Hollywood* by Paul Lichter (Simon & Schuster, 1976). The most exhaustive and detailed reference source currently available is *Elvis: His Life from A to Z* by Fred L. Worth and Steve D. Tamerius (Contemporary Books, 1990). The rating system employed here is a five-point scale, and in addition to being completely personal and arbitrary, it is intended only as a guide to the relative merit of each film in context of the Elvis Movie genre. Therefore, five stars (★★★★★) = Highly recommended, and one star (★) = For hard-core fans only.

Love Me Tender★★★★ (Twentieth Century–Fox, 1956. B&W, 95 minutes.)
Director: Robert D. Webb. Cast: Richard Egan, Debra Paget, Elvis Presley, Robert Middleton, Neville Brand. Songs: "We're Gonna Move," "Love Me Tender," "Let Me," "Poor Boy."

Loving You ★★★★★ (Paramount, 1957, Color, 101 minutes.)
Director: Hal Kanter. Cast: Elvis Presley, Lizabeth Scott, Wendell Corey, Dolores Hart. Songs: "Got a Lot o' Livin' to Do," "(Let's Have a) Party," "Teddy Bear," "Hot Dog," "Lonesome Cowboy," "Mean Woman Blues," "Loving You."

Jailhouse Rock ★★★★★ (MGM, 1957. B&W, 96 minutes.)
Director: Richard Thorpe. Cast: Elvis Presley, Judy Tyler, Mickey Shaughnessy, Vaughn Taylor. Songs: "Young and Beautiful," "I Want to Be Free," "Don't Leave Me Now," "Treat Me Nice," "Jailhouse Rock," "(You're So Square) Baby, I Don't Care."

King Creole ★★★★ (Paramount, 1958. B&W, 116 minutes.)
Director: Michael Curtiz. Cast: Elvis Presley, Carolyn Jones, Dolores Hart, Walter Matthau, Dean Jagger, Vic Morrow. Songs: "Crawfish," "Steadfast, Loyal & True," "Lover Doll," "Trouble," "Dixieland Rock," "Young Dreams," "New Orleans," "Hard Headed Woman," "King Creole," "Don't Ask Me Why," "As Long As I Have You."

G.I. Blues ★★ (Paramount, 1960. Color, 104 minutes.)
Director: Norman Taurog. Cast: Elvis Presley, Juliet Prowse, Robert Ivers, Leticia Roman. Songs: "G.I. Blues," "Doin' the Best I can," "Blue Suede Shoes," "Frankfurt Special," "Shoppin' Around," "Tonight Is So Right for Love," "Wooden Heart," "Pocketful of Rainbows," "Big Boots," "Didja Ever."

Flaming Star ★★★★ (Twentieth Century–Fox, 1960. Color, 92 minutes.)
Director: Don Siegel. Cast: Elvis Presley, Steve Forrest, Barbara Eden, Dolores del Rio. Songs: "Flaming Star," "A Cane and a High Starched Collar."

Wild in the Country ★★ (Twentieth Century–Fox, 1961. Color, 114 minutes.)
Director: Philip Dunne. Cast: Elvis Presley, Hope Lange, Tuesday Weld, Millie Perkins. Songs: "Wild in the Country," "I Slipped, I Stumbled, I Fell," "In My Way," "Husky Dusky Day."

Blue Hawaii ★★★ (Paramount, 1961. Color, 101 minutes.)
Director: Norman Taurog. Cast: Elvis Presley, Joan Blackman, An-

gela Lansbury, Roland Winters. Songs: "Blue Hawaii," "Almost Always True," "Aloha Oe," "No More," "Can't Help Falling in Love," "Rock-a-Hula Baby," "Moonlight Swim," "Ku-u-i-po," "Ito Eats," "Slicin' Sand," "Hawaiian Sunset," "Beach Boy Blues," "Island of Love (Kauai)," "Hawaiian Wedding Song."

Follow That Dream ★★ (United Artists, 1962, Color, 110 minutes.)

Director: Gordon Douglas. Cast: Elvis Presley, Arthur O'Connell, Anne Helm, Joanna Moore. Songs: "What a Wonderful Life," "I'm Not the Marrying Kind," "Sound Advice," "Follow That Dream," "Angel."

Kid Galahad ★★★ (United Artists, 1962. Color, 96 minutes.)

Director: Phil Karlson. Cast: Elvis Presley, Gig Young, Lola Albright, Joan Blackman, Charles Bronson. Songs: "King of the Whole Wide World," "This Is Living," "Riding the Rainbow," "Home Is Where the Heart Is," "I Got Lucky," "A Whistling Tune."

Girls! Girls! Girls! ★ (Paramount, 1962. Color, 106 minutes.)

Director: Norman Taurog. Cast: Elvis Presley, Stella Stevens, Jeremy Slate, Laurel Goodwin. Songs: "Girls! Girls! Girls!," "I Don't Wanna Be Tied," "We'll Be Together," "A Boy Like Me, A Girl Like You," "Earth Boy," "Return to Sender," "Because of Love," "Thanks to the Rolling Sea," "Song of the Shrimp," "The Walls Have Ears," "We're Coming in Loaded."

It Happened at the World's Fair ★ (MGM, 1963. Color, 104 minutes.)

Director: Norman Taurog. Cast: Elvis Presley, Joan O'Brien, Gary Lockwood, Vicky Tiu. Songs: "Beyond the Bend," "Relax," "Take Me to the Fair," "They Remind Me Too Much of You," "One Broken Heart for Sale," "I'm Falling in Love Tonight," "Cotton Candy Land," "A World of Our Own," "How Would You Like To Be," "Happy Ending."

Fun in Acapulco ★★ (Paramount, 1963. Color, 97 minutes.)

Director: Richard Thorpe. Cast: Elvis Presley, Ursula Andress, Elsa Cardenas, Paul Lukas. Songs: "Fun in Acapulco," "Vino, Dinero y Amor," "I Think I'm Gonna Like It Here," "Mexico," "El Toro," "Marguerita," "The Bullfighter Was a Lady," "No Room to Rhumba in a Sports Car," "Bossa Nova Baby," "You Can't Say No in Acapulco," "Guadalajara."

Kissin' Cousins ★★ (MGM, 1964. Color, 96 minutes.)

Director: Gene Nelson. Cast: Elvis Presley, Arthur O'Connell, Glenda Farrell, Jack Albertson. Songs: "Kissin' Cousins,"

"Smokey Mountain Boys," "One Boy, Two Little Girls," "Catchin' on Fast," "Tender Feeling," "Barefoot Ballad," "Once Is Enough."

Viva Las Vegas ★★★★ (MGM, 1964. Color, 85 minutes.)
Director: George Sidney. Cast: Elvis Presley, Ann-Margret, Cesare Danova, William Demarest. Songs: "Viva Las Vegas," "The Yellow Rose of Texas/The Eyes of Texas," "The Lady Loves Me," "C'mon Everybody," "Today, Tomorrow and Forever," "What'd I Say," "Santa Lucia," "If You Think I Don't Love You," "I Need Somebody to Lean On."

Roustabout ★★ (Paramount, 1964. Color, 101 minutes.)
Director: John Rich. Cast: Elvis Presley, Barbara Stanwyck, Joan Freeman, Leif Erickson. Songs: "Roustabout," "Poison Ivy League," "Wheels on My Heels," "It's a Wonderful World," "It's Carnival Time," "Carny Town," "One Track Heart," "Hard Knocks," "Little Egypt," "Big Love, Big Heartache," "There's a Brand New Day on the Horizon."

Girl Happy ★ (MGM, 1965. Color, 96 minutes.)
Director: Boris Sagal. Cast: Elvis Presley, Shelley Fabares, Harold J. Stone, Mary Ann Mobley. Songs: "Girl Happy," "Spring Fever," "Fort Lauderdale Chamber of Commerce," "Startin' Tonight," "Wolf Call," "Do Not Disturb," "Cross My Heart and Hope to Die," "The Meanest Girl in Town," "Do the Clam," "Puppet on a String," "I've Got to Find My Baby."

Tickle Me ★ (Allied Artists, 1965. Color, 90 minutes.)
Director: Norman Taurog. Cast: Elvis Presley, Julie Adams, Jocelyn Lane, Jack Mullaney. Songs: "Long Lonely Highway," "It Feels So Right," "(Such an) Easy Question," "Dirty, Dirty Feeling," "Put the Blame on Me," "I'm Yours," "Night Rider," "I Feel That I've Known You Forever," "Slowly But Surely."

Harum Scarum ★ (MGM, 1965. Color, 95 minutes.)
Director: Gene Nelson. Cast: Elvis Presley, Mary Ann Mobley, Fran Jeffries, Michael Ansara, Billy Barty. Songs: "Harem Holiday," "My Desert Serenade," "Go East, Young Man," "Mirage," "Kismet," "Shake That Tambourine, "Hey Little Girl," "Golden Coins," "So Close, Yet So Far."

Frankie and Johnny ★ (United Artists, 1966. Color, 87 minutes.)
Director: Frederick de Cordova. Cast: Elvis Presley, Donna Douglas, Harry Morgan, Sue Ane Langdon. Songs: "Come Along," "Petunia, the Gardener's Daughter," "Chesay," "What Every Woman Lives For," "Frankie and Johnny," "Look Out Broadway," "Beginner's Luck," "Down by the Riverside,/When the

Saints Go Marching In," "Shout It Out," "Hard Luck," "Please Don't Stop Loving Me," "Everybody Come Aboard."

Paradise, Hawaiian Style ★★ (Paramount, 1966. Color, 91 minutes.)
Director: Michael Moore. Cast: Elvis Presley, Suzanna Leigh, James Shigeta, Donna Butterworth. Songs: "Paradise, Hawaiian Style," "Queenie Wahini's Papaya," "Scratch My Back," "Drums of the Islands," "A Dog's Life," "Datin'," "House of Sand," "Stop Where You Are," "This Is My Heaven."

Spinout ★★ (MGM, 1966. Color, 93 minutes.)
Director: Norman Taurog. Cast: Elvis Presley, Shelley Fabares, Diane McBain, Deborah Walley. Songs: "Spinout," "Stop, Look and Listen," "Adam and Evil," "All That I Am," "Never Say Yes," "Am I Ready," "Beach Shack," "Smorgasbord," "I'll Be Back."

Double Trouble ★ (MGM, 1967. Color, 90 minutes.)
Director: Norman Taurog. Cast: Elvis Presley, Annette Day, John Williams, Yvonne Romain. Songs: "Double Trouble," "Baby, If You'll Give Me All Your Love," "Could I Fall in Love," "Long Legged Girl (with the Short Dress On)," "City by Night," "Old MacDonald," "I Love Only One Girl," "There Is So Much World to See."

Easy Come, Easy Go ★★ (Paramount, 1967. Color, 97 minutes.)
Director: John Rich. Cast: Elvis Presley, Dodie Marshall, Pat Priest, Pat Harrington, Jr., Elsa Lanchester. Songs: "Easy Come, Easy Go," "The Love Machine," "Yoga Is as Yoga Does," "You Gotta Stop," "Sing, You Children," "I'll Take Love."

Clambake ★★ (United Artists, 1967. Color, 98 minutes.)
Director: Arthur H. Nadel. Cast: Elvis Presley, Shelley Fabares, Will Hutchins, Bill Bixby. Songs: "Clambake," "Who Needs Money," "A House That Has Everything," "Confidence," "You Don't Know Me," "Hey, Hey, Hey," "The Girl I Never Loved."

Stay Away, Joe ★★★ (MGM, 1968. Color, 102 minutes.)
Director: Peter Tewksbury. Cast: Elvis Presley, Burgess Meredith, Joan Blondell, Katy Jurado. Songs: "Stay Away," "Stay Away, Joe," "Dominick," "All I Needed Was the Rain."

Speedway ★★ (MGM, 1968. Color, 94 minutes.)
Director: Norman Taurog. Cast: Elvis Presley, Nancy Sinatra, Bill Bixby, Gale Gordon. Songs: "Speedway," "Let Yourself Go," "Your Time Hasn't Come Yet, Baby," "He's Your Uncle, Not Your Dad," "Who Are You, Who Am I," "There Ain't Nothing Like a Song."

Live a Little, Love a Little ★★★ (MGM, 1968. Color, 90 minutes.)

Director: Norman Taurog. Cast: Elvis Presley, Michele Carey, Don Porter, Rudy Vallee, Dick Sargent. Songs: "Wonderful World," "Edge of Reality," "A Little Less Conversation," "Almost in Love."

Charro! ★★★★ (National General, 1969. Color, 98 minutes.)

Director: Charles Marquis Warren. Cast: Elvis Presley, Ina Balin, Victor French, Lynn Kellogg. Songs: "Charro!"

The Trouble with Girls ★ (MGM, 1969. Color, 105 minutes.)

Director: Peter Tewksbury. Cast: Elvis Presley, Marlyn Mason, Nicole Jaffe, Sheree North, Joan Carradine, Vincent Price. Songs: "Swing Low, Sweet Chariot," "The Whiffenpoof Song," "Violet (Flower of NYU)," "Clean Up Your Own Backyard," "Sign of the Zodiac," "Almost."

Change of Habit ★★★ (Universal, 1969. Color, 97 minutes.)

Director: William Graham. Cast: Elvis Presley, Mary Tyler Moore, Barbara McNair, Ed Asner. Songs: "Change of Habit," "Rubberneckin'," "Have a Happy," "Let Us Pray."

DOCUMENTARIES

Elvis-That's the Way It Is (MGM, 1970. Color, 97 minutes.)
Footage of Elvis in rehearsal and in performance at the International
Hilton, Las Vegas, July–September 1970.
Songs: "Mystery Train/Tiger Man," "Words," "The Next Step Is
Love," "Polk Salad Annie," "Crying Time," "That's All Right,"
"Little Sister," "What'd I Say," "Stranger in the Crowd," "How
the Web Was Woven," "I Just Can't Help Believin'," "You Don't
Have to Say You Love Me," "Bridge over Troubled Water,"
"You've Lost That Lovin' Feeling," "Mary in the Morning,"
"I've Lost You," "Patch It Up," "Love Me Tender," "Sweet Car-
oline," "Little Sister"/"Get Back," "Heartbreak Hotel," "One
Night," "Blue Suede Shoes," "All Shook Up," "Suspicious
Minds," "Can't Help Falling in Love."

Elvis on Tour (MGM. 1972. Color 93 minutes.)
Footage of Elvis's concert performances from a fifteen-city tour in
April 1972. Songs: "Johnny B. Goode," "See See Rider," "Polk
Salad Annie," "Separate Ways," "Proud Mary," "Never Been to
Spain," "Burning Love," "Lead Me, Guide Me," "Bosom of

Abraham," "Love Me Tender," "Until It's Time for You to Go," "Suspicious Minds," "I, John," "Bridge Over Troubled Water," "Funny How Time Slips Away," "An American Trilogy," "I Got a Woman"/"Amen," "A Big Hunk o' Love," "You Gave Me a Mountain," "Lawdy Miss Clawdy," "Can't Help Falling in Love," "Memories."

TELEVISION SPECIALS

Elvis made numerous appearances on television, particularly on network television variety shows in 1956–57. In addition to his celebrated appearances on "The Ed Sullivan Show," he also appeared on local television in the South ("Louisiana Hayride," "Grand Prize Saturday Night Jamboree") as well as on "Stage Show" (the Dorsey Brothers show), "The Steve Allen Show," and "The Milton Berle Show." While kinescopes are not available for all these appearances, portions of the Sullivan, Allen, and Berle shows do appear in a number of documentaries (see Elvis Goes to Hollywood). These black-and-white television images are invaluable testimony to the impact Elvis had on national television audiences. They provide a glimpse of what Elvis looked and sounded like in his prime, and his performance of "Hound Dog" on "The Milton Berle Show" of June 5, 1956, features a good measure of the bumping, grinding, corkscrew motions that outraged some viewers even though they are clearly done in a tongue-in-cheek spirit. Already at this early stage in Elvis's career, there is a sense of self-parody about his act, an element that would figure significantly in his performances later in life.

In addition to guest appearances on these and other television shows, Elvis also made three television specials of his own. These specials depict Elvis at three distinct stages of his career. The Elvis of these shows is clearly not the Elvis of the fifties or the Elvis of the movies; he is more mature, his music more polished and less aggressive. While many critics mourned the loss of Elvis the Rocker and groaned at the emergence of Elvis the Entertainer, he remained a remarkable performer, a compelling stage presence, and a solid box-office draw. Details are listed below.

Elvis Taped June 27, 1968, at NBC Studio 4 in Burbank and aired December 3, 1968. Producer/Director: Steve Binder. Musical Producer: Bones Howe. Choreography: Jaime Rogers and Claude Thompson. Costumes: Bill Belew. Songs: "Trouble"/"Guitar Man," "Lawdy Miss Clawdy," "Baby What You Want Me to Do," "Heartbreak Hotel"/"Hound Dog"/"All Shook Up," "Can't Help Falling in Love," "Jailhouse Rock," "Love Me Tender," "Where Could I Go But to the Lord," "Up Above My Head," "Saved," "Blue Christmas," "One Night," "Memories," Nothingville," "Big Boss Man," "Little Egypt," "If I Can Dream."

Elvis: Aloha from Hawaii Taped January 14, 1973, at the Honolulu International Center Arena and broadcast live by satellite around the world. The special was rebroadcast several times that year. Songs: "Paradise, Hawaiian Style," "See See Rider," "Burning Love," "Something," "You Gave Me a Mountain," "Steamroller Blues," "Early Morning Rain," "My Way," "Love Me," "Johnny B. Goode," "It's Over," "Blue Suede Shoes," "I'm So Lonesome I Could Cry," "I Can't Stop Loving You," "Hound Dog," "Blue Hawaii," "What Now My Love," "Fever," "Welcome to My World," "Suspicious Minds," "I'll Remember You," "Hawaiian Wedding Song," "Long Tall Sally"/"Whole Lotta Shakin' Goin' On," "Ku-u-i-po," "An American Trilogy," "A Big Hunk o' Love," "Can't Help Falling in Love."

Elvis in Concert Taped in June 1977, just two months before his death, this special was not broadcast until after his death, on October 3, 1977, on CBS. It consists of concert performances in Omaha, Nebraska, and Rapid City, South Dakota. Songs: "See See Rider," "That's All Right," "Are You Lonesome Tonight?," "Teddy Bear"/"Don't Be Cruel," "You Gave Me a Mountain," "Jailhouse Rock," "How Great Thou Art," "I Really Don't Want to Know," "Hurt," "Hound Dog," "My Way," "Early Morning Rain," "Can't Help Falling in Love."

THE LITERARY ELVIS

The following is intended as a general guide for the casual reader or potential Elvis scholar. While this volume is a small attempt to assemble a sampling of contemporary thought on Elvis, the serious student of Elvis phenomena will doubtless want to pursue some areas in further detail. The selected reading list contains all the material required to give the reader a solid background in the biographical details of Elvis's life as well as a firm grasp of some of the current critical and analytical thinking about the King. In addition to being invaluable as reference sources, all the books on the reading list are thoroughly readable and enjoyable books, all written with at least some degree of respect for both reader and subject matter. Following the selected reading list is a bibliography that is by no means complete but contains selections from a wide range of published material and should prove helpful if only as a starting point. The exploration of Elvis literature can be a frustrating and tedious venture, but persistence will be rewarded, often in the form of valuable insights from unexpected sources.

Biographies:

Elvis: A Biography by Jerry Hopkins, Simon & Schuster, 1972. The standard biography, this volume chronicles Elvis's life and career up to the early seventies, making it one of the few biographies with a genuinely upbeat ending. Published five years before Elvis's death, this straightforward account avoids the extremes of mawkish praise and bitter mudslinging that characterized many post-1977 biographies. Highly recommended as an introduction to Elvis.

Elvis: The Final Years by Jerry Hopkins, St. Martin's Press, 1981. In his second Elvis book, Hopkins completes the picture. Again, Hopkins avoids taking sides or making judgments, making for a depressing but reliable account of the King's decline and fall.

Elvis by Albert Goldman, McGraw-Hill, 1981. Without a doubt, this is the most controversial celebrity biography of all time, making its author a loathed and vilified figure among the devoted. Albert Goldman is the Salman Rushdie of the Elvis world, and his biography of John Lennon has only swelled his fiendish reputation. Rich in detail and painstakingly researched, Goldman's *Elvis* gleefully explores the dark underbelly of the Elvis myth. The problem here is that Goldman's research and insight is buried in endless pages of gruesome detail, and his sources are rarely cited in the text. What is intended as the debunking of a colossal myth ends up coming across as a sleazy exercise, albeit an impressive one. Ultimately, Goldman's message is undermined by his obvious dislike for both Elvis and his audience. Highly recommended, but only for those with open minds and strong stomachs.

Elvis: The Last 24 Hours by Albert Goldman, St. Martin's Press, 1991. Using Elvis's stepbrother as his primary source, Goldman reevaluates Elvis's final exit, asserting that Elvis deliberately overdosed by stockpiling his pills and taking them all at once. The book cites financial difficulties, health problems, and dread about the imminent publication of a biography (*Elvis: What Happened?*) written by three ex-bodyguards, which painted him as a violent, drug-addicted recluse, as reasons for Elvis's suicide. The circumstances surrounding Elvis's death will probably never be sorted out, and only Elvis himself could tell us whether he took his pills in a spirit of reckless pleasure seeking or suicidal depression, but in the meantime this theory is as good as any other.

Elvis and Me by Priscilla Beaulieu Presley with Sandra Harmon, Putnam, 1985. This book disappointed some readers by coming up rather short in the sex, drugs, and violence department, but it is nevertheless a fascinating firsthand chronicle of a teenager whose parents let her go to Memphis to live with and eventually marry the King of rock 'n' roll. This book is remarkably free of the shamelessly self-aggrandizing style that characterizes most first-hand accounts. Her narrative is surprising in its tone of warm but unsentimental reminiscence, and her levelheaded outlook, both as an author and as a main character, is impressive.

Picture Books:

Elvis Close-Up by Jay B. Leviton & Ger J. Rijff, Simon & Schuster, 1988. Photographer Leviton followed Elvis's every move for three days in Florida in August 1956 while on tour and captured Elvis in performance, in rehearsal, at meal times, and even in bed. This book amounts to a visual time capsule, a gorgeous black-and-white look at the brief moment when Elvis first came to our attention and everything was loose, live, and fresh. These photographs convey the innocence and the intoxicating sense of freedom Elvis brought to his first audiences.

Elvis: A Tribute to His Life by Susan Doll (contributing writer), Publications International, 1989. While the text of this large-format coffee-table-style volume provides a good general overview of Elvis's life and times, it is the photographs that set this book apart from all others. The selection and presentation of the photographs, which cover every stage of Elvis's life, is first-rate. In a field inundated by cheap and garish items, this book is a triumph of good taste and fine design.

General:

Elvis: His Life from A-Z by Fred L. Worth & Steve D. Tamerius, Contemporary Books, 1990. Trivia collectors Worth and Tamerius have assembled by far the best general reference source for Elvis facts and figures. In addition to an abundance of favorite-toothpaste-type entries, this book is encyclopedic in scope and contains exhaustive lists of records, bootlegs, chart listings, concert dates, film credits, television appearances, and much more. Even the most knowledgeable of Elvis fans will find new facts here. Excellent for reference, but it also makes for entertaining and informative browsing.

Elvis World by Jane and Michael Stern, Viking, 1987. Fearless explorers of American popular culture, the Sterns bring their wry wit and insight to this marvelous celebration of the Elvis phenomenon. *Elvis World* is richly illustrated and packaged in a glorious mock-tacky fifties style. From Elvis impersonators to Howard Finster's folk art to the photographs that document Elvis's ceaseless physical transformations, this book captures the true spirit of Elvisness; both the strange and the beautiful.

Criticism:

Lost Highway by Peter Guralnick, Godine, 1979. While not strictly about Elvis, this collection of portraits of American country, blues, and rockabilly musicians features the excellent essay "Elvis and the American Dream." Guralnick's assessment of Elvis centers around an exploration of the tension between the purity of the early rockabilly style and the throwaway attitude that characterized his movies and later recordings. He movingly conveys the sense of disillusionment at Elvis's frequent failure to live up to the promises of his youth, despite brief periods of renewed vitality. This line of critical thinking has since mutated into a familiar cliché in the hands of lazy critics and listeners, but Guralnick's handling of it is original and compelling. The book also features superb essays on Ernest Tubb, Howlin' Wolf, and many others, including lesser known but equally fascinating figures such as Cowboy Jack Clement and Sleepy LaBeef. *Lost Highway* is filled with rarely seen photographs and firsthand interviews with its subjects, and Guralnick's writing is both passionate and authoritative. Highly recommended not only as background reading for the Elvis student but for anyone interested in American music.

Mystery Train by Greil Marcus, Dutton, 1976. Neither history nor biography, *Mystery Train* traces the work of a handful of American musicians and examines the myths and legends that inform their work and their lives. Marcus's writing is part observation, part speculation, and part ranting and raving. What makes his work so exceptional is his acknowledgment of the unseen, the mysterious, and the supernatural, even as he tries to define the murky depths of American mythology. Elvis is the pivotal figure in *Mystery Train,* bridging the gap between the blues musicians of the thirties and forties and the rock musicians of the sixties and seventies. "Elvis: Presliad" looks at the American myths and cultural forces that brought Elvis into existence. This essay delves into the background of two of Elvis's most significant artistic achievements: his first recording sessions at Sam Phillips's Sun Studio in Memphis and his triumphant comeback in his 1968 NBC-TV special. Particularly interesting is Marcus's portrayal of Elvis as a self-conscious artist who, under Phillips's direction, actively searched for and perfected a sound. This is contrary to the more popular conception of Elvis as a primitive hillbilly who stumbled upon his new sound spontaneously and accidentally. "Elvis: Presliad" was written long after Elvis ceased to be an innovator and long before he became the Ultimate Dead Celebrity. There was never a more unlikely time for a serious assessment of Elvis Presley to be written, and Marcus's willingness to even attempt one is admirable. While the writing is often passionate, it is never sentimental. This is Elvis, without nostalgia or postmortem hysteria, a portrait of the Mystery Train's most mysterious passenger. Highly recommended.

BIBLIOGRAPHY

All About Elvis, Fred L. Worth & Steve D. Tamerius, Bantam Books, 1981.

All Shook Up: Elvis Day-by-Day, Lee Cotten, Peirian Press, 1985.

Are You Lonesome Tonight?, Dary Matera and Lucy de Barbin, Villard Books, 1987.

The Boy Who Dared to Rock, Paul Lichter, Doubleday, 1978.

The Complete Elvis, Martin Torgoff, ed., Delilah, 1982.

Elvis, Albert Goldman, McGraw-Hill, 1981.

Elvis, K. D. Kirkland, Bison Books, 1988.

Elvis, Dave Marsh, Rolling Stone Press, 1982.

Elvis, Richard Wooton, Random House, 1985.

Elvis After Life, Raymond Moody, Jr., Peachtree, 1987.

Elvis in Art, Roger Taylor, St. Martin's Press, 1987.

Elvis for Beginners, Jill Pearlman, Allen & Unwin, 1986.

Elvis: A Bio-Bibliography, Patsy Hammontree, Greenwood Press, 1985.

Elvis: A Biography, Jerry Hopkins, Simon & Schuster, 1972.

The Elvis Catalog, Lee Cotten, Doubleday, 1987.

Elvis Close-Up, Jay B. Leviton & Ger J. Rijff, Simon & Schuster, 1988.

Elvis '56, Alfred Wertheimer and Gregory Martinelli, Collier Books, 1979.

Elvis: The Films and Career of Elvis Presley, Steven and Boris Zmiijewsky, Citadel Press, 1976.

Elvis: The Final Years, Jerry Hopkins, St. Martin's Press, 1981.

Elvis and Gladys, Elaine Dundee, Macmillan, 1985.

Elvis: His Life from A to Z, Fred L. Worth & Steve D. Tamerius, Contemporary Books, 1990.

Elvis in Private, Peter Haining, St. Martin's Press, 1987.

Elvis in His Own Words, Mick Farren & Pearce Marchbank, Omnibus Press, 1982.

Elvis in Hollywood, Paul Lichter, Simon & Schuster, 1976.

Elvis: An Illustrated Biography, Rainer Walrahf and Heinz Plehn, Quick Fox, 1979.

Elvis: The Illustrated Record, Roy Carr and Mick Farren, Harmony Books, 1982.

Elvis: Images & Fancies, Jac L. Tharpe, ed., University Press of Mississippi, 1977.

Elvis, a King Forever, Robert Gibson & Sid Shaw, McGraw-Hill, 1987.

Elvis: The Last 24 Hours, Albert Goldman, St. Martin's Press, 1991.

Elvis: Man & Myth, Sarah Parker Danielson, Bison Books, 1990.

Elvis and Me, Priscilla Presley with Sandra Harmon, Putnam, 1985.

Elvis: Portrait of a Friend, Marty and Patsy Lacker and Leslie S. Smith, Wimmer Brothers, 1979.

Elvis Presley, Robert Love, Watts, 1986.

Elvis Presley, Todd Slaughter, Wyndham, 1977.

Elvis in Quotes, Sid Shaw, ed., Elvisly Yours, 1986.

Elvis: A 30-Year Chronicle, Bill E. Burk, Osborne Enterprises, 1980.

Elvis Through My Eyes, Bill E. Burk, Burk Enterprises, 1987.

Elvis: A Tribute to His Life, Susan Doll, Publications International, 1989.

Elvis, We Love You Tender, Dee Presley, Ricky, David and Billy Stanley, with Torgoff, Delacorte Press, 1979.

Elvis: What Happened?, Red West, Sonny West, Dave Hebler, & Steve Dunleavy, Ballantine Books, 1977.

Elvis World, Jane and Michael Stern, Viking, 1987.

If I Can Dream, Larry Geller and Joel Spector with Patricia Romanowski, Simon & Schuster, 1989.

The Illustrated Elvis, W. A. Harbinson, Grosset & Dunlap, 1975.

Is Elvis Alive?, Gail Brewer-Giorgio, Tudor, 1988.

King! When Elvis Rocked the World, Pete Nelson, Proteus, 1984.

Lost Highway, Peter Guralnick, Godine, 1979.

The Minstrel, Bernard Benson, Putnam, 1977.

Mystery Train, Greil Marcus, Dutton, 1976.

My Life with Elvis, Becky Yancey and Cliff Linedecker, St. Martin's Press, 1977.

Private Elvis, Diego Cortez, ed., FEY, 1978.

The Private Elvis, May Mann, Drake, 1975.

The Real Elvis: Good Old Boy, Vince Staten, Media Ventures, 1978.

Stark Raving Elvis, William McCranor Henderson, Dutton, 1984.

Starring Elvis, James W. Bowser, Dell, 1977.

Studies in Modern Music: Elvis Presley, Robert Matthew-Walker, Omnibus Press, 1972.

The Truth About Elvis, Jess Stearn with Larry Geller, Jove Books, 1980.

When Elvis Died, Neal and Janice Gregory, Communications Press, 1980.

Index